MVFOL

A MANUAL OF PAINTING MATERIALS AND TECHNIQUES

MARK DAVID GOTTSEGEN

*The University of North Carolina
at Greensboro*

HARPER & ROW, PUBLISHERS   NEW YORK

Cambridge   Philadelphia   San Francisco   Washington
London   Mexico City   São Paulo   Singapore   Sydney

FOR MY PARENTS

Executive Editor: Judith Rothman
Project Editor: Joan C. Gregory
Text Design: Rafael H. Hernandez
Cover Design: Betty Chow, Nicholas Bouyoukas, Karen Salsgiver
Text Art: Shelly Sacks
Production Manager: Willie Lane
Compositor: TAPSCO, Inc.
Printer and Binder: R. R. Donnelley & Sons Company

A MANUAL OF PAINTING MATERIALS AND TECHNIQUES

Library of Congress Cataloging-in-Publication Data

Gottsegen, Mark David.
    A manual of painting materials and techniques.

    Bibliography: p.
    Includes index.
    1. Artists' materials.   2. Painting—Technique.
I. Title.
ND1500.G6155   1987   750'.28   86-22911
ISBN 0-06-042421-4

87 88 89 90 9 8 7 6 5 4 3 2 1

CONTENTS

PART TWO   **PAINT MANUFACTURE AND PAINTING TECHNIQUES   205**

PART THREE   **PICTURE PROTECTION AND RESTORATION**   **319**

ILLUSTRATIONS

COLOR REPRODUCTIONS

The color reproductions are the best representations of the paintings and drawings that four-color printing can produce. It is not possible, however, to do full justice to art in this manner. The author strongly suggests a visit to a museum or gallery for a long, close look at actual objects.

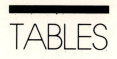

TABLES

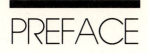

PREFACE

Knowledge of the materials of painting remains a neglected aspect of the education of many artists. There has recently been a revival of interest in craftsmanship, yet in much good painting today we see evidence of early deterioration and physical failure. I am hopeful that an interest in the craft of painting will keep pace with the attention artists now pay to the business aspects of their profession.

This book is first of all a reference work designed for practical studio use, but it is also a text that can serve as a guide for those who teach and study the materials of painting. Third, it may be of interest to collectors who wish to know more about how paintings are made.

The manual is a starting point for development as an individual artist, and a helpful addition to the mature artist's library.

Since this manual has grown out of a teaching situation, it is organized somewhat differently from others like it. Part One gives information about basic materials and methods for preparing and using them. It is the basis for Part Two, which covers the methods and techniques of individual processes. Part Three provides an overview of picture protection. It briefly describes how to mat and frame works of art and lists the types of damage that pictures may sustain.

This book could not have been written without the help and enthusiasm of a large number of people. I am first indebted to my teachers, all of whom contributed to my early development as a painter and to my interest in painting materials: David Aronson, Philip Guston, Morton Sacks, James Weeks, and most especially Reed Kay.

My thanks also go to those who have at one time or another commented on various parts of the manuscript, answered questions, or made suggestions or corrections. These include my colleagues in the American Society for Testing and Materials, Artists Equity Association, and the Inter-Society Color Council: Hilton Brown; Fred W. Billmeyer, Jr.; Vern Clark; Robert L. Feller; Ruth Johnston-Feller; Ed Flax; Mark Golden; Fred Gould; Barbara Keyser; Wally

Klarman; Elaine Koretsky; Henry W. Levison; Joy Turner Luke; Treva Pamer; Zora Sweet Pinney; Max Saltzman; Irving Shack; Al Spizzo; Peter Staples; Woodhall Stopford; John C. Weaver; and Tom Vonderbrink. Naturally any errors or omissions are mine, not theirs.

Various manufacturers and distributors willingly answered numerous questions and provided volumes of information, far beyond the normal call of duty: American Cyanamid; American Hoechst; Andrews/Nelson/Whitehead; Blythe Colours, Ltd.; Borden Chemical; Burlington Industries; Ciba-Geigy; Cities Service; Conserv-Art; Dow Chemical; E. I. Du Pont de Nemours; Ferro Corporation; Tara Materials; Glidden Pigments and Colors Group; M. Grumbacher; Harmon Colors; Harshaw Chemical; Hercules, Inc.; The Hollinger Corporation; Hunt Manufacturing; ICI Americas; H. Kohnstamm and Company; Alois K. Diethelm AG; Lefranc et Bourgeois; Binney and Smith; Martin/F. Weber; Mineral Pigments Corporation; Oudt Hollandse Olieverwen Makerij NV; Pfizer Minerals; Process Materials Corporation; Reckitt's Colours, Ltd.; Reichard-Coulston; Reichhold Chemicals; H. Schmincke and Co. KG; Sennelier; The Sheperd Chemical Company; Shiva, Inc.; Strathmore Paper Company; Sun Chemical; Union Carbide; Whittaker, Clark and Daniels, Inc.; and Winsor & Newton, Inc. I wish also to acknowledge with thanks the correspondence and personal contacts with staff members at the following institutions: the Art Conservation Program at the University of Delaware, the Conservation Center of the Institute of Fine Arts, the Cooperstown Art Conservation Program, the Courtauld Institute of Art of the University of London, the Fogg Art Museum, the Library of Congress, the Metropolitan Museum of Art, the Merrimac Valley Textile Museum, the North Carolina Museum of Art, and the Williamstown Regional Art Conservation Laboratory.

I am grateful for A. Doren's photography, and owe a debt to the Weatherspoon Art Gallery and the individual artists for their permission to reproduce the paintings and drawings in their collections. In addition, several other of my colleagues at UNCG deserve mention for their support of my efforts to muddy disciplinary lines: Walter Barker, Ben Berns, William Collins, Margaret Cecil, Von Eisenhardt, Robert Gerhart III, and particularly Joan Gregory. Naturally, I would never have done this without the enthusiasm of my students.

I owe many thanks to Jane Cullen for her encouragement and confidence in me. At Harper & Row, I am indebted to Fred Henry for his enthusiasm, help, and firm hand; to Diane Moran for keeping me in check; to Joan Gregory for her guidance, advice, and quiet determination; and to Robin Hessel, Naomi Collette, and Lilly Farkas for their devotion to the project. I also wish to thank Jeannine Ciliotta for her superb skill and blinding speed, and Susan Joseph for her incisive and thorough work.

Finally, I must express my gratitude to Patsy Allen, for her tolerance and affection.

Mark D. Gottsegen

INTRODUCTION

Studying the materials and processes of painting is one way to begin the study of the art. Since earliest times, painters have recorded information about how their works were made. Historical accounts have been of interest to artists and art historians, and until the latter part of the last century the study of the materials of art was a regular and continuing aspect of every organized training program for artists. The knowledge gleaned from this study gave an artist the means to choose materials wisely.

There is now a vast range of ready-made products within easy reach of most artists, and selecting what to use is no longer a simple affair. There are too many choices, and too many unknowns. Every product seems to offer advantages, and, quite naturally, advertisements for them do not dwell on possible shortcomings. Since it is the artist's responsibility to select paints, mediums, supports, brushes, and all the other studio paraphernalia intelligently, it is more important than ever that choices be made with some understanding of the properties and characteristics of the materials.

To express ideas clearly, a painter must be in control of the chosen medium. A brief encounter with a variety of materials while a student, and a firm grounding in the technical and procedural aspects of the craft, can help an artist choose the most appropriate medium and use it most effectively. Few artists will want to prepare materials from scratch after their student days, but an understanding of what is involved will give them the basis for selecting ready-made products. And it is entirely possible that certain homemade materials will become preferable to their store-bought approximations.

As an artist matures, his or her technical and stylistic requirements are likely to change. Familiarity with different materials will open more possibilities in the search for a technique, or combination of techniques, that best reflects the evolving style. Experimentation with the newer materials can be more successful if the artist understands their technical limitations, and this understanding grows directly from an understanding of the traditional materials. The pursuit of a new form of expression in a new medium is substantially bolstered by knowledge of time-tested procedures.

Artists must also be able to choose painting materials which, when properly assembled, result in durable works. Paintings are fragile and easily damaged by poor display or storage conditions. Even in the best of circumstances, pictures made with inferior materials will deteriorate rapidly. Pictures made with good materials but constructed without regard for the rules that govern their use can suffer premature deterioration. Most artists want their works to last. They have a responsibility to themselves and their patrons if they wish to have their ideas survive more than a few years. Restoration can be immensely expensive, and works that are under constant treatment may soon lose their original impact through subtle changes in appearance. Furthermore, artists whose paintings need repeated fixing may soon find themselves with poor reputations. Some museums are now beginning to have their conservation staffs assess potential acquisitions for "inherent vice"; those works that do not have a reasonable expectation of longevity may not be recommended for purchase.

This manual, then, is intended to be a guide through the maze of information about traditional and nontraditional painting materials and processes. There is no attempt to suggest esthetic approaches to painting, although successful artistic expression is greatly enhanced by a full command of technique. Rather, artists who use the manual should come away with a better idea of the practical whys and hows of selecting and using painting materials, and perhaps with some insight into the possibilities of their chosen form of expression.

HEALTH AND SAFETY NOTICE

This book makes suggestions about the use of materials, methods, and equipment, some of which can be hazardous to personal safety or health. Every effort has been made to provide sufficient cautions about recognized hazards. Since there is little conclusive evidence regarding the potential hazards of some art or craft materials, it is the responsibility of the individual artist to establish the necessary safe practices and to determine whether the material or method should be used. Be sure to consult manufacturer's or distributor's Material Safety Data Sheets whenever possible.

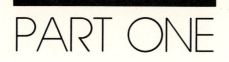

PART ONE

BASIC TOOLS AND MATERIALS

All artists, no matter how talented, need to know about their materials if their work is to last; they need to know the properties, advantages, and disadvantages of what they use to support a painting and to preserve it. In Part One, we look at the painter's basic materials—supports, sizes and grounds, binders, solvents and thinners, varnishes, and preservatives. These basic materials, often invisible to viewers, play a crucial role in how well and for how long those viewers will be able to enjoy the painting and see it as the artist intended it to be seen.

CHAPTER 1

SUPPORTS

In painting, the basic substrate which carries the image is called a *support*. This is, in fact, the most important structural element in a painting, for if it fails, the painting probably will not survive. Over the centuries, artists have used a whole range of supports—walls, wood panels, stretched canvas, glass, metal sheets, paper, to name just a few. Each of the variety of support materials imparts a character to the surface of the picture. If the support is a smoothly finished surface, the picture will exhibit a smooth surface; if the support has a pronounced texture, the picture will show some of this texture.

Many supports for easel painting can be purchased already prepared. There is extreme variation in the quality and durability of these products—the most expensive materials are often on display right next to the cheapest. It is therefore worth considering the nature of the raw materials and undertaking the preparation of supports in your own studio. A degree of quality control can be exercised, and you can develop combinations of supports and grounds that meet your own needs.

Home preparation of supports is neither expensive nor difficult. If the durability of a painting is often dictated by the durability of the support, then any effort expended in gaining knowledge about the support's composition and performance is worthwhile.

Whatever the support chosen, whether ready-made or homemade, it should satisfy these minimum requirements.

1. The support should age without becoming so brittle or fragile that it will suffer from exhibition, handling, or proper storage.

2. The support should be able to withstand the effects of atmospheric changes. Under reasonably variable conditions of relative humidity (RH) and temperature, the support should expand, contract, or warp as little as possible.

3. The support should have enough absorbency and *tooth* to provide a good *key* for the kinds of paints and grounds applied to it.*

RIGID SUPPORTS

In the history of Western painting, rigid supports were used long before the adoption of flexible fabric supports: cave walls come immediately to mind. By many accounts, one of the earliest uses of a rigid support separate from a wall is in the portraits that decorated the coffins of Egyptians in the Fayum era, between the first and third centuries A.D. Since then, artists have endeavored to find suitable supports for their paintings.

This section will examine several major types of rigid support and will describe the methods used for bracing and for surface preparation. For a complete discussion of walls used as supports for painting, see Chapter 16, "Mural Techniques."

SOLID PANELS

Painters in the Renaissance developed the use of wooden panels for religious works into a special craft. Thick, solid, hard- and semi-hardwoods such as oak, mahogany, and poplar were used for altarpieces. Sophisticated joinery, heavy framing, and continual treatment through the centuries by conservators have combined to ensure the physical survival of these works. Panels made of solid wood, however, present complicated problems.

Wood is a cellular material. In the central core of a tree, these cells store water. When the wood is cut into boards and allowed to dry for a long period of time, the cells eventually give up most of their moisture. However, the cell walls and cavities remain capable of absorption and are constantly expanding and contracting according to the moisture content of the surrounding atmosphere. After many years of gradual drying, the cells become more or less stable.

If wood planks are cut radially from a log (Figure 1.1), the stresses of expansion and contraction are more or less equalized between the two faces of the panel. Tangentially sawn planks impose unequal tension on the faces, because of the arrangement of the grain, and can lead to defects such as warping, twisting, cupping, splitting, and cracking. Even radially sawn planks can be affected this way. Figure 1.1 shows that tangential sawing is by far the most economical way to obtain the greatest number of boards from a log; it is rare to find radially sawn planks at the average lumberyard. Even when they can be found, radially sawn boards must be seasoned for several years in a stable environment—the modern kiln-drying seasoning method employed today does not produce a fully seasoned wood.

---

* Reed Kay, *The Painter's Guide to Studio Methods and Materials,* © 1983, pp. 4, 32, 94, 173–186. Adapted by permission of Prentice-Hall, Inc., Englewood Cliffs, New Jersey.

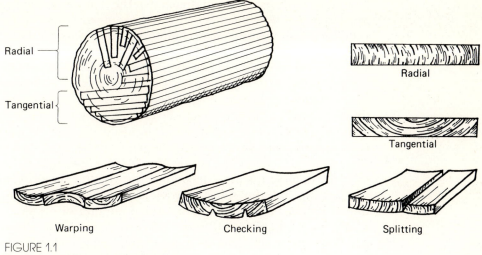

Radial

Tangential

Radial

Tangential

Warping   Checking   Splitting

FIGURE 1.1
Radial and Tangential Sawing

Top left: The top half of the log is sawn radially, the lower half, tangentially.
Top right: End view of a radially sawn board; of a tangentially sawn board.
Bottom: Defects of solid wood panels: warping, checking, splitting.

Well-seasoned hardwoods such as mahogany or white oak are preferred for easel painting panels; semi-hardwoods and softwoods like poplar or pine should be avoided. The board should be at least 1 inch (2.5 cm) thick; thinner boards will not resist structural deformation over a long period of time.

The panel should be sealed against moisture penetration by applying a size and ground to all edges and both sides. To slow down the expansion and contraction of the wood further, apply a layer of paint used in the picture to the back of the panel to equalize the tensions on the faces of the panel.

Because few large hardwood trees are now harvested, and the width of a board is limited by the size of a tree, it will probably be difficult to find boards of substantial width. Several boards may be glued together at the edges, with tongue-and-groove joints, to form a larger panel. But if the joints are not perfectly made, they will certainly split or crack. Bracing systems (also known as *cradles*) applied to the rear of solid wood panels invariably lead to cracking, because the braces hold the panel far too rigidly against the stresses in the wood grain.

LAMINATED PANELS

Laminated panels are a useful alternative to the inconvenience, expense, and risk of preparing and using solid woods. Plywood is the most common of the laminated woods. These boards are available in large sizes and varying thicknesses, and are made of both soft and hard woods.

The structure of plywood is such that the stresses caused by moisture and grain are lessened, if not eliminated. Thin layers of wood veneer, peeled from a tree by rotating the log against a sharp knife, are glued together so the grain of each layer is at right angles to the grain of those adjacent to it. The number of layers will vary according to the thickness of the board, but the minimum is three; the arrangement of the layers works to reduce warping and shrinking.

The inner layers of most plywoods are thicker and sometimes composed of a different wood from the outside layers. This is particularly true when the outer veneers are expensive hardwoods. It is possible to find die boards, five-ply boards of hardwood, with all the layers composed of the same wood and of equal thickness, used for making dies (Appendix D). In addition, different types of glue are used to laminate the plys, depending on whether the plywood is for interior or exterior use. Exterior grade plywood is superior for its resistance to moisture, but the smoothest surface finishes are found on interior grades.

The most accessible and least expensive plywood has a pine veneer. If at least one side is perfectly smooth—free of seams, plugs, fillers, and knots—this may be a satisfactory surface. Softwood grains do have a tendency eventually to show through thinly applied paint layers; hardwood veneers of birch, maple, walnut, or mahogany are less likely to show this fault.

The necessary thickness of a plywood panel can be determined by the size of the proposed picture. A small picture might require a panel only ¼ inch (6 mm) thick, a large one might require a panel of up to 1 inch (2.5 cm) thick. A thin panel for a picture larger than about 24 inches (61 cm) on one side will require bracing against warpage. (Bracing plywood does not cause the problems associated with bracing solid wood panels because of the multidirectional grain in the panel.) The bracing is carried out by glueing 1- by 2-inch (2.5 × 5 cm) strips of wood around the outside edges of the back of the panel, using a strong carpenter's glue and C-clamps. Cross-bracing the middle of the longer side may also be indicated. Neither nails nor screws are used, since they must be put through the face side of the panel to work effectively and will eventually rust or pop through the ground and paint layers. The best way is to assemble the bracing as a separate unit and then glue it to the rear of the panel.

The exposed edges of the plywood should also be treated against moisture penetration, which could cause the delamination of the layers. Sand the edges and seal them with a size, the ground, and paint, just as you might treat the edges of a solid wood panel.

LAMINATED PAPER BOARDS

Paper boards are made from wood waste or wood pulp. They are thick, somewhat dense, and lack the distinct layering of plywood. Laminated boards are sold under a variety of trade names, such as Upson Board or Beaver Board. Illustration board and the commercial framer's inexpensive mat board are more common types that have paper layers glued to the face surfaces.

Paper boards should be considered temporary supports. Because of their high acidity and weak physical structure, they will deteriorate quickly after exposure to normal atmospheric conditions; no amount of preservation or stabilization will prevent the deterioration. They should not be used as substrates, nor should they be used as collage materials. The discoloration and brittle appearance of added papers and paper boards in much twentieth-century painting is evidence of how poorly the materials survive. Furthermore, it is not a good idea to use these products for studies or sketches; you can easily be seduced by the surface quality or absorbency of the material and end up doing work that is intended to be permanent. If you wish to do throwaway studies, be sure to discard them.

MUSEUM BOARD

A mat board made from 100 percent linen or cotton rags, or from deacidified and buffered paper pulp, is a different and far more reliable species of paper board. This material is usually an off-white or cream color, although other colors are now available. The boards have distinct layers (two, four, six, or eight layers)—the same coloration throughout all the layers—and no paper facing on the surfaces. This type of laminated board can be used successfully with a number of painting techniques and is an excellent support. Museum board does not have much structural strength, however, and so the two-ply boards should be matted and displayed like works done on paper. The four-, six-, or eight-ply boards can be displayed the same way or mounted on a wooden panel for rigidity.

POROUS BOARDS

Boards such as Homosote or Cellotex are made of materials similar to those found in the inferior laminated paper boards—paper or wood pulp. These materials also deteriorate rapidly and cannot be considered suitable for permanent works. They are also structurally weak, too porous, loosely textured, and offer little in the way of physical support for a painting.

CHIPBOARDS

These heavyweight boards are made of ground wood chips, pressed and glued together into large panels about the same size as the standard plywood panels. While chipboards are structurally sound, panels of any significant size are disproportionately heavier than other rigid supports. The storage, transportation, and exhibition problems of using such a heavy support should be taken into account. One product, with the trade name Aspenite, has much larger chips in its matrix, which allow for sufficient structural strength and a much thinner panel. This type of chipboard is also known as wafer board.

One must remember that chipboards were designed for construction and industrial use, not for artists, so there should be some doubt about the permanence of the products. It may be wiser to avoid their use until their reliability as artists' materials can be verified.

HARDBOARDS

Hardboard panels are made of shredded, compacted, and compressed wood fibers. The fibers are burst apart under steam pressure, and the resulting pulp is formed into sheets; only the natural adhesive found in the wood—lignin—holds the mass together. The method of manufacture produces a dense, one-layer substitute for solid wood that does not have a grain. The panels are therefore less likely to warp and are resistant to penetration by atmospheric moisture.

A widely available brand called Presdwood is made by the Masonite Corporation. Two finishes, Tempered and Untempered, are of interest to the artist. Tempered Presdwood is impregnated with an oily substance to make it more moisture-resistant, and can be recognized by its dark brown color and hard surface. Untempered Presdwood is light brown in color and considerably less dense than the tempered variety, since it lacks the oily addition.

Either type of hardboard panel can be successfully used as a painting support. Because the Tempered Presdwood has an especially hard and nonabsorbent surface, it must be sanded vigorously to provide a good mechanical key for a painting ground. Untempered Presdwood should be lightly sanded to break up its surface fibers; because it is less dense and more absorbent than Tempered Masonite, it is more susceptible to moisture penetration and mechanical damage.

Both these types of hardboard are made by other companies using more or less similar manufacturing processes. The panels come in varying thicknesses, but are more readily found in ⅛-inch (4 mm) and ¼-inch (6 mm) sizes. The standard width is 4 feet (126 cm). The length of a panel can be 8 feet, 10 feet, or 12 feet (241, 304, or 365 cm). Small panels can be used without an auxiliary support, but all panels may warp if uneven tension is exerted by a painted layer on only one side, and larger panels will bend and deform from their own weight. Bracing will easily lessen this problem.

CORED BOARDS

The principal disadvantage of panels, especially large ones, is their weight. Boards with a lightweight core between two permanent surfaces seem to offer a way of overcoming this disadvantage.

One type of cored board, which has a plastic foam core with white paper surfaces, is used extensively as a backing for framed pictures. The board itself is not very rigid and warps easily. Archival-quality (suitable for permanent use) foam-cored boards are now available, but the usual type is of questionable durability.

A hollow-core door, cored with a honeycomb of treated cardboard and faced with clear hardwoods, can be useful if there are no seams on at least one side. Custom services can provide panels like this made with a variety of surfaces: hardwood, hardboard, and even museum board. The one difficulty with this kind of structure is altering the size: if it is cut to a special size, the exposed edge will lose the support of the surrounding framework and will have to be replaced (Figure 1.2).

METALS AND GLASS

At one time or another both metal and glass surfaces have been used for painting, although the practice is much less common today. In Holland during the sixteenth and seventeenth centuries, artists sometimes did small paintings on copper or other metals; in the twentieth century, Jackson Pollock painted on glass. Examples such as these survive, however, only because of extensive restoration treatment.

The problems with these nonabsorbent supports relate to the meticulous surface preparation required to provide a key for the following layers of paint. Glass must be etched or sandblasted to give it tooth; even then, getting a good key between the support or ground is difficult. Metals will often rust or corrode beneath their primings even if the surfaces are sufficiently roughened.

Aluminum is one metal that seems to be a good substrate for the acrylic polymer emulsion paints—the metal and the paint appear to react to temperature changes in a similar fashion (they have the same thermal coefficient of expansion), and the paint-aluminum reaction produces excellent adhesion. If an aluminum panel surface is thoroughly sanded and degreased, it can be primed with an acrylic polymer emulsion ground and painted with acrylic emulsion paints. Process Materials Corporation offers a cored substrate that has a honeycombed inte-

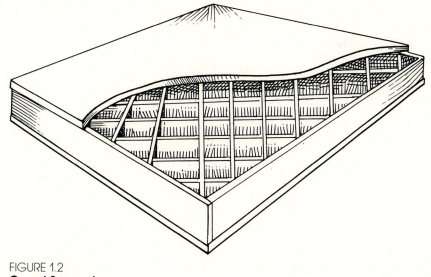

FIGURE 1.2
Cored Support
With a lightweight honeycomb interior.

rior with aluminum skins; Fine Arts Stretchers and Services offers aluminum honeycombed panels with either aluminum or polyester skins. As one might expect, the prices for these types of supports are very high (see Appendix D).

BRACING A RIGID SUPPORT

Panels of plywood or Masonite should be braced on the back side to help prevent bending or warping caused by the weight of the panel or uneven tension between the painted and the unpainted sides. Bracing will also guard against the shredding or denting of the panel edges.

The following list includes the materials needed for the two primary types of bracing, simple and lap joint (Figure 1.3). The wood for bracing should be straight-grained and free from knots, twists, or warps. The boards can be softwoods like white pine, fir, or redwood, or a harder wood like yellow pine. You can use 1- by 2-inch or 1- by 3-inch (2.5 × 5 cm or 2.5 × 7.5 cm) boards, but remember that these are nominal measurements. The actual size of a 1- by 2-inch board is only ¾- by 1½-inch (1.9 × 3.8 cm).

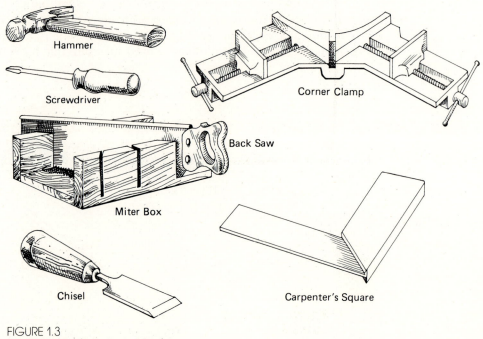

Hammer

Screwdriver

Corner Clamp

Back Saw

Miter Box

Chisel

Carpenter's Square

FIGURE 1.3
Tools for Making Panel Braces

Clockwise, from top right: corner clamp, carpenter's square, chisel, miter box and back saw, screwdriver, hammer.

MATERIALS

1. Bracing strips, 1- by 2-inch (2.5 × 5 cm).
2. Corner and T-irons, with flathead wood screws.
3. Hammer and screwdriver.
4. Back saw and miter box.
5. A sharp, wide chisel.
6. A carpenter's square.
7. C-clamps.
8. Corner clamps.
9. A good-quality, strong carpenter's glue. The yellow glues are stronger than the less moisture-resistant white glues. Contact cement may also be used, but avoid the solvent-laden variety (toxic solvents are used); use the water-based kind.

SIMPLE BRACING

In this technique, the bracing parts are cut to fit the outside dimensions of the panel. The joints of the bracing are not attached to each other, but are glued separately to the panel.

1. Measure the dimensions of the panel.
2. Cut the bracing to the measured lengths with the back saw and miter box. Check the cut ends with the carpenter's square to be sure that they are perfectly square. If the panel is large, cut extra pieces for cross-bracing.
3. Lay the panel face down on a table or the floor and assemble the bracing on it to see that it fits. All the butt joints should be snug and square.
4. Spread the glue evenly and thinly on each piece of the bracing and reposition them on the back of the panel.
5. Pile weights on the bracing or, better, clamp them with the C-clamps. Allow the assembly to dry overnight. If contact cement is used, clamping will probably not be necessary.

This type of bracing is adequate for many applications. Its only disadvantage is that, because the joints between the members of the bracing are not rigidly connected, it does not provide a tight support for the panel. The jointing can be improved by attaching them using corner and T-irons (Figure 1.4).

LAP JOINT BRACING

This technique, which calls for a bit more carpentry skill, produces stronger joints and a better independent structure for the bracing.

1. Measure the dimensions of the panel and cut the bracing members to these lengths. Notice that the strips overlap.
2. Cut laps, also known as dados, for all the joints by sawing halfway through

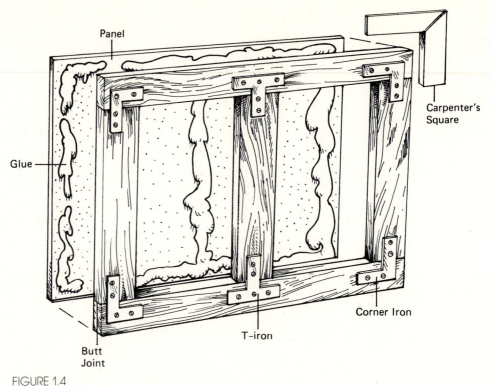

FIGURE 1.4
Simple Bracing for a Rigid Support
Bracing is built as a separate unit with butt joints, and glued to the rear of the panel.

the end of each overlapping piece and chiseling away the scrap. Each joint will now be a lap joint, which is stronger than a butt joint (Figure 1.5).

3. Assemble the bracing and glue it to the panel in the same way as for the simple method. The joints may be screwed and glued, or attached with the corner and T-irons (Figure 1.6).

SURFACE PREPARATION

Before receiving a size and ground, the surface of the panel should be roughened by a light sanding with fine sandpaper. The edges of the panel may be beveled slightly with a file or rounded with sandpaper to prevent a stiff ground layer from chipping off (Figure 1.7). Thoroughly dust the sanded panel before applying any coatings.

Aluminum panels are also easily sanded. Take care to abrade the surface thoroughly and evenly—an electric orbital sander is a great help. Gently file the edges to remove the burrs left when the panel was cut.

Wood and aluminum panels should be wiped with a cloth dampened in dena-

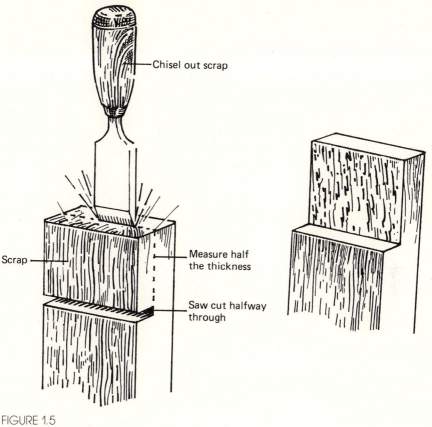

FIGURE 1.5
Lap Joint

tured ethyl alcohol or mineral spirits to remove residual grease or oils. *Caution:* Alcohol is a health and fire hazard and should be used with plenty of ventilation.

FLEXIBLE SUPPORTS

Supports made of textiles or paper—flexible supports—have advantages over rigid supports: They are lightweight and portable; they can be constructed in a much greater variety of sizes; and they are generally more easily treated if they need to be repaired. But because flexible supports are also much thinner than panels, they are more susceptible to atmospheric and mechanical damage. Depending on the specific material, most textiles and papers are unstable in response to atmospheric changes. Constant movement resulting from fluctuations in temperature and humidity can contribute to the physical deterioration of a relatively rigid painted layer. To counteract the instability of fabrics, they can be supported

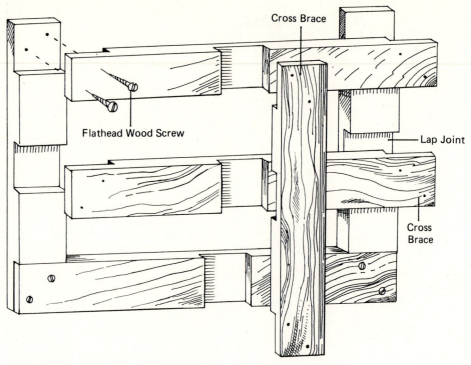

Cross Brace

Flathead Wood Screw

Lap Joint

Cross Brace

FIGURE 1.6
Lap Joint Bracing for a Rigid Support
Screw and glue all joints.

by chassis (strainers or stretchers) or mounted on a rigid panel substrate. Both techniques are described later in this section.

TEXTILES

Fabrics such as silk have been used in the Orient since ancient times as supports for paintings in ink and watercolor. Linen and cotton came into general use in Europe in the Middle Ages. Other sorts of woven fabric have been used as a basis for painting at one time or another. Today, artists chiefly use cotton, linen, and a few of the synthetic fabrics. *Canvas* is a term often applied to cotton materials, or even as a designation for a finished picture (whether on cotton, linen, or synthetic), though its true definition is much more general: a firm, closely woven cloth.

COTTON DUCK

Cotton duck is made of the fibers of the fruit of the cotton plant. It is widely available and a popular support for painting, although it has definite disadvan-

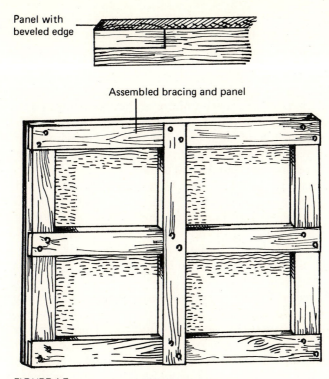

Panel with beveled edge

Assembled bracing and panel

FIGURE 1.7
Assembled Lap Joint Bracing and Panel

Top detail: Beveled edge of the panel—the angle of the bevel is exaggerated.

tages. Cotton fibers are quite short and resistant to stretching; they suffer rapid degradation when subjected to atmospheric stresses, especially when the fabric made from them is stretched tightly on a frame (as in a painting); and the fibers, no matter how white and pure, show a measurable color change after relatively little exposure to light (less than ten years).

Cotton is, however, widely used. Many forms are currently used in painting. The medium to heavy weights—on the order of 10 ounces per square yard (284 gm/m²) and tightly woven—are used in artistic paintings. Raw cotton duck should be washed before using to rid it of the mill-applied sizings, and should be prestretched before attaching it to an auxiliary stretcher system to remove the crimp in the weave.

Thin cotton, such as bed sheeting or muslin, is also sometimes used as a support—especially by those who are thinking of economy. But this cotton is not economical in the long run, as it is much too structurally weak to support a paint film unless backed by a rigid panel substrate.

Some artists object to the mechanical appearance of the cotton weave, although this objection is largely esthetic; some styles of painting may demand that the fabric's texture be unassertive. Regardless of esthetic concerns, cotton should be considered an inferior material in comparison to other fabric supports now available.

LINEN

Linen is made from the woven fibers of the flax plant and is distinguished from cotton by its color—a dull brownish-green—and its usually pronounced and irregular texture. Individual linen fibers are considerably longer and springier than those of cotton; the material is therefore somewhat more durable and has a livelier feel when it is stretched on a frame.

The physical problems of linen have long been discounted because of its relatively better performance when compared to cotton. However, studies on the mechanical properties of linen and cotton when combined with sizings and primings show them to be equally poor supports for oil painting. Nonetheless, linen is the most favored support today, and when properly supported by an auxiliary system and used with the right kind of paint, it can still be a valuable and useful material.

There is considerable variety of weave texture and weight available in linen, from very coarse and heavy to fine and light. Usually the heavier grades are chosen for large pictures, while the lightweight linens are satisfactory for small works or for mounting on a panel. Whichever grade you choose, select a linen made for artists' use. Look for a close weave, where the threads of warp and fill (weft) are of equal weight, and avoid blends of linen and other materials such as cotton or the synthetics, since different threads will have uneven tension when stretched and will show unequal reactions to environmental changes. If the blend is in the thread, and exists in equal weight ratio in the warp and fill, the combination can be satisfactory. Practically speaking, many of these blends are usually too thin for general artistic use (see Appendix D).

SYNTHETIC FABRICS

The major disadvantage of a fabric support is its continual movement in response to atmospheric change. Some manufacturers of artists' and conservators' materials are investigating the use of synthetic fabrics to replace the natural ones.

Polyester fabrics seem to be the most promising alternative, since they are nonabsorbent (and therefore do not react to humidity) and stable at normal temperatures. Polyester fabrics do have a tendency to sag at higher than normal temperatures. Fredrix Artist Canvas, an American manufacturer, markets a pre-primed polyester support called Polyflax. It also produces a cotton and polyester blend—a blend in the thread. Both are primed with a heat-set acrylic polymer emulsion ground which is tightly keyed to the nonabsorbent support. Fredrix also markets a dyed polypropylene fabric, also preprimed with a thermoset acrylic emulsion ground, which, in color at least, resembles linen (see Appendix D).

Fiberglass fabrics, both the chopped strand mat and the woven cloth, might provide another alternative to the natural fabrics, though neither has been fully tested in conditions under which artists would use it. Neither stretches very well. The other synthetics (acrylics, nylons, acetates, sarans) show rapid deterioration on exposure to light and so are probably unsuitable.

OTHER FABRICS

Burlap, jute, and hemp are coarse-textured, heavy, short-fibered textiles that have been used for painting. Works done on these fabrics usually deteriorate very quickly, for the materials are too absorbent, brittle, and short-lived. For a rough-textured support, it is better to choose a rough linen.

PREPRIMED TEXTURES

Many fabrics can be bought already prepared with a size and/or ground. This can be both tremendously convenient and economical. Since there is wide variation in preprimed supports, however, pay particular attention to choosing the best quality.

It is most common to find cotton duck preprimed with an air-dried or thermoset (heat-cured) acrylic or vinyl emulsion ground. Look at the backs of these products to inspect the fabric. It should be of substantial weight and have a tight, close weave. One may find during such an inspection that the ground is actually holding together a thin, insubstantial fabric. This is an indication of poor quality.

Single- or double-primed linen, with a glue size and an oil ground, is also on the market. The basic expense of the ingredients and labor in the preparation of these materials will generally ensure that the manufacturer has made a better-quality support (see Chapter 2 for an admonition about glues). Here again, check the back of the support to see that the fabric is closely woven and substantial. You can also check the adherence and flexibility of the ground by rolling a corner of the material, ground side out, between forefinger and thumb. An oil ground will usually crack under such an extreme test. If it does not powder or separate from the support, it should be satisfactory.

Note that many textiles preprimed with an oil ground, especially a lead-in-oil ground, have a grayish color instead of the brilliant white expected in a ground coating. This is because oil grounds turn yellowish with age, so manufacturers add a tint to hide this defect. Lead-in-oil grounds suffer even more because the lead pigment can turn yellowish when stored in dark or humid conditions, and since preprimed textiles are stored in rolls, this frequently happens. An untinted ground that has yellowed will regain its former whiteness once it is stretched and exposed to daylight for a few days. But a ground that has been tinted during manufacture will remain gray.

Preprimed supports with oil grounds should be stretched before being stored in the studio. Long storage in rolls allows the ground layer to grow brittle—a natural characteristic of the oil. Subsequent stretching of a preprimed fabric that has been stored rolled up may crack the ground, especially where it is bent over the chassis. Cracking exposes the fabric to stress from paint layers and atmospheric conditions, and can lead to future separation of the ground and paint from the support.

PAPER

When properly prepared, paper can be an excellent support for a variety of media. The paper should be made of 100 percent cotton or linen rag fibers, or one of the newer cellulose pulp papers that are buffered against atmospheric acid (they are called acid-free or pH neutral). These conditions must be met if the papers are to resist yellowing and embrittlement. Certainly, cheap newsprint and the various plain white drawing bond papers are not permanent materials unless they can be certified to contain no wood pulp or acids (a simple test for the acidity of papers can be found in Appendix B).

Papers are useful as sketching supports for oil painting, but they should not be considered permanent. A boardlike 400 pound watercolor paper might prove durable for a while, but even such a strong support will eventually be stained and damaged when the oil penetrates its fibers. Papers can be primed with a ground such as an acrylic polymer emulsion "gesso" to protect them against the oil, but priming will so obscure the surface quality of the paper—which is the reason for using it in the first place—that one might as well use a different support or a different paint.

The advantages of paper are that it is accessible and inexpensive. But it is physically fragile; paintings done on it should be carefully handled and stored (see Chapter 17 and Appendix B).

CANVAS BOARDS

Most supply shops carry canvas boards and primed paper as supports for painting, but they are of doubtful quality and the serious artist will avoid them. Primed paper is sold in tear-off tablets and has a cloth weavelike texture imprinted on its surface: it is both cheaply made and impermanent. Canvas boards use the thinnest cotton or muslin glued to cheap pulp cardboard, primed with an acrylic emulsion that also serves to fill the gaps in the material's thin weave. These materials are technical disasters.

While it is possible to find well-constructed custom canvas boards made of permanent materials, one can easily prepare one's own at less expense and be equally assured of a durable product.

CHASSIS FOR STRETCHING TEXTILES

To lessen the movement of a textile support, as mentioned earlier, fabrics used for painting are stretched on an auxiliary chassis. There are two types of chassis: the strainer and the stretcher.

STRAINERS

The homemade *strainers* described below are convenient, inexpensive, and easy to make. Because their rigid corners restrain the movement of the mounted textile, and because this can sometimes lead to the cracking or flaking of oil paint, strainers have not enjoyed a good reputation. But plenty of oil paintings on linen, sized with glue, primed with lead white in oil, and stretched on strainers have survived for well over a hundred years without significant damage to the paint. While strainers can pose a threat to oil paintings, they can be used successfully if the paintings receive proper care, and are more than satisfactory for other types of flexible paints.

A strainer is easily built in the studio. It is usually constructed from 1- by 2-inch (2.5 × 5 cm) or 1- by 3-inch (2.5 × 7.5 cm) clear lumber in the same manner used for building a panel bracing, with one important difference. A lip, or bevel, must be added to the front edge of the chassis to hold the textile away from the frame. If the fabric were to remain in contact with the full width of the strainer frame during the painting process, an annoying, or even damaging, line would appear on the painting. The bevel can be made by sawing it into the chassis edges with a table saw, or by adding it as a separate component using quarter-round molding.

MATERIALS FOR SAWED BEVEL

1. 1- by 2-inch (2.5 × 5 cm) or 1- by 3-inch (2.5 × 7.5 cm) pine, fir, or other straight softwood, free of twists, warps, or knots.
2. Table saw.
3. Miter box and back saw.
4. Corner irons, with screws.
5. Hammer and screwdriver.
6. Carpenter's square.
7. Corner clamps.
8. Carpenter's glue.

METHOD

1. Use the table saw to cut a bevel into the face side of the boards. Leave a lip about ½-inch (1.3 cm) wide exposed on the face of the board; this will be the area of contact for the fabric.
2. Cut the boards to length and miter their ends to 45 degree angles with the miter box and back saw.
3. Assemble the chassis using the corner clamps to get 90 degree angle corners. Glue the joints and use the corner irons to hold them rigid. Add cross-bracing to the back of the chassis if any side is over 24 inches (60.8 cm) long; cross-bracing will prevent bowing-in of the chassis as the textile is stretched on it (Figure 1.8).

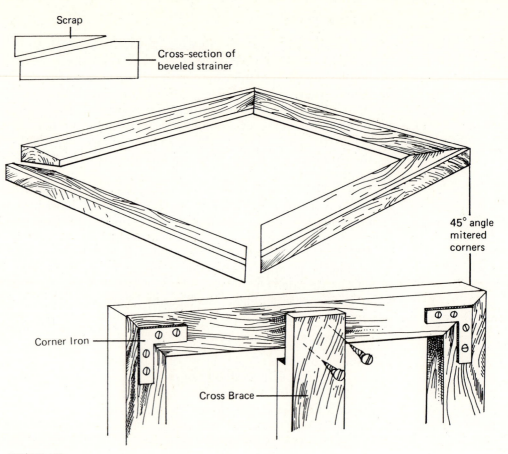

FIGURE 1.8
Beveled Strainer

Top left: Cross-section of strainer member, with bevel ripped out on a table saw.
Middle: Assembly with 45° angle mitered corners.
Bottom: Attachment of a lap-jointed cross brace.

MATERIALS FOR QUARTER-ROUND MOLDING

1. Wood for the chassis, of the same size chosen for the beveled strainer.
2. Miter box and back saw.
3. Corner irons, with screws.
4. Hammer and screwdriver.
5. Carpenter's try square.
6. Corner clamps.
7. Carpenter's glue.
8. ½-inch (1.3 cm) quarter-round wooden molding.
9. ¾-inch (1.9 cm) brads or finishing nails.

METHOD

1. Construct the strainer as for bracing the back of a panel. Miter the corners or make lap joints; glue them together and use the corner irons on the back for rigidity. Use the corner clamps to be sure that the corners are 90 degree angles. Construct cross-bracing, using lap joints, if the size of the strainer warrants it.
2. On the face side of the strainer, measure for and cut the quarter-round molding. Lay the molding around the outside edges of the strainer so the rounded profile of the molding faces the inside of the strainer. Miter the ends of the quarter-round for a flush, square fit.
3. Apply the carpenter's glue to the bottom of each molding strip and nail it into place (Figure 1.9).

STRETCHERS

A stretcher is a set of machine-made wooden rails, with beveling at the edges and mitered, mortise-and-tenoned corners. The mortise-and-tenoned corners allow a set of four bars to be fitted together without glue or screwed-on supports. The stretcher system can therefore expand and contract with the movement of the mounted fabric. Most stretcher systems have small slots in the inside corners of the chassis into which keys can be inserted (two keys for each corner). These keys provide a means for retensioning the fabric if it sags. But the keys should not be overused.

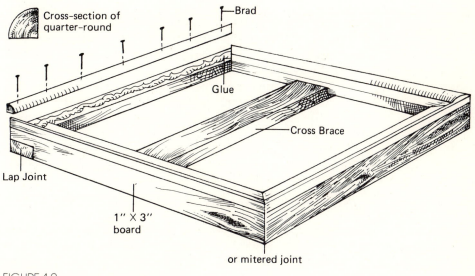

Cross-section of quarter-round

Brad

Glue

Cross Brace

Lap Joint

1″ × 3″ board

or mitered joint

FIGURE 1.9
Strainer with Quarter-Round Lip

Top left: Cross-section of a quarter-round.
Bottom: Attachment of quarter-round to strainer, with brads and glue.

Most fabrics have a tendency to sag in conditions of high humidity and to shrink when the humidity goes down. If one keys out a sagging picture when the humidity is high—so that the picture is drum-tight in high humidity—it can be exposed to great stress when the humidity goes down. This can place a strain on a relatively rigid paint film, especially after many cycles of high and low humidity. The strain causes cracking, loss of adhesion, and the like. Keying out should therefore be avoided if possible. If the picture is sagging too much, keying out should be done only when the humidity is low.

Despite these drawbacks, stretcher systems are popular and attractive: They are easily disassembled, rearranged, and reused, and they are convenient and relatively inexpensive.

Ready-made stretcher bars come in two sizes. The smaller and most common is about ¾-inch thick and 1½ inches wide (1.9 × 3.9 cm), with beveling on both front and back. Sometimes these bars can be found with a keyable cross-brace for the middle of the long side of a chassis.

The larger bars are not as readily available at retail stores, but can be had through various mail-order suppliers (see Appendix D). These are about 1½-inches thick and 2½ inches wide (3.9 × 6.9 cm) and have the bevel only on one side; they also come with corner keys (Figure 1.10). This size is excellent for large pictures, where the greater expanse of fabric needs a stronger support. Both sizes are usually well made, but it is wise to inspect individual bars before purchase for defects such as warping, twisting, or cracks in the joints.

Custom-made stretcher bar systems can be made from several companies, who will make up a chassis to exact dimensions (see Appendix D). These systems feature harder and clearer wood in their construction, and ingenious mechanical devices at the corner and cross-bar attachments that can maintain precise tension on the fabric support. The expense of these custom systems usually prohibits their use by the average artist, but they are widely used by conservators and museums.

One manufacturer of artists' supplies, M. Grumbacher, makes Stretcher Cleats and Cross Bar Cleats that can be used to simulate the action of keyable bars on a homemade strainer. The cleats are aluminum wedges that slide on screws fastened to the mitered corners of a strainer. They spread the corners of the strainer and angle the face of the fabric away from the inside edges of the bars. The cleats allow an artist to build an acceptable stretcher from plain wood (Figure 1.11).

STRETCHING A TEXTILE

There are a number of ways to stretch a fabric onto a chassis. Any system that produces a flat, smooth, taut surface will do. Stretching a preprimed fabric requires slightly more effort than stretching raw fabric because priming stiffens the fabric's surface. If stretching is difficult, use upholsterer's stretching pliers (Figure 1.12) to achieve the desired result. A textile that will later have an acrylic emulsion ground applied also needs to be stretched rather tightly, because the acrylic primer will not shrink the fabric as much as a glue size. Linen or cotton

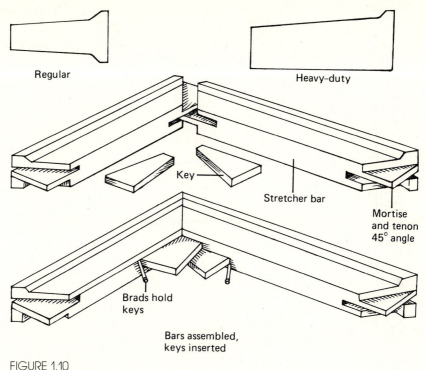

Regular

Heavy-duty

Key

Stretcher bar

Mortise
and tenon
45° angle

Brads hold
keys

Bars assembled,
keys inserted

FIGURE 1.10
Stretcher Bars and Keys

Top left: Cross-section of regular stretcher.
Top right: Cross-section of heavy-duty stretcher.
Middle: Bars and keys—note mortise and tenon 45° angle mitered corners.
Bottom: Assembled, with brads holding keys.

duck that will be sized before the ground is applied should not be tightly stretched (it is sometimes better to do it without using the pliers) because the size shrinks the fabric considerably. If the fabric is too tightly stretched, the shrinking action can break the joints of the chassis.

Methods of fastening the material vary. Some artists prefer to use No. 4 or No. 6 blue steel carpet tacks and a magnetic tack hammer. The tacks hold very well even when they begin to rust, and are the traditional fasteners. Some artists prefer to use staples because a staple gun is faster and can be used with one hand; if you use staples, choose a gun that can shoot heavy-duty fasteners.

The following is a description of one method of stretching a textile—raw, unprimed linen—using tacks, onto a chassis of ready-made stretcher bars.

MATERIALS

1. Four stretcher bars with keys.
2. Linen, cut so it is a piece about 2 inches (5 cm) larger on each side than the assembled chassis.

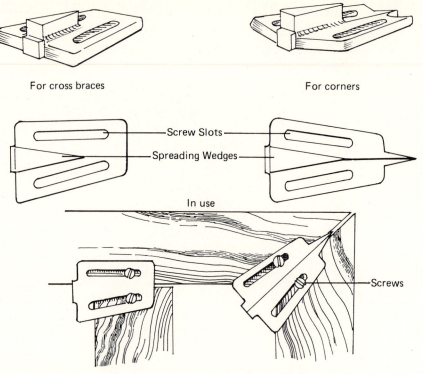

For cross braces   For corners

Screw Slots

Spreading Wedges

In use

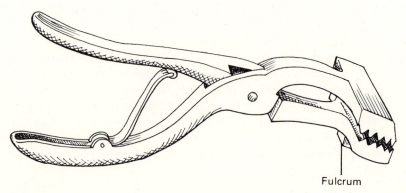

Screws

FIGURE 1.11
Grumbacher's Cross-Bar Cleats and Stretcher Cleats

Fulcrum

FIGURE 1.12
Stretching Pliers

3. A carpenter's square.

4. A tack hammer with one magnetic head and one plain head.

5. No. 4 or No. 6 blue steel carpet tacks.

6. Stretching pliers.

METHOD

1. Assemble the chassis. Make sure the corners are 90 degrees by checking them with the square, or use the inside corner of a square doorframe to check or measure the length of the two diagonals to see that they are equal. Secure the corners of the chassis by driving a tack through the joints, or use some scrap wood as a temporary brace. (Be sure to remove the tacks or bracing after stretching the fabric.) If the size of the chassis requires it, attach a cross-brace between the centers of the longer sides.

2. Place the linen on the floor or a table and smooth it out. Center the chassis on the linen so that there is an equal amount of excess material on all sides. The weave of the linen should be parallel to the sides of the chassis.

3. Find the center of each bar, by eye or by measuring. Fold the linen over the bar on one side and tack it to the center of the outside edge of the bar. Drive this and all the rest of the tacks about halfway in, so they can be removed later if necessary.

4. Tack the linen to the center of the opposite bar. Follow the same procedure with the other two sides.

5. Stand the chassis on one edge and remove the center tack. With the pliers, grasp the excess linen and stretch it across the edge of the bar. Replace the tack, using the magnetic head of the hammer to hold the tack for the first blow. Do the same to the adjacent side. Notice the diamond-shaped wrinkle in the surface of the fabric.

6. About 2 inches (5 cm) on either side of the first tack, drive two more tacks. Do the same on the opposite side, stretching the linen taut before placing the tacks and using the same tension to keep the weave parallel to the bars. Estimate the distance between the tacks by using the width of the plier jaws.

7. Do the same with the adjacent sides, being sure to place the tacks directly opposite their counterparts. This will ensure even tension. Pull slightly away from the center, toward the corners, when stretching the material. Continue in this manner, placing the tacks at even intervals, until the linen is stretched onto the chassis up to the corners (Figure 1.13).

8. Neatly fold the corners as in Figure 1.14 and tack the linen into the heavier part of the joint. When facing the rear of the chassis, the heavier part of the joint will be the lower edge on the right and the upper edge on the left. The corner fold illustrated not only looks neat, but is an advantage when the picture is inserted into a frame: bulging excess material at the corners makes secure framing difficult.

9. If you are satisfied that the linen is properly stretched, without wrinkles,

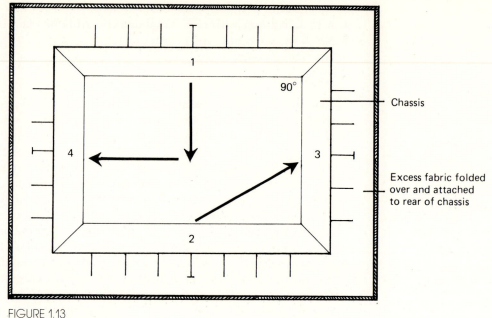

FIGURE 1.13
Stretching Diagram

sags, ripples in the weave, or warps in the chassis, drive the tacks in completely. If there are defects, remove the tacks at that point and restretch.

10. Tack the excess linen to the back of the chassis. Do not trim it off at the edges of the bars, because this will make future restretching of the material extremely difficult.

Some artists find it more convenient to make the attachments on the rear of the stretcher instead of the edges—it is much easier to stand the stretcher on edge. It

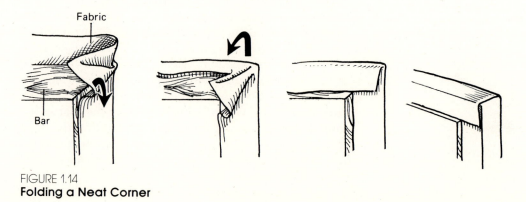

FIGURE 1.14
Folding a Neat Corner

is an acceptable practice, provided you realize that extra strain is put on the material by stretching it over two edges instead of one.

Whatever system is used, a properly stretched fabric should lie flat when placed on the floor. If one corner is raised up off the floor, this indicates that the support is warped—usually the result of uneven stretching tension.

Place the keys in the slots at the rear corners of the chassis. They can be held in place with small brads. Remember that using them can be harmful for the picture.

TEXTILE MOUNTING

The homemade version of those cheap canvas boards described earlier combines a rigid panel substrate with the desirable surface qualities of a flexible material. Since painting with oil on flexible fabrics can be risky, this laminated arrangement might be the best support for easel painting on fabric.

The disadvantages of mounting a textile on a panel include the difficulties of making repairs to the back of the textile, the potential for the lamination to separate due to air bubbles or moisture penetration between the layers, and the weight of the combination. But good technique can at least prevent delamination.

Two methods are given below. One uses the common and easily obtained hide glue adhesive (also called a size), the other a less common but more effective wax-resin adhesive similar to those used by some conservators.

BASIC MATERIALS

1. Panel substrate. (If hardboard, sand, bevel the edges, and brace if necessary.)
2. Fabric (linen, cotton) cut to a size about 2 inches (5 cm) larger on all sides than the panel.
3. The adhesive: a strong hide glue, as described in Chapter 2, or a wax-resin adhesive made as follows:
   a. Melt 7 parts by weight of Be Square No. 175, a microcrystalline petroleum wax with a high melting point (see Appendix D) in a double boiler until liquid. Do not allow it to burn. *Caution:* Wax vapors are harmful and flammable.
   b. Add 1 to 2 parts by weight of damar varnish. Stir until homogenized. Apply while warm.
4. A bowl for the glue.
5. A large housepainter's brush.
6. A hard rubber brayer.

HIDE GLUE METHOD

1. Make the glue and put it into the bowl.
2. Brush the glue onto the panel and cover it generously.

3. Dip the fabric into the glue so that it is thoroughly wet. Wring out the excess glue.
4. Position the fabric on the panel. Fold the flaps over the panel's edges and onto the back.
5. Use the brayer to roll the surface and edges of the panel to be sure the fabric is completely adhered. Start at the center of the panel and work toward the edges; this will force trapped air bubbles out.
6. Put a coating of the glue on the back of the panel.
7. Allow the panel to dry overnight. It will need no further preparation except priming.

WAX-RESIN ADHESIVE METHOD

1. Make the adhesive.
2. Brush it onto the panel thinly, to cover completely.
3. Brush it onto the fabric thinly, to cover completely. Work quickly—this adhesive dries by cooling.
4. Press the fabric onto the panel, fold the edges over to the back, and roll the front of the panel vigorously with the brayer to ensure complete contact. A hand-held heat lamp will soften adhesive that dries too quickly.
5. Allow the panel to dry and cure overnight.
6. To prepare the panel for receiving a ground, first wipe it gently with a rag dampened in mineral spirits to dissolve and remove excess adhesive. Allow it to dry before priming.

The hide glue method is best for general use and is the easiest to make and apply, but the fabric may come loose from the panel if moisture penetrates. The wax-resin method makes a waterproof system, but one that is susceptible to solvents like mineral spirits and gum turpentine. It is also more difficult to control during application.

CHAPTER 2

SIZES AND GROUNDS

Most painting supports need further surface treatment before they can be used. Preprimed textiles already have a prepared surface and need only be mounted on an auxiliary support; papers being used for aqueous techniques generally do not need further attention. But untreated supports, flexible and rigid, are usually too absorbent to allow the controlled application of paint. Therefore intermediate layers, a size and a ground, are first applied.

SIZES

A *size* is a thin solution, often a weak glue but sometimes a resinous mixture, which is brushed directly onto the support (see Glossary). A correctly made and applied size will permeate the support surface without coating it—it will not form a distinct, separate layer.

The incorrect application of a size can cause damage to the picture. A glossy film of size may prevent a good mechanical bond between the support and further applications of coatings. A weak bond may lead to cracking and loss of the paint film. A size that is too weak, on the other hand, will allow the paint binder to be absorbed into the support: weakly bound paint may crumble or powder off the support.

A size is essential if the grounds or paints are based on linseed oil. Linseed oil dries by oxidizing, and can disintegrate or embrittle an unprotected paper or fabric support.

As the term implies, sizes shrink a stretched fabric support so that it fits tightly on its chassis. Some materials used as sizes do this better than others, and some, like hide glue, are so powerful that they have a tendency to overwhelm the other physical components of a painting. Of course, this depends on the conditions under which they are used.

HIDE GLUE

This is a glue made from animal skins and bones. Its popular name is *rabbitskin glue.* It comes in the form of tough, leathery sheets, roughly ground granules, or finely ground powder. The dry glue is mixed with hot water to make a powerful adhesive, a binder for paints, and a size.

Recipes for making the hide glue solution are affected by the age and source of the dry glue: a fresh glue will be stronger than one which has been in storage for a long time. The formulas in this section take this factor into account by allowing leeway in their measurements.

MATERIALS *(Figure 2.1)*

1. The dry glue.
2. Cold tap water.
3. A double boiler or other clean metal container.
4. An electric hotplate. The hotplate should have a rheostat so the temperature can be controlled. It should also have a metal cover over the heating element to lessen the danger of fire.
5. A glass quart measure, graduated in 1 ounce (or milliliter) divisions.
6. A wooden spoon or stick for stirring.
7. A 2- to 3-inch (5 to 7.5 cm) housepainter's brush, for application.

Hide glue is now known to be far stronger than any other component in an oil painting on fabric (the other components are the paint and the fabric). Hide glue is hygroscopic—it tends to absorb and expel atmospheric moisture, even when apparently dry—and its response to changes in relative humidity can be extreme. It shrinks greatly when humidity is low, and sags considerably when the humidity is high. Both responses put undue stress on a relatively rigid and brittle dried oil paint layer, especially when it has been painted on a flexible support and stretched on a chassis. The oil paint has little choice but to crack under these conditions, and the obvious result is the slow and inevitable destruction of the picture. Nonetheless, hide glue is a valuable adhesive for certain applications: very diluted, it will weakly size a strong paper; when formulated properly, it can be used to mount a fabric support on a panel; and it has been used as the binder for pigments in a paint called, variously, size paint or distemper.

HIDE GLUE SIZE FOR A SUPPORT

As a size, hide glue may be prepared according to one of two methods; the difference is in the way the amount of glue to be used is measured. The prepared glue can then be applied to a stretched fabric or to a panel.

METHOD A: DISPLACEMENT MEASUREMENT

1. Put 16 ounces (480 ml) cold tap water in the quart (liter) measure.
2. Add dry glue to the water to raise its level by about 1½ ounces (45 ml).

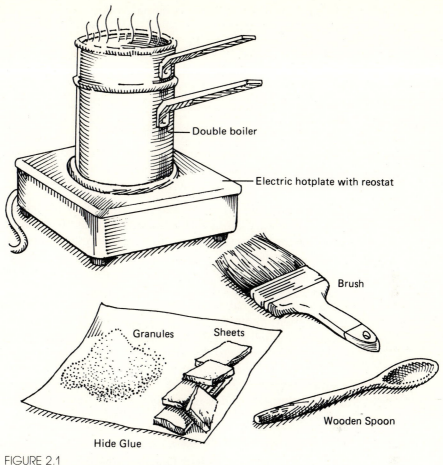

— Double boiler

— Electric hotplate with reostat

Brush

Granules   Sheets

Wooden Spoon

Hide Glue

FIGURE 2.1
Materials for Making Hide Glue Size

Clockwise, from bottom right: Wooden spoon, imported sheet hide glue, granular domestic hide glue, reostat-controlled hotplate, double boiler, brush.

3. Add additional water to the mixture to bring its level up to the 32-ounce (960 ml) mark.

4. Soak the glue until it has absorbed water and swelled. If the glue is granulated or powdered, three hours of soaking should be enough; if it is sheets, soak it overnight. Stir the glue occasionally to keep it from sticking together in a lump.

5. Place the glue and water mixture in the top of the double boiler. Put water in the bottom pot—the water will melt the glue and insulate it from the direct application of heat.

6. Heat the mixture gently on the hotplate. Do not allow it to boil. Remove it from the heat when it has melted completely, and use it while it is hot.

7. If the glue boils while it is being made, it will lose its adhesiveness and should be discarded.

METHOD B: VOLUME/VOLUME MEASUREMENT

1. Place about 1 part by volume of the dry powdered glue into 10 parts cold tap water.
2. Soak and heat as in method A.

APPLICATION TO A STRETCHED FABRIC

This application is not recommended when the textile is to be primed and painted with oil-based paints. Since it is a widely used procedure, however, it should be done correctly.

1. Be sure the fabric is clean and not too tightly stretched.
2. Brush the warm, dilute glue onto the fabric. Begin in the center and work toward the edges. Apply the glue thinly and uniformly so that it appears to sink into the weave. Brush the size onto the edges of the support and around to the back of the chassis. This will glue the fabric to the back of the bars and keep frayed edges from raveling.
3. Since a single coat of glue may leave a number of pinholes through which subsequent applications of paint can seep, a second, very thin coat of size can be applied when the first is dry.
4. If the fabric sticks to the stretchers, release it by running a blunt knife or a stiff paper card along the back of the support, between the bars and the fabric (Figure 2.2).
5. Allow the size to dry naturally. Do not force it to dry by applying heat, direct sunlight, or air.

APPLICATION TO A PANEL

1. Sand and dust the panel; bevel its edges. If the surface is waxy-looking, wipe it off with a rag dampened in denatured ethyl alcohol or mineral spirits and allow it to dry. *Caution:* Alcohol is a toxic health and fire hazard; use with plenty of ventilation and keep away from sparks or flame.
2. Apply thinly, as to a stretched fabric. The edges and the back of the panel should also be covered—this will retard moisture penetration and equalize shrinkage and stress on both faces of the panel.

Whichever support has been used, you should check to make sure that the glue has been applied properly. To do so, hold the support at an angle to a strong light and look at the dried surface. It may have an overall sparkle, but it should not show any shiny, reflecting spots—these indicate a too-heavy application of the glue. The shiny spots can be removed by wiping them with a rag dampened in warm water. Insufficient coverage can also be noticed if the support is held up in front of a strong light. Pinholes indicate that a second thin coat of size is needed.

Leftover glue can be stored in a clean, covered glass jar in the refrigerator. It

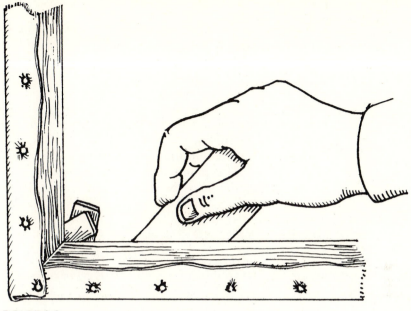

FIGURE 2.2
Preventing the Fabric from Sticking to the Bars

Slip a card between the rear of the fabric and the stretcher bars.

will decompose after about two weeks; its odor becomes stunningly unpleasant, and it must be discarded. Glue that has cooled will jell. In most instances it is necessary to melt the gel by gentle heating in order to use it again. Reheating will drive off some of the water and increase the strength of the glue; a little hot water added to the solution will return the glue to its proper concentration. Softly jelled glue can be applied without reheating by using the edge of a large spatula to spread the size thinly over the support. Be sure to use enough pressure to force the gel into the weave.

Hide glue in a thin film will gradually harden from its jelled state as the balance of the water evaporates. As noted, however, it is hygroscopic, and will continue to absorb and expel atmospheric moisture. In the past it was recommended that the film be further cured and made somewhat more moisture-resistant by lightly spraying the support with a weak solution of formaldehyde in water. It has recently been found that formaldehyde is a possible carcinogen; its use is no longer recommended.

HIDE GLUE SIZE FOR PAPER

Some papers made specifically for aqueous painting techniques need no further surface preparation. Other papers, which are not presized, can have this weak solution applied.

METHOD

1. Put 1 part dry glue into 10 parts cold water, and soak and heat as before.
2. When the solution has formed, stir it into 30 additional parts of warm water. The final proportion is 1 part glue to 40 parts water, by volume.

APPLICATION

1. Put the weak glue solution in a tub or tray large enough to hold the paper.
2. Immerse the paper in the glue—several sheets can be done at once—and soak for several hours.
3. Remove each sheet and drain off the excess glue. Lay the sheets flat on a large sheet of glass or smoothly sanded plywood, and leave until dry. It is important that the paper be allowed to dry naturally at room temperature —do not force-dry with heat lamps, heaters, or sunlight.

HIDE GLUE FOR MOUNTING FABRIC ON A PANEL

To prepare hide glue for the mounting technique described in Chapter 1, combine about 3 parts by volume of dry glue with 10 parts cold water; then soak and heat as usual.

OTHER MATERIALS FOR SIZE

Hide glue is the traditional size material, but recent studies show that it poses definite dangers under certain circumstances. Other adhesives may be substituted for hide glue for making a protective size. Most of them are easier to make and use; some are safer from the standpoint of physical stability, and are not subject to organic decomposition; many are more expensive.

When chosing an alternative, be aware of the principle of reversibility. A film-forming material such as a size or varnish that is reversible—that is, may be easily removed by dissolving it with its original diluent—is sometimes preferred to one that is resistant to removal.

REVERSIBLE SIZES

These reversible sizes are easily removed when redissolved in their diluents. They all provide a measure of protection for the support and will reduce its absorbency; a few shrink (size) a stretched fabric as they dry; some can be used on a fabric or paper to which oil paints will be applied; some may pose stresses similar to those of hide glue.

Gelatin   Powdered gelatin is a refined relative of hide glue, prepared from the same source. It may be purchased through scientific supply houses. Edible gelatin, found in supermarkets, can also be used. Gelatin yellows upon ageing; its stress characteristics are similar to those of hide glue (being of the same composition but weaker); and, when dry, is attractive to molds and insects. The formulas for making, using, and storing a gelatin size are approximately the same as for hide glue.

Starch Vegetable flours such as those derived from rice and wheat may be used to make weak glues. These are adequate, but inconsistently effective, sizes. They lose their adhesiveness after a long period; they decompose in storage; and they are susceptible to molds and insects.

To make, mix 1 part by volume of the flour into 2 to 3 parts cold water and blend into a smooth paste. Stir this paste into 3 parts boiling water slowly enough to avoid forming lumps. Allow the mixture to cool.

For brushing onto a support, thin 1 part of the starch glue with 5 to 10 parts cold water—or enough water to make the solution very thin. This size does not have to be heated, but should be made fresh each time.

Methyl Cellulose This is a methyl ether of cellulose, the basic constituent of plants. It comes in the form of a flaky, somewhat spongy white powder, and is dissolved in cold water to make a glue. It need not be heated to dissolve, remains liquid when cool, does not decompose in storage, and is not as attractive as the other materials to insects and molds (see Appendix D). Methyl cellulose powder has a shelf life of about one year, after which time its adhesive power diminishes. The prepared glue will have a longer life if it is made with distilled water.

To make a methyl cellulose size, add 24 parts cold water to 1 part of the powder. Mix and stir into a smooth syrup. Thin 1 part of the syrup with 10 to 20 parts cold water to make the size.

Acrylic Solutions Gelatin, starch, and methyl cellulose are all hygroscopic to some degree; acrylic resins are not. Polymerized acrylic resins (see Chapter 3) are dissolved in a solvent to produce syrupy solutions. One variety that is reversible is Acryloid B-67MT, made by the Rohm and Haas Company, with the resin dissolved in mineral spirits.

The solution is thinned for application by brush by adding about 5 to 10 parts by volume of solvent to 1 part acrylic resin solution. For spray applications, further dilution is necessary. The fabric should be tightly stretched. Do not heat the solution.

Caution: The solvents used in acrylic solutions can be health and fire hazards. Do not use them near an open flame. When spraying these solutions, wear a vapor mask rated for organic mists, solvent-proof rubber gloves, splash goggles, and a smock or long-sleeved shirt. Local exhaust ventilation is also recommended.

IRREVERSIBLE SIZES

Once dry, these materials are not easily removed by their original diluents; stronger solvents must be used. They protect the support and reduce its absorbency, but do not shrink the fabric. They are very effective substitutes for hide glue.

Acrylic Emulsions Polymerized acrylic resins can be emulsified in water. They can be used as a protective sealer and are available wherever acrylic emulsion paints are sold under various proprietary names. Use the "matte medium" variety for this purpose.

About 2 parts water and 1 part medium are mixed and applied with a brush; for spraying, thin with more water. The fabric support should be tightly stretched, and the size should not be heated. The size remains liquid and does not decompose in storage. Store the size in a tightly covered plastic container to prevent evaporation, and avoid freezing. Metal containers will rust.

Acrylic emulsions are considered relatively safe to use, but sometimes the vapors can produce an allergic reaction. Use all synthetic polymer emulsions with adequate ventilation—at least three complete air changes in the room per hour. Check the container label for the product's health hazard certification by the Art and Craft Materials Institute.

Polyvinyl Acetate Emulsions Polymerized vinyl acetate (PVA) resin, finely dispersed in water, is readily recognized as the common white glue used for paper and wood. Some of the PVA emulsions reportedly yellow on exposure to ultraviolet light; archival PVA emulsions reportedly do not yellow. When exposed to water, PVA emulsion films cloud—turn from translucent to nearly opaque white—but do not lose their film properties.

Mix 5 to 10 parts water with 1 part PVA emulsion, depending on whether it will be brushed or sprayed, and apply to the support. The size should not be heated. It will not decompose in storage, nor does it attract insects or molds. Store in plastic containers, and avoid freezing. *Note:* Neither the PVA nor the acrylic emulsions form perfectly continuous films when diluted for application as a size. They are apt to be full of pinholes; two thin coats are recommended.

GROUNDS

The next intermediate layer between a support and subsequent films is a *ground,* sometimes also called a *primer.* A ground is unnecessary for some painting techniques—in transparent watercolor, for example, the white paper is both support and ground. Sometimes the artist's aims are better realized when the paint is applied directly to an unprimed support. An example is the effect obtained when diluted acrylic emulsion paint is used to stain raw cotton duck. Whether to use a ground is often an esthetic question, but it is important to be aware of the technical considerations. The yellowing of the cotton duck, for instance, will quickly change the color balance of the original picture: Morris Louis's paintings have shown this change over the last twenty or so years.

Most supports will be unevenly absorbent, even if they have been correctly sized. It is difficult to predict the results of a paint film laid on an unevenly absorbent surface: The loaded brush may not respond to the painter's touch and skip and drag across the support in an uncontrolled way; the paint film may show areas of glossiness or dullness that were not intended. A ground will ensure that a particular kind of paint will perform with reasonable predictability.

A ground is also a structural element, a key for the paint films—a toothy coating for the paint to grip—and a definite layer between the support and the paint. If the support should deteriorate, a paint film somewhat isolated by a stable ground layer can more easily be stabilized. Without a ground, treatment is much more difficult.

Perhaps most important is the color of the ground and its effect on the color of the painting. Many paint films, particularly those in an oil vehicle, grow more transparent as they age. If the ground is white, the hues in the painting will retain their relative value relationships and may even grow more intense as the film becomes transparent. If the support is unprimed or the ground itself is pigmented and dark, the increasing transparency of the paint film will eventually lower and alter the picture's color system.

In summary, grounds should meet these following requirements:

1. The grounds should be white. A middle tone wash of color can be applied to the ground to reduce its brilliance, but the ground itself should not be tinted.

2. The ground should have a tooth. A toothy surface can be obtained by slightly underbinding the ground so that pigment particles project above the binder film, or by using pigment particles of varying sizes. A ground should also be somewhat absorbent.

3. A ground should be an even and thinly applied coating, without pinholes or other application defects that leave areas of the support uncovered.

4. When applied to a flexible support, the ground should not be too much affected by the continuous movement (expansion and contraction) of the support. Brittle grounds such as glue gesso need rigid supports.

GROUNDS FOR FLEXIBLE SUPPORTS

Several types of primers meet the requirements for a ground when applied to flexible supports. They are divided into two principal categories, oil grounds and acrylic emulsion grounds.

OIL GROUNDS

The traditional ground for oil painting is called an oil ground. Although ingredients for oil grounds have been altered in present-day commercial formulas, the basic constituents of the original material are lead white pigment and linseed oil. Unlike titanium white, zinc white, and titanium and zinc mixtures, lead white in oil can be prepared in the studio, but its toxicity makes it unsuitable for use by those who are inexperienced in working with hazardous materials.

Lead White in Oil Lead white (basic carbonate of lead) is one of the earliest pigments and was, until the middle of the nineteenth century, the only white pigment that would remain opaque when mixed with oil. Its virtues are that it is dense and opaque; it forms tough, relatively flexible and fast-drying films in linseed oil; and it uses very little oil when mixed into a coating material, thus satisfying the requirement that an oil ground be lean, or underbound. Its faults are that it is *toxic* when ingested, absorbed through breaks in the skin, or inhaled. It can turn dark when exposed to sulfide pigments or hydrogen sulfide in the atmosphere. Its films in oil, which become transparent with age, grow progressively rigid as they age—a fault more of the oil than the pigment. The harmful aspects of lead white can be avoided by good hygiene, sensible and cautious work habits, and protective equipment. The darkening effect is reduced to a negligible level when the pigment is properly encased in a binder like linseed oil—and lead white is not used with binders other than those that thoroughly encase it.

A stiff paste of lead white in linseed oil is available from Triad Paint and Chemical (see Appendix D) in large quantities, though the outlawing of lead-based paints for general home use has made the paste harder to get. Artists who wish to use lead-in-oil grounds can: (1) make their own (not recommended for those unfamiliar with handling toxic materials); (2) modify an artists' white lead oil paint so that it meets the requirements of a ground; (3) purchase an artists' white lead oil paint that has been specially formulated for use in underpainting or as a ground; or (4) purchase the paste from a supplier. The last two options are recommended for those who wish to avoid handling the dry white lead pigment.

Lead White in Oil Paste

MATERIALS FOR PREPARING LEAD WHITE IN OIL PASTE

Warning: Do not attempt this procedure unless you are thoroughly familiar with the proper handling of toxic materials (Figure 2.3).

1. Protective equipment.
   a. NIOSH-approved toxic dust mask.* The mask should have replaceable filters and tightly cover both nose and mouth.
   b. Latex or nitrile rubber gloves.
   c. Goggles for eye protection.
   d. Long-sleeved shirt or smock with closed collar and cuffs. Store the smock in the studio so it does not carry toxic powders into living quarters.
   e. A barrier hand cream such as Barracaide (Mentholatum Company) or Cover-Derm (Lab Safety Supply Company). Barrier creams should not contain solvents.
2. Lead white pigment.
3. Barium sulfate pigment, an inert pigment that gives the mixture tooth; also called barytes.
4. Artists' grade alkali-refined linseed oil.
5. A spatula or a long, stiff palette knife.
6. A glass slab, approximately ¼ inch by 18 inches by 24 inches (7 by 460 by 610 mm). The size depends on the amount of paste to be made.

---

* National Institute of Occupational Safety and Health.

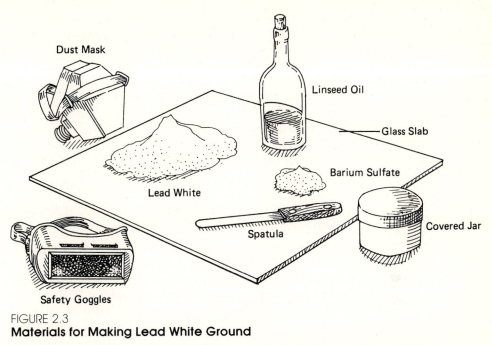

FIGURE 2.3
Materials for Making Lead White Ground

Clockwise, from bottom left: Goggles, dust mask, lead white pigment, linseed oil, barium sulfate, spatula, large covered container. Everything is sitting on a glass slab.

7. Large, wide-mouthed glass jar with cap. A pharmaceutical ointment jar, opaque white or amber-colored, is excellent.

8. Inert plastic sheet, such as Saran Wrap. Common household plastic food storage bags can be cut into sheets and will also work.

METHOD

1. Wear the protective devices. Apply the barrier cream to hands, wrists, and forearms, working it under the fingernails. Allow it to dry. Put on the gloves and smock. Put on the mask and goggles. The discomfort of the equipment is something to get used to, and is preferable to the discomfort, pain, and cost of a chronic illness.

2. Combine 10 parts by volume of the lead white with 1 part barium sulfate. Handle the dry lead white pigment with care: Do not agitate it so much that dust is raised.

3. Place the combined pigments on the slab and add 1 part by volume of the linseed oil. The total proportions are 1 part oil to 11 parts pigment.

4. Rub the ingredients with the spatula until a very stiff paste is formed. Be sure all the particles are wet by the oil; rub hard. If a little more oil is needed, add it drop by drop. Keep the oil content to the absolute minimum.

5. Scrape the paste into the storage jar. Tap the jar on the table top to make any trapped air bubbles rise to the surface, and to ensure that the paste is firmly packed. If the paste does not fill the jar, press the plastic film down on its surface to exclude air.

6. Cap the jar and store until ready for use. If the paste does not come into contact with air, the mixture should keep for a long time.

7. Clean off the slab with a small amount of mineral spirits. Wash with scouring soap and water. Rinse and dry thoroughly.

8. Rinse gloves. Remove smock and store in a plastic bag. Remove goggles and mask. Wash hands and arms with soap and water, using a scrub brush.

MATERIALS FOR MODIFYING LEAD WHITE IN OIL PAINT

Warning: Do not attempt this procedure unless you are thoroughly familiar with the proper handling of toxic materials.

1. Any brand of artists' lead white paint. It may be called by various names, such as flake white or white lead. Be sure that the binder is linseed oil. Other oils may contain additives to increase the drying rate.

2. The same protective equipment and other materials listed under lead white in oil paste.

METHOD

1. Wear the protective devices.

2. Empty the entire contents of the tube of paint onto the slab. Consider this to be 10 parts by volume.

3. Add 1 part by volume lead white pigment and 1 part barium sulfate pigment. Handle the dry lead white pigment with care.

4. Mix and rub the ingredients until a stiff paste is formed. If more pigment is needed to absorb excess oil, add lead white, not barium sulfate. Do not add more oil.

5. Scrape the paste into the jar and pack as described above. If the paste does not fill the jar, use the plastic film to exclude air.

6. Clean up as before.

Other Pigments and Oils for Grounds Titanium white, zinc white, and titanium and zinc combinations are pigment mixtures used by commercial manufacturers in oil grounds that are sold ready to apply. These pigments have considerable advantage over lead white: They are whiter, do not change hue or value when kept in the dark, and are nontoxic. In linseed oil, however, these pigments form less durable paint films. Poppyseed oil, safflower oil, or other nonyellowing drying oils, combined with driers and solvents, can be used as the vehicles in these commercial preparations. The products are useful as paints and grounds, but their formulation is more complex than the simple lead white in linseed oil mixture and should not be attempted in small-scale studio situations.

A pigmented oil modified alkyd resin under the trade name Oil Painting Primer is sold by Winsor & Newton. The primer is thinned with mineral spirits or gum turpentine and can be applied in the same way as the lead white ground. The alkyd grounds are potentially significant improvements over the traditional oil grounds: The binder is nonyellowing, the vehicle is more flexible than straight linseed oil, and the drying time is shorter. The alkyd ground should be used only for alkyd or oil paints.

Application of an Oil Ground to a Fabric Support   The application of an oil ground is simple, though some practice is necessary to achieve a thin, uniform coating. The resulting surface is unique in its texture, look, and effect on a painting.

MATERIALS

1. A stretched and sized but unprimed fabric.
2. A stiff bristle brush.
3. A palette knife or spatula.
4. Pure gums spirits of turpentine or mineral spirits.
5. A lead white in oil paste: homemade, a modified artists' lead white paint, or a tubed or canned lead white in linseed oil. Use other white oil or alkyd paints only if they are designed specifically to be used as grounds. A home-made paste should have as little oil in it as possible. Using a manufactured paste or modified tube paint will prove to be expensive; the consolation is that an oil ground has no real substitutes.
6. A container for mixing the primer large enough to store leftover primer.
7. Plastic film to cover the leftover primer.

METHOD

1. Be sure the fabric is well stretched and sized; the sizing should be allowed to dry for 24 hours before applying the ground. Remove any surface dust or dirt.
2. Use a barrier cream on the hands and arms if making large quantities of primer: the thinners, gum turpentine or mineral spirits, can be allergenic agents when in contact with the skin. Observe the previous precautions about handling lead white.
3. Put enough paste for two coats of ground into the container. The exact amount will depend on the number or size of the supports being primed.
4. Thin the paste to a smooth brushable consistency by adding some thinner a bit at a time. Some writers have compared the proper consistency to that of whipped cream—the paste should stand in peaks.
5. Use the bristle brush to apply the priming to the support. Do a small area at a time and work the priming thoroughly into the weave of the fabric. Cover the entire front of the support, and coat the edges where the fabric

turns over the chassis. This will prevent oil paint from seeping into the support; paint that bleeds over the edges of the painting will make the support brittle even when it is sized well. It is not necessary to cover the fabric on the back of the bars.

6. When the support is covered, use the knife or spatula to scrape off the excess primer. This should be done before the primer has a chance to set up, and should leave a very thin, even coating. Avoid leaving marks from the stretcher bars by using your fingers to push the fabric gently away from the bars. Discard the scraped-off primer.

7. Store the remaining primer in its container. Pack it down and press the plastic wrap over the surface to exclude air.

8. Wash hands and forearms thoroughly—use a scrub brush.

9. Put the support in a dry, well-lit room for a few days. Drying will take any where from four days to two weeks; humid conditions and low temperatures will retard drying.

10. When the first coat is dry, apply a second coat in the same way as described above. To remove any raised nap or fuzz, lightly sand the support with fine sandpaper before giving it the second coat. *Caution:* the dust raised by sanding contains lead white pigment, which is toxic. Wear a dust mask. A single coat of priming is desirable if the support is thin or has a fine weave. Double priming is recommended for heavier weaves, or to obscure the weave.

11. The double primed support should be left to dry for about two weeks, more or less. Some writers suggest a curing time of 6 to 12 months before an oil-primed support is used. During this time, lead white grounds may darken or yellow if stored in darkness or conditions of high humidity. The effect is reversible: Expose the primed support to sunlight in a warm, dry room for a few days, and it will be bleached back to its former whiteness.

ACRYLIC EMULSION GROUNDS

Acrylic emulsion grounds are called gesso by their manufacturers, although they neither contain the same ingredients nor show the surface qualities of a true gesso.

The synthetic emulsion grounds are a mixture of white pigment (usually a titanium-zinc combination), barium sulfate pigment (or chalk, mica, silica, or marble dust—all used to give the mixture tooth), and the acrylic resin dispersed in water. The grounds are brilliant white, very adhesive, and retain flexibility and toughness as they age. They may be applied to most permanent supports—provided the support is not oily or greasy—both flexible and rigid, and are used as a foundation for a wide variety of media. They should not be applied over a hide glue size. Application and cleanup are easy and convenient, because water is the diluent.

Although the acrylic emulsion primers work well with most media, their physical properties may preclude their use under oil paints. Oil paint films grow increasingly rigid and brittle with age; the acrylic emulsion films remain pliant and flexible. Over a period of time, the increasingly different degrees of flexibility may cause the oil paint to separate from the ground. Therefore it is advisable to avoid using the acrylic primer under large oil paintings on fabric supports. For paintings over 3 square feet in area (2.4 m^2), use an oil ground. Of course, it is possible to avoid this problem by painting on a rigid support or fabric mounted on a rigid substrate.

The following formula describes the technique for applying an acrylic emulsion ground to a support. But before beginning, it is important to be aware of some points.

As this primer dries, some fabric shrinkage can occur, so the support should be stretched firmly, but not too tight. Sizing is not required—the primer is impervious to oil paint.

The acrylic emulsion primer appears to sink into and conform with the weave of the textile—much more so than an oil primer. This effect can be countered by applying the ground, unthinned, with a large spatula or a rubber squeegee (like the kind used by window washers). The primer will be forced into the weave but removed from the top of each thread. Several coats will produce a smoother surface. Up to five or more coats of ground can be applied with a brush, with each coating applied at right angles to the layer beneath, to produce a smoother surface. Some commercial acrylic emulsion grounds are harder and less absorbent than an oil ground. A light sanding of the final coat will roughen the surface to give it some tooth.

Although acrylic emulsion primers can be used on most permanent supports, the support must be free of oily or greasy films. For this reason, acrylic grounds should not be applied over old oil paintings in an attempt to salvage and reuse the support; there is always the chance that the ground will not adhere and will later separate from the old painting.

Finally, it is unlikely that the acrylic emulsion primers (and paints) are significantly dangerous, but their use in certain circumstances can be annoying. Some emulsions give off an ammonia odor; this should not be breathed. Use both the primers and the paints with plenty of ventilation and read cautionary labels carefully. Some products may by now be certified by the Art and Craft Materials Institute. In general, exercise normal caution when handling the materials, and wash up thoroughly.

MATERIALS

1. A tightly stretched, unsized, unprimed support.
2. Any brand of acrylic emulsion primer, usually labeled acrylic gesso.
3. 2- to 3-inch (5–7.5 cm) housepainter's brush.
4. Water.

METHOD

1. The primer can be used as it comes from the container or it can be slightly thinned by adding a small amount of water; do not add more than about a tablespoon of water per quart of primer.
2. Brush the primer on, beginning at the center of the support and working toward the edges. Coat the edges where the fabric turns over the chassis. Brush in all directions and finish by smoothing the surface with parallel brush strokes. Allow the priming to dry for at least an hour.
3. Lightly sand the surface, after waiting overnight, if desired. A second coat may be applied, but do not thin the primer. Allow the second coat to dry overnight before using the support.
4. Cleanup is easy. Wash the tools and equipment in warm, soapy water. Do not allow the primer to dry on the tools—the acrylic emulsion is insoluble in water once it dries. If this should happen, paint removers available from some artists' materials companies can dissolve the dried emulsion.

GROUNDS FOR RIGID SUPPORTS

The grounds described above can be applied to rigid supports as well as flexible ones. The surfaces of these grounds, however, tend to be slicker and less absorbent on rigid substrates. A ground perfectly suited for rigid supports is made from a combination of chalk, pigment, and hide glue. This is the traditional glue gesso; the word *gesso* is Italian for gypsum, or plaster.

Gesso grounds are smooth, hard, and white, do not yellow with age, and are quite absorbent. They are suitable for a side variety of oil- and water-based media, as long as the absorbency of the surface is adjusted for the type of paint. Because they are hard and brittle, gesso grounds should be applied only to rigid supports such as the hardboards. They can also be applied to fabrics or papers that have been mounted on a rigid support.

The recipes for gesso vary in measurements and proportions. Some call for equal parts of chalk and pigment, others reduce the amount of pigment; some require that the glue be fairly strong, others recommend a weak glue. The chalk provides bulk, and the pigment provides opacity and whiteness.

Glue strength is important. A weak glue may not bind the chalk and can produce a ground that is soft and crumbly. A glue that is too strong will make a ground that is too hard or that cracks when it has dried. These defects become apparent as soon as the gesso dries. Observe the effects of the recipes and make adjustments accordingly, and remember that the source and age of the hide glue can affect its performance.

The grade of the chalk is also important. All chalk is composed of calcium carbonate, derived from natural deposits of limestone or dolomite, with textures ranging from fine to coarse. Common whiting, found in hardware or paint supply stores, may be too rough to make a smooth gesso. Grades labeled "gilder's whiting" or "Paris white" are smoother, finer-grained varieties. Artificial chalk, also called precipitated chalk, is the smoothest of the available chalks—it consists of very small, uniform particles. Precipitated chalk is less dense than natural chalk, so less is needed in the following recipes.

GLUE CHALK GESSO

There are two ways to prepare glue chalk gesso; they differ only in the way the glue is combined with the filler. Because, when mixing chalk and glue, it is vital to avoid bubble formation, the first method may be preferable to the second. The slow and laborious nature of the first technique seems to reduce bubbling. In the second approach, the temptation is to hurry and pour the glue in too quickly. If there are bubbles in the gesso when it is applied, pinholes or tiny pits will appear in the drying surface as the bubbles burst. These pits cannot be easily removed, nor can they be easily covered up by subsequent coats of gesso. They will show through thin coats of paint as dark specks.

Avoid breathing the chalk or pigment dusts. Neither the pigment nor the chalk is a significant hazard, but inhaling any dust can be irritating to the lungs and a possible source of chronic health problems.

MATERIALS

1. Dry hide glue.
2. Titanium white pigment or zinc oxide pigment.
3. Natural or precipitated chalk.
4. Water.
5. Double boiler and hotplate.
6. Graduated quart or liter measure.
7. Wooden spoon.
8. Fine mesh kitchen strainer.
9. Fine cheesecloth.

METHOD

1. In a separate container, mix the filler. Avoid raising dust and breathing it during this operation. The proportions of chalk to pigment can vary, though generally little pigment is needed. Try using 4 parts chalk and 1 part pigment, by volume. However it is mixed, the total volume of the filler should be equal to that of the glue solution. That is, for every 1 part of glue, make 1 part filler. If a coarse natural chalk is being used, increase the volume of the filler to about 1½ times that of the glue. In this case, the filler-to-glue ratio is 3 to 2 (Figure 2.4).
2. Add 2 parts by volume of the dry glue to 10 parts cold water. Allow to soak 3 hours to overnight, and heat gently in the top of the double boiler until the glue dissolves. Remove it from the heat, but keep it warm.
3. Slowly sprinkle the filler through the strainer into the warm glue. To prevent the formation of air bubbles, add small amounts at a time. As the filler absorbs the glue it will sink to the bottom of the pot.

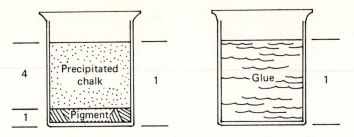

1 : 1

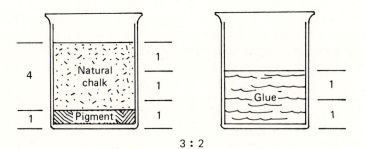

3 : 2

FIGURE 2.4
Filler-to-Glue Combinations for Glue Gesso

Top: 1:1 proportion. *Left,* 4 parts chalk to 1 part pigment.
Bottom: 3:2 proportion. *Left,* 4 parts chalk to 1 part pigment.

4. When all the filler has been added, gently stir the mixture with the wooden spoon. Avoid vigorous agitation or rapid stirring, both of which can cause air bubbles. The color and texture of the gesso should be like that of light coffee cream.
5. If the gesso has coarse particles or bits of undissolved glue floating on the surface, strain it through the cheesecloth before using it.

ALTERNATIVE METHOD OF COMBINING THE GLUE

1. Instead of sprinkling the filler into the glue, add the glue to the filler. Place the container of filler in a hot water bath. Add a small amount of glue to the filler—enough to make a thick paste. Mix the paste with the wooden spoon until it is smooth and free of lumps.
2. Slowly add the rest of the glue in a thin, intermittent stream, while gently stirring with the spoon.
3. Strain if gritty.

Application of a Gesso Ground   The procedure for applying gesso either to a rigid support or to a mounted fabric is simple. Because the product may be somewhat disappointing at first, the best way to learn about gesso and its application is through experience. Make and use it a few times, then note the results. Keep the following in mind as you proceed.

The pigment chalk portion of the gesso has a tendency to settle to the bottom of the pot. It is necessary to stir the mixture from time to time during application to keep the pigment and chalk in suspension in the glue.

If the gesso cools during application, the pot may be returned to the hotplate to warm it. Continuous heating, however, will evaporate water from the mixture and make it too thick to apply easily. If the gesso thickens, add a little warm water. Do not add more glue.

Leftover gesso can be stored in a cool place and will keep for about two weeks. Cool gesso will jell; to use, gently reheat on a hotplate. If it is too thick, add a little warm water.

The finished gesso surface should be somewhat soft, but not so soft that it can be easily scratched by a fingernail. If it can be easily scratched, or too easily sanded, there is not enough glue in the mixture. If sanding is difficult, there is too much glue in the mixture. Dilute with warm water mixed with a bit of chalk. It is a good idea to test the strength of the gesso on a piece of scrap wood before applying it to a panel.

If the panel is correctly braced, the coating on the back can be eliminated. If the panel is not braced, you can be a bit frugal with the gesso by substituting an X-shaped coating for a full layer (Figure 2.5).

The finished gesso ground is very absorbent. Absorbency is required for some painting techniques, but should be adjusted for others by applying a size. The size can be made of a very thin glue solution, or a dilute varnish resin, acrylic emulsion, or acrylic solution. When the size is colored with pigment or paint to tint the ground to a middle tone, it is sometimes called an *imprimatura* or a *veil:* an imprimatura can be applied to any kind of ground, not just gesso.

To make a size for the gesso ground, dilute 1 part by volume of the chosen material with 2 to 3 parts of its diluent. Brush it onto the ground in liberal amounts, and before it has a chance to dry, wipe it off with a soft cloth. This will produce a thin continuous film which will not interfere with the mechanical bond between the paint and the ground. Incorporate color into the veil before applying it to the support.

MATERIALS

1. Warm gesso mixture.
2. Panel, prepared as recommended in Chapter 1. The panel should be sized with a regular strength hide glue and allowed to dry overnight.
3. 2- to 3-inch (5 to 7.5 cm) housepainter's brush.
4. Fine sandpaper wrapped around a wooden block.

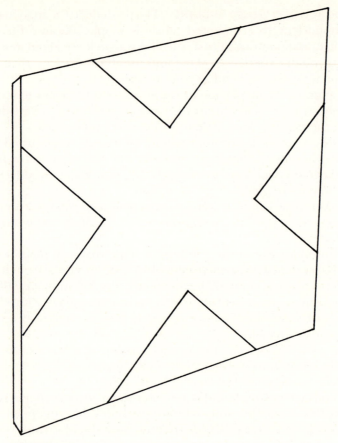

FIGURE 2.5
X-Shaped Coating of Gesso on the Back of a Gessoed Panel

5. Soft cotton cloth.
6. Stainless steel spoon.

APPLICATION TO A RIGID SUPPORT

1. Apply the first coat of gesso to the front of the support by scrubbing it on with the brush. Lay the brush aside and massage the entire surface of the gesso with the fingertips; this will work it into the panel and remove any air bubbles (Figure 2.6). If the panel has no bracing, coat the rear with a layer of gesso to equalize the tension between front and back. Allow to dry.
2. Apply the second coat with a fully charged brush: lay down strokes parallel to each other and to one edge of the panel. Do not stroke back and forth as though painting a wall; overpainting will pick up or roughen previous strokes. Coat the rear of the panel. Allow it to dry—each succeeding layer will take slightly longer.

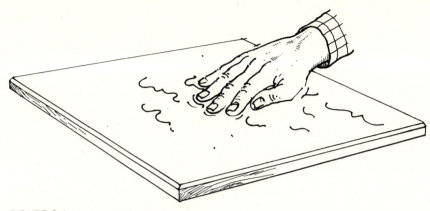

FIGURE 2.6
Massaging the First Coat of Gesso

3. Apply the third coat in the same manner, but with the strokes at right angles to those in the coat below (Figure 2.7). Coat the rear and allow the panel to dry.
4. Continue in this way, applying fresh coats as soon as the previous one is dry, making the brushstrokes of each layer at right angles to the layer below. Between 2 and 10 layers of gesso may be applied, depending on the thickness and opacity of the mixture or the artist's requirements.
5. When the panel is dry, the surface may be sanded to remove superficial defects such as lumps or brushstroke ridges. Use fine sandpaper or garnet paper wrapped around a flat wooden block; sand with a circular motion. Do not breathe the dust raised during sanding. Dust off the surface of the panel before using.

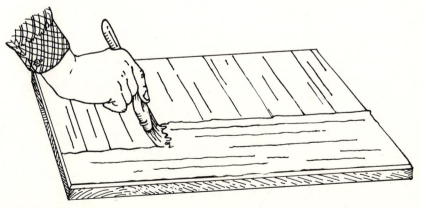

FIGURE 2.7
Coats of Gesso Perpendicular to Each Other

6. The gesso may be polished. Dampen a soft cotton cloth with water, wring it out, and fold it into a small pad. Rapidly polish the panel using gentle, circular, strokes. Be sure not to polish too long in one spot; the damp pad may dissolve the gesso right down to the bare support. Polishing will produce a smooth, eggshell-like surface.
7. For a harder, ivorylike finish, burnish the polished gesso with the back of a stainless steel spoon (Figure 2.8).

APPLICATION TO A MOUNTED FABRIC

1. Mount thin muslin, cotton, or fine linen, onto a panel, as instructed in Chapter 1.
2. Follow the same procedures outlined above, but apply only one or two coats of gesso. Do not obscure the weave of the fabric.
3. When the gesso has dried, scrape or sand it down so that the weave of the fabric is visible, while its interstices remain filled. This will give a somewhat textured surface.

GESSO AND OIL EMULSION GROUNDS

Commonly called half-chalk grounds, emulsions of gesso and linseed oil are sometimes suggested for artists who want to combine the virtues of the oil ground (toughness and flexibility) with those of the gesso ground (whiteness and absorbency). If correctly made, a half-chalk ground may be flexible enough to survive the continual movement of a fabric support.

The problem with using a half-chalk ground is that it combines the defects of its components along with the virtues: The oil yellows and tends to separate from the emulsion, and the glue chalk's inherent brittleness may cause it to flake off the support.

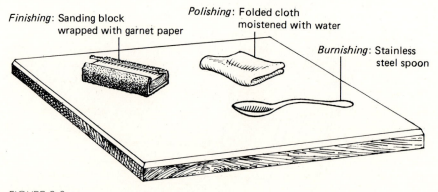

Finishing: Sanding block wrapped with garnet paper

Polishing: Folded cloth moistened with water

Burnishing: Stainless steel spoon

FIGURE 2.8
Finishing the Surface of a Gessoed Panel

Sitting on the panel: Sanding block wrapped with garnet paper, folded cloth moistened with water, stainless steel spoon.

It is possible to apply this ground to a rigid panel that has been mounted with a finely woven fabric.

MATERIALS

1. Panel mounted with fabric.
2. Standard glue gesso.
3. Artists' grade alkali-refined linseed oil or stand oil.
4. Wooden spoon.
5. Housepainter's brush.

METHOD

1. Add no more than 1 part by volume of the linseed oil to 3 parts of the warm gesso. Pour the oil slowly, in a thin stream, stirring all the while with the wooden spoon; stir rapidly enough to emulsify the mixture, but not so rapidly as to cause air bubbles. This is somewhat like making mayonnaise. The proportions of oil to gesso should not exceed 1 to 4. Stand oil is more viscous than alkali-refined linseed oil—slightly more will be needed.
2. When the oil is fully incorporated into the gesso, allow the mixture to rest for a few minutes before applying it to the panel. If the oil rises to the surface, stir it again.

APPLICATION

1. Use the brush to coat both sides of the panel smoothly. Allow it to dry for several days.
2. Before applying the second coat, warm the gesso and stir it gently. Coat both sides of the panel again, and allow it to dry for about a week before using.
3. The surface of the dry half-chalk gesso can be smoothed by sanding. It is considerably harder than a regular gesso.

Half-chalk grounds tend to separate because the glue in the solution is not a good emulsifier. To aid in emulsification, ¼ ounce by weight (7 gm) of ammonium carbonate—available in any pharmacy—crushed into a smooth paste with a little water, can be added to 1 quart (960 ml) of the solution. Warm the mixture until the smell of ammonia dissipates. *Caution:* Ammonia is toxic. Do not inhale the vapors; avoid handling the ammonium carbonate paste with the bare hands. Even when the emulsion is helped along by the addition of ammonium carbonate, the oil may still rise to the top of the drying ground.

When it is applied to a mounted fabric, the half-chalk ground can be finished in the same way as a plain gesso ground. As it ages, the ground will turn yellow.

Half-chalk grounds on stretched, sized fabric supports will at first appear to be as white as the plain gesso and as supple as an oil ground. The ground will yellow and become brittle with age, and if the oil content is too little, the ground may separate from the support. The layers of ground should be applied very thinly.

These admonitions suggest that there is little advantage in using a half-chalk ground. Its manufacture cannot be precisely controlled, and the product is often erratic.

PREPARED GESSO GROUNDS

There are proprietary mixtures of chalk, pigment, and dry glue to which only the correct amount of warm water need be added. If they are made of pure ingredients in the correct proportions, commercial preparations are convenient to use. The support must still be sized, and since glue gesso is inexpensive and easy to make, it hardly seems economical to pay a premium price for someone else's simple labor. Custom-made gesso panels are also available; usually the binder in these is casein-based and is sometimes harder than when made with hide glue. Again, a gesso panel can be made from scratch less expensively.

Because hide glue decomposes, those gessoes on the market in liquid form must use some other adhesive binding, such as the acrylic emulsion. These binders have handling and surface characteristics much different from glue gesso.

Flat interior water-based wall paints with latex or casein binders are sometimes suggested as substitutes for gesso or even the acrylic emulsion primers. Since these materials are not made for art applications and have relatively little durability, they should not be used for anything that is to be permanent.

Tables 2.1 and 2.2, which follow, provide a quick reference to supports and grounds.

TABLE 2.1
RIGID SUPPORTS

Support	Sizes								Grounds				Durability	Other Comments
	Glue	Gelatin	Starch	Methyl Cellulose	Acrylic Solution	Acrylic Emulsion	PVA Emulsion	Oil	Oil	Acrylic Emulsion	Glue-Chalk Gesso	Gesso-Oil		
SOLID WOOD														
Hardwood	X	X	X	X	X	X	X	X	X	X	X	X	Fair	Solid panels crack easily
Softwood	X	X	X	X	X	X	X	X	X	X	X	X	Fair	Crack easily; will show grain through paint
LAMINATED														
Plywood	X	X	X	X	X	X	X	X	X	X	X	X	Good	Hardwood veneers preferred
Paperboard	X	X	X	X	X	X	X	X	X	X	X	X	Poor	Not recommended
Museum board	X	X	X	X	X	X	X			X			Very good	Dilute glue and gelatin sizes: prepare and preserve properly
pH neutral cardboard	X	X	X	X	X	X	X			X	X		Very good	Same cautions as for museum board
pH neutral binder's board	X	X	X	X	X	X	X			X	X		Good	New material; durability presumed good
pH neutral corrugated	X	X	X	X	X	X	X			X			Very good	Not recommended; framing only
Die board	X	X	X	X	X	X	X	X	X	X	X	X	Very good	Excellent but heavy; best 100% hardwood
CHIPBOARD														
Small flake				X	X	X	X		X	X	X		Fair–Good	Industrial material: adhesive and structure weak; heavy
Large flake				X	X	X	X		X	X	X		Fair–Good	Same as small flake; lighter weight
HARDBOARD														
Plain (untempered)	X	X	X	X	X	X	X	X	X	X	X	X	Very good	Soft and porous; edges fragile; must be braced
Impregnated (tempered)	X	X	X	X	X	X	X	X	X	X	X	X	Excellent	Surface must be sanded; must be braced
CORED BOARDS														
Impregnated paper core														
Plywood surface	X	X	X	X	X	X	X	X	X	X	X	X	Very good	Wood veneer grain may show through; cut edges need filling
Hardboard surface	X	X	X	X	X	X	X	X	X	X	X	X	Excellent	Sand surface; attach wooden surround
Paper surface				X	X	X	X	X	X	X	X	X	Very good	Fragile surface; needs thick paper; attach wooden surround

TABLE 2.1 *(continued)*

	Sizes							Grounds					
	GLUE	GELATIN	STARCH	METHYL CELLULOSE	ACRYLIC SOLUTION	ACRYLIC EMULSION	PVA EMULSION	OIL	ACRYLIC EMULSION	GLUE-CHALK GESSO	GESSO-OIL	DURABILITY	OTHER COMMENTS
Aluminum core													
Hardboard surface	×	×	×	×				×	×		×	Excellent	Sand surface; attach wooden surround
Polyester surface	×	×	×	×				×	×		×	Excellent	Sand surface; attach wooden surround; deteriorates in ultraviolet light
Aluminum surface				×			×		×			Good	Sand surface; degrease; acrylic emulsion paints only; oxidizes
Foamed core													
No surface													Not recommended; use for backing matted works if archival
Paper surface													Not recommended; use for backing matted works if archival
METALS													
Copper				×	×	×	×	×	×			Good	Sand surface; brace if large; oxidizes beneath paint
Steel			×	×	×	×	×	×	×			Good	Same as for copper; can rust; best for porcelain enamel
Aluminum				×	×	×	×	×	×			Good	Same as for copper; use only acrylic emulsion paints
GLASS									×			Excellent	Adhesion problems: etch or sandblast surface
WALLS													
Interior													
Wood			×	×	×	×	×	×	×			Good	Grain pattern and joints can show; cracking and warps
Plaster		×	×	×	×	×	×	×	×			Very good	Settling causes cracks; moisture causes deterioration
Wallboard	×	×	×		×		×	×	×			Very good	Paper covering must be coated; acrylic emulsion paints best
Exterior													
Wood					×	×	×	×	×			Fair–Good	Moisture deterioration and grain pattern show-through
Brick					×	×	×	×	×			Very good	Moisture and efflorescence; must be isolated from ground
Concrete						×	×	×	×			Very good	Ground not imperative; may effloresce if impure; should be sized
Stucco							×		×			Very good	Size and ground not imperative; may effloresce; susceptible to moisture

54

TABLE 2.2
FLEXIBLE SUPPORTS

	Sizes							Grounds				DURABILITY	OTHER COMMENTS
	GLUE	GELATIN	STARCH	METHYL CELLULOSE	ACRYLIC SOLUTION	ACRYLIC EMULSION	PVA EMULSION	OIL	ACRYLIC EMULSION	GLUE-CHALK GESSO	GESSO-OIL		
PAPER													
Newsprint												Poor	Not recommended for permanent work
Bleached cellulose												Fair	Bleach and/or sulphite content contribute to deterioration
Rag "content"	×	×	×	×	×	×	×	×	×			Fair–Good	If balance of ingredients are stable and pH neutral, % rag unimportant
100% rag	×	×	×	×	×	×	×	×	×			Very good	Sizing and buffers should be alkaline and appropriate for rag fiber used
Rag "content," pH neutral	×	×	×	×	×	×	×	×	×			Very good	Same as rag "content" papers; alkaline is better than "neutral"
Nonrag, pH neutral	×	×	×	×	×	×	×	×	×			Poor–Excellent	Check package label for contents
Museum board	×	×	×	×	×	×	×	×	×			Very good	Check package label for contents
Drawing	×	×	×	×	×	×	×	×	×			Variable	Durability depends on content
Watercolor	×	×	×	×	×	×	×	×	×			Variable	Generally excellent; check for "right" and "wrong" sides
Illustration	×	×	×	×	×	×	×	×	×			Variable	Durability depends on content; smooth white filler may be acidic or alkaline

Note: What constitutes the "best" paper is often a matter of esthetics. Papers can be well made with shoddy materials or poorly made with excellent materials. There are more than 2000 varieties of art papers available (see Appendix B). Any paper can be used, provided it is well made of excellent materials of proven durability. Consider: buffering against atmospheric acidity; length of fibers and wet strength; whether the paper has been sized during manufacture or after, and the type of sizing material; thickness and weight of the paper for the proposed technique; whether colored paper is lightfast; the water used in the papermaking process. Ask questions of the retailer, wholesaler, or manufacturer.

TABLE 2.2 (*continued*)
FLEXIBLE SUPPORTS

	Sizes							Grounds				DURABILITY	OTHER COMMENTS
	GLUE	GELATIN	STARCH	METHYL CELLULOSE	ACRYLIC SOLUTION	ACRYLIC EMULSION	PVA EMULSION	OIL	ACRYLIC EMULSION	GLUE-CHALK GESSO	GESSO-OIL		
TEXTILES													
Cotton													
Muslin	×	×	×	×	×	×	×	×	×	×	×	Good	Should be mounted; short-fibered; embrittles and yellows
Duck	×	×	×	×	×	×	×	×	×	(×)	(×)	Good	Short-fibered; embrittles, yellows; (X = if mounted *only*)
Linen	×	×	×	×	×	×	×	×	×	(×)	(×)	Good–Excellent	Fragile; long-fibered; large variety of weights and textures (X = if mounted *only*)
Hemp, jute, burlap												Poor	Not recommended
Silk	×	×	×	×	×	×						Excellent	Variable texture weaves; strong but light; grounds will obscure surface
Synthetics													
Acrylic					×							Fair	Deteriorates in light
Fiberglass					×			×				Good	Stretches poorly; poor adhesion
Polyester								×				Good–Excellent	Thermoset ground manufacturer-applied: best adhesion; sags in high heat
Polypropylene								×				Good–Excellent	Thermoset ground manufacturer-applied: best adhesion; can deteriorate in light

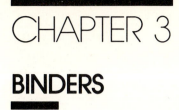

CHAPTER 3

BINDERS

A *binder* is an adhesive liquid that distinguishes one paint from another. It is different from a *vehicle,* which is the entire liquid content—volatile and nonvolatile—of a paint system.

A binder can be spread by brush, spray, knife, or any other means. It dries into a more or less continuous layer. This layer, or film, attaches the coloring agent to the support. If the binder is strong enough, it can be worked up into a relatively substantial thickness, though most serve their purpose well when applied as a thin film.

Mayer lists four functions of a binder:*

1. *Executive*   The binder allows the paint to be applied and spread out.

2. *Binding*   The binder locks the coloring agent into a film, protecting it from atmospheric or mechanical forces and from being disturbed by the application of further coats of paint. Many binders do this well; some, like the water gum binders, are notably weak.

3. *Adhesive*   The binder attaches the coloring agent, or pigment, to the ground.

4. *Optical*   The binder brings out the chromatic character of the pigment, giving it a different optical quality than it had in its dry state. This last quality is significant, for it makes an ultramarine blue in oil look distinctively different from the same ultramarine blue in, say, watercolor. *Refraction,* the bending of light rays as they pass from one medium to another, contributes to this difference.

The *refractive index* is a numerical representation of the relationship of the angle of a ray of light in air—relative to the surface it strikes—to the angle of the

---

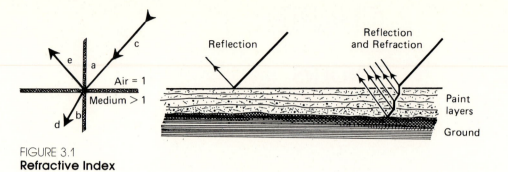

FIGURE 3.1
Refractive Index

Left: Refractive index is the ratio of the sine of the angle of incidence (a) to the sine of the angle of refraction (b) of the ray of light; c = incidence ray, d = refracted ray, e = reflected ray.
Right: Simple reflection on the left, refraction (simplified for clarity) and reflection on the right.

ray once it passes through or into another medium (Figure 3.1). When light strikes a translucent surface like a paint film, some of the light is reflected and some passes through the surface. The more light reflected, the higher the refractive index of the surface (or medium); the less light reflected—and therefore the more that penetrates or passes through—the lower the refractive index. Air has a refractive index of 1. Every other medium is less transparent and so has a higher refractive index, but some are more transparent than others. The following binders and mediums are listed in order of increasing transparency according to refractive index:

Molten beeswax
Damar varnish solution
Linseed oil
Poppyseed oil
Gum turpentine
Hide glue in water
Gum arabic in water
Water

From this list you can see why ultramarine blue looks different in water color (gum arabic) than it does in oil.

In *The Painter's Guide to Studio Methods and Materials,* Reed Kay explains that binders must meet certain criteria to function successfully:*

1. The binder must not change color as it ages, thereby changing the color of the paint. Many binders (linseed oil, for instance) yellow or darken as they age, mainly as a result of exposure to ultraviolet light.

---

* Reed Kay, *The Painter's Guide to Studio Methods and Materials,* © 1983, pp. 4, 32, 94, 173–186. Paraphrased by permission of Prentice-Hall, Inc., Englewood Cliffs, New Jersey.

2. The binder should also not activate a radical color change in the coloring agent. This is usually not a problem, although some binders that are alkaline can bleach certain pigments.

3. The binder should retain its strength as it ages. Storage conditions and ultraviolet light play a part in deteriorating a paint's binding strength.

4. The binder should remain structurally stable with the passage of time, resisting cracking, peeling, flaking, and so on, and should have a good degree of chemical and atmospheric stability once it has dried. Atmospheric conditions—light, temperature, humidity, pollution—all affect the structural integrity of a binder film.

5. After a binder has dried, it should not be easily dissolved by mild solvents used in normal cleaning or conservation operations. Watercolors and pastels will be easily destroyed by the injudicious use of plain water.

6. A binder should not be unusually hazardous (toxic or flammable) when handled with normal caution. Some paints can be harmful, but it is usually the solvent content of the whole vehicle—not the binder—that makes them hazardous. Read the container label for any cautions. This is simple common sense; to use any material in ignorance is to invite trouble.

Despite the lack of a perfect binder, many materials work very well when used appropriately. These can be divided into two classes: natural binders and synthetic binders.

NATURAL BINDERS

Liquids that can be used as paint binders are abundant in nature. Some of them, the plant gums in particular, have been used for thousands of years.

DRYING OILS

Drying oils are plant oils, squeezed mainly from seeds or nuts, which dry by oxidation. That is, the oil absorbs oxygen from the air and solidifies into a tough, leathery film. As it oxidizes, a drying oil also polymerizes. Its molecular structure changes so that once it has solidified, it is a substance quite different from its original form. (A *polymer* is composed of two different *monomers* chemically linked at the molecular level and repeated in chains.) A unique characteristic of the drying oils and similar polymers—most of the synthetic emulsions, for example—is that they cannot be changed back into their original state by dissolving them in their original diluents.

LINSEED OIL

Linseed oil is the most widely used of the drying oils. It is pressed from the seeds of the flax plant (*Linum usitatissimum*), the same plant that is the source of linen fibers. It can be processed into a variety of forms useful to artists. Its advantages are that it is a good film former, giving tough, resilient paint films, and it is compatible with a huge number of colorants. Its disadvantages include yellowing and embrittlement, which occur with age and exposure to light and are nearly unavoidable, and the apparent darkening of the paint film when it is stored in the dark, an effect reversed by reexposure to light.

Linseed and other drying oils contain relative percentages of the following:

1. *Linoleic acid*   An unsaturated fatty acid
2. *Linolein*   A component of linoleic acid that induces the drying properties of the oil
3. *Linolenic acid*   An unsaturated fatty acid

It has been claimed that a large percentage of linolenic acid in linseed oil contributes to its yellowing, and a large percentage of linoleic contributes to an oil's relatively short drying time.

In spite of its disadvantages, linseed oil has been used for nearly five centuries, far longer than any other complex and popular binder (see Appendix D).

Cold-Pressed Linseed Oil   Made by crushing the flax seed under great pressure, this variety is considered to be the most pure and desirable linseed oil for making oil paints because of its pale color and good wetting ability. Its color ranges from a pale strawlike yellow to a deeper, golden yellow. It is considered a "good drier"; it dries comparatively fast. Cold-pressed linseed oil was at one time the oil normally used by commercial paint makers for artists' paints. Because of the high cost and low yield of cold pressing, however, refined, steam-pressed linseed oil has largely replaced it.

Steam-Pressed Linseed Oil   Nineteenth-century producers found that steam heating the seeds before pressing gave a greater yield of oil. The quality of the oil was somewhat reduced by the addition of water vapor from the steam, so several refining techniques have been developed to make an oil that is comparable to the cold-pressed variety:

1. Acid-refined linseed oil is a steam-pressed oil that has been treated with sulfuric acid to remove the mucilaginous matter (called foots) and other impurities caused by the extraction process.
2. Alkali-refined oil is treated with alkali to reduce the acidity, then water-washed to remove the precipitated salts. This is the preferred treatment for oils to be used in artists' paints.
3. Solvent extraction is a technique for removing the oil from the seeds that leaves most of the impurities behind, and is the most modern and widely employed method for producing oil.

Stand Oil   A partially polymerized but unoxidized oil is made by heating linseed oil to about 570° F (300° C) in the absence of oxygen. Stand oil is also called heat-bodied oil. It is not a good binder because it is too viscous, but it is an excellent addition to painting and glazing mediums. It yellows less than other forms of linseed oil and has good leveling properties. Its film gives a smooth, enamel-like surface without brushmarks.

Sun-thickened Linseed Oil   This is an older process for refining linseed oil, dating from the Renaissance, in which equal parts of linseed oil and water are thoroughly mixed and exposed to strong sunlight for a few weeks. The oil produced is viscous, somewhat bleached, and a pretty good drier. The oil is partially polymerized and slightly oxidized; it is a good leveler.

To make a sun-thickened linseed oil, mix equal parts cold-pressed or alkali-refined linseed oil and water in a clear glass bottle by thoroughly shaking them together. Cover the mouth of the bottle with a cheesecloth cap and put it on a window sill with a southern exposure so that it gets full direct sun. Agitate the mixture occasionally. After several weeks, depending on the amount of light, the oil will thicken and become paler. Drain off the water, using a funnel or a gravy separation pitcher, and filter the oil through several layers of fine cheesecloth. Store in a tightly closed glass jar. Keep air out of the jar as the oil is used by raising the oil level to the top of the bottle with glass marbles (Figure 3.2).

Washed Oil   Cold-pressed linseed oil can be water-washed to remove some impurities. The process does not increase the viscosity or the drying rate of the oil. Here is how it is done:

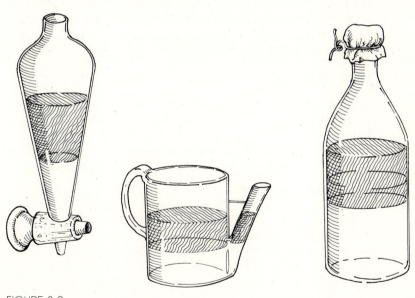

FIGURE 3.2
Separating Oil and Water

Left to right: Separatory funnel, oil floating on water; gravy separating cup, oil floating on water; bottle with a cheesecloth cap for sun thickening, oil floating on "foots" (if oil is also being washed) floating on water.

1. Put 1 part oil and 1 part water in a glass bottle, leaving an air space. Shake until thoroughly mixed.
2. Let the mixture sit; after several hours it will separate into three layers. The top layer is oil, the middle is mucilage, and the bottom is water.
3. Pour off the oil, being careful to leave the layers of mucilage and water behind.
4. Repeat to clarify the oil further.

Other Forms of Linseed Oil   Raw linseed oil (unprocessed), blown linseed oil, and boiled linseed oil are of interest to the housepainter, not the artist. These varieties have been treated with air or heat or both to make them dry more quickly. Though they physically resemble stand oil—they are thick and viscous—they have a tendency to darken and grow brittle quickly. Linoxyn, a semi-solid type of oxidized linseed oil, is the basis for linoleum floor coverings.

SAFFLOWER OIL

Safflower oil is pressed from the seeds of the safflower plant (*Carthamus tinctorius*) found in the Near East and cultivated for the dye extracted from its blossoms. It is grown commercially in North America as a source of a paint oil and an edible oil. It is classified as a semi-drying or a drying oil, according to the reference, but it can be used in artists' paints by the addition of small amounts of driers. Since it is a pale oil and yellows less than linseed oil (its linolenic content is smaller), it is sometimes used in lighter colored paints, specifically the whites. It has been suggested that safflower oil becomes more brittle more quickly than does linseed oil (see Appendix D).

POPPYSEED OIL

Poppyseed oil is extracted from the seed of *Papaver somniferum,* the poppy plant. It is a pale, nearly colorless oil that is also used in making artists' whites and light-colored paints (especially the pale blues). Poppyseed oil dries rather slowly, and some sources claim that it is susceptible to cracking. A well-known European manufacturer, Blockx, uses poppyseed oil in its line of artists' paints (see Appendix D).

WALNUT OIL

A drying oil expressed from walnuts (*Juglans regia*) has been used by artists who make their own paints. Walnut oil is nonyellowing and dries at a rate comparable to that of safflower and poppyseed oils. Like many nut oils, walnut oil does not store well—it will turn rancid unless refrigerated. Because demand for it is low, it is expensive (see Appendix D).

SOYBEAN OIL

Soybean oil, also known as soya bean oil, is a semi-drier from the soybean plant (*Soja hispida*), grown throughout the world. It dries much more slowly than linseed oil, but has been successfully incorporated into synthetic binders to ensure flexibility. Winsor & Newton's alkyd paints have a synthetic soybean-type oil as a constituent of the alkyd resin binder. Soybean oil yellows less than linseed oil (see Appendix D).

TUNG OIL

Tung oil is extracted from the Chinawood tree (*Aleurites fordii, A. montana,* or *A. cordata*) and is also known as Chinawood oil. This is a rapid drier which has a tendency to bloom (frost) and yellow; it is used in the furniture industry.

SEMI-DRYING OILS

Corn, olive, peanut, and other types of vegetable oils familiar to cooks are generally classified as semi-drying oils. They do dry, but very slowly, and are sometimes used in cheap housepaints (where they should be thought of as adulterants). Semi-driers are not recommended for permanent painting, although they can be made to work for throwaway sketches on paper if the artist has pigments to disperse in them. Be sure to throw the sketches away.

NONDRYING OILS

Nondriers, like motor oil or castor oil, never form a completely dry film—they will remain tacky and soft for years. Asphaltum, a colored petroleum derivative, was used in the nineteenth century as a painting medium or additive because of its pleasing color and handling characteristics: it was a total disaster for the paintings. Nondrying oils should never be used in permanent painting.

Castor oil comes from the castor bean (*Ricinus communis*) and is almost water-white, soluble in alcohol, and highly viscous. It can be changed into a drying oil by chemically dehydrating it (removing the hydrogen) to form dehydrated or dehydrogenated castor oil. It has been proposed that this oil be used in artists' paints, but there is little information about its performance.

WAXES

Waxes from animal, vegetable, and mineral sources have long been used as protective coatings, binders, infusers, ingredients in painting mediums, adhesives, and stabilizers for mixtures of pigments and binders. They are versatile and stable, and they do not generally oxidize at normal temperatures. They are not subject to decay in the normal sense, although they obviously react to extremes in temperature—they crack when cold and melt when hot. Also, they do not attract insects, bacteria, or molds. Waxes are waterproof but soluble in organic solvents. They "dry" by solidifying from the liquid state.

BEESWAX

Beeswax in the honeycomb form is familiar to everyone. When the honey is centrifuged out, a crude yellow wax is left which can be melted and filtered. The bleached white variety is melted, formed into thin sheets, and bleached by sunlight. The bleaching process also raises the melting point of the wax. Bleached white beeswax is the artist's choice for most techniques calling for wax ingredients—it is the binder for encaustic paints. Its melting point (MP) is around 145° F (63° C), (see Appendix D).

CARNAUBA WAX

This comparatively hard wax is scraped from the leaves of a Brazilian palm tree. The various commercial grades are bleached, yellow, or gray. It is an ingredient in some automobile waxes. The grades are variable in quality, so its use in art is confined mostly to conservation processes, where it is used as a hardener. MP: 183° F (84° C).

SPERMACETI

Spermaceti is a fish oil wax extracted from the head cavity of the sperm whale, among other species. It has a clean, crystalline character, and a low melting point. It has been replaced by synthetic varieties for most uses. It is not recommended, because of efforts to save the whales. MP: 120° F (49° C).

CANDELILLA

Candelilla wax is found on the leaves of a plant grown in the southwestern portion of North America. It is similar in many respects to carnauba wax, but is not quite as hard. It is used in varnishes, waterproofing processes, and paint removers—it is primarily an industrial material. MP: 154° F (68° C).

JAPAN WAX

Japan wax is obtained from the berries of a species of sumac tree native to Japan and China, but it is not actually a wax. In its chemical composition, it is more like an oil. It is used in the cosmetics industry and as an adhesive in wax recipes for some art-related work. MP: 125° F (52° C).

OZOKERITE

Ozokerite is a natural mineral wax found in the Americas, Europe, and South Africa. Its properties are variable, but it does find its way into a proprietary wax emulsion manufactured for the artist called Dorland's Wax Medium (see Appendix D). MP: 138–194° F (59–90° C).

OTHER WAXES

A number of manufactured waxes (such as the polyethylene waxes) are used in the preparation of wax crayons and watercolors, and as matting agents for varnishes.

WATER-SOLUBLE BINDERS

Plant gums, glues, and animal by-products that dissolve in water have been used for centuries as adhesives and paint binders. Most are hygroscopic and easily redissolved in water, and some are plastic and durable enough to work admirably in permanent painting.

Gums are exuded or tapped saps from trees or shrubs and either dissolve in warm water or swell into a jellylike mass called a *colloid solution.* They usually require the addition of a *plasticizer* to make them more flexible in a paint binder, though some can be used alone.

Vegetable glues like the starches and cellulose mentioned in Chapter 2 are adequate for many applications, but they are not strong enough for permanent painting. They will serve well, in a pinch, for studies or sketches.

Animal by-products can be made into very strong glues, some of which have been used as binders. On rigid supports with absorbent grounds, they make interesting but difficult-to-handle paints.

GUM ARABIC

This is more formally known as gum acacia; it exudes from incisions made in the bark of the acacia tree, found in Australia and Asia, but principally in Africa. Many writers claim that the best types come from Africa—these are known by the name of their place of origin. Gum Senegal and gum Kordofan are examples.

Gum arabic is dissolved in hot water and used as an adhesive (common librarian's mucilage is boiled gum arabic), as a "stop-out" in lithographic printing techniques, as a size, as an ingredient in candies, and as the binder in opaque and transparent watercolors and pastels. In most uses, a plasticizer is added to the formula, since the gum film is rather brittle.

GUM TRAGACANTH

This gum comes from the shrub *Astragalus,* found in the Middle East and western Asia. It swells into a translucent colloid in hot water. The gel is pressed through a filter, and the liquid is used as a stabilizer for coating emulsions and as a binder for pastel chalks. Gum Tragacanth is also used in foods, as a thickener.

GUM KARAYA

Gum Karaya comes from *Sterculia urens,* a plant found in India. It superficially resembles gum Tragacanth, and is sometimes used as a substitute for it.

DEXTRIN

Dextrin is one of the starches used in some artists' materials as binders or additions to vehicles. It is a water-soluble adhesive prepared from wheat starch. Other starches, or flours such as from rice or potatoes, are similarly prepared and used.

Dextrin is sometimes the binder in tempera poster colors, and in "designer's gouaches" as an addition to the gum arabic binder. It is also used as a glue in conservation and restoration.

HIDE GLUE

Aside from being used as a size, hide glue has been used as a paint binder (distemper paints). It is difficult to use because it so readily redissolves: Overpainting tends to pick up or muddy the dried paint layers below.

NATURAL EMULSIONS

An *emulsion* is a liquid composed of two parts: an aqueous (watery) part, and an oily, greasy, resinous, or fatty part. Emulsions of two normally immiscible (unmixable) ingredients can be made with any two dissimilar ingredients, but artists' emulsions usually have water as one of the components. In an emulsion, either oil in water or water in oil, small droplets of one liquid are dispersed uniformly throughout the other liquid. The dispersion is held constant by an ingredient called an emulsifier, a material that modifies the surface tension of the two liquids to stabilize the mixture.

Natural emulsions make versatile paint binders, within limitations. Though they are water-resistant and not hygroscopic, the films are not waterproof.

WHOLE EGG

Hen's eggs consist of yolk and white, both of which are emulsions. The yolk contains egg oil, a watery solution of albumen, and lecithin, an efficient emulsifier found in many food products, both natural and manufactured. Albumen is the main constituent of the egg white and is an advantageous ingredient. It coagulates under the influence of heat and light. Whole eggs can be used in vehicles for a variety of egg tempera and egg–oil emulsion tempera paints.

EGG YOLK

The plain egg yolk, cleaned of the white and separated from its sac, is a well-known natural emulsion binder. It contains the same ingredients as the whole egg, but in different proportions. When thinned with water, it is used as the binder for the classic and unusually delicate egg tempera paint.

GLAIR

Glair is the white of a hen's egg, separated from the yolk. It is beaten until frothy, mixed with a little water, and allowed to stand until the froth subsides. Glair makes a weak and little-used binder that spoils quickly. It has been used for centuries as the adhesive for gilding and as the binder for paints for manuscript illumination.

CASEIN

When the butterfat is removed from milk, it becomes skim milk. When skim milk is soured—naturally, by the addition of an acid, or by coagulating it with the enzyme rennet—and the curd is extracted and dried, the lumpy yellowish powder that results is called casein. The powder is dissolved in hot water with the help of an alkali additive (either ammonium carbonate or ammonium hydroxide) and makes a clear, syrupy solution that can be used as a binder, the ingredient in glue gessoes, a size, and an excellent strong furniture glue (see Appendix D).

CATALYTIC BINDERS

When calcium carbonate (chalk) is roasted to drive off its water content, calcium oxide (lime) is produced. Lime can be mixed into water, with which it reacts to form calcium hydroxide—slaked lime. Slaked lime, mixed again with water to form a soft white paste and enough sand to stabilize the mixture, is troweled onto prepared walls and used while damp as the substrate and binder for the classical mural technique called *fresco.*

Pigments ground with water are brushed onto the wet slaked lime plaster, where they are absorbed into the wall and become a part of it; only pigments resistant to the alkaline lime can be used. Further reaction occurs first as the wall dries out, and second as the calcium hydroxide combines with carbon dioxide to return eventually to its native form, calcium carbonate.

The process of *fresco* (Italian for "fresh") painting is fairly well understood, but the medium is not used often today for two reasons: preparation, materials, and labor can be very expensive; and our modern atmosphere, polluted as it is with acidic compounds, will destroy an unprotected fresco painting in a short time. Any surface protection applied over the painting will defeat the main objective, which is to have a huge decorated surface that can be seen, without the interference of reflections, from all angles. Indoor murals, in environments which have a regulated atmosphere, are still a possibility. But it takes resources (financial, technical, and esthetic) to consider attempting this kind of painting.

SYNTHETIC BINDERS

Synthetic materials that can be altered to meet the requirements of paint binders are a product of late nineteenth- and early twentieth-century technology. Derived from petroleum by-products, natural gas, or other organic sources, and from mineral sources, the synthetic paint binders have opened up a versatile range of possibilities for the painter. Many of these are industrial materials, and the requirements for a binder of artists' paints are more particular than those for some industrial applications. Only since the 1940s has much research been done on the use of the synthetics as artists' materials—several companies have produced reliable paints from them—and only in recent years has there been a concerted effort to do more research. It is imperative that the painter who wishes to experiment with the new developments be aware of their pitfalls as well as their advantages.

Resins is a term associated with the word *synthetic,* and bears definition here. There are two kinds: natural and synthetic. They are both more or less transparent, fusible materials. The term can be used to describe any polymer that is a basic material for paints. They are sometimes flammable, and they are soluble in organic solvents, but not usually in water.

VINYL RESINS

Vinyl resins are derived from ethylene, distilled from crude petroleum. The term *vinyl* also refers to the many compounds that contain the vinyl group and include vinyl acetate, vinyl chloride, and the polymerized variations of them, polyvinyl acetate (PVA), polyvinyl chloride (PVC), and polyvinyl chloride acetate (PVCA). Other resins useful to artists are also relatives of vinyl: co-polymers (a combination of two polymers) of the PVAs and the PVCAs, the acrylic resins, the methacrylate resins, the polystyrene resins, and so on. The chemistry is complex.

Most vinyls are characterized by their durable, nonyellowing (if they are not already yellowish) properties, and by the fact that they are soluble only in volatile and toxic solvents. This last factor should prohibit the prudent artist from using them in raw form. They are used in industry as coatings, plastics, and sheetings.

The vinyl resins are of interest to artists, however, when they are polymerized or co-polymerized and emulsified with water. In this form they are safer—and readily recognized in their most common form as white glue. This all-purpose adhesive for wood and paper is marketed under many different trade names and can be used as a size, and in a pinch as a binder for sketch paints. The archival variety can be used as a collage glue, or in conservation framing. The polyvinyl acetate emulsions (PVAEs) form rather porous though water-resistant films. Manufacturers of artists' acrylic emulsion paints may use the PVAEs, or derivatives of them, in their co-polymer or ter-polymer (three polymers) emulsion vehicles.

ACRYLIC RESINS

The acrylics are a subgroup of the vinyls. The basic constituent is acrylic acid. Polymerization of the acrylic acid molecule leads to various forms of plastics; the polymers can also be linked to other polymers to make co- or ter-polymers. These variations can be dispersed in water to form a type of emulsion.

The straight acrylic resins, methyl methacrylate in particular, have been used in paint binders for quite some time, since the Rohm and Haas Company introduced them to industry in the early 1930s. In their solid form, these resins are familiar under the trade names Lucite and Plexiglas. The first accepted artists' paint application of the straight acrylic resin solution binder was in Leonard Bocour's Magna paints, which appeared on the market in the late 1940s. Rohm and Haas's American trade names for the syrupy *acrylic solutions* dissolved in a solvent are the Acryloids. Most of these syrups are 45 to 50 percent resin solutions in dangerous solvents like toluene or other aromatic hydrocarbons (Acryloid B-72). Some are soluble in less dangerous solvents such as mineral spirits (Acryloid B-67MT) or VM&P Naphtha (Acryloid B-67 and Acryloid F-10).

When the acrylic resin is polymerized and dispersed in water, the common name for the product is *acrylic polymer emulsion*. Artists' paints made with this binder, sold on an industrial scale under such trade names as Rhoplex (Rohm and Haas), are exceptionally adhesive and durable. There are many different forms of Rhoplex; Rhoplex AC-33, AC-34, and possibly a few of the other 30 or so varieties are the most used in making artists' paints. Henry Levison's Liquitex paints, originally manufactured by Permanent Pigments (now Binney and Smith), were the first accepted acrylic emulsion paints. The dried paint films exhibit a tendency to absorb atmospheric moisture like their porous PVAE cousins; they must be varnished with an acrylic solution varnish to protect them. The acrylic emulsion binders are also not as clear as the straight acrylic solutions, nor even as clear as the linseed oils, even though they are advertised as being clear. Observe the difference between the oils and acrylic emulsions by spreading out samples of the same colors in the two different vehicles. The acrylic emulsion paint may look a bit lighter, or perhaps a bit "chalky," compared to the oil paint.

The acrylic polymer emulsion paints have come to be known simply as the acrylics. This is unfortunate, since the term can mean either acrylic solution or acrylic emulsion. Nonetheless, the paints have become one of the most useful and popular products available to artists.

ALKYD RESINS

When a polyhydric alcohol (commonly, glycerol) and a polybasic acid (commonly phthalic anhydride, derived from coal or petroleum) are condensed together, the product is a complex ester called an *alkyd*. This plastic resin can be modified by the addition of synthetic or natural vegetable oils, for increased flexibility, for use as a paint binder.

The alkyd resins have been in commercial industrial applications for about 30 years in automobile finishes and interior house paints. In the late 1970s Winsor & Newton introduced an alkyd-based artists' paint, modified with what it calls a "synthetic soya bean-type" drying oil, and thinned with mineral spirits or gum turpentine. An American company in California, PDQ (Paints Dry Quick), has also marketed a similar paint.

The alkyd paints are a significant addition to the variety of materials offered to the artist mainly because of two factors: the drying time is faster than oil, though slower than the acrylic emulsions; and the binders and mediums are clear and theoretically nonyellowing. Although they have been tested extensively for more than twenty years by Winsor & Newton, the paints have yet to prove themselves in wide use by artists over a similar period. Nonetheless these new paints seem very promising for those who like the convenience of relatively quick-drying paints, but prefer the clarity and brilliance of an oil-like vehicle.

SILICATES

Silicate binders are generally used in industrial situations, but some writers on artists' materials have suggested that they may have possibilities as binders for outdoor mural paints.

These paints are based on sodium, potassium, lithium, or ethyl silicate, are thinned with water or water plus a little alcohol, and resemble a volatile thinner when unpigmented. Only Kurt Wehlte, in Germany (in the 1950s and 1960s), conducted much research into its art applications, and while he extolled the paints for their durability and reliability, conservators have expressed doubts about their long-term survival.

Practically speaking, the silicate paints are difficult to handle, but no more so than the fresco paints. They are alkaline, and only alkali-proof pigments can be used. The binder—depending on the variety—must be made fresh each day, since the catalytic reaction that results cannot be stopped (see Appendix D).

Table 3.1, which follows, provides a quick reference to binders.

TABLE 3.1
BINDERS

COMMON NAME	Cold-pressed linseed oil	Steam-pressed linseed oil	Linseed stand oil	Sun-thickened linseed oil
TYPE	Natural drying oil	Natural drying oil, alkali-refined	Natural drying oil	Natural drying oil
SOURCE	*Linum usitatissimum* flax seed, pressed cold	*Linum usitatissimum* flax seed, steam-pressed	*Linum usitatissimum* flax seed, heated without oxygen; not oxidized	*Linum usitatissimum* flax seed, processed as in text
COLOR/APPEARANCE	Pale Y to darker YO	Pale Y to darker YO	Pale Y	Pale Y
USE	Binder, ingredient in mediums	Binder, ingredient in mediums	Ingredient in mediums	Ingredient in mediums
REFRACTIVE INDEX	Relatively low	Relatively low	Relatively low	Relatively low
VISCOSITY	Low to medium	Low to medium	Medium to high	Medium to high
THINNER/SOLVENT	Mineral spirits, gum turpentine; stronger	Mineral spirits, gum turpentine; stronger	Mineral spirits, gum turpentine; stronger	Mineral spirits, gum turpentine; stronger
REVERSIBILITY	Not with original thinner	Not with original thinner	Not with original thinner	Not with original thinner
pH	Slightly acidic	Slightly acidic; refining reduces acidity	Relatively neutral, depending on refining	Slightly acidic unless water-washed
For Oils				
Linoleic	Average	Average	Average	Average
Linolein	Higher (good drying)	Average	Higher (good drying)	Higher (good drying)
Linolenic	Average	Average	Average	Average
DURABILITY				
Interior	Good–excellent	Good–excellent	Good–excellent	Good–excellent
Exterior	Fair	Fair	Fair	Fair
Rigid support	Good–excellent	Good–excellent	Good–excellent	Good–excellent
Flexible support	Fair	Fair	Fair	Fair
RESISTANCE TO:				
Water	Good	Good	Good	Good
Acid	Poor	Poor	Poor	Poor
Alkali	Fair	Fair	Fair	Fair
Pollutants	Fair	Fair	Fair	Fair
Ultraviolet light	Fair	Fair	Fair	Fair
Decay	Good	Good	Good	Good
HAZARDS				
Health	n/a	n/a	n/a	n/a
Fire (flash point)	Over 500°F (260°C)	Over 500°F (260°C)	Over 500°F (260°C)	Over 500°F (260°C)
OTHER COMMENTS	Excellent for making paints; good wetting ability; good drying; expensive; color varies	Most used for commercial and home paintmaking; average drier; less costly; only a fair binder, but in use for more than 500 years—reliable	Good for mediums, poor for vehicles; less color change over time than other linseed oils; good drier; levels—will not show brushstrokes	Similar to linseed stand oil but easily homemade

Note: n/a = not applicable; NR = not recommended; MSDS = Material Safety Data Sheet; P/CD = *Paint/Coatings Dictionary.*

TABLE 3.1 (*continued*)
BINDERS

COMMON NAME	Washed linseed oil	Safflower oil	Poppyseed oil	Walnut oil
TYPE	Natural drying oil	Natural semi-drying oil	Natural semi-drying oil	Natural drying or semi-drying oil
SOURCE	*Linum usitatissimum* flax seed, processed as in text	*Carthamus tinctorius*, native of India	*Papaver somniferum*, opium plant	*Juglans regia*, walnuts
COLOR/APPEARANCE	Pale Y	Pale Y	Very pale Y	Pale (varies)
USE	Ingredient in mediums	Binder in light colors and whites, with driers added	Binder in whites and light colors, w/driers added	Binder for oils, if sufficient quantities available
REFRACTIVE INDEX	Relatively low	Low	Low	Low
VISCOSITY	Medium to high	Low to medium	Low to medium	Low
THINNER/SOLVENT	Mineral spirits, gum turpentine; stronger	Mineral spirits and stronger	Mineral spirits and stronger	Mineral spirits and stronger
REVERSIBILITY	Not with original thinner	Not with original thinner	Not with original thinner	Not with original thinner
pH	If thoroughly washed, relatively neutral	Relatively neutral	Relatively neutral	Relatively neutral
For Oils				
Linoleic	Average	Higher than linseed oil	High; slow drier	High; slow drier
Linolein	Higher if polymerized	Low	Average	Average
Linolenic	Average	Low; does not yellow as much as linseed oil	Average	Low; relatively nonyellowing
DURABILITY				
Interior	Good–excellent	Good–excellent	Good–excellent	Good
Exterior	Fair	Fair–good	Fair	Fair
Rigid support	Good–excellent	Good	Good	Good
Flexible support	Fair	Fair–good	Fair–good	Fair–good
RESISTANCE TO:				
Water	Good	Good	Good	Good
Acid	Poor	Poor	Poor	Poor
Alkali	Fair	Fair	Fair	Fair
Pollutants	Fair	Fair	Fair	Fair
Ultraviolet light	Fair	Fair	Fair	Fair
Decay	Good	Good	Good	Good
HAZARDS				
Health	n/a	n/a	n/a	n/a
Fire (flash point)	Over 500°F (260°C)	Very high	Very high	Very high
OTHER COMMENTS	Easy method of home refining a linseed oil; some commercial alkali-refined oils improve in color when water-washed	Edible oil; used with driers; yellows less than linseed oil but may embrittle faster	Edible oil; used more in Europe (Blockx—Belgium); poor drier—may crack	Edible oil; used in Renaissance to make nonyellowing oil for paint; expensive; comparable to safflower and poppyseed oils

TABLE 3.1 (continued)
BINDERS

COMMON NAME	Soybean oil	Perilla oil	Tung oil	Corn, olive, and peanut oils
TYPE	Natural semi-drying oil	Natural drying oil	Natural drying oil	Natural nondrying oils
SOURCE	*Soja hispida,* soybean plant	*Perilla ocymoides* and *Perilla nankinensis* (Asia)	*Aleurites fordii, montana, or cordata,* Chinawood tree	Corn, olives, and peanuts
COLOR/APPEARANCE	Pale Y	Pale Y	Medium Y or YO	All very pale Y
USE	Plasticizing oil for alkyd resin-based paints (w/driers)	Use varies	Furniture finishes	Cooking; cheapening extenders for housepaints
REFRACTIVE INDEX	Low	Low	Medium	All low
VISCOSITY	Low to medium	Low to medium	Low to medium; depending on processing	All low
THINNER/SOLVENT	Mineral spirits and stronger	Aliphatic hydrocarbons	Mineral spirits and stronger solvents	n/a
REVERSIBILITY	Not with original thinner	Aromatic hydrocarbons	Fair	n/a
pH	Relatively neutral	Varies from neutral to slightly acidic	Relatively neutral	n/a
For Oils				n/a
Linoleic	High	High	Low; fast drier; frosts	
Linolein	Average	Higher than linseed oil	Average	
Linolenic	Slightly lower than linseed oil	Low; yellows less than linseed oil	High; yellows	
DURABILITY			NR	NR
Interior	Good	Excellent		
Exterior	Good	Fair		
Rigid support	Good–excellent	Excellent		
Flexible support	Good	Fair–good		
RESISTANCE TO:			NR	NR
Water	Good	Excellent		
Acid	Poor	Poor		
Alkali	Fair	Fair		
Pollutants	Fair	Fair		
Ultraviolet light	Fair	Fair		
Decay	Good	Good		
HAZARDS				
Health	n/a	? n/a	Do not ingest	n/a
Fire (flash point)	Very high	Very high	High	Very high
OTHER COMMENTS	Edible oil used in long-oil alkyds for paints containing up to 70% soy oil—more like resin-modified oil paints than industry designation as "oil-modified alkyd"	Industrial use; experimental use only in artists' paints	Use *only* to finish frames —not in paint	Found in the cheapest products; not for artists' use

TABLE 3.1 (*continued*)
BINDERS

COMMON NAME	Castor and dehydrogenated castor oils	Mineral oil	Beeswax	Carnauba wax
TYPE	Natural oils nondrying; semi-drying	Petroleum derivative	Natural wax	Natural wax
SOURCE	*Ricinus communis*, castor bean seed	Refined "high molecular weight hydrocarbon" (P/CD)	Bees' honeycombs	Brazilian palm; many varieties
COLOR/APPEARANCE	Both nearly colorless	Colorless	Dark Y to W, depending on degree of refinement	Y to Gray to bleached W
USE	Plain: extender; dehydrogenated: plasticizer and experimental use	Medicinal	Binder for encaustics and certain crayons; ingredient in emulsions, surface waxes	Auto wax and conservation
REFRACTIVE INDEX	Both low	Low	High when solid; low when liquid	High when cold; low when hot
VISCOSITY	Both high	Varies, but generally high	High when cold; low when hot	High when cold; low when hot
THINNER/SOLVENT	Strong solvents	n/a	Mineral spirits	Variable
REVERSIBILITY	n/a	n/a	Excellent; if hardeners added, more resistant	Variable
pH	n/a	n/a	Quite neutral	Relatively neutral
For Oils Linoleic Linolein Linolenic	n/a	n/a		
DURABILITY	NR	NR		
Interior			Excellent	NR
Exterior			Fair–poor	NR
Rigid support			Excellent	NR
Flexible support			Fair–poor	NR
RESISTANCE TO:				
Water	NR	NR	Excellent	NR
Acid			Good	NR
Alkali			Good	NR
Pollutants			Good	NR
Ultraviolet light			Good	NR
Decay			Excellent	NR
HAZARDS				
Health	n/a	n/a	Do not overheat; avoid breathing vapors	n/a; do not overheat
Fire (flash point)	Very high	Very high	Vapors flammable	Vapors flammable
OTHER COMMENTS	Dehydrogenated form may prove useful; considered experimental	Not for artists' use; does not dry	Excellent artists' material. Paint films can be too soft if overused or hardeners not used	Hardener for conservation adhesives; could be used to harden beeswax mixtures; poor color stability

74

TABLE 3.1 (*continued*)
BINDERS

COMMON NAME	Spermaceti	Candelilla	Japan wax	Ozokerite
TYPE	Natural wax	Natural wax	Natural wax	Natural wax
SOURCE	Sperm whale head cavity and other species; rare	Plant wax	Far Eastern species of sumac; berries	Natural mineral wax; Europe; Australia; Americas
COLOR/APPEARANCE	Clean W	Pale Y or Y to GBr	Oily W wax	Variable, but refined varieties are W
USE	NR: Save the Whales	Electric insulation; paint removers, etc. (P/CD)	Cosmetics and conservation	In proprietary mixtures like Dorland's Wax Medium
REFRACTIVE INDEX	High when cold; low when hot	High when cold; low when hot	High when cold; low when hot	High when cold; low when hot
VISCOSITY	High when cold; low when hot	High when cold; low when hot	High when cold; low when hot	High when cold; low when hot
THINNER/SOLVENT	Variable	Variable	Variable	Mineral spirits
REVERSIBILITY	Good	Good	Good	Good
pH	Neutral	Relatively neutral	Neutral	Relatively neutral
For Oils Linoleic Linolein Linolenic				
DURABILITY				
Interior	NR	NR	NR	Good
Exterior	NR	NR	NR	Fair–poor
Rigid support	NR	NR	NR	Excellent
Flexible support	NR	NR	NR	Fair
RESISTANCE TO:				
Water	NR	NR	NR	Excellent
Acid	NR	NR	NR	Fair
Alkali	NR	NR	NR	Fair
Pollutants	NR	NR	NR	Good
Ultraviolet light	NR	NR	NR	Good
Decay	NR	NR	NR	Excellent
HAZARDS				
Health	n/a	n/a; do not overheat	n/a; do not overheat	n/a; do not overheat
Fire (flash point)	Vapors flammable	Vapors flammable	Vapors flammable	Vapors flammable
OTHER COMMENTS	Formerly widely used; now wisely preserved in live whales	In paint removers, allows active materials to coat vertical surfaces without flow; not artists' material	More like oil than wax; not artists' material; could be used in wax-based adhesives for art-related work	Relatively soft wax combined with oils and resins in wax soaps for artists' use. Use in minimum quantities with care; wax soaps can give films that are easily damaged

TABLE 3.1   (continued)
BINDERS

COMMON NAME	Microcrystalline wax	Gum acacia (gum arabic)	Gum Tragacanth	Gum Karaya
TYPE	Petroleum wax	Natural, water-thinned	Natural, water-thinned	Natural, water-thinned
SOURCE	Petroleum	Sap from several species of acacia trees	Shrub *Astragalus;* Middle East and Western Asia	*Sterculia urens;* Asian plant—resinlike exudation
COLOR/APPEARANCE	W; variably high MP	Pale Y dusty lumps or crushed powder	Pale Y tears; W crushed powder; translucent pale Y colloidal solution	Pale Y tears; W crushed powder; pale Y colloid
USE	Ingredient in adhesive mixtures for conservators	Binder; adhesive; thickener; lithographic stop-out	Binder (pastel); thickener	Substitute for gum Tragacanth
REFRACTIVE INDEX	High when solid; low when liquid	Low	Low as binder	Low as binder
VISCOSITY	High when solid; low when liquid	Medium–high	Medium–high as colloid solution; low in binder solution	Medium–high in colloid solution; low in binder solution
THINNER/SOLVENT	Aliphatic hydrocarbons and higher solvents	Water	Water	Water
REVERSIBILITY	Good	Good	Good	Good
pH	Neutral	Slightly acidic	Slightly acidic	Relatively neutral

For Oils
     Linoleic
     Linolein
     Linolenic				

DURABILITY				
Interior	Excellent	Excellent	Excellent	Excellent
Exterior	Fair	Poor	Poor	Poor
Rigid support	Excellent	Excellent	Excellent	Excellent
Flexible support	Fair–good	Excellent—in *thin* films	Excellent—in *thin* films	Excellent—in *thin* films
RESISTANCE TO:				
Water	Excellent	Poor	Poor	Poor
Acid	Fair	Poor	Poor	Poor
Alkali	Fair	Poor	Poor	Poor
Pollutants	Good	Poor	Poor	Poor
Ultraviolet light	Fair–good	Fair	Fair	Fair
Decay	Excellent	Fair–good	Fair–good	Fair–good
HAZARDS				
Health	n/a; do not overheat	n/a; beware of mixtures	n/a; beware of mixtures	n/a; beware of mixtures
Fire (flash point)	Vapors flammable	n/a	n/a	n/a
OTHER COMMENTS	Conservation adhesives; very soft at room temperature—must have hardeners added	Excellent binder; thick films will not work; hygroscopicity will encourage cracking and mold growth	Excellent, versatile, but weak binder; thick films will not work; hygroscopicity will encourage cracking and mold growth in thick films	Similar to gum Tragacanth

TABLE 3.1 (*continued*)
BINDERS

COMMON NAME	Dextrin	Methyl cellulose	Hide glue	Whole egg
TYPE	Natural, water-thinned	Processed natural	Natural	Natural emulsion
SOURCE	Partially hydrolized starch	Methyl ether of cellulose, natural plant material	Animal bones, hides, hooves, cartilage, etc.	Fowl
COLOR/APPEARANCE	W powder	White flaky powder	Hard brown sheets or granules	Like a raw egg
USE	Additive for water-thinned vehicles; adhesive; cheap binder	Thickener, stabilizer, cheap binder, and adhesive	Strong adhesive; binder for "size" paints	Binder for egg-oil emulsions
REFRACTIVE INDEX	Low–medium as binder	High when dry; medium when prepared	Low–medium when prepared	Low in vehicle
VISCOSITY	Low when thinned; high when thickened	Low thin; High thick	Low heated; high gelled	Low
THINNER/SOLVENT	Water	Water	Water	Water; hot water
REVERSIBILITY	Good	Good	Good	Poor; destroyed by water, not reversed
pH	Relatively neutral	Neutral	Relatively neutral	Neutral
For Oils				
Linoleic				
Linolein				
Linolenic				
DURABILITY				
Interior	Fair–good	Good–excellent	Good	Excellent
Exterior	Poor	Poor	Poor	Poor
Rigid support	Good	Good–excellent	Excellent	Excellent
Flexible support	Fair	Fair	Poor	Poor
RESISTANCE TO:				
Water	Poor	Poor	Poor	Fair
Acid	Fair	Fair	Fair	Poor
Alkali	Fair	Fair	Fair	Poor
Pollutants	Poor	Fair	Fair	Fair
Ultraviolet light	Poor	Fair–good	Poor	Good
Decay	Poor	Good–excellent	Poor	Fair–good
HAZARDS				
Health	n/a	n/a	n/a	n/a
Fire (flash point)	n/a	n/a	n/a	n/a
OTHER COMMENTS	Found in best commercial transparent watercolors as thickener or binder extender; used alone, not a good binder; good, cheap, temporary adhesive	Many varieties; similar to starches but more stable and resistant; good but weak adhesive	Traditional textile support size, now thought hazardous because too strong; replace with synthetics	Excellent binder and ingredient in egg-oil emulsion vehicles

TABLE 3.1 (*continued*)
BINDERS

COMMON NAME	Egg yolk	Glair	Casein
TYPE	Natural emulsion	Natural emulsion	Natural emulsion
SOURCE	Fowl	Fowl	Dried skim milk curd
COLOR/APPEARANCE	Y	W, slightly translucent	W to Y powder; clear syrup when prepared
USE	Binder for pure egg tempera	Binder for manuscript illumination paints	Binder for casein and casein gesso, adhesive
REFRACTIVE INDEX	Low in vehicle	Low	Low
VISCOSITY	Medium–high	Low when prepared	Low–high, depending on dilution
THINNER/SOLVENT	Water; hot water	Water	Water; stronger for dried films
REVERSIBILITY	Same as whole egg	Good	Poor: destroyed by scrubbing w/ water
pH	Neutral	Neutral	Alkaline
For Oils			
Linoleic			
Linolein			
Linolenic			
DURABILITY			
Interior	Excellent	Good	Excellent
Exterior	Poor	Poor	Poor
Rigid support	Excellent	Good	Excellent
Flexible support	Poor	Poor	Poor
RESISTANCE TO:			
Water	Fair	Poor	Fair
Acid	Poor	Poor	Poor
Alkali	Poor	Poor	Poor
Pollutants	Fair	Fair	Fair
Ultraviolet light	Good	Fair	Good
Decay	Fair–good	Fair–good	Fair–good
HAZARDS			
Health	n/a	n/a	n/a; solutions alkaline
Fire (flash point)	n/a	n/a	n/a
OTHER COMMENTS	Excellent classical binder for egg tempera; *cannot be duplicated by acrylic emulsions*	Classic binder for manuscript paintings; can also be used as a size and adhesive for gilding	Excellent adhesive and binder, inconvenient to prepare; *cannot be duplicated*

TABLE 3.1 (continued)
BINDERS

COMMON NAME	Slaked lime (calcium hydroxide)	Vinyl resins		Acrylic resins	
TYPE	Natural catalytic	Synthetic resin; lacquer		Synthetic resin	
SOURCE	Roasted calcium carbonate + water (see text)	Ethylene; crude petroleum; large variety		Vinyl derivative; large variety	
COLOR/APPEARANCE	Dull W putty	Large clear lumps that fracture like glass; in emulsion, milky W		Large clear lumps or W powder; in emulsion, milky W	
USE	Support, ground, and binder for *fresco buono*	Variety of uses		Variety of uses	
REFRACTIVE INDEX	n/a	Low, depending on form		Low, depending on form	
VISCOSITY	High in putty; lime water has low viscosity	High when solid; low–medium in solution or emulsion		High when solid; low–medium solution or emulsion	
THINNER/SOLVENT	Water; water destroys lime walls	Aromatic hydrocarbons, ketones for solutions; water for emulsions unless dry		Aliphatics for solutions; water for emulsions unless dry	
REVERSIBILITY	Poor; destroyed by water if improperly applied	Good in solution; poor in emulsion		Good in solution; poor in emulsion	
pH	Alkaline	Neutral in solution; alkaline in emulsion		Neutral in solution; alkaline in emulsion	
For Oils Linoleic Linolein Linolenic					
DURABILITY		Solution	Emulsion	Solution	Emulsion
Interior	Excellent	Good	Good	Excellent	Good–excellent
Exterior	Poor	Fair	Fair–good	Good	Fair
Rigid support	Excellent	Excellent	Excellent	Excellent	Excellent
Flexible support	Poor	Fair	Fair–good	Fair	Good–excellent
RESISTANCE TO:					
Water	Poor	Excellent	Fair	Excellent	Fair
Acid	Poor	Excellent	Poor	Fair	Poor
Alkali	Poor	Fair	Poor	Fair	Poor
Pollutants	Poor	Good	Fair	Fair–good	Fair
Ultraviolet light	Good	Fair	Fair	Fair	Fair
Decay	Good	Excellent	Excellent	Excellent	Excellent
HAZARDS					
Health	Very alkaline; can burn	Major hazards w/solvents		Major hazards w/solvents	
Fire (flash point)	n/a Fn/a	Varies; solvent hazard		Varies; solvent hazard	
OTHER COMMENTS	Excellent mural material under right environmental conditions; inconvenient and expensive to prepare	Solutions hazardous because of solvents; emulsions safer but good only for adhesives; see MSDSs for hazards		Solutions hazardous because of solvents, but can make good paints; use only solution which can be thinned with mineral spirits; see MSDSs for hazards; emulsions excellent for artistic uses; see MSDSs for hazards	

TABLE 3.1 (continued)
BINDERS

COMMON NAME	Alkyd resins	Latex	Silicates
TYPE	Synthetic resin	Natural or synthetic emulsion	Silicate
SOURCE	Condensed ester of a polyhydric alcohol and a polybasic acid	Natural fine dispersion of rubber or resin in water (e.g., fig milk)	Pure silica; dissolved in a solvent or dispersed as a colloid in water
COLOR/APPEARANCE	Y to YR, depending on modifier	Milky W	Clear or bluish fluid
USE	Major industrial use as paint binder	Binder	Industrial binder; experimental for artists
REFRACTIVE INDEX	Low to medium	Medium–high liquid; low–medium dry film	Low
VISCOSITY	High—in artists' paint vehicle, low to medium	Low–high, depending on vehicle contents	Low until hydrolysis; medium–high until dry
THINNER/SOLVENT	Varies, but in artists' binders, mineral spirits; higher aromatics for dried films	Water; higher solvents when dry	Varies, from water to mineral spirits to alcohol
REVERSIBILITY	In oil-modified binder, only aromatics can be used: poor reversibility	Poor	Not possible
pH	Oil-modified: slightly acidic	Alkaline	Alkaline to *very* alkaline

For Oils
      Linoleic
      Linolein
      Linolenic			

DURABILITY		Depends on type	Depends on type
Interior	Excellent	Good–excellent	Excellent
Exterior	Good	Fair–good	Excellent
Rigid support	Excellent	Good–excellent	Excellent
Flexible support	Good–excellent	Good–excellent	Poor
RESISTANCE TO:			
Water	Excellent	Good	Good
Acid	Fair	Fair	Fair
Alkali	Fair	Fair	Fair
Pollutants	Good	Good	Excellent
Ultraviolet light	Good	Fair	Good
Decay	Excellent	Good	Excellent
HAZARDS			
Health	n/a; misuse or abuse	n/a; vehicle contents	Silica causes silicosis; binder can cause burns
Fire (flash point)	Very high flash point	n/a	Varies from n/a to flammable
OTHER COMMENTS	With more than 50% oil in vehicle, paints are really oil paints; versatile, nonyellowing (with proper oil content), quick-drying, less apt to crack than linseed oil binders; better color development than acrylic emulsions; underrated	Generic term for wide variety of water-based dispersions of particles of rubber or resin in water; *common latex housepaint is not an artists' material*	Potential exterior mural paint binder; "one package" systems require only pigment dispersion, application similar to fresco; serious hazard; see MSDSs for hazards and *follow all instructions*

CHAPTER 4

SOLVENTS AND THINNERS

Thinners and solvents are used for diluting binders, for thinning paints to working consistency, for cleaning up around the studio, for dissolving varnish resins or waxes, and as cleaning agents in the conservation or restoration of paintings. They are usually *volatile*—they rapidly evaporate large amounts of the material into the air—and leave little or no residue behind.

The Artist's Handbook lists the requirements for artists' thinners:*

1. A thinner should be completely volatile, leaving no residue.
2. A thinner should evaporate at a uniform rate.
3. When used in the process of painting, a thinner should not have a solvent effect on dried paint layers. In many cases, this is difficult to control.
4. A thinner should not induce a chemical reaction with the other materials or ingredients to which it is exposed. Neither should the products of any reactions that do occur be harmful to the user (see 6 below).
5. A thinner should mix completely with all the other materials with which it is used; precipitates (residues) should not be formed.
6. Vapors given off by a thinner or solvent should be nontoxic. Few thinners or solvents meet this requirement—many present both acute and chronic hazards to those who are careless or ignorant about their proper use.
7. When used as a solvent, the material should have a complete solvent action.
8. The solution produced by a solvent should be stable.

FIRE HAZARDS

Most thinners and solvents are flammable, and some are extremely dangerous for this reason. An indication of a liquid's flammability is expressed by its *flash*

---

* From *The Artist's Handbook*, revised edition, by Ralph Mayer. Copyright © 1981 by Bena Mayer, Executrix of the Estate of Ralph Mayer. Reprinted by permission of Viking Penguin, Inc.

point—the lowest temperature at which a solvent gives off vapors that can be ignited by an open flame or spark. Here are classifications of flammability, based on the flash point of a solvent:

Combustible	Flash point 100–150° F (38–65° C)
Flammable	Flash point 20–100° F (−7 to 38° C) (consider this room temperature)
Extremely flammable	Flash point around 20° F (−7° C)
Explosive	Flash point around 10° F (−12° C)

To avoid the danger of fire when using solvents, be aware of the following precautions:

1. Know the flash point of the solvent, or determine the flammability of the liquid by reading the container label carefully.

2. All container labels should have complete information, including any cautions about hazards other than fire, with instructions for the treatment of injuries or overexposure and warnings about proper storage. Do not transfer solvents to unlabeled containers.

3. Purchase solvents and thinners in the smallest quantities practical, generally no more than a gallon (3.8 l) at a time. There is little need to buy larger quantities, but if you must, then store them in fireproof steel cabinets that have a provision for automatically extinguishing fires. Lab Safety Supply has a good selection of these expensive devices (see Appendix D).

4. Store solvents in their original containers, tightly closed, away from sources of heat (including direct sunlight), and out of the pathway to an exit from the studio.

5. Keep even small containers of solvents closed when working—open them only to remove the solvent or use the thinner.

6. Never smoke in the presence of solvents.

7. Heating and ventilating equipment (exhaust fans) should have explosion-proof motors, and all other electrical equipment should be in excellent condition, with properly grounded wiring.

8. Dispose of soaked rags and materials properly. The ideal container is one with a self-closing top, made of steel, that is fireproof or self-extinguishing. Empty the container every day to avoid a buildup of flammable vapors.

9. Have a good-quality carbon dioxide or dry chemical fire extinguisher located in a prominent place, preferably near the exit and away from the storage area.

HEALTH HAZARDS

The health hazards of solvents are perhaps more significant than the fire hazards. Much has been made of these potential hazards in recent years; in industry they have been more extensively studied than in the arts. In the fine arts, familiar materials are often repackaged into containers much smaller than the package in which the original material was shipped, with less specific and less detailed cautionary labeling. Furthermore, the uses to which artists put solvents or thinners —not to mention other potentially harmful materials—are frequently variable, uncontrolled, unknown to the manufacturer or distributor of the product, and conducted somewhat carelessly. When a product is used carefully, with full understanding of its dangers, there is less cause for concern.

Exposure to the hazards of solvents and thinners can occur in three ways: by absorption through the skin, by aspiration (breathing in) of the liquid or inhalation of the vapors into the lungs, and by ingestion. The various solvents and thinners have varying degrees of hazards, and can have either acute toxic effects (those which produce symptoms of injury immediately after exposure) or chronic toxic effects (producing symptoms of injury only after prolonged exposure, even to low levels). The toxicity of solvents can be put into three general categories:

1. *Highly Toxic* These solvents can produce major injury, or death, from a single incident of acute exposure. Skin damage or a severe allergic reaction can be produced by absorption through the skin. Brain damage or severe irritation of the nose, throat, and lungs can result from inhalation. Fatal injury can result from the aspiration or ingestion of small amounts. These materials can also produce chronic severe damage from regular exposures to smaller amounts over a sustained period of time.

2. *Toxic* Toxic solvents may have a less severe acute effect during a single exposure to smaller amounts than highly toxic materials, but should still be considered extremely hazardous. The injuries may be minor but permanent; dermatitis from skin absorption is a good example. The inhalation of toxic vapors can cause headaches, nausea, and lung irritation. Aspiration or ingestion can be fatal unless immediate and massive first aid is applied. Repeated exposure to small amounts of a toxic material can have the same results as a single acute exposure to a highly toxic material.

3. *Harmful* Slightly toxic solvents or thinners are harmful, producing minor injury that can be treated by removal from contact with the material. An allergic skin reaction to a solvent can be avoided by not using it, or by protecting the skin from contact with the appropriate gloves or creams. Intoxication from inhaling harmful solvent vapors can be reversed by removing the victim to fresh air. Serious injury can still result from overexposure to large amounts of harmful solvents.

The chronic effects of exposures to solvents are more difficult to assess than the acute effects, which usually show up immediately. Some of the illnesses that have been shown to result from exposure to materials with a chronic toxic effect include the following:

1. Sterility.
2. Birth defects and/or harm to a developing fetus.
3. Harm to a nursing infant.
4. Various forms of cancer.

5. Allergic skin or lung reactions.
6. Personality changes or mental injury.
7. Damage to organ systems such as the blood, liver, heart, lungs, or brain.

To avoid injury when using solvents, follow this advice.

1. *Always* know the content(s) of the solvents or thinners in use. If the container is improperly labeled, do not use the solvent. Write to the manufacturer and ask for the Material Safety Data Sheets (MSDSs) on the material in question. These sheets provide some information about the harmful or hazardous content of the material, although they cannot be considered 100 percent reliable. If the manufacturer cannot or will not supply information about the material, do not use the product—there is no reason to risk serious injury. If at all possible, avoid the use of highly toxic solvents altogether. *Note:* Material Safety Data Sheet information applies not only to solvents but to other types of materials as well. If there is a question about the labeling of *any* product used in the studio, request a MSDS from the manufacturer.

2. Wear splash goggles, or a full face mask, and gloves when using more than small amounts of a solvent. The proper glove for the particular solvent must be chosen, since some gloves will permit particular solvents to penetrate (see Table 4.1 for this information). Barrier creams can be used under gloves for additional protection, or for short-term protection for bare skin when using small amounts of the solvent. *Never* use solvents to clean hands.

3. Use the proper ventilation to remove solvent vapors from the studio. The phrase "adequate ventilation" is on almost every solvent label, but its meaning is not always explained. An open window is generally not enough; there must be cross-ventilation to remove the vapors. Cross-ventilation directs the flow of air away from the face and out of the studio. A general exhaust fan, placed in a window, can provide air changes in a room if there is another window or door opposite that can let in fresh, uncontaminated air. A general exhaust fan should be used only with harmful solvents. To remove highly toxic or toxic vapors, direct local exhaust is recommended: Either a laboratory hood or a flexible duct system can be used. If neither general nor direct local exhaust systems are feasible, you can use an organic vapor mask, provided with the correct cartridge filter. Figure 4.1 shows examples of correct and incorrect exhaust setups, and of organic vapor and air-supply protective masks. Appendix D gives sources for this equipment.

The importance of knowing the hazards of using solvents cannot be overemphasized. It is, however, equally necessary to keep a perspective about them: The average painter will have no need, in the normal course of events, to use the more dangerous solvents and thinners. Most painters live quite happily using only water, gum turpentine, mineral spirits, and occasionally alcohol or "lacquer thinners." Most precautionary advice is founded on *common sense.* Ignorance is perhaps more dangerous than any particular solvent—even a relatively harmless solvent can be abused.

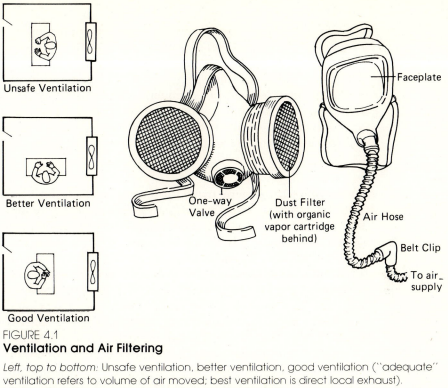

FIGURE 4.1
Ventilation and Air Filtering

Left, top to bottom: Unsafe ventilation, better ventilation, good ventilation (''adequate'' ventilation refers to volume of air moved; best ventilation is direct local exhaust).
Middle: Organic vapor mask, covering nose and mouth.
Right: Full-face air-supplied respirator, covering the entire face.

Follow the advice given here and in the more specific and detailed accounts found in books such as *Artist Beware.* Ask questions if labeling seems incomplete. Use protective equipment, and have the telephone number of a poison control center on hand.

COMMON SOLVENTS

The more common solvents encountered in a painting studio are discussed below. For quick reference to technical information, see Table 4.1. For more detailed information on the less common solvents, consult one of the texts specializing in this kind of information, such as *Artist Beware.* For medical advice, see your doctor or call a local poison control center. The relative toxicity ratings of the solvents below are adapted from *Artist Beware.**

---

* Copyright © 1979 by Dr. Michael McCann. Reprinted by permission of Watson-Guptill Publications.

WATER

Water is called the universal solvent—it is the thinner most often used by artists for many studio procedures. It is the thinner for the watercolors, casein, tempera, acrylic polymer and polyvinyl acetate emulsions, and fresco.

Distilled water is often specified for the preparation of binders for water-thinned paints, since dissolved mineral salts in ordinary tap water can affect the performance or durability of the paint. Where local water is soft, there should be no problem, and distilled water (not spring water or mineral water) is usually available at supermarkets or pharmacies.

GUM TURPENTINE

Turpentine is the general name for several products distilled from the sap of pine trees: the longleaf yellow pine (*Pinus palustris*) or the loblolly pine (*Pinus taeda*). The whole crude sap, or oleoresin, was originally called turpentine, but now the word usually refers only to the more volatile spirit, or liquid.

Gum turpentine (or turps) is properly called Pure Gum Spirits of Turpentine. It is distilled from the sap of live pine trees and for artistic use must be *anhydrous*, or water-free. Fresh turpentine is colorless or slightly yellow and has a distinctive odor; as it ages, it turns yellow and its odor grows sharper and more pronounced. Gum turps bought in a hardware store, where the stock turnover is rapid, is usually fresher than the smaller amounts found in art supply stores.

A slightly gummy residue is left behind as gum turpentine evaporates. This is partly the result of polymerization and oxidation, and does little harm to mixtures in which it is used. Fresh turps is better in this respect.

Gum turpentine is classifiable as a harmful solvent. Some varieties are more harmful than others (depending on the species of tree) and require a health hazard warning label to be certified by the Art and Craft Materials Institute. This applies only to turpentines marketed as art supplies, not to turpentines sold in hardware stores. It is reasonably safe with regard to fire hazards, with a flash point of around 95° F (35° C): flammable. It should be stored in closed, opaque containers, away from heat and light. The vapors can be irritating to the nose, throat, and eyes, and skin contact should be minimized: some people develop severe skin allergies to gum turpentine. Do not use gum turpentine to clean brushes or hands.

The other varieties of turpentine are steam-distilled wood turpentine, from pine scraps or stumps; sulfate wood turpentine; and destructively distilled wood turpentine. None of these is as pure or as useful as the pure spirits of gum turpentines. They may often contain water and can be much more irritating than gum turpentine.

PETROLEUM PRODUCTS

A variety of solvents that painters use are derived from petroleum, the components of which are separated by fractional distillation. All are varieties of hydrocarbons, and painters are generally concerned with two classes: *aliphatic hydrocarbons* and *aromatic hydrocarbons.*

The aliphatic solvents are considered less volatile and less active than the aromatics, although they may contain a percentage of aromatics in the less pure grades. Gasoline and kerosene are included in this group. The aromatics include benzene and naphthalene. They are quite volatile and consequently more active solvents. Most are highly flammable and some are highly toxic.

ALIPHATIC HYDROCARBONS

Mineral Spirits   This is a refined distillate of petroleum with a low aromatic content, known by the general designation of "paint thinner." It is usually sold under a proprietary name like P & W Paint Thinner. Its properties are similar to those of gum turpentine, but with several advantages: It does not leave a gummy residue when it evaporates; it does not deteriorate with age; it is less likely to affect those with an allergic reaction to gum turpentine; and it is much less expensive than gum turpentine. It can replace gum turps for those studio operations which do not involve damar or other hard resins or varnishes. Mineral spirits can be classified as harmful, though when ingested can be highly toxic. The flash point is 85–105° F (30–40° C): flammable.

Varnish Maker's and Painter's Naphtha   Also known as VM&P Naphtha, this solvent is more volatile than mineral spirits and is used occasionally as a substitute for it. The name "benzine" is still sometimes used as a name for VM&P Naphtha but should not be, since it can be easily confused with the highly toxic "benzene," an aromatic hydrocarbon solvent. The naphthas should be used with care, since they can contain aromatic additives. VM&P Naphtha can be classified as harmful, though when ingested it can be highly toxic. The flash point is 20–55° F (−7 to 13°C): flammable.

Kerosene   This is a fuel oil that is sometimes used as a cleanup solvent. It can leave behind a greasy residue as it evaporates, and is not suitable for studio use. The proprietary solvent Varsol is only slightly better; it can be used for cleanup, but should not be used as a thinner or diluent in paints or varnishes. Kerosene is harmful; when ingested it can be highly toxic. The flash point is 100–165° F (38–74° C): combustible.

Gasoline   This is chemically a good paint thinner, but many varieties contain additional ingredients such as lead or benzene that make it very dangerous to use. In addition, it is a serious fire hazard. Gasoline is highly toxic. The flash point is −50° F (−46° C): explosive.

AROMATIC HYDROCARBONS

Benzene   This dangerous and explosively flammable solvent was formerly found in many commercial solvent-thinned products; the odor was familiar to users of rubber cement. Now the solvent used in that product is usually n-hexane. Benzene should never be used in an artist's studio. It is highly toxic. The flash point is 12° F (−11° C): explosive.

Xylene Used as a solvent in picture conservation and restoration and sometimes found in fast-drying marker inks, xylene is less toxic and flammable than benzene, but its use should be avoided where possible. Xylene is toxic. The flash point is 75° F (24° C): flammable.

Toluene Toluene is found as the solvent in some commercially prepared spray varnishes and fixatives. Use these very carefully; avoid using the solvent alone. Toluene is toxic. The flash point is 45° F (7° C): flammable.

Note: Commercial brands of benzene, xylene, and toluene can be labeled benzol, xylol, and toluol. Unless they are chemically pure (called C.P.), they may contain small amounts of each other as additives. Commercial "lacquer thinners" can also contain one or more of these aromatics, with the label giving a nonspecific phrase like "contains aromatic hydrocarbons." Generally, none of these solvents need be used by the average painter.

N-Hexane This solvent is now used in many brands of rubber cement. It is harmful, though ingestion can cause a toxic reaction. The flash point is −70° F (22° C): explosive. Use with caution in rubber cements.

ALCOHOLS

The alcohols find minor use among artists as resin solvents, wetting agents, and cleaners.

Ethyl Alcohol This is also called ethanol or grain alcohol, and usually contains a small proportion of water. Absolute alcohol, or 100 percent anhydrous (water-free) alcohol, contains no water, and can be had through chemical supply firms. Denatured ethyl alcohol, available in paint supply and hardware stores, contains ingredients to make it poisonous—small amounts of gasoline, methyl alcohol, or other solvents. Denatured ethyl is most often used for studio operations. Ethyl alcohol is harmful; denatured ethyl alcohol is toxic. The flash point is 54–60° F (12–16° C): flammable.

Methyl Alcohol Also called methanol or wood alcohol, with the same general solvent properties as ethyl alcohol, it has significantly higher toxicity. It should not be used in the studio. Methyl alcohol is highly toxic by ingestion. The flash point is 54–60° F (12–16° C): flammable.

Glycerine This is a trihydroxy alcohol also known as glycerin or glycerol—a nonvolatile, syrupy alcohol that bears little resemblance to its cousins. Glycerine is used in commercial coatings as a plasticizer and finds the same use in manufactured and homemade paints containing brittle binders, principally watercolors. Glycerine is neither toxic nor flammable.

KETONES

The ketones are a group of organic solvents used in paint and varnish removers and as lacquer and plastic solvents. They are considerably stronger in their solvent action than some of the aromatic hydrocarbons; some of them are more hazardous than the aromatics, some are less. What is called "lacquer thinner" may contain one or more of the ketones.

Acetone This is the most familiar of the ketones, and it is used as a solvent for a variety of natural and synthetic resins and recommended by some writers as a "quick-dry" solvent for cleaning brushes. Acetone should be classified as harmful. Its flash point is −4 to 15° C (−19 to −10° C): explosive. Avoid its use when possible because of the fire hazard.

Methyl Ethyl Ketone This is also known as MEK and has many of the same solvent properties as acetone, although it is not as volatile. It is used as a vinyl resin solvent. MEK peroxide is a derivative of MEK, used as a catalytic additive for polyester resins; it is highly toxic. Methyl ethyl ketone should be classified as toxic to harmful. The flash point is 24–30° F (−4 to −1° C): flammable.

Methyl Butyl Ketone Also known as MBK or 2-hexanone, this is a solvent that is less flammable but more hazardous than MEK. Methyl butyl ketone should be classified as highly toxic. The flash point is 73–97° F (23–35° C): flammable.

Methyl Isobutyl Ketone Also known as MIBK or hexone, this is a ketone solvent with moderate hazards. Methyl isobutyl ketone should be classified as harmful to toxic. The flash point is 74° F (24° C): flammable.

Cyclohexanone Also called hexanone, it is known as the chemical basis for a ketone resin varnish supplied with Winsor & Newton's alkyd resin paints. The solvent form (not the varnish form) should be classified as toxic; highly toxic by inhalation. The flash point is around 111° F (44° C): combustible.

MISCELLANEOUS

The following solvents are other materials that artists may encounter but that are not generally found in the average studio. It is helpful to be aware of them—but remember that this is not a comprehensive list.

Cellosolve This solvent sometimes finds its way into acrylic polymer, co-polymer, or ter-polymer emulsion binders in very small amounts. Cellosolve is a proprietary name for this water-miscible solvent. Cellosolve should be classified as harmful, though by ingestion it is toxic. The amounts in commercial emulsions are not significant with regard to this classification. The flash point is 107° F (42° C): combustible.

Carbitol This is also a proprietary solvent with properties and uses similar to Cellosolve. Carbitol should be classified as harmful, though by ingestion it is toxic. The amounts in commercial emulsions are not significant with regard to this classification. The flash point is 205° F (96° C): combustible.

Ethylene Glycol This is a type of alcohol used in emulsion dispersions as a plasticizer; it provides stability to the emulsion if it is frozen. (It is also used as an antifreeze for automobile radiators.) Ethylene glycol should be classified as harmful, though by ingestion it is toxic. The amounts found in commercial emulsions may be significant depending on the proprietary formula of the manufacturer, but generally speaking the material does not pose a serious threat. The flash point is 232° F (111° C): combustible.

CHLORINATED HYDROCARBONS

Chlorinated hydrocarbons are used as degreasing agents, and as solvents for plastics and waxes. Some are flammable; some decompose in the presence of a flame to form the toxic gas phosgene. Some are suspected carcinogens—in laboratory tests they can cause cancer in animals. The chlorinated hydrocarbons should be avoided. A typical list follows, giving the flash point (FP), whether the solvent decomposes into phosgene, and its general toxicity classification according to *Artist Beware.* But to repeat: *Do not use these solvents.*

Name	Flash point	Toxicity
Tetrachloroethane	Decomposes into phosgene	Highly toxic
Carbon Tetrachloride (dry-cleaning fluid)	Not flammable	Highly toxic
Chloroform (anesthetic)	Decomposes into phosgene	Highly toxic
Trichloroethylene (batik wax solvent)	Decomposes into phosgene	Highly toxic
Ethylene dichloride	65° F (18° C)	Highly toxic
Methylene chloride (commercial paint stripper)	Not flammable	Toxic
Ortho-Dichlorobenzene	165° F (74° C)	Toxic
Monochlorotoluene	120° F (52° C)	Toxic
Perchloroethylene	Decomposes into phosgene	Highly toxic
Methyl chloroform	Decomposes into phosgene	Highly toxic

For quick reference to the technical aspects of solvents and thinners, their uses, hazards, and cautions about them, consult Table 4.1, which follows.

TABLE 4.1
SOLVENTS AND THINNERS

COMMON NAME	Water		Distilled water		Pure Gum Spirits of Turpentine		Steam-distilled turpentine	
TYPE	Aqueous		Aqueous		Nonaqueous; should be anhydrous		Nonaqueous but may contain water	
SOURCE	Ground water		Distilled; also de-ionized		*Pinus palustris* or *Pinus taeda;* many species of pine		Ground pine wood pulp; lumber industry by-product	
COLOR/APPEARANCE	Clear		Clear		Very pale Y when fresh		Darker Y than Pure Gum Spirits	
USE	"Universal solvent"; polluted water may contain dissolved heavy metals		Mainly for "clean" techniques		Diluent for oils and alkyds; damar solvent		Commercial use	
HAZARDS							NR	
Flash point	n/a		n/a		95° F (35° C)		95° F (35° C)	
Fire hazard rating	n/a				Flammable		Flammable	
Health hazard rating by route of entry	Acute	Chronic	Acute	Chronic	Acute	Chronic	Acute	Chronic
Absorption		n/a		n/a	H	H	H	H
Aspiration					HT	HT	HT	HT
Ingestion					T	T	T	T
Inhalation					H	H	H	H
ACUTE EFFECTS		n/a		n/a	Skin irritation; severe lung damage; aspiration can be fatal		Same as Pure Gum Spirits, but can be more acute	
CHRONIC EFFECTS		n/a		n/a	Skin allergy or rash; vapors may sensitize skin		Same as Pure Gum Spirits, but can be more acute	
TYPE OF VENTILATION (Explosion-proof motors)		n/a		n/a				
General (3 air changes/hour)					×			
General exhaust					×, preferred		×	
Local direct exhaust								
Fume hood								
BARRIERS		n/a		n/a				
Type of respirator Dust								
Organic vapor					×, if spraying		×, at least	
Air-supplied								
Goggles or other eye protection					×, when spraying		×	
Type of glove Latex/neoprene rubber								
Nitrile rubber					×		×	
Solvent-proof cream					×, if sensitive		×	
OTHER COMMENTS	Soft tap water can be used; avoid hard water, mineral water, sea water		For procedures where dissolved metallic salts could affect paint; "clean" diluent for sensitive water-thinned paints		Relatively safe, but avoid if possible; certain species of tree more likely to cause adverse reaction; use mineral spirits		Not an art material; likely to contain other materials that could cause more severe reactions	

Note: H = harmful; T = toxic; HT = highly toxic; NR = not recommended; C.P. = chemically pure.

TABLE 4.1 *(continued)*
SOLVENTS AND THINNERS

COMMON NAME	VM & P Naphtha		Mineral spirits		Kerosene (kerosine)		Gasoline (leaded and unleaded)	
TYPE	Nonaqueous		Nonaqueous		Nonaqueous; may contain water		Nonaqueous	
SOURCE	Petroleum distillate		Petroleum distillate		Petroleum fuel oil; distilled aliphatic hydrocarbon		Petroleum fuel oil; distilled aliphatic hydrocarbon	
COLOR/APPEARANCE	Clear		Clear		Greasy W to pale Y		Clear to pinkish	
USE	Paint thinner; cleanup		Cleanup; thinner; resin solvent		Fuel; cleanup		Fuel	
HAZARDS								
Flash point	20–55° F (−7 to −13° C)		85–105° F (30–40° C)		100–165° F (38–74° C)		−50° F (−46° C)	
Fire hazard rating	Flammable		Flammable		Combustible		Explosive	
Health hazard rating by route of entry	Acute	Chronic	Acute	Chronic	Acute	Chronic	Acute	Chronic
Absorption	H	T	H	H	H	T	T	HT
Aspiration	HT	HT	HT	HT	HT	HT	HT	HT
Ingestion	HT	HT	HT	HT	HT	HT	HT	HT
Inhalation	T	T	H	H	T	T	HT	HT
ACUTE EFFECTS	Skin irritation; slight narcotic; aspiration can be fatal		Skin irritation; slight narcotic; aspiration can be fatal		Skin irritant; narcotic; aspiration can be fatal		Ingestion or aspiration can be fatal; skin defatting; narcotic	
CHRONIC EFFECTS	Skin irritation; vapors harmful		Skin irritation; vapor concentrations can be harmful		Skin irritation; vapor concentrations can be harmful		Brain damage; skin defatting; other organ damage	
TYPE OF VENTILATION (Explosion-proof motors)								
General (3 air changes/hour)	✕, at least		✕, at least		✕, at least			
General exhaust	✕, preferred		✕, preferred		✕, preferred			
Local direct exhaust							✕	
Fume hood							✕, preferred	
BARRIERS								
Type of respirator Dust								
Organic vapor Air-supplied	✕, at least		✕, when spraying		✕		✕	
Goggles or other eye protection	✕		✕, when spraying		✕		✕	
Type of glove Latex/neoprene rubber								
Nitrile rubber	✕		✕		✕		✕	
Solvent-proof cream	✕		✕		✕		✕	
OTHER COMMENTS	Not an art material; mineral spirits cleaner and safer, though has same hazards		Good general-purpose solvent with excellent characteristics		Not an art material; greasy and dirty		Very dangerous material; good solvent, *but do not use*	

TABLE 4.1 *(continued)*
SOLVENTS AND THINNERS

COMMON NAME	Benzene (benzol)		Xylene (xylol)		Toluene (toluol)		n-Hexane	
TYPE	Nonaqueous; may not be C.P.		Nonaqueous; may not be C.P.		Nonaqueous; may not be C.P.		Nonaqueous; may not be C.P.	
SOURCE	Distilled petroleum aromatic hydrocarbon		Distilled petroleum aromatic hydrocarbon		Distilled petroleum aromatic hydrocarbon		Distilled petroleum aromatic hydrocarbon	
COLOR/APPEARANCE	W (clear)		W or slightly Y		W (clear)		W (clear)	
USE	Solvent		Solvent; found in some rapid-dry felt-tip markers		Solvent; found in some spray varnishes		Solvent; may replace highly toxic benzene in some rubber cements	
HAZARDS								
Flash point	12° F (−11° C)		75° F (24° C)		45° F (7° C)		−70° F (−22° C)	
Fire hazard rating	Explosive		Flammable		Flammable		Explosive	
Health hazard rating by route of entry	Acute	Chronic	Acute	Chronic	Acute	Chronic	Acute	Chronic
Absorption	HT	HT	H	H	HT	HT	H	T
Aspiration	HT	HT	HT	HT	HT	HT	T	T
Ingestion	HT	HT	HT	HT	HT	HT	T	T
Inhalation	HT	HT	HT	HT	HT	HT	T	T
ACUTE EFFECTS	Carcinogenic: *do not use*		Skin, eye, nose, throat irritant; concentrated vapors—heart failure		Same as for Xylene		Same as for Xylene	
CHRONIC EFFECTS			Skin defatting; possible organ damage		Same as for Xylene		Same as for Xylene	
TYPE OF VENTILATION (Explosion-proof motors)								
General (3 air changes/hour)								
General exhaust							×, at least	
Local direct exhaust			×		×		×, preferred	
Fume hood	×, mandatory		×, preferred		×, preferred			
BARRIERS								
Type of respirator Dust								
Organic vapor			×		×		×, at least	
Air-supplied	×, mandatory		×, preferred		×, preferred		×, preferred	
Goggles or other eye protection	×		×		×		×	
Type of glove Latex/neoprene rubber								
Nitrile rubber	×		×		×		×	
Solvent-proof cream	×, under gloves		×, under gloves		×, under gloves		×	
OTHER COMMENTS	A human carcinogen; *do not use;* do not confuse with the old name for VM&P Naphtha, ben*z*ine		Odor familiar to users of solvent-based markers; use general exhaust at least		Use caution when spraying: use general exhaust at least		Not as hazardous as the former solvent for rubber cement (benzene), but use with caution	

TABLE 4.1 (continued)
SOLVENTS AND THINNERS

COMMON NAME	Ethyl alcohol (ethanol)		Denatured ethyl alcohol		Methyl alcohol (methanol)		Glycerine (glycerol)	
TYPE	Nonaqueous; may contain water; hygroscopic		Nonaqueous; hygroscopic; contains toxic materials		Nonaqueous; hygroscopic; may be contaminated		Nonaqueous; hygroscopic	
SOURCE	Distilled from grain		Distilled from grain		Distilled from grain		Trihydroxy alcohol, distilled from grain	
COLOR/APPEARANCE	W liquid		W		W		Viscous W with sweet odor	
USE	Solvent		Solvent		Solvent and fuel		Plasticizer	
HAZARDS								
Flash point	54–60° F (12–16° C)		54–60° F (12–16° C)		54–60° F (12–16° C)		Not flammable	
Fire hazard rating	Flammable		Flammable		Flammable		n/a	
Health hazard rating by route of entry	Acute	Chronic	Acute	Chronic	Acute	Chronic	Acute	Chronic
Absorption	n/a	H	H	H	H	T		n/a
Aspiration	T	T	HT	HT	T	T		
Ingestion	H	T	HT	HT	HT	HT		
Inhalation	n/a	H	T	T	HT	HT		
ACUTE EFFECTS	Intoxication; aspiration into lungs can be very harmful		Intoxication; euphoria; coma; organ damage depends on denaturant		All effects of ethyl plus fatal coma, severe organ damage, blindness		n/a	
CHRONIC EFFECTS	Liver and other organ damage				All effects of ethyl; chronic effect can be fatal		n/a	
TYPE OF VENTILATION (Explosion-proof motors)							n/a	
General (3 air changes/hour)	×		×					
General exhaust	×, preferred		×, preferred					
Local direct exhaust					×			
Fume hood					×, preferred			
BARRIERS							n/a	
Type of respirator								
Dust								
Organic vapor	×, if spraying		×, when spraying		×			
Air-supplied					×, preferred			
Goggles or other eye protection	×, when spraying		×, when spraying		×			
Type of glove								
Latex/neoprene rubber	×		×		×			
Nitrile rubber	×, preferred		×, preferred		×, preferred			
Solvent-proof cream	×		×		×, under gloves			
OTHER COMMENTS	Grain alcohol, about 90% alcohol and 10% water (180 proof), safer and easier to get than 100% ethyl; 100% ethyl better for anhydrous needs; not a safe material		More commonly used than ethyl; easier to get; *poisonous:* use with caution		A toxic solvent; avoid its use		A safe alcohol	

TABLE 4.1 (continued)
SOLVENTS AND THINNERS

COMMON NAME	Ethylene glycol (ethylene alcohol)		Propylene glycol (1, 2 propanediol)		Acetone (propanone; dimethyl ketone)		Methyle ethyl ketone (MEK; 2-butanone)	
TYPE	Nonaqueous; hygroscopic		Nonaqueous; hygroscopic		Nonaqueous; miscible with water		Nonaqueous	
SOURCE	Dihydric alcohol distilled from grain		Dyhydric alcohol distilled from grain		Gas distilled; other sources		Gas distilled; other sources	
COLOR/APPEARANCE	Viscous W liquid or opaque waxy solid		Viscous W liquid or opaque waxy solid		W liquid		W liquid	
USE	Plasticizer		Plasticizer		Solvent		Solvent	
HAZARDS								
Flash point	Not flammable unless heated: *do not heat*		Not flammable unless heated: *do not heat*		−4 to 15° F (−19 to −10° C)		24–30° F (−4 to −1° C)	
Fire hazard rating					Explosive		Extremely flammable	
Health hazard rating by route of entry	Acute	Chronic	Acute	Chronic	Acute	Chronic	Acute	Chronic
Absorption	H	H	Little harm unless heated: *do not heat*		Little harm	Unknown	H	H
Aspiration	T	T			T	T	H	H
Ingestion	HT	HT			Little harm	Little harm	Little harm	Little harm
Inhalation	n/a	n/a			Little harm	Little harm	H	H
							MEK-peroxide, a derivative of MEK, is highly toxic	
ACUTE EFFECTS	Ingestion can be fatal		Current research indicates not harmful		Intoxication; skin irritation or drying		Same as acetone	
CHRONIC EFFECTS	Chronic ingestion of small amounts can lead to organ damage				Same as acute *Do not drink alcohol while using acetone*			
TYPE OF VENTILATION (Explosion-proof motors)								
General (3 air changes/hour)	×		×					
General exhaust								
Local direct exhaust					×, fire hazard		×, fire hazard	
Fume hood								
BARRIERS								
Type of respirator								
Dust								
Organic vapor	×		×		×, when spraying		×, when spraying	
Air-supplied								
Goggles or other eye protection	×		×		×, if spraying		×, if spraying	
Type of glove								
Latex/neoprene rubber					×		×	
Nitrile rubber	×		×					
Solvent-proof cream	×		×, instead of gloves		×, instead of gloves		×, instead of gloves	
OTHER COMMENTS	Additive for some artists' acrylic emulsion paints; little need in average studio		Additive for some artists' acrylic emulsion paints; little need in average studio; less than 1% by weight concentration in tubes of paint, but paint should not be heated or eaten		Dangerously explosive but not a health hazard		Very flammable but not a health hazard; use with caution	

TABLE 4.1 (continued)
SOLVENTS AND THINNERS

COMMON NAME	Methyl butyl ketone (MBK; 2-hexanone)		Methyl isobutyl ketone (MIBK; hexone)		Cyclohexanone (hexanone)	
TYPE	Nonaqueous		Nonaqueous		Nonaqueous	
SOURCE	Gas distilled; other sources		Gas distilled; other sources		Gas distilled; other sources	
COLOR/APPEARANCE	W liquid		W liquid		W liquid	
USE	Solvent		Solvent		Solvent; polymerized form: resin varnish	
HAZARDS						
Flash point	73–95° F (23–35° C)		74° F (24° C)		111° F (44° C)	
Fire hazard rating	Flammable		Flammable		Combustible	
Health hazard rating by route of entry	Acute	Chronic	Acute	Chronic	Acute	Chronic
Absorption	HT	HT	T	T	H	H
Aspiration	HT	HT	T	T	HT	HT
Ingestion	HT	HT	T	T	Little harm	Little harm
Inhalation	HT	HT	T	T	HT	HT
ACUTE EFFECTS	Intoxication; weakness and nerve damage		Intoxication; narcosis; skin, eye, nose, throat irritation		Intoxication; skin, eye, nose, throat irritation	
CHRONIC EFFECTS	General deterioration of nervous system		Same as acute; more severe irritation		Organ damage	
TYPE OF VENTILATION (Explosion-proof motors)						
General (3 air changes/hour)						
General exhaust						
Local direct exhaust	✕		✕		✕, preferred	
Fume hood	✕, preferred		✕, preferred			
BARRIERS						
Type of respirator						
Dust						
Organic vapor	✕		✕		✕, preferred	
Air-supplied	✕, preferred		✕, preferred			
Goggles or other eye protection	✕		✕		✕, if spraying	
Type of glove						
Latex/neoprene rubber	✕		✕		✕	
Nitrile rubber	(dissolved in MBK)					
Solvent-proof cream	✕, under gloves		✕		✕	
OTHER COMMENTS	Very hazardous to health; *do not use* if possible		Safer than MBK but still hazardous; avoid in average studio; *do not use*		Not useful as a solvent; more useful in the form known as a "ketone resin varnish"	

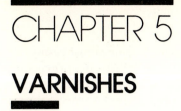

CHAPTER 5

VARNISHES

Varnishes are solutions of natural or synthetic resins that dry to a solid, relatively transparent, and continuous film when spread thinly on a surface. According to the composition of the solution, the films exhibit varying qualities of gloss, protective ability, flexibility, and durability.

Artists use two major categories of varnishes: the simple solution varnishes and the cooked oil varnishes. Lacquers and enamels, varnishlike coatings that are often pigmented, are classified by some as a third category of varnish.

SIMPLE SOLUTION VARNISHES

The solution varnishes are made by dissolving the resin in its appropriate solvent. They are sometimes called "cold cut varnishes" because no heating is involved: if alcohol ("spirits of wine") is used as the solvent, the varnish may be called a "spirit varnish."

Solution varnishes dry by simple evaporation. Theoretically, the dried films are reversible and can be reliquefied by using the original solvent; practically, this is not always the case.

Simple solution varnishes are easily made at home (examples are damar in gum turpentine and shellac in alcohol). The concentration of a natural resin varnish made by solution is called a "cut." The cut is determined by the proportion of the weight of the resin to a gallon volume of the solvent: the phrase "5 pound cut" means that 5 pounds (2.3 kg) of the resin were dissolved in 1 gallon (3.8 l) of the solvent. A 5 pound cut is the usual concentration for simple solution varnishes.

COOKED OIL VARNISHES

Cooked oil varnishes are more complex solutions of resins melted in heated oils, with the addition of driers and thinners. The drying process is also more complex: The solvent evaporates and the oil polymerizes and oxidizes. The dried films are consequently much harder than the solution varnish films, and are not easily reliquefied with the original solvent because of the change in the nature of the oil content.

Controversy over the use of cooked oil varnishes has centered on the fact that they contain heated oils, which apparently have a tendency to darken and embrittle more rapidly than unheated oils. Furthermore, the hard resins used in their manufacture are more variable in quality than the softer resins, and do not easily reliquefy. This would be significant if the cooked oil varnish were to be used as a final coating on a finished work, where its removal would be desirable when the work needs to be cleaned. If the cooked oil varnish is to be incorporated into a painting medium, its potential irreversibility would be an advantage.

The production of cooked oil varnishes is restricted to large-scale manufacturing processes, where the precise mixture of potentially harmful ingredients can be easily monitored. The heating of solvents and oils also presents significant health and safety hazards; cooked oil varnishes should not be homemade. An example of a cooked oil varnish is linseed oil–copal.

LACQUERS AND ENAMELS

These varnishlike coatings are widely used in industry and have found sporadic application in artistic painting.

LACQUERS

Lacquers can be based on nitrocellulose or other cellulose derivatives dissolved in strong solvents such as acetone; they have more recently been based on the vinyls and their derivatives—the acrylics—again using strong, volatile solvents. The rapid drying time of lacquers, particularly when they are sprayed in very thin coats on rigid substrates, makes them useful in high-speed production processes. But unless they are applied under carefully controlled conditions, their usefulness, insofar as durable artistic painting is concerned, is relatively limited. The older nitrocellulose lacquers showed a marked tendency to crack, darken, yellow, and lose adhesion. The newer lacquers must still be applied with a great deal of care, lest they too crack or lose adhesion.

ENAMELS

Enamels are industrially prepared combinations of varnish and oil that are usually pigmented. When they are applied in thin, uniform layers on a rigid support, commercial enamels will perform reasonably well. They are noted for their leveling properties, which produce smooth surfaces with good gloss. However, the requirement that enamels be applied in thin films does not necessarily lend itself to the free-flowing brushstrokes used in some painting styles, and violating this rule about their use can lead to the paint's wrinkling, creeping, or cracking. Commercial manufacturers of enamels frequently change production formulas and pigments, and they sometimes use materials that are not durable.

USES OF VARNISHES

Varnishes are used for different purposes, in combination with other materials, and in different strengths. Here are some uses of a varnish.

FOR PICTURE PROTECTION

A varnish is used as a top coating on a finished painting to give a consistent appearance to the surface and to protect the painting from dirt, dust, and other atmospheric impurities. To function well in this capacity, a varnish chosen for use as picture protection should meet the requirements listed below, which are adapted from an article by Rutherford J. Gettens in the November 1934 issue of the *Journal of Chemical Education,* quoted in *The Artists' Handbook.** Even after more than five decades, these requirements still stand as desirable.

1. A varnish should provide protection from atmospheric impurities. Dust and chemical pollutants, even in air-conditioned environments, can wreak havoc on a painting by discoloring and disfiguring or pitting and physically detriorating the picture surface. A varnish should take the brunt of this damage—its removal during cleaning saves the picture.

2. A varnish should expand and contract in response to atmospheric changes. This is particularly important if the varnish is used on a picture painted on a flexible support. Brittle lacquers do not make good picture varnishes.

3. A varnish should preserve the elasticity of the painting. A brittle varnish can easily transfer its mechanical action to inflexible areas of the painting.

4. The varnish should be transparent and colorless. This almost goes without saying, except that many varnishes have a slight tinge of color. Damar is distinctly yellow—and gets yellower as it ages. Acrylic emulsions marketed as varnishes are translucent when wet, but dry to a state somewhere between transparent and translucent.

5. The varnish film should have the capacity to be applied in a thin layer. A thin coating of varnish will not disturb any textural effects on the surface of the painting; a thick coating is apt to change color more rapidly or present such a reflective surface that the work cannot be easily seen. A thin coating is less likely

---

* From *The Artist's Handbook,* revised edition, by Ralph Mayer. Copyright © 1981 by Bena Mayer, Executrix of the Estate of Ralph Mayer. Reprinted by permission of Viking Penguin, Inc.

to crack as it expands and contracts. Too thin a coating, however, may be too easily removed or may deteriorate too rapidly.

6. A varnish should be reversible. The conservation or restoration of a painting often includes the removal of embedded surface dirt by carefully removing the varnish coating. Many varnishes do not remain soluble in their original solvents, even though they were once thought to, so their removal requires stronger agents which may be dangerous for the paint underneath. Some varnishes grow less soluble by such slow degrees that the fact that they are not entirely reversible is unimportant; if the surface of the varnish is removable, then the purpose may be served. Some conservators insist that a varnish be completely removable.

7. The varnish should not cloud. This defect is also known as "bloom," and results from the penetration of water vapor into the film or condensation of water vapor within the film. The appearance is similar to frosted glass—a whitish or bluish veil seems to grow over the surface of the work. A varnish can bloom because it attracts water vapor: mastic varnish's solvent is alcohol, which is hygroscopic. Bloom can also be the result of faulty application: A cloudy, humid day is not a good day to varnish a painting, because water vapor can be trapped beneath the drying film.

8. A varnish should have the proper degree of gloss. Gloss is an attractive quality, and a hard gloss gives the surface to which dust and dirt will not stick (soft, glossy varnishes are sticky enough to attract dirt). But glossy paintings are hard to see unless they are lighted carefully. Matte surfaces are easier to view, but they have a microscopic texture which allows the deposit of surface durt. Semi-gloss surfaces are a reasonable alternative; waxing a glossy surface is also a good alternative—the wax is matte and is easily removed from the varnish.

No varnish is yet capable of meeting all these requirements, and research into the problem of varnishes continues. Some varieties of acrylic solution varnishes hold promise, although it has been shown recently that some of them also become insoluble on exposure to ultraviolet light by a process called cross-linking. (One methacrylate, Acryloid B-67MT, does not apparently cross-link.) The ketone resin varnishes, derived from cyclohexanone and recently introduced by Winsor & Newton, are a promising alternative—though they eventually become insoluble, they do so more slowly than the acrylics. Damar resin dissolved in gum turpentine, while subject to yellowing and embrittlement with ageing, is still recommended to the artist who wishes to manufacture and use varnish-containing painting mediums, but it is not recommended as a final varnish coating.

The usual concentration for a heavy picture varnish is a 3 pound cut, which can be reduced to a 2 pound cut for a lighter varnish.

AS A RETOUCH VARNISH

A retouch varnish is a simple solution varnish greatly thinned with its solvent and applied in extremely thin films. Its purpose is to retrieve the original color appearance of wet paint on an in-progress oil painting where the paint has dried out or appears to have sunken in. *Sinking-in* is the result of a too-absorbent or unevenly absorbent ground, which starves the paint layer of its binder; sinking-in occurs more often, and is a more serious problem, in oil painting than in any other technique.

The retouch varnish is applied only to those areas of the picture that require it—not as a continuous film over the entire surface of the painting—and makes color-matching of fresh paint to dry paint much easier. Application is by soft brush or by spraying. Spraying may be a health and fire hazard because of the solvent in the retouch.

More than one coat of a retouch varnish may often be necessary to accomplish the wet look but avoid the heavy buildup that could produce a glossy layer. The point is to change the refractive index of the dried paint, not interfere with the structure of the painting.

The usual concentration for a retouch varnish is a 1 pound cut.

AS AN INGREDIENT IN OTHER MIXTURES

Varnish can be used in painting or glazing mediums, emulsion binders, and in some wax vehicles to impart hardness and a degree of gloss to the painted films. When using simple solution varnishes in these mixtures, there is a chance of producing a paint film that is easily redissolved by overpainting, or a whole painting that is subject to embrittlement, or a picture that could be damaged during a cleaning process. Using a cooked oil varnish as an ingredient in a medium may prevent dissolution of the paint layer, but it could also lead to darkening and embrittlement if the hard varnish resin is unreliable. The usual recommendation is to use a solution varnish, but to keep the varnish content of the medium as small as possible. In a 10 parts by volume medium, use no more than 1 part solution varnish. If the medium contains a thinner, do not count the thinner as part of the volume measure; in other words, keep the varnish content of a medium to about 10 percent, excluding the thinner. As parts of emulsion or wax vehicles, the varnish content may be slightly higher.

The usual concentration of the varnish used in a medium or binder is a 5 pound cut.

AS A SIZE

A greatly diluted varnish solution can be used to size an absorbent surface, as noted in Chapter 2. Some resins, such as the acrylics or shellac, can be diluted and used as fixatives for chalk or pastel drawings as well. A pigmented size is called an *imprimatura*.

The usual concentration for a varnish used as a size is a 1 pound cut.

NATURAL RESINS

Natural varnish resins are hard or semi-hard exudations from trees, insect secretions, or fossil deposits formed by decaying vegetation. They are shipped as hard lumps that may vary in color, shape, toughness, solubility, and quality. Few are soluble in water (gum arabic, a water-soluble gum, can be made into a varnish). The names of the resins can be derived from their places of origin or the ports that ship them.

When buying natural resins, look for batches of large, clean pieces. Crushed or powdered resin may mean that the patch has been accidentally adulterated with dirt, twigs, or other debris. The small sacks of dry resin found in art supply stores are usually fairly clean.

DAMAR

Damar resin, also spelled *dammar,* is tapped from the Damar fir tree (Dipterocarpaceae family) found chiefly in Indonesia and Malaya. It appears in stores as clear or slightly yellowish, dusty lumps about 1 to 2 inches (2.5–5 cm) in diameter. Gum turpentine is the solvent of choice for the artist; other solvents either dissolve the resin incompletely or are not safely kept in the average studio.

Making damar varnish is simple. The standard 5 pound cut can be made in gallon lots, but this is usually too large a volume for the small user. Instead, use an equivalent proportion of 10 ounces (280 gm) of damar resin to 1 pint (480 ml) of gum turpentine.

MATERIALS

1. A large, wide-mouthed glass jar with a lid. The jar should be of a size so that the resin will be completely submerged in the gum turpentine.
2. A square of fine-mesh cheesecloth, and some string.
3. 10 ounces (280 gm) damar resin (see Appendix D).
4. 1 pint (480 ml) pure gum spirits of turpentine.

METHOD

1. Wrap the resin in the cheesecloth and tie it into a bag with the string. Leave a length of string by which to hang the bag.
2. Punch a hole in the center of the jar lid.
3. Pour the gum turpentine into the jar.
4. Place the bag of resin in the gum turpentine and thread the string through the hole in the jar lid.
5. Screw the lid on and pull the string to raise the bag. It should hang freely, not touching the sides or bottom of the jar. Tie the string to a pencil or nail to hold the bag in place (Figure 5.1).
6. Allow the resin to dissolve—it will take a day or two. If the bag sticks to the sides of the jar, it may be dislodged by raising and lowering it a few times. Agitation will also hasten the solvent action of the gum turpentine.
7. When all the resin has dissolved, remove the bag and discard it. There will be a fair amount of debris no matter how clean the dry resin appeared. If some of the debris has filtered out of the bag into the varnish, allow the solution to settle for a few days. Then decant it through a cheesecloth filter

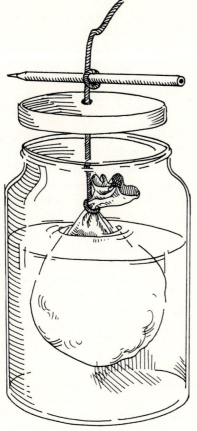

FIGURE 5.1
Making Damar Varnish

into another container. Store the varnish in a warm, dry place in an airtight container.

OBSERVATIONS

1. In all phases of the varnish-making operation, water must be kept from the varnish. Water in the gum turpentine, in the jar used for making the solution, or even water vapor in the atmosphere on very humid days may cause a dried varnish film to bloom.

2. A homemade damar varnish may not be as clear and pale as the kind purchased in stores (at 5 to 10 times the cost of the homemade kind). Natural waxes in the resin can cause the solution to appear cloudy, but when the film dries, the wax will be transparent. Techniques for precipitating or dissolving the wax recommended by some writers usually call for the addition of acetone. Since the undissolved wax is transparent when dried and has little structural effect on the dried film, there seems little point in going to the effort.

3. Damar varnish yellows with age, and its films become brittle. This is caused by exposure to ultraviolet light, present in most lighting systems, and is nearly unavoidable unless you use special filters over lamps used to light the work. Yellowing and embrittlement are also caused by oxidation, which in turn is encouraged by exposure to ultraviolet light. While damar is a reversible varnish, its repeated removal and replacement as to counteract yellowing is a significant problem for conservators charged with the care of a work, since the process can be harmful to the painting.

Raymon H. LaFontaine, in *Studies in Conservation,* 24 (1979), suggests that the addition of an anti-oxidant will slow the yellowing rate of the resin. After study, he concluded that Irganox 565, a product of Ciba-Geigy Canada, Ltd., dissolved into a solution of damar and toluene or xylene (these two solvents are better, in his opinion, than gum turpentine, which may also contribute to the yellowing of damar) will slow the yellowing. Spraying is the recommended application procedure, since the volatile solvents have a high rate of evaporation. The prepared solution reportedly has a shelf life of only a few days.

The use of an anti-oxidant may be the answer for those who wish to continue to use damar varnish, but using toluene or xylene in the home studio is not recommended because both are health and fire hazards; spraying solvent-containing solutions increases the risk. Manufacturers of varnish solutions in this country are studying the possible use of anti-oxidants in their own commercial formulations.

MASTIC

Mastic resin is collected from pistachio trees (*Pistachia lentitiscus*), which grow in the Mediterranean region of southern Europe. The resin comes in the form of small, roundish "tears," or drops, clear when fresh and yellowish if aged (see Appendix D).

Mastic can be dissolved in alcohol or gum turpentine, but not in mineral spirits. It forms an easily manipulated, glossy varnish. But it is known for an inclination to bloom, darken, and yellow with age; it is therefore in less favor than damar. It is easily made in the studio using the same procedures as for damar.

A painting medium popular in the nineteenth century was made by combining a thick solution of mastic varnish with linseed oil that had been cooked with lead white pigment. The mixture, called Meglip, gave a pleasing feel and look to oil paints that were mixed with it, although it eventually caused a great many film defects in the paintings on which it was used. Mastic resin should be used only as a simple solution varnish, not as an addition to painting mediums.

SANDARAC

Sandarac is a hard resin collected from the alerce tree (*Calitris quadrivalis*), found in North Africa. It comes in the form of yellowish tears that are soluble in alcohol and stronger solvents to form a hard, brittle varnish. It was formerly used as a protective coating or ingredient in mediums. Because it is best replaced with damar resin, it is little used today.

COPAL

Copal resins are exuded from living plants and then fossilized. Some are hard, some are soft, and the group as a whole is so large and ill-defined that the label copal can be used only in the most general way. The copals have varying degrees of cold solubility in solvents such as alcohol, but are most familiar to artists as manufactured cooked oil varnishes, mixed with linseed oil and driers.

The varnish films produced by some of the cooked-oil mixtures made with the hard copals are glossy and somewhat brittle, with a reported tendency to darken and crack with age. Furthermore, they are made with a drying oil and so are not reversible in simple solvents. Other forms of copals may not suffer these deficiencies.

The arguments and discussions about copal, which went on for years, may now be moot; copal resins, mined mainly in Africa, are no longer being shipped, and the varnishes and mediums made with them may no longer be produced. But since it is still possible to find examples of "copal painting mediums" in art supply stores, one should consider how they might be used. Copals may be used in small proportions by volume in simple painting mediums. Do not use copals for final varnishes. Products called Kopal painting mediums (note spelling) contain no copal resins.

SHELLAC

Shellac is a secretion from the insect *Laccifer lacca,* scraped from twigs and branches of several species of trees found in India and Indochina. The resin may be reddish-orange in hue, although the color can range from a deeper brown to a milky white; the more refined, the lighter the color.

The solvent for shellac is denatured ethyl alcohol, which gives a cloudy solution. When the solution is allowed to settle and the clear upper portion is decanted, the result may be used in diluted form as a fixative for drawings and pastel paintings, or as a size for absorbent surfaces. It should not be used as a final or retouch varnish coating, nor as an ingredient in mediums, because it rapidly yellows and grows brittle.

The following fixative can be made from shellac purchased in a hardware store, already in solution with alcohol. White shellac resin in powder form can also be used, although it is unlikely that the material will be found easily (try chemical supply houses and expect to pay a high price).

MATERIALS

1. A good grade of bleached white shellac. The usual concentration is a 4 pound cut.
2. Denatured ethyl alcohol. If anhydrous too, so much the better.

3. A glass jar with a plastic-lined cap. Metal caps will react with the shellac, darkening it.

METHOD

1. Dissolve 1 part by volume of the shellac in 5 parts by volume of the alcohol. Place the shellac in the jar first, then add the alcohol.
2. Shake the mixture from time to time, and then let it settle overnight.
3. Decant the clear, very slightly yellow liquid from the settled precipitate. The clear liquid is the stock solution and must be stored in a glass container away from contact with metal. The stock solution will keep about six months before it begins to yellow; make a new stock and discard the yellowed solution. (Do not discard the settled white precipitate; use it to shellac the insides of homemade frames.)

To use the fixative, dilute 1 part of the stock solution with between 5 and 10 parts of denatured alcohol. The concentration will vary with the material being fixed. Try these proportions: powdery charcoal and pastels: 5 to 1 solution to alcohol, or pencil or graphite: 10 to 1 solution to alcohol. Apply the fixative by spraying, but remember that the solvent, alcohol, is a health and fire hazard. (The same precautions hold true for commercial fixatives.) For spraying techniques and equipment, see Chapter 17, pp. 327–331.

SYNTHETIC RESINS

Some of the synthetic resins discussed in Chapter 3 hold the promise of becoming accepted as useful varnishes for paintings. The acrylic solutions, dissolved in such solvents as toluene, xylene, or mineral spirits, have been shown to be clear, durable, and tough. In fact, proprietary spray fixatives have used some of the acrylic resins in solution with toluene and other solvents for years (one well-known brand name is Krylon), and there seems to be wide market acceptance of these products.

ACRYLIC RESINS

The solutions of acrylic resins, available from Rohm and Haas (see Appendix D), can be diluted and used as varnishes. Acryloid B-72 or B-67 are probably the versions used in proprietary spray varnishes because they are soluble in fast-drying toluene; but toluene is a health and fire hazard and normally should not be kept in the studio. Acryloid F-10 and Acryloid B-67MT are soluble in VM&P Naphtha and mineral spirits, respectively, which could make them safer for home use. But it has been reported that they cross-link and become insoluble, thus violating the principle of reversibility, which is a requirement for a picture varnish. Acryloid B-67MT is soluble in mineral spirits and so far does not exhibit a tendency to cross-link quickly. Since it remains reversible, it is probably the best choice for use as a final varnish.

Acryloid B-67MT can be had as a dry resin, a white powdery material, or as a 45 to 50 percent solids solution in mineral spirits. The latter is probably the best form to have it in, since the price difference between the two forms is negligible and the solution is easier to obtain. B-67MT in solution is a viscous, syrupy solution that must be diluted for use: Try a proportion of about 10 parts by volume of mineral spirits to 1 part by volume of the resin solution, adding the mineral spirits to the solution in small amounts while stirring. Do not stir too vigorously, or bubbles will form, and the bubbles will take a long time to rise out of a thick solution. The solution can be brushed on paintings as a final coating, or sprayed on paintings or dusty drawings as a fixative. Again, the health and fire hazard precaution applies when spraying.

None of the acrylic resins should be presumed to be miscible with linseed or other natural oils and resins. Therefore, do not use them as ingredients in oil or other natural binder painting techniques; damar resin is still the best for that. The acrylic solution varnishes can be used with the acrylic solution paints and with alkyd paints.

Various acrylic emulsion varnishes are also on the market, and the Rhoplex variations may be available from Rohm and Haas (see Appendix D).* The proprietary versions come in gloss and matte finishes; they make excellent ingredients to mix with the acrylic polymer emulsion paints, to use as sizes when greatly thinned with water, and to use as collage adhesives. They should not be used as final varnishes on acrylic emulsion paintings: They are porous and admit atmospheric moisture, dust, and smoke; they are not soluble in mild solvents; and they are translucent, not transparent. Instead, use an acrylic solution varnish for a protective coating on acrylic emulsion paintings.

VINYL RESINS

The vinyl resins are soluble only in solvents too hazardous to be used by the average artist. The polyvinyl acetate emulsions, dispersed in water, have the same drawbacks as the acrylic emulsions.

KETONE RESINS

Winsor & Newton has marketed a ketone resin varnish under the name Winton Picture Varnish. There is a gloss version and a matte version, which contains a wax additive to reduce gloss. The ketone resin varnishes are for use only as final protective coatings, not as painting mediums. Winsor & Newton's other versions

---

* Because of questions of liability or misuse, such products may be available only to industrial users and manufacturers.

of the ketone resin varnishes are called Artists' Picture Varnish, Barbola Varnish, Griffin Picture Varnish, Winton Matt Varnish, and Winton Retouching Varnish. All contain the ketone resin, white spirit (mineral spirits), and in the matte version, wax.

ALKYD RESINS

The alkyd resins are used only in painting and glazing mediums, not in final varnish coatings. Prepared alkyd painting and glaze mediums are available from PDQ and Winsor & Newton (see Appendix D).

Table 5.1, which follows, provides a quick reference to varnishes.

TABLE 5.1
VARNISHES

COMMON NAME	Damar (dammar, damer)	Mastic	Sandarac
SYNONYM OR OTHER NAME	Gum Damar	Gum Mastic	
SOURCE	*Dipterocarpaceae,* Damar fir tree	*Pistachia lentitiscus,* Pistachio tree	*Caltris quadrivalis,* alerce tree
TYPE	Natural solution	Natural solution	Natural solution
COLOR/APPEARANCE	Yellowish lumps; Y solution	Small W tears; pale Y solution	Y tears; pale Y solution
REFRACTIVE INDEX	Low–medium	Low–medium	Low–medium
USES			
Ingredient	×	×, but NR	×, but NR
Picture	×, but NR	×	
Retouch	×		×, but NR
Size	×		
REVERSIBILITY SOLVENT	Fair–good (solvent) gum turpentine and higher aromatics; damar cross-links	Fair–good (solvent) alcohol and aromatics	Fair–good (solvent) alcohol and aromatics
DURABILITY			
Interior	Good	Fair–good	Fair–good
Exterior	Poor	Poor	Poor
Rigid support	Good	Good	Good
Flexible support	Fair	Fair–good	Fair–good
RESISTANCE TO			
Water	Fair–good	Poor–fair	Poor–fair
Acid	Poor	Poor	Poor
Alkali	Poor	Poor	Poor
Pollutants	Good	Fair	Fair
Ultraviolet light	Fair	Poor–fair	Poor–fair
Decay	Good	Good	Good
HAZARDS			
Fire (flash point)	Resin not flammable	Resin not flammable	Resin not flammable
Health	Harmful when sprayed	Harmful when sprayed	Harmful when sprayed
OTHER COMMENTS	Good in ingredient mixtures; no longer thought to be good as final varnish	Should not be used—blooms; newer synthetics far better	Not recommended as an art material

Note: NR = not recommended.

TABLE 5.1 *(continued)*
VARNISHES

COMMON NAME	Copal	Shellac	Acrylic solution
SYNONYM OR OTHER NAME			Synvar (Weber); Soluvar (Liquitex); Acryloid B-67MT, etc.
SOURCE	Fossil resin; various sources	*Laccifer lacca,* insect secretion	Esters of acrylic acid, methacrylic acid, or acrylonitrile
TYPE	Natural cooked oil, w/solvents, driers	Natural solution	Synthetic acrylic
COLOR/APPEARANCE	Pale Y to dark RY; clear lumps	Dark R flakes or powder; bleached, Y, W solution	W powder; clear syrup solution
REFRACTIVE INDEX	Low–medium	Low–medium	Low
USES			
Ingredient	×, but NR		×
Picture	×, but NR		×
Retouch	×, but NR		×
Size		×, or fixative	×
REVERSIBILITY SOLVENT	Fair (solvent) alcohol and aromatics	Fair–good alcohol	Good–excellent (solvent) mineral spirits; alcohol; aromatics
DURABILITY			
Interior	Good–excellent	Fair	Excellent
Exterior	Poor	Poor	Good
Rigid support	Good	Good	Excellent
Flexible support	Fair–good	Poor	Excellent
RESISTANCE TO			
Water	Good	Fair	Good
Acid	Poor	Poor	Good
Alkali	Poor	Poor	Good
Pollutants	Fair	Poor–fair	Very good
Ultraviolet light	Poor–fair	Poor	Very good
Decay	Good	Fair	Excellent
HAZARDS			
Fire (flash point)	Resin not flammable	Resin not flammable	Very high
Health	Harmful when sprayed	Harmful when sprayed	Free monomers may be released from drying film
OTHER COMMENTS	Original not easily available; beware alternate spellings ("Kopal" is not copal); replaced by new synthetics	Cheap alternative as a fixative; questionable durability; not recommended	Usual commercial product complex combination of methyl methacrylate, iso- or butyl-methacylate and "other ingredients" (50%, 40%, and 10% by weight); many varieties; *do not confuse with acrylic emulsion*

TABLE 5.1 *(continued)*
VARNISHES

COMMON NAME	Vinyl solution	Ketone resin	Silicone
SYNONYM OR OTHER NAME	Many proprietary names	Winsor & Newton trade names: Winton®, etc.	Varni-Sil (Conserv-Art)
SOURCE	Ethylene; petroleum	Cyclohexanone derivative	Methylphenyl polysiloxane (polysiloxane)
TYPE	Vinyl resin	Ketone resin	Silicone
COLOR/APPEARANCE	Clear W or Y lumps W powder; clear solution	Pale W or milky solution	Colorless solution "nonglare gloss" finish
REFRACTIVE INDEX	Low	Low–medium	Low
USES			
Ingredient		×, perhaps	
Picture		×	×
Retouch	×	×	×
Size	×		
REVERSIBILITY	Good	Good	Good
SOLVENT	Aromatics	Mineral spirits and aromatics	VRS-1: trichlorotrifluoroethane, halogenated hydrocarbon
DURABILITY			
Interior	Good	Excellent	Good
Exterior	Fair	Not tested	Fair–good
Rigid support	Excellent	Excellent	Excellent
Flexible support	Fair	Good–excellent	Excellent
RESISTANCE TO			
Water	Good	Good	Excellent
Acid	Fair	Good	Fair
Alkali	Fair	Good	Fair
Pollutants	Good	Good	Good
Ultraviolet light	Fair	Good	Excellent
Decay	Excellent	Good	Excellent
HAZARDS			
Fire (flash point)	Solvent hazard	High; solvent hazard	41° F (8° C) extremely flammable
Health	Major health hazards with solvents	Spray mist may be toxic; skin irritant	Hazardous material, as defined by FHSA
OTHER COMMENTS	Not recommended because of solvent hazard; *do not confuse with the less-hazardous vinyl emulsions*	Relatively new— manufacturer-tested only; promising new material	New product, developed by General Electric (silicone) and Du Pont (solvent), adapted by Conserv-Art; *silicone and solvent are HAZARDOUS and should not be used without correct laboratory procedure;* consult MSDSs

CHAPTER 6

BALSAMS, DRIERS, RETARDERS, PRESERVATIVES

BALSAMS

Balsams are the thick, viscous, saplike exudations from plants also known as oleoresins. They do not form hard lumps like the varnish resins, but have a soft, sometimes semi-liquid consistency. Like the varnishes, they can be mixed with the oils and solvents used in oil painting. They do not mix with water.

When balsams dry by evaporation, they remain relatively reversible. They are usually used as additives to painting mediums in oil and encaustic techniques, and can be used as the oily ingredient in egg tempera emulsions. There are a few varieties to consider but only one, Venice turpentine, is widely used today.

Gum Thus Gum thus is the oleoresin from one of the American long-leaf yellow pines from which gum turpentine is distilled. It has been used as a plasticizer in commercial varnishes, but should not be used in artistic painting. The rosin content causes darkening.

Strasbourg Turpentine Strasbourg Turpentine is tapped from the silver fir (*Abies pectinata*) or white fir tree and is the European equivalent of Venice turpentine.

Burgundy and Jura Turpentines Both varieties are European, and are not usually found in this country.

Venice Turpentine Venice turpentine is tapped from the European larch tree (*Larix europea* or *Larix decidua*), and is sometimes called Larch turpentine. Supplies of Venice turpentine are readily found in America. Venice turpentine is a good additive for oil painting mixtures because it contributes to the stability of the films: it is relatively nonyellowing and, because of its slight rosin content, more flexible than many resins. It is an excellent addition to egg tempera emulsions and encaustic mediums in place of the usual varnish resins.

Copaiba Balsam Copaiba balsam comes from several types of South American trees of the genus *Copaifera.* It is a slow-drying oleoresin—a poor additive for oil painting mediums, which dry slowly enough. Proprietary oil painting restorers often contain copaiba balsam, whose application to an old, dried-out looking oil paint film increases the refractive index and so improves the appearance of the paint. Eventually the balsam dries out and the process must be repeated; meanwhile, as the sticky balsam dries, it collects airborne dust.

DRIERS

Driers—also called siccatives—are added to oil paints to make them dry faster. They are composed of metallic salts, dissolved in a solvent, which promote oxidation by forcing, accelerating, or starting the absorption of oxygen.

Most writers agree that driers are harmful to oil paint films (especially when used to excess by an individual artist), since they can darken or weaken the dried paint. But then they go on to recommend ways they can be used safely. The slow drying of oil paint is one of its natural attributes—one many artists find desirable. Since there are now other paints that can come close to the optical effects of oil paints but dry faster (the alkyds and the acrylic solution paints), it seems foolhardy to risk the early deterioration of an oil paint by using driers.

Of the driers available, Manganese Linoleate is the one characterized as "least harmful." Driers are used in the commercial production of some oil paints, where they are necessary to produce a full line of colors which will dry at about the same rate, and where the careful addition of small amounts can be monitored accurately.

RETARDERS

Retarders are liquids that slow the drying of oil paint so that wet-into-wet painting effects can be accomplished over a longer period of time. Plant oils, sweet-smelling liquids which are actually like very slow-drying thinners, have been used as retarders. The most commonly mentioned is oil of cloves. If an artist wishes to retard the drying of an oil paint, it is probably better to add a slower drying oil to the painting medium: poppyseed oil can work. Keep the proportion of slow-drying oil to the rest of the painting medium low—around 10 percent.

Retarding the drying of other paints is sometimes desirable. Both types of acrylics and the alkyds are occasionally found to dry too rapidly for certain techniques. In this case, use one of the proprietary additives made by the company that manufactures the paints. In the acrylic emulsion paints, most retarders contain proportions of jelled glycols; retarders for the acrylic solution and alkyd paints may have beeswax added. In all cases, avoid the addition of too much of the retarder, lest the resulting paint films become too soft.

Any discussion of balsams, driers, and retarders may have become academic. There are now a number of products made for the alkyd paints which can be mixed with oils to provide the same results as the natural additives. If not over-used, these products may be superior—more durable and reliable.

PRESERVATIVES

Materials that prevent or inhibit the growth of microorganisms in water-containing products are called *preservatives*. Preservatives are used in many packaged food products, and in some manufactured paints. They are also recommended additions to some homemade paints.

The preservatives used in manufactured paints are necessary in order to ensure a reasonable shelf life. Artists who make their own paints do not necessarily need to add preservatives unless they are making a considerable volume of the paint; preservatives must be used in such small percentages that controlling their addition to a pint (0.47 l) of binder requires precise measuring tools not often found in the studio.

Preservatives themselves no longer have a very good reputation. Some, like formaldehyde, mercury, and the phenols, are suspected of being health hazards and should be avoided. A few have been approved for use in food products by the Food and Drug Administration of the U.S. Government; they can be used if absolutely necessary. Small amounts of the following FDA-approved preservatives can be had through Conservation Materials Ltd. (see Appendix D): Cuniphen 2778-I and Cunilate 2174-NO. These preservatives are used in a concentration of about 0.50 percent or less, based on the weight of the binder or adhesive. Cuniphen does contain a phenol, so it should be used with caution despite the FDA approval.

Using preservatives is a questionable practice except on an industrial scale. It is better to avoid the problem by making small volumes of the mixtures that might require them, and then storing them properly and using them without delay.

For quick reference to technical aspects of varnishes, see Table 6.1, which follows.

TABLE 6.1
BALSAMS, DRIERS, RETARDERS, PRESERVATIVES*

COMMON NAME	Gum Thus	Strasbourg Turpentine	Venice Turpentine	Copaiba Balsam
SYNONYM OR OTHER NAME				
TYPE	Balsam	Balsam	Balsam	Balsam
SOURCE	Sap of American long-leaf yellow pine	*Abies pectinata,* silver fir	*Larix europea,* or *larix decidua,* the European larch	*Copaifera*
USE	Commercial plasticizer for varnish	Plasticizer for oils, egg temperas, encaustics	Same as Strasbourg turpentine	Oil paint film "rejuvenator"
COLOR/APPEARANCE	Y syrup	Pale to deep Y syrup	Pale to deep Y syrup	Dark Y
REFRACTIVE INDEX, IF APPLICABLE	Low–medium	Low–medium	Low–medium	Low–medium
EFFECTS	Darkens paint	Increases film resolubility; can cause yellowing	Same as Strasbourg turpentine	Very slow drier; increases refractive index of oil
DURABILITY				NR
Interior	Good	Good	Good	
Exterior	Fair	Poor	Poor	
Rigid support	Excellent	Excellent	Excellent	
Flexible support	Fair	Fair–good	Fair–good	
RESISTANCE TO				NR
Water	Good	Good	Good	
Acid	Fair	Fair	Fair	
Alkali	Fair	Fair	Fair	
Pollutants	Fair	Fair	Good	
Ultraviolet light	Poor	Fair–good	Fair–good	
Decay	Good	Good	Good	
HAZARDS				
Fire (flash point)	Very high	Very high	Very high	Very high
Health	Varieties from certain pines can be allergenic	Varieties from certain pines can be allergenic	Varieties from certain pines can be allergenic	Varieties from certain pines can be allergenic
OTHER COMMENTS	Not an art material; raw gum source of gum turpentine; rosin content causes darkening	Use with caution; overuse can contribute to later technical problems	Use with caution; overuse can contribute to later technical problems	Not recommended as an art material

Note: NR = not recommended; n/a = not applicable.
* Preservatives are generally not necessary in small-scale studio operations. It is far better to make and use fresh materials.

TABLE 6.1   *(continued)*
BALSAMS, DRIERS, RETARDERS, PRESERVATIVES

COMMON NAME	Manganese linoleate	Essential plant oils: oil of cloves, oil of lavender, etc.	Various proprietary names
SYNONYM OR OTHER NAME			
TYPE	Drier	Retarder	Retarder
SOURCE	Metallic salt of manganese in solution with solvents	Oils expressed (pressed) from plants	Mixtures of gelled propylene or ethylene glycol; beeswax may be added
USE	Drier for oil paint and linseed oil mediums	Retards drying of oil paints	Retard drying of alkyds or acrylic emulsions
COLOR/APPEARANCE	Thin dark V or P liquid	Varies from pale Y to RY	Pale W, translucent gel or liquid
REFRACTIVE INDEX, IF APPLICABLE	Low in thin films or weak concentrations	Low	Low–medium, depending on concentration
EFFECTS	If used to excess darkens, embrittles, weakens oil film	If used to excess softens oil films	Soft films if used to excess; paint that never dries

DURABILITY
  Interior
  Exterior
  Rigid support
  Flexible support
	Not tested	NR	Inert

RESISTANCE TO
  Water
  Acid
  Alkali
  Pollutants
  Ultraviolet light
  Decay
	Not tested	NR	Inert

HAZARDS
  Fire (flash point)
  Health
	Solvent flammable
	Metallic salts can be allergenic; nausea from ingestion
		n/a unless in solvent
		n/a unless in solvent
			n/a
			Do not ingest; protection needed for spraying

OTHER COMMENTS	Not recommended for use with oil paints—use a faster drying paint, or drier-type pigments with oil: see Table 7.1	Not recommended because of unreliable properties; use a slower drying oil instead	Use with caution; basically unnecessary

TABLE 6.1 *(continued)*
BALSAMS, DRIERS, RETARDERS, PRESERVATIVES

COMMON NAME	Vinegar	Formaldehyde	Mercuric chloride
SYNONYM OR OTHER NAME			
TYPE	Preservative	Preservative	Preservative
SOURCE	Impure, dilute acetic acid (5%)	Formalin: 40% formaldehyde, 55% water, 5% methanol	Mercuric chloride
USE	Preservative for homemade vehicles	Preservative	Preservative
COLOR/APPEARANCE	Clear liquid	Clear liquid strong odor	n/a
REFRACTIVE INDEX, IF APPLICABLE	Low	Low	n/a
EFFECTS	Soft films if used to excess	Weak films if overused	n/a

DURABILITY
  Interior
  Exterior
  Rigid support
  Flexible support
	NR	NR	NR

RESISTANCE TO
  Water
  Acid
  Alkali
  Pollutants
  Ultraviolet light
  Decay
	NR	NR	NR

HAZARDS
  Fire (flash point)
  Health
	
	n/a
	n/a at 5%
		
		n/a
		May be carcinogenic; do not use
			
			n/a
			Highly toxic; do not use

OTHER COMMENTS	Not an art material; make fresh materials and do not use preservatives	*Do not use this material*	*Do not use this material*

TABLE 6.1   (*continued*)
BALSAMS, DRIERS, RETARDERS, PRESERVATIVES

COMMON NAME	2,2′ methylene bis (4-chlorophenol)	Copper 8-quinolin-oleate	Sodium benzoate
SYNONYM OR OTHER NAME	Cuniphen 2778-I (trade name)	Cunilate 2174-NO (trade name)	
TYPE	Preservative	Preservative	Preservative
SOURCE	Same as common name	Same as common name	Same as common name
USE	Preservative	Preservative	Preservative
COLOR/APPEARANCE	Dark YR liquid	Pale G	W powder
REFRACTIVE INDEX, IF APPLICABLE	Low	Low	n/a
EFFECTS			n/a
DURABILITY	n/a	n/a	n/a
Interior			
Exterior			
Rigid support			
Flexible support			
RESISTANCE TO	n/a	n/a	n/a
Water			
Acid			
Alkali			
Pollutants			
Ultraviolet light			
Decay			
HAZARDS			
Fire (flash point)	n/a	n/a	n/a
Health	Low degree of human toxicity; FDA-approved	FDA-accepted for food use	FDA-approved for food use; overdose may cause nausea
OTHER COMMENTS	Use at less than 0.50% concentration by weight of the solution; make fresh materials	Use at less than 0.15% concentration by weight of solution; make fresh materials	Use at less than 5% concentration by weight of solution

CHAPTER 7

PIGMENTS

Pigments are small particles of colored material that are insoluble in water, oils, and resins. When suspended in liquid binders or vehicles, they form paint. With a few exceptions, the same pigments are used in all paints; it is the binder or total vehicle that accounts for the differing kinds of paint.

HISTORY

In prehistoric times, early humans found many colorants in the minerals occurring in soils and clays. Cave paintings using red and yellow colored clays, black from charred wood or bones, and white from chalk deposits, date from at least 15,000 B.C.

As long ago as 8000 B.C., artists in Egypt had discovered how to process natural minerals, animal products, and vegetable matter into useful and fairly stable colorants for paints. Examples of the early Egyptian color range include reds from iron and cinnabar (a mercury ore), yellows from iron and arsenic ores, greens and blues from copper ores, purples and red purples from *Rubia tinctorum* (the madder plant), black from charcoal and burned animal fats, and white from chalk.

The 1500 years after the birth of Christ saw the development of more sophisticated means for processing raw materials into pigments or pigmentlike colorants. White lead, a precipitated lead carbonate, is probably the most well known early artificial pigment that is still in demand and in wide use today. Iron oxides were mined extensively in Italy and processed by heating, *levigating* (water washing), and other mechanical means into a range of red, yellow, green, and red-purple hues which are still some of the most useful colorants artists have. A green copper carbonate produced verdigris; resinous materials made reddish dyes (Dragon's blood); vegetable and animal materials made ever more interesting reds, yellows, blues, and greens (sepia, bistre, cochineal, tumeric, saffron, sap green, Indian yellow, quercitron, indigo); more involved mineral processing produced smalt (potassium glass and cobalt oxide), King's yellow (arsenic sulfide), and the well-known ultramarine blue (*lapis lazuli*).

In 1704 the first modern pigment, Prussian blue, was discovered. In rapid succession over the next 150 years, there appeared dozens of colors that replaced the less stable, more costly or rare, and more dangerous of the earlier pigments. These are now almost indispensable to the modern artist. They include cobalt blue (1802), synthetic ultramarine blue (accidentally discovered in 1828), viridian green (1838), cadmium yellow (1846), and zinc white (first produced in 1751 but not commercially available until about 1850).

The modern era may have started with the development of the synthetic organic "coal-tar" dyes by William Perkins in 1856, although these colors, due to their fugitive nature, quickly got a bad reputation. In 1868 the first synthetic duplication of a natural organic colorant, alizarin crimson, was marketed and accepted by artists; it replaced the reputedly less stable rose madder (also called madder lake) and greatly improved the violet side of the artist's palette.

The last quarter of the nineteenth century, and the first 25 years of this century, saw tremendous improvement in the color range and durability of processed mineral and synthesized organic pigments. The production of the phthalocyanine colors (blue and green, in 1928 and 1935, respectively), very stable and powerful colorants, more or less led to a renewed interest in synthetic organic pigments. Today, the synthesized organics make up the largest share of colorants used in industry and are extensively tested for use in artists' paint lines. Some of the new organics are excellent and valuable additions to the artist's list of choices.

STANDARDS FOR ARTISTS' PIGMENTS

The pigments and dyes used by industry are not expected to last forever—or even as long as ten years in some applications. These colorants need not be durable in light to any great extent, and they may not be required to stand up to other kinds of exposure. But the pigments used in artists' paints must have special qualities that guarantee durability over long periods of time. The word *permanent* is often used to describe one of the requirements of an artists' paint. *Permanent* means "continuing or enduring without fundamental or marked change"—an apt description of what one usually expects of a painting. But unless the conditions of exposure and use of the paint, or painting, are given and understood, the term has little meaning.

For a pigment to be suitable for use in an artists' paint, it must meet these requirements, adapted from *The Painter's Guide to Studio Methods and Materials**
and *The Artist's Handbook:*†

1. A pigment must be a fine, smooth powder. Many older pigments, such as smalt, were rather rough, granulated materials. Smalt ground too fine is colorless; in order to retain its hue and other color characteristics, it had to be kept in a relatively crude state.

2. A pigment should not alter in hue (color), chroma (intensity of the color), or value (the lightness or darkness of the color) when exposed to normal conditions of light over a long period of time. "Normal" conditions are not easy to define; we think of museum conditions as being the standard—dim natural north daylight or low-power incandescent light. Pigments should be able to withstand continuous exposure to controlled low-level light for at least a century without showing a visually detectible change. If a pigment does not alter after test exposures equivalent to the 100-year real-time exposure, it can be considered *lightfast.* Some of the changes in a pigment are not detectible unless the colorant is measured instrumentally.

3. A pigment should not react chemically with the other paints or supplementary materials to which it is exposed. These materials include the binder, varnishes, thinners or solvents, glaze or painting mediums, grounds, and other pigments. When viridian green is used in acrylic emulsion vehicles, for example, it can "break" the emulsion—cause it to separate. Lead white and zinc oxide are also unstable in the acrylic emulsion vehicles; only titanium white is used.

4. A pigment should not react to the changes in normal atmospheric conditions. Lead white has a tendency to turn brown or darken to a gray when exposed to hydrogen sulfide (a component of polluted air found in some modern cities): it is only used in oily or resinous binders that encase it thoroughly in a waterproof vehicle to prevent its exposure to moisture and pollutants.

5. A pigment should form a tough, stable film with the binder. No pigment is perfect in all binders. Pigments that do not meet this requirement in one binder sometimes meet it in another; pigments that cannot meet this requirement at all usually reveal their defects shortly after the paint is manufactured. Some pigments *flocculate:* They rise to and project above the surface of a dried paint film, and powder off. Others *agglomerate:* They coagulate into lumps and resist dispersion in the binder. These defects can be the result of faulty manufacturing processes, occurring most often with the complex acrylic emulsion binders, but can also be controlled through careful monitoring.

---

* Reed Kay, *The Painter's Guide to Studio Methods and Materials,* © 1983. Paraphrased by permission of Prentice-Hall, Inc., Englewood Cliffs, New Jersey.

† From *The Artist's Handbook,* revised edition, by Ralph Mayer. Copyright © 1981 by Bena Mayer, Executrix of the Estate of Ralph Mayer. Reprinted by permission of Viking Penguin, Inc.

6. A pigment should not migrate or bleed through dried paint layers. *Migration* is the action of a pigment or dye moving through a dried paint film and thereby discoloring it. *Bleeding* is the result of the action of the binder, vehicle, or solvent used in the vehicle leading to the diffusion of a colorant. Neither trait is desirable. Some dye-based organic colorants easily bleed or migrate—those used in artists' paints should not.

7. A pigment should be "full strength," without added inert ingredients that adversely affect its color or handling. Many pigments, especially the synthetic organics, must be reduced: They are such powerful colorants that they can easily overwhelm the other hues in the palette. The phthalocyanines, for example, are such strong tinters that they can be reduced by 60 to 75 percent without harming their color properties. (This kind of extension should not be considered an adulteration of the colorant.)

8. A pigment should be nontoxic when properly handled. Pigments are dusty powders that can hang in the air and be inhaled if mishandled. Always avoid inhaling the pigment dust, even if the pigment itself is not harmful; wear a dust mask. Check Tables 7.1, 7.2, and 7.3 for the potential hazards of particular pigments, and note that for every pigment there is the instruction to avoid dust.

9. A pigment should be supplied by a reliable manufacturer that is willing to provide information about the colorant's origins, quality, test results, and other characteristics. The manufacturer of the raw pigment is usually willing to supply this information (see Appendix D). Retailers or repackagers are less often capable of providing the information, merely because they know only what they are told by their suppliers. The artists' paint manufacturers are in a similar situation, although they make a genuine effort to provide as much information as possible.

A nonpartisan reference to pigments such as *The Pigment Handbook* or the *Colour Index* can provide a great deal of useful information about colorants. But no reference source is complete, especially regarding the newer pigments, because the field is subject to research and rapid development.

COLOR

The most obvious attribute of pigments is their color. A pigment's color will determine its use in a particular painting, while its physical attributes determine its suitability for a particular kind of painting.

Color theory is not a simple subject, despite myriad attempts on the part of artists and writers to make it so; a complete discussion of it would require another book. There are some good elementary texts on the subject of color theory—see the list in the Bibliography. But it is necessary to delve into color theory a little to understand the importance of pigment choice.

Color is technically divisible into three parts: hue, value, and chroma. *Hue* is the name by which we distinguish one color from another: red, yellow, green, blue, purple, black, white, and the intermediate mixtures of those hues. *Value,* also called lightness, refers to the apparent lightness or darkness of one color in relation to another—that is, black is darker than white and so is regarded as having a lower value. *Chroma* is the apparent intensity (saturation) of a color in relation to another color of the same value. A red of the same lightness as a yellow may be less intense (lower in chroma, or grayer) than the yellow, since it must have more white added to it to make it the same value as the yellow. Adding white does not always lower chroma, however; adding a little white to a full-strength dioxazine purple will raise the chroma. Chroma is often the most difficult attribute of color to understand—but practice applying the theory, using actual visual examples, can easily clear up misunderstandings.

The existence of light makes it possible to perceive color. Light is a form of electromagnetic energy, energy in wave form, and is the only part of the electromagnetic spectrum visible to the naked eye. Other types of electromagnetic energy include ultraviolet light, radio waves, infrared light, and microwaves (see Figure 7.1, the spectrum). Visible light is a tiny part of the spectrum, about 300 nanometers in length (a *nanometer* is a unit of length equivalent to 10^{-9} meters used to measure a wavelength of light—a radio wave may be measured in meters, a substantially larger unit). Each hue has a separate narrow band of wavelengths within the spectrum. A modern measuring device such as a spectrophotometer, which can separate the wavelengths in the visible spectrum, can be used to measure the light precisely and determine a hue accurately.

Light and the hues within it are not visible until the light strikes a surface. If all the light is absorbed into the surface, as it might be if it struck a piece of black velvet, our perception is of black. But practically speaking, there is always some reflectance, however little. If all the light is reflected from the surface, say from a

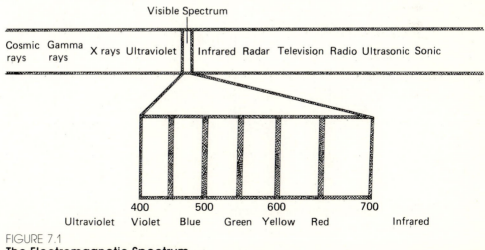

FIGURE 7.1
The Electromagnetic Spectrum

The visible portion of the spectrum is between about 400 nanometers and about 700 nanometers.

pressed cake of dry magnesium oxide pigment, the perception is of white. Again, in fact, there is always some absorption, so that it is hard to get a 100 percent pure white. Under certain specified light conditions, smoked magnesium oxide (sometimes pressed dry barium sulfate) is the closest practical thing to "pure" white. If equal parts of each wavelength are absorbed by the object, the perception is of a neutral (hue-less) gray. If most of the light rays pass through the object, the perception is that the object is transparent or translucent (partly transparent); this particular attribute is related to the refractive index of a material and is quite variable. If there was really total transparency, we would not perceive the object at all. Finally, if only some of the wavelengths are reflected and most are absorbed, we perceive a particular hue; the blue wall absorbs all of the other wavelengths and reflects only blue (Figure 7.2).

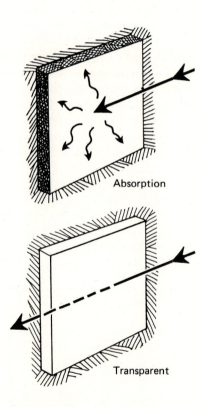

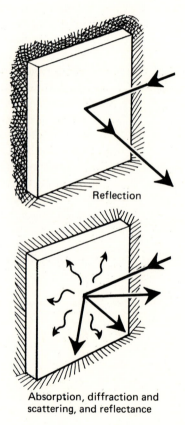

FIGURE 7.2
Different Actions of Light

Top left: "Pure" black; complete absorption of light.
Top right: "Pure" white; complete reflection of light.
Bottom left: "Pure" transparency; light passes completely through (object not visible).
Bottom right: Most common—light absorbed, diffracted and scattered, and reflected.

Reflected light is therefore how we see. When we look at a painting, we can see how very complex reflection can become (Figure 7.3): there is not only reflection, but also refraction, diffraction or scattering (two very similar light actions), some *transmittance* (light reflecting off lower layers of the painting, through glazed layers), and *specular reflection* (mirrorlike reflections that can interfere with perception of a hue—whitish reflections from the surface of a curved glass bottle are specular reflections). A slide of the same painting will always look somehow "purer" than the actual work—assuming it's a good slide—because it is missing the interference specular reflection can cause.

Color mixture systems differ according to their application. In lighting for the theater, one deals with transmitted colored lights reflecting from colored surfaces (the costumes, the scenery). Different colored lights in a theater seem to project a single colored light onto the stage: This system whereby, say, two colored lights mix to produce a third color is called *additive color.* Additive color happens in nature as well. Up close, the leaves on a tree will be seen to have a rather large variation in hues, but from a distance the hues blend into one generalized green. In color television projection systems, tiny dots of colored light blend into various hues. And in Seurat's painting, tiny dots of pure colorants seem to mix and blend into different hues when seen from the proper distance. Actually, though, this is not purely additive color, since energy has not been added, as in color television. Seurat's paintings used what is now recognized as a *partitive* color system; a yellow dot next to a blue dot in this system will yield a gray with a greenish cast when viewed from a distance, not as pure a green as one might expect.

Additive mixtures, when they are from transmitted light, are always brighter than the separate hues used to make the mixtures. In the example of Seurat's work, in which the mixture is partly additive and from reflected instead of transmitted light, the mixtures appear duller. The additive primary colors, taken from the spectrum of visible light, are red, green, and blue. Magenta is red plus blue, cyan is blue plus green, and yellow is red plus green. This last mixture is difficult to comprehend unless one sees it. Set up three slide projectors side by side and use colored theatrical gels as color filters over the projector lenses. If the colored gels are of the correct spectral wavelengths, you can easily demonstrate how this

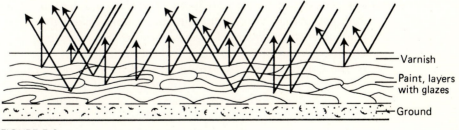

FIGURE 7.3
Action of Light on the Surface of a Painting
Refraction, diffraction (and scattering), reflectance.

works (gels of nearly the correct wavelengths are available from Edmund Scientific—see Appendix D). It is essential to understand additive color if you wish to understand fully how painters can use color.

Subtractive color is the kind of color most people are familiar with: Red plus blue gives purple, blue plus yellow gives green, yellow plus red gives orange, and so on. This is because the color of most things is determined by what light is absorbed into the object's surface and what is reflected. Since some of the light rays are absorbed, they can be considered to be *subtracted* from white light—hence the term subtractive color. A mixture of artists' paints is a subtractive mixture. If the paints are mixed into thick, opaque films, the mixture is called *complex* subtractive color, due to the complexity of light's actions on the paint, as seen in Figure 7.3. These mixtures will always be darker and duller (lower in value and chroma) than the pure hues used to make the mixture. If the color mixtures are made with thin, transparent glazes, as in the paintings of Maxfield Parrish and many of the Pre-Raphaelite painters, the mixture is called *simple* subtractive color. Simple subtractive color mixtures are used in modern four-color printing processes (using cyan, magenta, yellow, and black inks of varying degrees of transparency plus the white of the paper). Subtle, simple, and "beautiful" color harmonies are quite possible from this limited range of hues.

In fact, the subtractive primary colors are magenta, cyan, and yellow: *red* is magenta plus yellow, *green* is yellow plus cyan, and *blue* is cyan plus magenta. Using the three-projector demonstration in proving the issue of additive color will reveal that these mixtures work. However, beginners are less apt to use the simplest mixtures possible—and, of course, will not be familiar with which pigments are opaque or transparent, nor with which pigments are appropriate for mixing which hues. The result is most often complex subtractive mixtures involving reflectance, refraction, and scattering. These complications, as described above, lead to the loss of chroma (duller mixtures) and the loss of value (darker mixtures). Overly complicated color mixtures, where many different colors are mushed together in a desperate attempt to match the hue of the thing observed, may give rise to what painting teachers call "muddy color."

The additive and subtractive primary colors explained above are quite interrelated; in fact, they are complementary. The complement of red is cyan, the complement of green is magenta, and the complement of blue is yellow. In the additive system, two complementary colors mixed together will yield white. In the subtractive system, however, where the complement of red is green, the complement of blue is orange, and the complement of yellow is purple, mixtures of the complements give subtle grays which are sometimes neutral in hue and sometimes tinged with one or the other of the parent hues.

This explanation can easily lead to an understanding of why artists have always used the simpler red, yellow, and blue color mixing system. Most artists don't know why they use the simpler system except that it works. The fact that it can produce all of the intermediate hues—orange, green, and purple—and that the complementary and tertiary mixtures give the desirable and necessary neutral hues is a good enough reason to use the system.

When pigments are mixed into binders of various refractive indices, various color effects are seen. If the binder is yellowish, as linseed oil is, the result of adding a very light blue or white pigment is not necessarily desirable. That, of course, is why some manufactuers disperse their white and light colors in safflower or poppyseed oil, both of which are less yellow than linseed oil. And that is one of the reasons why the alkyd, acrylic solution, and acrylic emulsion paints were developed.

The differences between the same pigment in different binders is apparent when we compare a blue in oil paint with the same blue in pastel—the pastel, consisting of almost pure pigment, with a little binder, appears lighter and brighter. A more subtle but still perceptible difference can be seen by comparing the same blue in oil with the same blue in an acrylic emulsion binder: The acrylic emulsion hue is slightly lighter (and less yellow), since the binder is less transparent than the oil binder. It is true, of course, that the acrylic emulsion binders are also "underloaded" with pigment because the emulsions are more sensitive than oil. An obvious lesson in this is to compare a dry blue pigment with the same blue dispersed in any transparent binder. The binder affects the hue, value, and chroma of the pigment.

The color of the light striking the pigment also affects its hue, value, and chroma. All light is colored to some extent. We may think of sunlight being transmitted through a light cloud cover at noon as the purest white light there is, because the cloud cover scatters all wavelengths to mix white light. That is the specification of white light used in most modern technical color measurement (specified by color temperature: 6500° Kelvin). Light coming through a north-facing window is 7500–12,000° K, and is the light of choice in most artists' studios. Consider this, however: The picture is painted in this cool north light, which is decidedly bluish, and then exhibited in a gallery where it is lit by bright yellow spotlights. No wonder so many artists get a shock when they put their pictures on a gallery wall! By knowing the attributes of light, color, and pigments, you can make appropriate adjustments in studio lighting. And by knowing how to use all of the foregoing, you may begin to understand the incredible complexity of color theory. Interested painters are encouraged to consult the available texts for a further understanding of technical color.

COLOR SYSTEMS

In an attempt to make order out of this chaos, color systems were invented. They began with Newton, who described colored light transmitted through a prism, and advanced through Goethe, J. C. Le Blon, James Clerk Maxwell (who in 1855 published data and test methods which proved that red, green, and blue were the additive primary colors, and on whose work all modern color reproduction methods are based), Chevereul (who published a color circle most artists use today in 1839), and Ostwald.

In 1905 an artist from Baltimore named Albert H. Munsell developed and published *A Color Notation,* a more sophisticated and less restrictive attempt to organize color than any system previously published. In 1929 the Munsell Foundation published the *Munsell Book of Color,* an extensive expansion and revision of the original. In 1976 the *Munsell Book of Color* was published in a glossy edition (glossy color can be more extensive in chroma and value than matte color), which has become a standard reference. In 1979 the Scandinavian Colour Institute's Natural Colour system was adopted by the Swedish Standards Institution. In 1977 the Optical Society of America (OSA) produced a set of color samples based on a system developed by its Committee on Uniform Color Scales; the OSA Uniform Color Scales are the most complicated and extensive of the color systems, and so far have not, like the Munsell and the Natural Colour System, been widely distributed. The point is that these various systems are simply alternative samplings of the same abstract "color space"—a theoretical three-dimensional model of color. Color space is easily explained by the Munsell system, which is published in this country and available for purchase (see Appendix D), and to which many users refer when they specify color. Its concept is relatively simple.

MUNSELL NOTATION

Munsell's system of color notation, as it is known, places all hues in five categories: red, yellow, green, blue, and purple, in that order. It then places intermediate steps between each of the basic categories: yellow red, green yellow, blue green, purple blue, and red purple. Between each of the 10 hues there are 10 further divisions, producing a total of 100 possible hues. Arranged in the familiar color circle, the order can be written like this, with red at the top: red (R), yellow red (YR), yellow (Y), green yellow (GY), green (G), blue green (BG), blue (B), purple blue (PB), and red purple (RP)—the letters in parentheses are the symbols for the hues.

For the 10 divisions of each of the 10 hues, a number is placed in front of the hue symbol, as in 5R. The number, in this case a 5, places the hue in relation to all the other hues around the circle: 5R means that the hue is neither purplish, since it is 5 steps beyond 10RP, nor yellowish, since it is 5 steps before 10R. In sequence then, the Munsell color circle reads as follows: 5R, 10R, 5YR, 10YR, 5Y, 10Y, 5GY, 10GY, 5G, 10G, 5BG, 10BG, 5B, 10B, 5PB, 10PB, 5P, 10P, 5RP, 10RP (see Figure 7.4 for a graphic representation of the circle and hue order). It is possible to divide the steps even further by using the decimal system: 5.5R is no longer pure red, but has an ever-so-slight tinge of yellow.

All the hue steps are placed around the perimeter of the circle. Progressing in toward the center are the chroma steps: the closer to the center, the lower the chroma (the duller the hue); the farther from the center, the higher the chroma (the brighter the hue). There are provisions in most representations of the Munsell color circle for 18 steps of chroma, with the option of going to decimal places between each step if necessary. Practically speaking, few artists' quality pigments

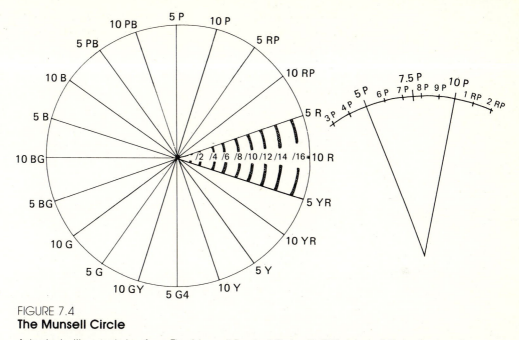

FIGURE 7.4
The Munsell Circle

Adapted with permission from *The Munsell Book of Color,* © 1976, Munsell Color Corporation.

are capable of chroma above about a 16. In the Munsell system, chroma is represented by a slash with a number following: /10.

In a two-dimensional color circle there is no provision for showing value, the third component of color. In Munsell notation there is a provision for numerical representation of value, but one must visualize the third dimension. The standard color circle represents a view of the Munsell Color Tree sliced through its center at value 5. There are 4 steps more above it, and 5 steps more below it for a total of 10 steps: 1 is the lowest value (darkest), and 10 is the highest (lightest). Naturally there is the option of using decimal divisions between each value step. The value step number is placed before the slash chroma notation and the full notation looks like this: 5.5R 10/2, which could be described as a very light, dull, slightly yellow red. In more familiar terms, this would be a very light orangish pink, or peach.

The Munsell color space is not symmetrical, as were many of the previously published systems. It is not a sphere, nor is it an equilateral pyramid; the space defined by the range of hues is lopsided. There are bulges outward in areas of high chroma and depressions in areas of low chroma. Therefore, one would never encounter a notation such as this: 5R 10/16, a very bright, perfectly red pink. Normal reds just cannot be very light and very bright at the same time; fluorescent pigments can sometimes come close to this, but they are a special case, and furthermore they cannot be used in permanent painting because they quickly lose their brilliance. (For a graphic representation of the lopsided Munsell color space, see Figure 7.5.)

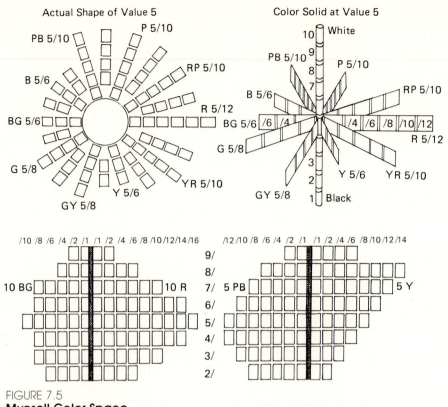

FIGURE 7.5
Munsell Color Space

Adapted with permission from *The Munsell Book of Color,* © 1976, Munsell Color Corporation.
Top left: Actual shape of value 5.
Top right: The color solid at value 5.
Bottom left and right: The chroma and value gamuts of four different hues, showing the varying form of color space.

The *Munsell Book of Color,* glossy edition (1976), contains 40 constant hue charts with about 1500 removable, numbered, glossy color chips. Using the book as a tool for understanding color order, color systems, harmonies, and contrasts is one of the most valuable exercises an artist can undertake. It is, unfortunately, an expensive tool—but most good university libraries should have a copy. The Munsell Foundation also publishes a student edition, which contains fewer, matte, unnumbered loose chips and hue charts; this set must be put together, in order, by the student, which is also a valuable excersise (see Appendix D).

In contrast to the simplicity of the Munsell system, consider the OSA Uniform Color Scales. They can be thought of as an orderly sampling of a variously colored mist filling a room that has no defined perimeter. The geometric arrangement is such that one can move in the space in at least 12 different directions, as opposed to only 3 in Munsell. Using the Munsell system, it is possible to specify exactly what color one is talking about without resorting to subjective descriptions such as "peach," or "sky blue," even though that is what artists have always done and will always do. Whether it is necessary for an artist to be able to do this is debatable and is really a question of technique, esthetics, or philosophy. One manufacturer of artists' paints, however, does use Munsell's system on its tubes of oil and acrylic emulsion paints: Liquitex (formerly Permanent Pigments). It even went so far as to develop a "modular color system" paint using the Munsell theory. The notation on the labels is simplified, to be sure, but useful nonetheless. Ironically, Liquitex's effort to label correctly will go unnoticed by all those who do not understand, or have made no effort to understand, color order systems.

CATEGORIES OF PIGMENTS

Pigments are traditionally named in a number of ways: for their inventors, for their place of origin, for the port from which they have been shipped, for their use, for their chemical derivation or composition, or for their resemblance to something else. Examples of this, respectively, are Scheele's green, Turkey brown, Solferino, Underpainting White, cadmium red, cerulean blue (sky blue). Many of these names survive today.

This is a confusing system, since the names of many colors refer only to the hue, not the pigment. In the case of sap green, for instance, the original colorant was a very fugitive dye made from buckthorn berries. Today's sap green resembles the hue of the original but is chemically and physically different and, perhaps, more permanent.

A more sensible way of naming pigments has been suggested by other writers, and that is to use the chemical names of the constituent materials. That suggestion is good, but has its drawbacks. Many pigments are composed of a number of different materials; some of the names of the substances used to make pigments are cumbersome and relatively meaningless; some of the organic pigments have a group name, with many variations under the same designation; and, most compelling, several pigments have a traditional common name so familiar that to change it might be confusing to users. A good example of the latter case is the name Prussian blue. There are two forms of Prussian blue, one called Prussian and one called Milori; the Milori variety is the better pigment, but to change the name after nearly 300 years of continuous use would not be helpful.

A further alternative, now used by manufacturers subscribing to the new paint standard (see pages 145–147), is to use the common name of the pigment and the *Colour Index* name of the pigment. The CI name is a number code by which one can refer to a specific pigment and its composition, source, and manufacturer.

A way to begin recognizing the basic differences between types of pigments is to categorize them by origin. Here are the generally accepted categories of pigments, with subcategories, adapted from the *Colour Index* definitions:*

CATEGORIES BY ORIGIN

INORGANIC

These are "colored, insoluble compounds of mainly inorganic composition" and include the elements, oxides, salts, and complex salts. All are usually simply called minerals, although this is less specific. As a group, the inorganic pigments are considered highly durable in most painting processes, though some of the processed natural mineral pigments and manufactured mineral pigments are exceptions.

Earth Colors or Natural Mineral Colors   These are crude ores colored mainly by iron but also by other metals, which are mined, washed, pulverized, and sometimes heated to produce different hues. They are characterized by low chroma, low to moderate tinctorial (tinting) strength, varying value ranges, and hues ranging from yellow to red, with some very dull red purples and greens. Natural deposits of white chalk can also be called earths.

Processed Natural Mineral Colors   These are generally metallic ores treated alone or in conjunction with other metals, with heat or by chemical reaction, to produce more sophisticated and purer hues. Their appearance runs the gamut of hues, values, and chromas from very bright, light hues to very dark, dull hues. This is a large category.

Manufactured Mineral Colors   These are duplications of the natural mineral colors or the processed natural mineral colors, made by synthesizing the components in a laboratory. They are similar in appearance to the processed mineral colors.

ORGANIC

These are "concentrated organic colorings with no salt-forming groups" composed mainly of arrangements of carbon atoms and carbon-based molecules. The significant difference between the organics and the inorganics is that the organics are mostly transparent soluble dyes, while the inorganics can be transparent, translucent, or opaque, but are discrete, characteristically shaped particles with an inherent color. For an organic colorant to function as a pigment, it must be a particle; dyes can bleed and migrate unless they are fixed in a particle form.

Animal-Derived Organics   These are made by extracting from or processing animal remains. Bone black is made from charred bone; sepia is from the ink of a

---

* This, and the information in Table 7.1, is adapted from the *Colour Index* with permission of the publishers, The Society of Dyers and Colourists, Bradford, England, and the American Association of Textile Chemists and Colorists, Research Triangle Park, NC, USA.

squid; cochineal (carmine) is extracted from the dried body of an insect; Indian yellow is from the urine of cows force-fed mango leaves. These are usually (but not always) bright, vivid hues of an unstable nature with poor durability.

Vegetable-Derived Organics   These are made from vegetable matter, produced in the same way as the animal-derived organics. They have the same general hue characteristics and the same shortcomings, with some exceptions.

Synthetic Organics   These are synthesized copies of the hues found in animal- and vegetable-derived organic colorants. Made in laboratories under controlled conditions, they run the gamut of hues, values, and chromas—although they are usually thought of as bright, transparent colors—and they also run the gamut of durability from poor to excellent.

FORMS OF ORGANIC PIGMENTS

There are two physical forms of organic pigments, toners and lakes.

A *toner* is a concentrated organic colorant, usually a water-soluble dye, chemically or electrically "fixed" on a precipitate. A *precipitate* is an inert, colorless (or nearly colorless) particle. Aluminum stearate and aluminum hydrate are examples. Since toners are water-soluble, and since they are very concentrated, they may bleed and migrate despite being attached to a precipitate. They are not ordinarily found in the better lines of artists' paints because of this defect, although there is evidence that they have been used by some manufacturers to brighten otherwise duller hues.

Lakes are similar to toners, being precipitated on an inert carrier like aluminum stearate, except that there is no "extra" dye, and the precipitate is considered a necessary part of the pigment.

EXTENSION OF PIGMENTS

Both organic and inorganic pigments may be "extended," whereby the colorant is diluted with more precipitate or inert than is necessary, in order to increase the volume yield of the colorant. While increasing the volume, extending a pigment also decreases its color strength. Sometimes, as with the phthalocyanines, extending the colorant is necessary. Sometimes it is not necessary: in this case an extended pigment should be considered as having been adulterated or cheapened. In the student grades of artists' paints extended pigments are common, which is why the paints are cheap. In professional lines adulteration is rare; extension of pigments is done only to those that require it.

TRANSPARENCY, TRANSLUCENCY, AND OPACITY

A batch of pigment by itself is usually seen as a pile of opaque colored powder. Microscopically, the individual pigment particles have a much different character. The synthetic organic lakes precipitated on an inert carrier are usually of regular and repetitious form and, if dry, opaque in reflected light or translucent in transmitted light. When they are put into a wet medium such as a paint binder, however, they are quite transparent and glow like colored glass if viewed as a thinly spread-out film on a white substrate.

The inorganic pigments, by contrast, exhibit all sorts of particle shapes, from crystalline forms to irregular rocklike chunks. They also have varying degrees of opacity from fully opaque, to semi-opaque (translucent), to completely transparent. The size of the particle is also important in some cases: When smalt is ground too finely it is weaker in hue, lighter in value, and a low chroma—almost totally useless in a liquid vehicle.

Whether the pigment itself is transparent, translucent, or opaque can be important in choosing the colorant for a particular use. In practice it is possible to make a normally opaque pigment look transparent by grinding it into a dust and very thoroughly dispersing it in its binder. That is the case with transparent watercolor, where many pigments which are opaque display marvelous transparency. An ordinarily transparent pigment can give opaque effects if the paint layer is built up to a thickness—a technique possible only in some painting processes. When choosing a pigment for a glazing technique, it is always preferable to select a transparent pigment, since it allows more light to pass through it and thus produces a richer, more "resonant" appearance.

MASSTONE AND UNDERTONE

The masstone and undertone of a pigment is related to its transparency, translucency, or opacity. The hue of a pigment, seen as a pile of dry powder or dispersed in a vehicle and spread out in a thick, opaque film, is called *masstone.* It is also sometimes called *body color,* although this term can refer to a painting technique (gouache) and therefore is confusing.

When the pigment is dispersed in a vehicle and spread out into a thin, translucent layer, one can see the *undertone.* The undertone of the hue can also be seen when the pigment is mixed into a tint with white, and when the colorant is thinned with a medium and spread out into a transparent film, as is done with transparent watercolors.

The masstone and undertone of many pigments are the same, but there are sometimes differences between these attributes in particular single pigments. Rose madder, for instance, has a deep red hue in masstone but a rosy, slightly bluish hue in undertone, depending on the variety (there are about 12 varieties of rose madder). When choosing a pigment for a glazing or other transparent painting technique, it is helpful to be familiar with any differences between the masstone and undertone of the pigment. Most painting processes make use of both color effects, although some are best expressed when only one or the other is exploited. Since there are often several different varieties of a particular pigment, it is helpful to make one's own assessment of the material's undertone and masstone; attempts to add these attributes to a list of pigments often leads to confusion when the variety within a particular pigment is great.

TESTS: SOLUBILITY, TINTING STRENGTH, AND LIGHTFASTNESS

Artists who wish to try new pigments, or are unfamiliar with the special characteristics of the colors they use, may wish to conduct some simple tests. These tests are by no means quantitative, but they can be a relative measure of quality.

SOLUBILITY

The solubility of a pigment in various liquids can be important when determining in which vehicles the pigment will function properly. A pigment that is soluble in water, for instance, will not work in any vehicle which contains water or for which water is the thinner or solvent. To test a pigment for solubility, place a small amount of the powder in a tall, clear glass jar. Fill the glass halfway with the solvent in question—water, mineral spirits, denatured ethyl alcohol, vinegar (for acidic vehicles), ammonia water (for alkaline vehicles)—cap the jar tightly, and shake the mixture thoroughly until the pigment is dispersed in the solvent. *Note:* Denatured ethyl alcohol is a health and fire hazard; ammonia is a health hazard (to make ammonia water, mix 1 part household ammonia with 10 to 20 parts tap water); do not breathe the vapors of either alcohol or ammonia.

Allow the pigment to settle overnight, or until it is completely settled to the bottom of the glass. If the solvent has been slightly colored by the pigment so that it is not the same color as it was before adding the pigment, the pigment is soluble in that liquid. The pigment might not be good to use in a vehicle that has the liquid as a part, or for which the liquid is a thinner or solvent.

TINTING STRENGTH

In simple terms, tinting strength is the ability of a colorant to affect the hue of another colorant to which it has been added. It is also a measure of how strongly a color will tint a standard white. The method given here is a subjective, qualitative test, but it provides a good means by which an artist can compare two manufacturers' paints for strength.

The test method requires the use of a standard white paint. In the example below, where several different cobalt blue oil paints are compared, a single white oil paint is used for mixing all the tints.

MATERIALS

1. A large tube of artists' titanium white in oil. (The kind of oil does not matter: this is a test of color strength, not a test of vehicle contents.)
2. Several different brands of oil paint labeled cobalt blue. Do not use paints labeled "Cobalt Blue Hue," since these will not contain cobalt pigment.
3. A clean glass or porcelain-on-steel palette, and spatulas for mixing.
4. A wall-scraper with a flexible steel blade, modified with layers of black plastic electrician's tape at each end to make an aperture (Figure 7.6).

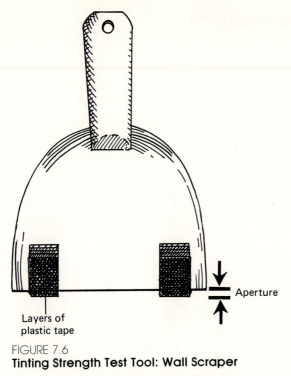

Aperture

Layers of
plastic tape

FIGURE 7.6
Tinting Strength Test Tool: Wall Scraper

Layers of plastic tape at each end of the blade built up to give a narrow aperture.

5. Kitchen measuring spoons: 1 tablespoon and a ⅛ teaspoon.
6. White posterboard sealed with two coats of acrylic emulsion gesso. (If the posterboard had a glazed finish, it need not be sealed.) Cut the posterboard into strips about 4 by 8 inches (10 × 20 cm).
7. A clipboard for holding the strips of posterboard while making the draw-down.

METHOD

1. Measure out 2 tablespoons of the white paint and ⅛ teaspoon of one of the cobalt blue paints. Mix together thoroughly and completely on the palette to make a tint.
2. Place one of the strips of posterboard on the clipboard, positioning it in the center and making sure that it is held firmly by the clip.
3. Place a volume of the cobalt blue tint oil paint near the top of the strip of posterboard and spread it lightly across the width of the strip with a palette knife.
4. Hold the clipboard down with one hand and use the other to hold the wall scraper. Put the wall scraper blade in front of the pile of paint and hold it at about a 45° angle. Draw the blade down over the tint, pressing firmly and evenly (Figure 7.7).

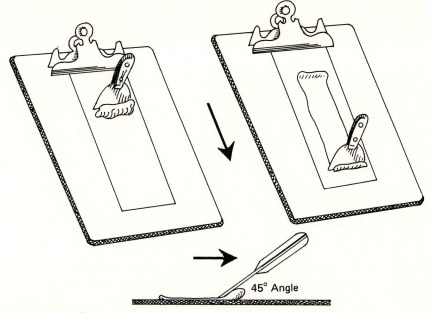

FIGURE 7.7
Making a Drawdown with a Wall Scraper

5. Remove the blade and the excess paint. Clean the blade. Observe that a uniform, opaque film of the paint mixture has been deposited down the center of the strip of posterboard.
6. Make a second mixture of the white with another brand of cobalt blue, using steps 1 to 5 above. Make a third, fourth, fifth, and sixth drawdown using these procedures, if there are that many paints to compare.
7. The paints can be compared while they are wet and again after they dry (about 3 to 7 days at room temperature). Once the strips are dry, they can be trimmed with scissors so all the edges are straight. The comparisons should be made in natural north daylight, with the light striking the surfaces of the samples at an angle to lessen surface reflection (Figure 7.8). The differences between the brands of cobalt blue paints will become evident due to the heavy reduction of the color with white; the weaker tinters will be noticeably lighter in value. Cobalt blue paints of similar tinctorial strength but from different manufacturers may be strikingly different in cost—if both paints are equivalent, there may be no reason to buy the more expensive one beyond brand loyalty.

LIGHTFASTNESS

Testing for lightfastness (relative light permanence) of a colored material is important to the artist, who is always concerned with the durability and permanence of his or her work.

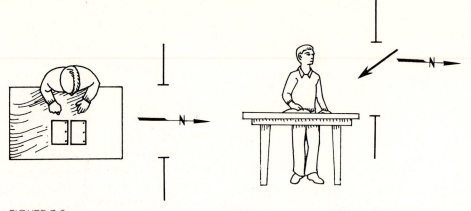

FIGURE 7.8
Position of Viewer Looking at Comparative Drawdowns

Artists can use paints like oils, acrylic emulsions, acrylic solutions, and alkyds with some degree of confidence regarding lightfastness. This is especially true if the container labels give the generic names of the pigment(s) used in the paint, and if the manufacturer certifies on the label that the paint conforms to a standard and lists the lightfastness rating of the paint (see the following section, "Standardization of Artists' Paints"). Paints that have generic names for the pigments on their labels but do not certify compliance with a standard can also be used, but with less confidence.

Some traditional coloring materials, like watercolors and pastels, and many nontraditional materials, like colored pencils and colored markers and inks, should be tested. Nontraditional media are not often standardized and may contain experimental ingredients, use different composition formulas from batch to batch, and be labeled permanent without sufficiently explaining what permanent means. With growing interest in the use of these nontraditional materials, there should be some means of testing their reliability without having to rely solely on a manufacturer's promotional literature.

Two very simple lightfastness tests can be performed. The first, and easier, is the one most often recommended in a manual like this. The second is slightly more complicated, but gives more reliable and predictable results.

LIGHTFASTNESS TEST 1

This is an adequate test in the grossest sense, but does not take into account the many variables that can be encountered in testing different types of colorants: different kinds of colorants are applied differently, and to different kinds of supports. Also, some paints are not used straight out of the tube, but are more often used in mixtures (tints) with white or as transparencies. This method does not adequately test these paints under normal use conditions. Neither is there a way to rate the results of this test as other than "good" or "bad." Some colorants might fall into a category between the two, which would make them acceptable under certain conditions; this test cannot distinguish these colorants.

Other considerations, such as the effect of heat, humidity, and darkness on the control sample, or the effects of the particular binder on the colorant, are not adequately addressed by this test.

MATERIALS

1. The colored medium to be tested: paints, colored pencils, colored inks, and so on.
2. Strips of fairly heavy, smooth-surfaced white paper. If possible, use a non-yellowing rag paper: paper that yellows will affect your judgment about possible changes in the colored material. The strips should be large enough to handle easily, but not so large as to require lots of colorant to cover them completely. Strips about 1 by 4 inches (2.5 × 10 cm) should do it.

METHOD

1. Completely cover a strip of the heavy paper with the colored material to be tested. A different strip should be used for each color. Cover the strip with as much color as possible to make an opaque (or nearly opaque) coating. With colored pencils this will not be possible, but get a thorough coating anyway. With transparent watercolors, a thick, opaque coating is not desirable (and not a good test of what is supposed to be a thin, transparent paint), but try to get a deep, richly colored hue while maintaining some degree of transparency.
2. Cut the strip in half, leaving two 1 by 2 inch (2.5 × 5 cm) chips. Write the identification of each chip (color name, code number, manufacturer) on the back, and place one in a drawer or in a book to remove it from the light. Put the other chip on a backboard of some kind and expose it to full sunlight in a south-facing window. Any kind of daylight exposure will do, but south sunlight is the most intense and will shorten the test time.
3. Check the exposed sample against the sample kept in the dark at periodic intervals. Note any changes in the one exposed to sunlight.
4. After a few months, compare the samples more closely, under natural daylight (north light, preferably). Any clearly perceptible change will indicate that the colored material in question is not entirely lightfast.

LIGHTFASTNESS TEST 2

The second method tries to take into account some of the deficiencies of the first. It uses a measuring device to separate the results into categories of lightfastness; it specifies that paints normally applied as opaque or translucent films be mixed with white, to make a more severe test of the colorant as a tint; and it specifies appropriate supports for different media.

This method is based on the International Standards Organization Recommendation 105, published as British Standard BS1006:1971,* and on work done by Dr. Robert L. Feller, of the Center on the Materials of the Artist and Conservator, Carnegie-Mellon Institute of Research, Pittsburgh.†

This is a simple test which is subject to many variables, not the least of which is the observer's experience in viewing color differences. It is a subjective, qualitative test. Unless both the samples and standards in the method below (see steps 6 and 7) are masked with a neutral gray card, changes in adjacent strips of color may affect the interpretation of the results. To avoid this possibility, paint a piece of paper with the Liquitex Neutral Gray paint described in the method and cut a slot in it that is the same size as the sample and standard strips. Compare the samples and standards by viewing them through this isolating mask.

Here are some additional points: the test does not expose all colorants in tints with white, a kind of exposure that is universally agreed to be a more severe test of a colorant's lightfastness. The test does not provide a method of making colorant films of a uniform thickness. And the test does not evaluate the physical durability of the binders, vehicles, or other media in which the colorants are carried, nor is it possible to separate what hue/value/chroma changes occur in the vehicle from those that occur in the colorant. In addition to the references cited below, artists may wish to consult the following test methods, which have application to this type of evaluation:

AATCC Test Method 16C-1974: "Colorfastness to Light: Daylight." Published by the American Association of Textile Chemists and Colorists, PO Box 12215, Research Triangle Park, NC 27709.

ASTM G24-73: "Standard Recommended Practice for Conducting Natural Light Exposures Under Glass." Published by the American Society for Testing and Materials, 1916 Race Street, Philadelphia, PA 19103.

MATERIALS

1. The British Blue-Wool Standard Textile Fading Cards. These can be obtained from TALAS (see Appendix D). The cards are about 1¾ inch by 4¼ inches (44.5 × 130 mm), with eight strips of wool cloth glued in horizontal

---

* "Methods for the Determination of the Colour Fastness of Textiles to Light and Weathering," British Standards Institution, 2 Park Street, London W1A 2BS, England.

† "Felt-tipped Markers and the Need for Standards of Lightfastness for Artist' Colorants," *Bulletin of the American Group-IIC*, 8, No. 1 (1967), pp. 24–26; and "Further Studies on the International Blue-Wool Standards for Exposure to Light," submitted to the ICOM Committee for Conservation, Zagreb, Yugoslavia, October 1978.

The technique described has been under development since 1981 and may eventually appear as a Standard Test Method of the American Society for Testing and Materials (ASTM). The principal difficulty with it is in reaching agreement among several observers in different locations about the ratings and categories. Artists Hilton Brown, Joy Turner Luke, and Zora Sweet Pinney have contributed significantly to the development of the method.

bands down the length of the card. Each strip is colored with a blue dye of a known lightfastness. The top strip, Standard #1, is the least lightfast; the bottom strip, Standard #8, is the most lightfast. Each standard, beginning with Standard #1 and moving down the scale, takes approximately twice as long to change as the standard immediately preceding. The cards are very sensitive to light. They should be kept in complete darkness until they are ready to be used in the test: wrap them in black paper, put them in an envelope, and store the package in a drawer or dark closet. High temperature and humidity may affect the blue dyes.

2. A support appropriate for the material being tested. The support material should be stable, white and nonyellowing, and of known composition, so that any changes in the colorant will not be affected by unpredictable changes in the support. For testing oil paints, use 100 percent rag or other neutral pH paper, primed with a light ground of acrylic emulsion gesso. For other paste paints, such as the alkyds, acrylic emulsion, acrylic solution, casein, tempera, or opaque watercolors, use a plain, unprimed white 100 percent rag paper. For transparent watercolor, use a watercolor paper, 100 percent rag, white, with not too prominent a surface texture. A very rough paper surface will interfere with a clear interpretation of the color changes. For most other colored materials, use a smooth, plain white, 100 percent rag or neutral pH paper.

3. The colored materials to be tested.

4. A stiff backboard to which the samples are attached.

5. Stiff cover strips to protect the unexposed portion of the colored samples: wooden lattice strips, inexpensive wooden rulers, or thin aluminum panels can be used.

6. Any brand of artists' alizarin crimson oil paint. This is a control. Since it is known that alizarin crimson is just below the cutoff point for acceptable lightfastness, any color with less lightfastness than alizarin crimson certainly should not be used to make permanent works of art. Be sure of getting the true alizarin pigment by choosing a brand that gives the *Colour Index* identification on the label. The *Colour Index* identification of this pigment is Pigment Red 83/Colour Index Number 58000 (PR83/58000) (see Table 7.1). Also buy any brand of artists' titanium white oil paint (PW6/77891).

METHOD

1. On the white support, paint out strips of each color of the material to be tested. Use the normal application techniques for the particular medium; that is, transparent watercolors should be washed on in a film of average transparency, pastels stroked on in a consistent manner, and so on. Very transparent coatings will change quickly. Identify each strip of color: brand name, code number, color name, and so on. Paints normally applied as opaque or translucent films—oils, acrylic emulsions, acrylic solutions,

alkyds, temperas, caseins, opaque watercolors—should be applied as tints with white, since this is the customary way of applying the paints while making a picture. To make a consistent tint of each color, use the white of the particular paint being tested and mix it with the colored paint to match a Munsell Value 7. Liquitex makes a Neutral Gray (Value 7) acrylic emulsion paint that can be used as a reference. Fill in a strip of the sample sheet with the alizarin crimson oil mixed to a Munsell Value 7 with the titanium white oil.

2. Attach the support with the colored samples to the backboard. Use tape, glue, tacks, or clips. Attach the Textile Fading Card to the backboard near the color samples.

3. Cover half of the samples and half of the Textile Fading Card with the cover strip(s). Be sure to cover the written identification as well. The cover must be stiff enough and securely attached so that it lies flat and does not allow light to leak underneath. Figure 7.9 gives a suggested arrangement of samples, cards, and covers.

4. Stand the backboard with the samples and the card attached in a south- or southwest-facing window, with the top of the board tilted back so that sunlight will reach the entire surface. North daylight, or other diffuse daylight, will be sufficient for testing the most fugitive colorants—but the testing time will be considerably extended in diffuse lighting conditions.

5. To identify the extremely fugitive colors in a set of samples, it may be necessary to check them, by gently lifting the cover strip, at daily intervals during the first month of exposure. With an unobstructed south-facing exposure and clear, sunny days, noticeable change may occur in one day. Any color samples that begin to show change when Standards 1, 2, or 3 on the Textile Fading Card show change are not lightfast and should not be used for permanent works of art. After approximately two months of exposure, check the color/contrast of Standard 6. When a change in the color of Standard 6 can just be perceived, the test is complete. At this point, also check for a change in the alizarin control. It may take anywhere from six weeks to as long as a year for Standard 6 to change, depending on the time of the year (whether the sun is high or low in the sky), weather conditions, geographic location, and the temperature and relative humidity of the room in which the tests are conducted.

6. When Standard 6 has just begun to change, check all the color samples for changes. The changes may not be limited to fading; a loss or gain of chroma or a complete change in hue may be observed. The samples that do not show a change by the time Standard 6 shows a perceptible change can be considered to have very good lightfastness. This is good enough for colorants that will be shown indoors in average lighting.

7. To assign a rating to the colorants, compare the changes in them with the range of changes shown on the Textile Fading Card. Find the standard

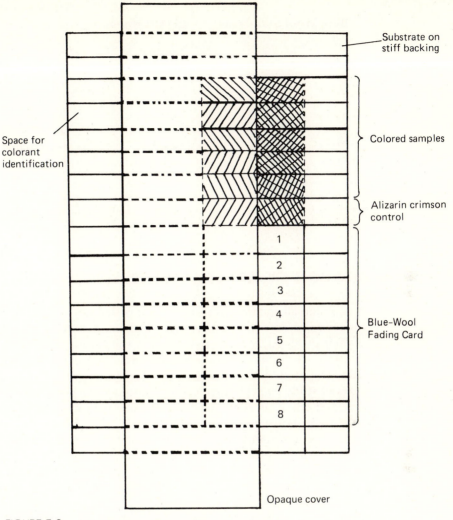

Substrate on stiff backing

Space for colorant identification

Colored samples

Alizarin crimson control

1
2
3
4
5
6
7
8

Blue–Wool Fading Card

Opaque cover

FIGURE 7.9
Layout of a Panel for the Simple Blue-Wool Test

Opaque covering over half of each test sample, the alizarin control, the Blue-Wool Fading Card, and the colorant identification.

that shows the same degree of change as the colored sample. If, for example, a sample fades the same amount as Standard 3 faded, it is given a rating of 3.

Use the following list to assign a lightfastness rating to the samples, once they have been given a number rating according to the blue-wool standards:

Blue-Wool Standards	Lightfastness	Approximate Lifetime (Years)
1	Fugitive	Less than 20
2	Fugitive	Less than 20
3	Fugitive	Less than 20
4	Fair	20 to 100
5	Fair	20 to 100
6	Very good	About 100 (more or less)
7*	Excellent	More than 100
8*	Excellent	More than 100

* In order to rate colorants as excellent, it will be necessary to extend the test exposure until Standards 7 or 8 change. Any colors that do not change by the time Standard 7 or 8 changes can be rated excellent.

THE STANDARDIZATION OF ARTISTS' PAINTS

A commercial standard for artists' paints that could serve as a purchasing guide for artists, and provide a means by which manufacturers could certify the quality of their products, was first published by the National Bureau of Standards (NBS) in 1942. The standard, called Commercial Standard 98-42 (CS98-42), was initially proposed by the Massachusetts Art Project of the WPA in 1938. After five years of study by artists, American manufacturers of artists' materials, conservators, and other interested parties, the standard was adopted as a voluntary guideline by the industry.

The "Paint Standard" was important for both artists and manufacturers. It established performance and composition standards for professional-grade oil paints. It promulgated a table of nomenclature and a system of labeling in an attempt to eliminate the confusion found in traditional methods of labeling. And it proposed requirements for the best professional grades of oil paints so that artists could be assured of some objective measure of quality.

In 1962 the standard was revised and reissued as Commercial Standard 98-62, with the addition of a few new pigments and the listing of some new materials under study that were being considered for addition to later revisions. CS98-42, however, remained essentially unchanged for over 40 years. Since the time of its publication and minor revision in 1962, four new binders have been developed and extensively marketed: the oil-modified alkyds, acrylic solutions, acrylic emulsions, and polyvinyl acetate emulsions. The acrylic emulsion binders have become immensely popular. In addition, scores of pigments, mostly synthetic organic types, have been introduced by pigment manufacturers. CS98-62 has become virtually obsolete; few companies adhere to its guidelines because they are no longer relevant.

In 1976, members of Artists Equity Association, of Washington, DC, a nonprofit organization of professional visual artists, contacted the NBS about a possible revision of CS98-62. The NBS gave its blessing to the project, but could not offer the services of a support staff to conduct testing. Committees within the American Society for Testing and Materials (ASTM) and the Inter-Society Color Council (ISCC) were then formed to study CS98-62 and coordinate its revision. The ISCC is an organization of groups and individuals who have an interest in color and color science, and ASTM, well known to many industries, is the largest independent standards-writing body in the world. ASTM undertook to sponsor the new Paint Standard, and the ISCC actively supported the revision work.

Beginning in 1976, members of both groups, which include several major American and European artists' materials manufacturers, a number of artists organizations, and individual artists, chemists, paint technologists, conservators, and teachers, met several times a year to discuss changes proposed for the new standard, to report on the progress of individual studies in areas of CS98-62 that needed revision, and to examine new materials and information which could be included in the new standard. The results of these efforts were published by ASTM in 1984, and include the following:*

ASTM D4302, "Standard Specification for Artists' Oil and Acrylic Emulsion Paints"
ASTM D4303, "Standard Test Methods for Lightfastness of Pigments Used in Artists' Paints"
ASTM D4236, "Standard Practice for Labeling Art Materials for Chronic Health Hazards"

ASTM D4302

This standard specification describes labeling, composition, physical properties, and performance requirements for artists' oil and acrylic emulsion paints, and covers pigments, vehicles, and additives for both types of paint.

The labeling requirements are of greatest interest to the artist. The following information will appear on every container label:

1. The complete identification of the pigment(s) contained in the paint, specified by common name, *Colour Index* name, and additional terms needed to identify the colorant(s). Placement of this information—whether on the front or back of the container—is also specified. Manufacturers are encouraged to include a simple chemical description of the colorant(s) where label size permits, but are required by the specification to give this information in company publications (like catalogues). In the case of pigments which have been duplicated by other colorants, the manufacturers are required to indicate the substitution by using

---

* From ASTM Standards D4302-84, D4303-84, and D4236-84, © American Society for Testing and Materials, by permission of the publisher.

the term "hue" after the name of the color, and by giving the name of the actual pigment used directly under the name of the color. For example:

Cadmium red hue
(Quinacridone)

Where a manufacturer has used a mixture of pigments to make a proprietary hue, all the pigments in the mixture must conform to the specification, and the mixture itself must pass the requirements of the specification. Furthermore, the paint must be labeled in accordance with the previous requirement. For example:

Permanent green
(Ultramarine blue, Cadmium-barium yellow)

2. An identification of the vehicle—either the vegetable origin of the oil and its method of refinement for oil paints, or the type of emulsion for acrylic emulsion paints.

3. The lightfastness rating of the pigment(s) in the paint, either Lightfastness I (excellent) or Lightfastness II (very good). Only those pigments that appear in a table of suitable pigments can be used in paints conforming to the specifications. The suitable pigments table is derived from tests done by a method given in ASTM D4303, and lists the *Colour Index* name of the pigment, its lightfastness rating in both oil and acrylic emulsion vehicles (the rating may differ, depending on the vehicle), the common name of the pigment and its chemical class or a simple chemical description, and its *Colour Index* number. Newly introduced pigments must pass the test in ASTM D4303 to be placed on the suitable pigments table. An appendix to the table lists Lightfastness III (fair) pigments. These pigments are not suitably permanent for use in artists' paints, but are listed in the interest of establishing common terminology. Pigments such as alizarin crimson, Hooker's green, and certain varieties of naphthol red, thioindigoid magenta, and dioxazine purple are listed here.

4. The volume contents of the container (required by law).

5. A statement certifying that the contents conform to the labeling requirements of the Federal Hazardous Substances Act (for acute hazards) and ASTM D4236 (for chronic hazards).

6. A statement certifying that the contents conform to ASTM D4302.

7. The manufacturer's name and address, or the importer's name and address and the country of origin.

In addition to this labeling information, there are methods given for testing artists' oil and acrylic emulsion paints for various physical and performance characteristics. The types of allowable additives to the vehicles are described, as are the reasons for adding inert pigments. Acceptable consistencies, fineness of grinds, freeze-thaw stability, and drying times are also given.*

---

* Artist's professional alkyd and transparent watercolor paints will soon be added to this standard; test methods are under development.

ASTM D4303

This standard test method describes the various tests on artists' pigments used to derive the table of suitable pigments given in ASTM D4302. If a manufacturer wishes to conform to ASTM D4302, these tests must be performed on the pigments, either by the manufacturer or by an outside contractor.

Aside from giving complete instructions on the preparation of samples for testing, the method describes the types of exposures allowable for the test. Each pigment must be exposed to at least two tests: an outdoor exposure in sunlight in Florida, and an indoor exposure to a fluorescent lamp apparatus or a xenon-arc fadeometer. All the methods of measurement (by instrument, not by visual comparison), calculation, and interpretation of results are given in the test, as well as instructions for determining the lightfastness categories of the test pigments.

Each time a manufacturer wishes to introduce a new pigment and list conformance to the standard, it must perform the tests given in ASTM D4303 on the new pigment.

ASTM D4236

This is a standard practice for labeling art materials for chronic health hazards (there is already a law covering acute hazards). It applies only to art materials packaged in small quantities for individual or small group use (it does not apply, for instance, to materials packaged in bulk bags), and it applies only to materials for the adult artist, not for children.

In order for a manufacturer to comply with this standard, product formulations must be submitted to a toxicologist for review; to protect trade secrets, the formulations and their review are confidential. The toxicologist takes into account the following information in determining the need for precautionary labeling: the chemical composition of the material, the current knowledge of the chronic toxic potential of the components and the full formulation, the amount of hazardous substance in the material, the chemical and physical form of the material, "reasonably foreseeable" uses of the material, the potential for the components of the material to react with each other, the potential for a chronic adverse health effect from the decomposition or combustion products resulting from the use of the material, and the opinions of various regulatory bodies on the potential for chronic adverse health effects from the use of the material.

Based on the conclusions of the toxicologist, labeling requirements are recommended. The requirements include the use of a signal word (WARNING), a list of the potential hazards from using the material, the name of the hazardous component(s), instructions for the safe handling and use of the product, and a list of any components in the material that could cause skin or respiratory sensitization. The label must also give the name of a source for more information about the health hazards of the material, such as instructions to contact a physician, a local poison control center, or a 24-hour toll-free poison control hotline.

Following the text of the standard is a list of the various chronic hazard statements, and a list of the precautionary statements that can be used on labels. If all the requirements of the standard are met, the manufacturer can claim compliance with a statement like "conforms to ASTM Practice D4236."

The Art and Craft Materials Institute (715 Boylston Street, Boston, MA 02116) is one approved certifying body for ASTM D4236. Manufacturers wishing to comply with the standard submit their formulations to the institute's toxicologist, and upon approval may use the institute's certification seal on their product labels.

SOME CONCLUDING OBSERVATIONS

All of these standards are voluntary, and manufacturers do not have to comply with them. Furthermore, a manufacturer may choose to have certain items in its line covered by the standards and let other items be marketed without submitting them to the standards' tests. For instance, a line of oil paints can contain alizarin crimson, a pigment which is not listed in the table of suitable pigments in D4302, as long as the label for that paint does not advertise compliance with D4302. Also, a material that conforms with D4302 automatically conforms with D4236 (and D4303), but a material that conforms to D4236 does not automatically conform to D4302. It is therefore necessary to read the compliance statements carefully to be sure of what the label is stating. Figure 7.10 shows typical paint labels under the new paint standard.

Copies of the individual ASTM standards can be obtained by writing to the American Society for Testing and Materials, 1916 Race Street, Philadelphia, PA 19103.

SPECIALTY PIGMENTS

Unusual pigments in some commercial lines of acrylic emulsion paints are mostly used for special effects. These include metallic, fluorescent, and interference pigments.

METALLIC PIGMENTS

The principal hues are gold and silver, with occasional variants of the gold in bronze, reddish, or greenish shades. The particles are metal flakes of aluminum or bronze, or mixtures of bronze and copper. If the particles are well dispersed in and completely surrounded by the paint vehicle, they should be adequately protected from oxidation, the main cause of discoloration.

FLUORESCENT PIGMENTS

In red, green, blue, and yellow hues, these are composed of dyes that absorb invisible ultraviolet light (some also absorb visible light), and then emit visible light of a longer wavelength than that absorbed. The colorant thus appears to glow. It has been shown that the fluorescents eventually lose their power to be excited by irradiation. The fluorescent effect will eventually fade—and the hue

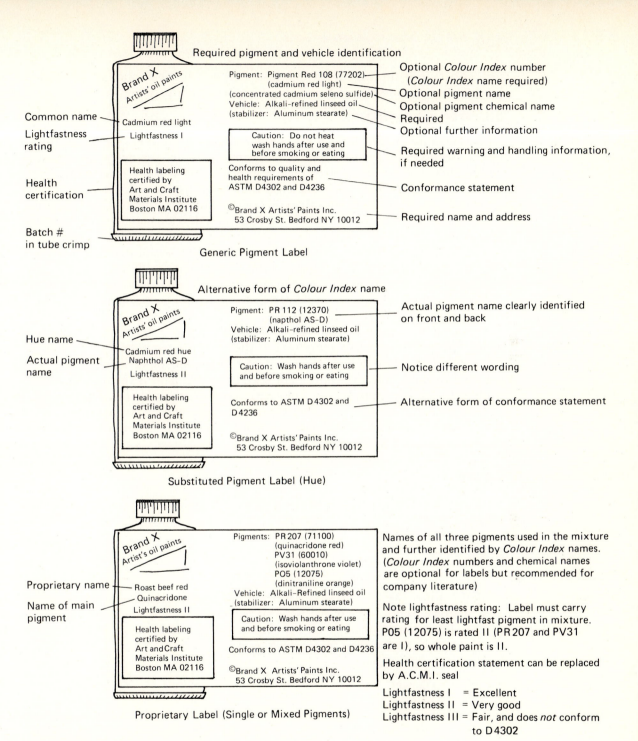

Required pigment and vehicle identification

Brand X Artists' oil paints

Pigment: Pigment Red 108 (77202) — Optional *Colour Index* number (*Colour Index* name required)
(cadmium red light) — Optional pigment name
(concentrated cadmium seleno sulfide) — Optional pigment chemical name
Vehicle: Alkali-refined linseed oil — Required
(stabilizer: Aluminum stearate) — Optional further information

Common name — Cadmium red light

Lightfastness rating — Lightfastness I

Caution: Do not heat wash hands after use and before smoking or eating — Required warning and handling information, if needed

Conforms to quality and health requirements of ASTM D4302 and D4236 — Conformance statement

Health certification — Health labeling certified by Art and Craft Materials Institute Boston MA 02116

©Brand X Artists' Paints Inc. 53 Crosby St. Bedford NY 10012 — Required name and address

Batch # in tube crimp

Generic Pigment Label

Alternative form of *Colour Index* name

Brand X Artists' oil paints

Pigment: PR 112 (12370) — Actual pigment name clearly identified on front and back
(napthol AS-D)
Vehicle: Alkali-refined linseed oil
(stabilizer: Aluminum stearate)

Hue name — Cadmium red hue
Actual pigment name — Naphthol AS-D
Lightfastness II

Caution: Wash hands after use and before smoking or eating — Notice different wording

Health labeling certified by Art and Craft Materials Institute Boston MA 02116

Conforms to ASTM D4302 and D4236 — Alternative form of conformance statement

©Brand X Artists' Paints Inc. 53 Crosby St. Bedford NY 10012

Substituted Pigment Label (Hue)

Brand X Artist's oil paints

Pigments: PR 207 (71100) — Names of all three pigments used in the mixture and further identified by *Colour Index* names. (*Colour Index* numbers and chemical names are optional for labels but recommended for company literature)
(quinacridone red)
PV31 (60010)
(isoviolanthrone violet)
PO5 (12075)
(dinitraniline orange)
Vehicle: Alkali-Refined linseed oil
(stabilizer: Aluminum stearate)

Proprietary name — Roast beef red
Name of main pigment — Quinacridone
Lightfastness II

Caution: Wash hands after use and before smoking or eating — Note lightfastness rating: Label must carry rating for least lightfast pigment in mixture. PO5 (12075) is rated II (PR 207 and PV31 are I), so whole paint is II.

Health labeling certified by Art and Craft Materials Institute Boston MA 02116

Conforms to ASTM D4302 and D4236 — Health certification statement can be replaced by A.C.M.I. seal

©Brand X Artists' Paints Inc. 53 Crosby St. Bedford NY 10012

Lightfastness I   = Excellent
Lightfastness II = Very good
Lightfastness III = Fair, and does *not* conform to D4302

Proprietary Label (Single or Mixed Pigments)

FIGURE 7.10
Labeling Requirements of ASTM Standards and How to Read a Label

may also fade if the dye is not lightfast. Because of their inherent instability, fluorescent colorants should not be used in permanent painting.

INTERFERENCE PIGMENTS

These pigments are also known as "pearlescent" or "iridescent" pigments. Interference seems to be the most appropriate name for them, as it describes how they work. Their color is dependent on the interference of light. Interference pigments are not particles in the usual sense, but thin transparent flakes coated with a film of a higher refractive index than that of the flake, for example, flakes of mica coated with a microscopically thin film of titanium dioxide pigment. These platelets, as they are called, will simultaneously reflect and transmit light, depending on their orientation toward the light source, the thickness of the paint film, the angle of the light to the paint film, and the refractive index of the platelets. The various colors—bluish, greenish, yellowish, and reddish—with a pearly luminescence and sense of depth, result from the strengthening or weakening of various light wavelengths.

Some manufacturers produce pigments with the appearance of a metallic but which are produced in the same way as the interference pigments. The same flakes of mica are used, but are coated with thin films of various mineral pigments. The appearance of paints made with these pigments is very close to those made with actual metals, but the colorants are not susceptible to oxidation, corrosion, or the other defects of the metal pigments. One artists' paint manufacturer, Golden Artist Colors, uses real stainless steel—a material that will not oxidize easily—for an unusual effect.

THE PIGMENT TABLES

Tables 7.1, 7.2, 7.3, and 7.4, which appear on the following pages, summarize important information about pigments and provide quick reference to that information. A brief explanation of each table, as well as keys to categories, terms, and abbreviations, is presented below.

PIGMENTS: TABLE 7.1

Table 7.1, pages 154–191, presents a survey of pigments that have been and are being used in artists' paints. Some of the pigments have been recently tested for the ASTM project. The pigments listed have a lightfastness rating only in oil or acrylic emulsion vehicles, and the type of oil or acrylic emulsion is not specified.

Symbols Used in Table 7.1

P	= Pigment		**P**	= Purple
N	= Natural		**B**	= Blue
M	= Metal		**G**	= Green
Y	= Yellow		**Br**	= Brown
O	= Orange		**Bk**	= Black
R	= Red		**W**	= White
V	= Violet		**n/a**	= Not available

NW = Not usable in water vehicles
LF = Lightfast type (manufacturer's code)
RS = Red shade (manufacturer's code)
SL = May darken in strong sunlight
SM = Sensitive to moisture
SS = Sensitive to hydrogen sulfide
CC = Concentrated cadmium (Paints containing concentrated cadmium pigments can have up to 15 percent barium sulfate pigment added for color control. The cadmium-barium pigments are further extended with extra barium sulfate.)

Categories and Terms in Table 7.1

ARTISTS' HUE   The common color name of the pigment.

COMMON NAME   The most common pigment name.

COLOUR INDEX NAME, NUMBER   Reference to the volume of *Colour Index* that gives each pigment's physical characteristics. The *Colour Index* is an internationally recognized reference to colorants of all types. The *Colour Index* name is written as a number, as in PY42 (Pigment Yellow 42—yellow ochre). The *Colour Index* number is the reference to the volume of the *Colour Index* that gives the pigment's composition, formulation, and sources of reference to the pigment. The number consists of five digits, as in 77493. The *Colour Index* name and number for yellow ochre would be written as PY42 (77493).

GENERIC NAME   The name of the pigment; given only if it is different from the common name.

PROPRIETARY NAME(S)   Any of the various names by which the pigment has been known; usually company or trade names.

SYNONYM(S)   Other common names for the pigment.

DATES/PLACES OF DISCOVERY   Available data about the origin of the pigment. Note that the discovery of some pigments did not occur at a specific moment in history, but evolved over a period of time.

CHEMICAL CLASS; CONSTITUENTS   The chemical class indicates whether the pigment is organic or inorganic; chemical constituents refer to the chemical contents of the pigment. Note that the data about chemical constituents is not very specific when it refers to organic pigments; this is because the usual representation of many of the organics is a diagram of the arrangement of the atoms within the molecules, or a series of long chemical designations (examples of which are given) that are relatively meaningless except to chemists.

SOURCE   Indicates the category of the pigment, simplified, with a comment in some cases about the pigment's being "processed." The pigment's source can be one of the following: natural organic, natural inorganic, synthetic organic, or synthetic inorganic.

TYPE   The following abbreviations are used to indicate the type of pigment. Note that some pigments may be of more than one type.

P = Particle   **L** =Lake
T = Toner   **E** =Extended

RESISTANCE TO: Rates the level of the pigment's resistance to various types of solvents and other liquids (adapted from the *Colour Index*).

MELTING POINT (°C)/STABILITY TO °C   Indicates both melting point temperature and temperature at which pigment may change color or deteriorate. For some pigments, information is included about the color it will become at a certain temperature.

LIGHTFASTNESS (CI/ASTM D 4302) The rating given the pigment by the *Colour Index* (CI) and the ASTM Paint Standard (ASTM D 4302), adapted into a simplified and direct categorization.

CI	**ASTM**	**Rating**
EX	I	Excellent
VG	II	Very good
G		Good
F	III	Fair
P		Poor

USE IN VEHICLES The usefulness of the pigment in various binders and/or vehicles, with specific comments on the pigment's effects in oil. An "×" across from a binder and/or vehicle indicates that the pigment is useful in that particular media; NT indicates that the pigment's usefulness in that media has not been tested; NR indicates that it is not recommended. The following abbreviations indicate the pigment's effects in oil:

Oil Absorption

> **L** = Low
> **M** = Medium
> **H** = High

Drying Rate

> **E** = Excellent **S** = Slow
> **G** = Good **VS** = Very slow
> **A** = Average

Film Properties

> **E** = Excellent **F** = Fair
> **G** = Good **P** = Poor

DRY REFRACTIVE INDEX The refractive index of the dry pigment, which is, of course, affected by the binder/vehicle/solvent combination in which it is dispersed.

> **L** = Low (transparent)
> **M** = Medium (semi-transparent)
> **H** = High (opaque)

DRY CHARACTERISTICS Indicates the hue range and so forth of the pigment. Standard symbols are used: R ▶ Y means *reddish to yellowish*.

HAZARDS Cautionary notes about hazards of pigments. *Note:* Avoid all pigment dusts.

OTHER COMMENTS Commentary on each pigment, including discussion of its major use (which may not be in artists' paints).

PIGMENTS OF HISTORICAL OR UNUSUAL INTEREST: TABLE 7.2

Table 7.2, pages 192–193, presents less-commonly known pigments, some of which have a long history of use. One may find these pigments still in use in some special cases, although the use is specific and not widespread. Some of the pigments presented in Table 7.2 are used as inerts, lake bases, or extenders; some are used in dry media such as colored pencils, pastels, or chalks, or as dyes for textiles; others are used as bases for gilding, as rough coats for pastel painting, as driers in industrial applications, or as special metallic or mineral additions to vehicles or binders.

Key for Table 7.2

P	= Pigment	**V**	= Violet
N	= Natural	**Bk**	= Black
M	= Metal	**E**	= Excellent
W	= White	**G**	= Good
R	= Red	**F**	= Fair
Y	= Yellow	**P**	= Poor
G	= Green	**NT**	= Not tested
B	= Blue		

HAZARDOUS PIGMENTS: TABLE 7.3

Table 7.3, pages 194–202, summarizes important information about hazardous pigments. Most pigments present a hazard in dry form as a dust. Exercise good hygiene in handling dry pigments by storing them in covered containers that are clearly labeled, and promptly replacing the covers after use; by not splashing dry pigments around so that the dust hangs in the air; and by avoiding overexposure to the dust. Once the pigments are dispersed in the medium, either a thinner or a binder, their hazards are considerably reduced.

The specific hazards of each pigment are generally more related to use and type of exposure than to content. There are, naturally, some exceptions. The lead-containing pigments should be handled with caution, even in paste form. Recently published accounts of the hazards of pigments have overstated the dangers associated with using some pigments, the cadmiums in particular, by not distinguishing various uses of the dry or paste materials. Be aware of how the pigment, or paint made with the pigment, is going to be used. If it is to be used in encaustic, for instance, check Table 7.3 to see if it can be safely heated without forming a metal fume (certain metal fumes can be toxic). Use, or abuse, of the pigment will be a factor in determining hazard if it contains a potentially toxic (acute or chronic) ingredient.

Finally, remember that there has never been a scientifically conducted study of how artists use their materials, and under what circumstances specific uses present hazards. Use Table 7.3 as a guide, but do not rely on it for medical advice. If in doubt, use caution and common sense.

DRYING RATES OF PIGMENTS IN OIL: TABLE 7.4

Table 7.4, page 203, presents a representative selection of the drying rates of pigments in oil; note that the drying rates and film qualities indicated in the table are only a guide, and that the drying rates are significant only in a linseed or poppyseed oil medium. Natural earth pigments are variable in drying rate and film quality, depending on the source of the ore and how carefully the ore is processed.

TABLE 7.1 **PIGMENTS**

ARTISTS' HUE	Yellow	Yellow	Yellow
COMMON NAME	**Arylide Yellow G Medium**	**Arylide Yellow 10G Light**	**Cadmium Yellow Light**
COLOUR INDEX **NAME, NUMBER**	PY 1 (11680)	PY 3 (11770)	PY 35 (77205)
GENERIC NAME	Acetoacetanilide AAA	Acetoacet-o-chloranilide	Cadmium Yellow
PROPRIETARY NAME(S)	Azo, Monoazo, Hansa G	Azo, Monoazo, Hansa 10G	
SYNONYM(S)	Hansa, Azo, Hansa G	Hansa, Azo, Hansa 10G	C.P. Cadmium Yellow
DATES/PLACE OF DISCOVERY	1909, Germany (?)	1911, Germany (?)	1840s
CHEMICAL CLASS; CONSTITUENTS	Organic; substituted anilines plus arylimides of acetocetic acid	Organic; substituted anilines plus arylimides of acetocetic acid	Inorganic; concentrated cadmium zinc sulfide
SOURCE	Synthetic organic	Synthetic organic	Processed mineral
TYPE	T, L, E	T, L, E	P, E (up to 15%)
RESISTANCE TO:			
Aliphatic Hydrocarbons	Fair	Poor	Excellent
Esters	Fair	Poor	Excellent
Ethanols	Fair	Poor	Excellent
Ketones	Fair	Poor	Excellent
Xylene	Fair	Poor	Excellent
Water	Good to Excellent (insoluble)	Good–Excellent (insoluble)	Very good
Linseed Oil	Excellent	Good	Excellent
HCl 5% (Acid)	Excellent	Excellent	Poor
Na$_2$CO$_3$ 5% (Alkali)	Excellent	Excellent	Good
Plasticizers	Excellent	Good	Excellent
Migration Through Dried Layers	NT	NT	Excellent
Soap Gel Bleeding	Excellent	Excellent	Excellent
MELTING POINT (°C)/ STABILITY TO °C	256/150, 20 minutes	258/150, 20 minutes	NT/Excellent
LIGHTFASTNESS (*CI*/ASTM D 4302)	VG/II	VG/II	EX/I
USE IN VEHICLES			
Oil; Oil Absorption; Drying Rate; Film Properties	✕; M; S; G	✕; M; S; G	EX; L; S; G
Acrylic Solution	✕	✕	✕
Acrylic Emulsion	✕	✕	✕
Transparent Watercolor	✕	✕	✕
Opaque Watercolor (Gouache)	✕	✕	✕
Temperas	✕	✕	✕
Casein	✕	✕	✕
Encaustic	✕	✕	✕
Frescos	✕	✕	NT
Experimentals/Pastel/Alkyds	✕ (test first)/✕/✕	✕ (test first)/✕/✕	✕/✕/✕
DRY REFRACTIVE INDEX	Medium	Medium	High
DRY CHARACTERISTICS	Bright Y, does not lose chroma when extended	Bright GY, does not lose chroma when extended	Bright Y → YR
HAZARDS	Avoid breathing dust	Avoid breathing dust	Avoid dust; do not heat—metal fumes toxic
OTHER COMMENTS	Used in all paints; may fade in weak tints; Hansa is a trade name (BASF Corporation) in Europe; may fade in weak tints	Slightly greenish Y, used to make bright green mixtures; Hansa is a trade name; may fade in weak tints	Used in all paints; sensitive to acidic environments; can be replaced by the cadmium-barium form

154

TABLE 7.1 PIGMENTS (continued)

ARTISTS' HUE	Yellow	Yellow	Yellow
COMMON NAME	**Cadmium-Barium Yellow Light**	**Cadmium-Barium Yellow** (Med, Dp)	**Cadmium Yellow** (Lt, Med Dp)
COLOUR INDEX NAME, NUMBER	PY 35:1 (77205:1)	PY 37:1 (77199)	PY 37 (77199)
GENERIC NAME	Cadmium-Barium Yellow Light	Cadmium-Barium Yellow	Cadmium Yellow
PROPRIETARY NAME(S)			
SYNONYM(S)			C.P. Cadmium Yellow (Chemically Pure)
DATES/PLACE OF DISCOVERY	1927	1927	1840s
CHEMICAL CLASS; CONSTITUENTS	Inorganic; cadmium zinc sulfide co-precipitated with barium sulfate	Inorganic; cadmium sulfide co-precipitated with barium sulfate	Inorganic; concentrated cadmium sulfide (CC)
SOURCE	Processed mineral	Processed mineral	Processed mineral
TYPE	P, E	P, E	P, E (up to 15%)
RESISTANCE TO:			
Aliphatic Hydrocarbons	Excellent	Excellent	Excellent
Esters	Excellent	Excellent	Excellent
Ethanols	Excellent	Excellent	Excellent
Ketones	Excellent	Excellent	Excellent
Xylene	Excellent	Excellent	Excellent
Water	Very good	Excellent	Very good
Linseed Oil	Excellent	Excellent	Excellent
HCl 5% (Acid)	Poor	Poor	Poor
Na_2CO_3 5% (Alkali)	Good	Good	Good
Plasticizers	Excellent	Excellent	Excellent
Migration Through Dried Layers	Excellent	Excellent	Excellent
Soap Gel Bleeding	Excellent	Excellent	Excellent
MELTING POINT (°C)/ STABILITY TO °C	NT/Excellent	NT/Excellent	NT/Excellent
LIGHTFASTNESS (*CI*/ASTM D 4302)	EX/I	EX/I	EX/I
USE IN VEHICLES			
Oil; Oil Absorption; Drying Rate; Film Properties	EX; L; S; G	✕; L; S; G	EX; L; S; G
Acrylic Solution	✕	✕	✕
Acrylic Emulsion	✕	✕	✕
Transparent Watercolor	✕	✕	✕ sensitive to acid/H_2O
Opaque Watercolor (Gouache)	✕	✕	✕
Temperas	✕	✕	✕
Casein	✕	✕	✕
Encaustic	✕	✕	✕
Frescos	NT	NT	NT
Experimentals/Pastel/Alkyds	✕/✕/✕	✕/✕/✕	✕/✕/✕
DRY REFRACTIVE INDEX	High	High	High
DRY CHARACTERISTICS	Bright Y → YR	Bright Y → YR	Bright Y → YR
HAZARDS	Same as PY 35	Avoid dust; do not heat— metal fumes toxic	Avoid dust; do not heat— metal fumes toxic
OTHER COMMENTS	Same as PY 35	Used in all paints; dense; not as expensive as pure (CP) cadmium	Used in all paints; sensitive to acidic environments; expensive, can be replaced by the cadmium-barium form without loss of chroma

TABLE 7.1 **PIGMENTS** *(continued)*

ARTISTS' HUE	Yellow	Yellow	Yellow
COMMON NAME	**Aureolin**	**Naples Yellow**	**Mars Orange**
COLOUR INDEX **NAME, NUMBER**	PY 40 (77357)	PY 41 (77589) (77588)	PY 42 (77492)
GENERIC NAME	Aureolin	Naples Yellow	Orange iron oxide
PROPRIETARY NAME(S)	Fischer's Salt	(Naples Yellow Hue)	Mars Orange
SYNONYM(S)	Indian Yellow (condemned) Cobalt Yellow	Giallolino; Antimony; Merimee's; Jaune Brilliant	
DATES/PLACE OF DISCOVERY	1848	c. 600 B.C.; 1700s	1800s
CHEMICAL CLASS; CONSTITUENTS	Inorganic; cobalt potassium nitrate	Inorganic; lead antimoniate	Inorganic; hydrated iron oxide precipitated
SOURCE	Processed mineral	Natural inorganic, processed mineral	Synthetic inorganic, processed mineral
TYPE	P	P	P
RESISTANCE TO:			
Aliphatic Hydrocarbons	Excellent	Excellent	Excellent
Esters	Excellent	Excellent	Excellent
Ethanols	Excellent	Excellent	Excellent
Ketones	Excellent	Excellent	Excellent
Xylene	Excellent	Excellent	Excellent
Water	Good	Excellent	Excellent
Linseed Oil	Good	Excellent	Excellent
HCl 5% (Acid)	Poor (darkens)	Poor, decomposes	Poor
Na$_2$CO$_3$ 5% (Alkali)	Poor (darkens)	Excellent	Excellent
Plasticizers	Excellent	Excellent	Excellent
Migration Through Dried Layers	Excellent	Excellent	Excellent
Soap Gel Bleeding	Excellent	Excellent	Excellent
MELTING POINT (°C)/ STABILITY TO °C	NT/Poor	NT/Excellent	NT/ Fair → R at 100+
LIGHTFASTNESS (*CI*/ASTM D 4302)	EX/II (oil only)	EX/I (oil only)	EX/I
USE IN VEHICLES			
Oil; Oil Absorption; Drying Rate; Film Properties	EX; M; A; G	EX; M; G; G	EX; M; AV; EX
Acrylic Solution	✕, test first	NT	✕
Acrylic Emulsion	P	NW	✕
Transparent Watercolor	✕	NW	✕
Opaque Watercolor (Gouache)	✕	NW	✕
Temperas	✕	test first	✕
Casein	✕	NW	✕
Encaustic	✕	✕	✕
Frescos	P	NW	✕
Experimentals/Pastel/Alkyds	✕/✕, test first/✕	✕, test first/NO/✕	✕/✕/✕
DRY REFRACTIVE INDEX	Low	High	High
DRY CHARACTERISTICS	Bright, weak Y	Dull Y → YR → RY	Dull RY → YR
HAZARDS	Avoid dust	Toxic; avoid dust	Avoid dust (iron)
OTHER COMMENTS	Poor tinting strength; poor opacity; used in glass and porcelain painting; useful in glazes	Excellent pigment; contains lead and is not used dry; expensive, many imitations— check label for contents	Dense; opaque; useful pigment; origin of ''Mars'' uncertain

TABLE 7.1 PIGMENTS (*continued*)

ARTISTS' HUE	Yellow	Yellow	Yellow
COMMON NAME	**Mars Yellow**	**Yellow Ochre**	**Titanium Yellow**
COLOUR INDEX NAME, NUMBER	PY 42 (77492)	PY 43 (42) (77492)	PY 53 (77788)
GENERIC NAME	Yellow iron oxide	Yellow ochre	Nickel-titanate
PROPRIETARY NAME(S)	Mars Yellow; Yellow Oxide		Titanium Yellow; Titanium Golden
SYNONYM(S)			
DATES/PLACE OF DISCOVERY	1800s	Prehistoric	Modern
CHEMICAL CLASS; CONSTITUENTS	Inorganic; hydrated iron oxide precipitated	Inorganic; iron oxide	Inorganic; combined oxides of nickel, antimony, and titanium
SOURCE	Synthetic inorganic, processed mineral	Natural inorganic, processed mineral	Synthetic inorganic, processed mineral
TYPE	P	P	P
RESISTANCE TO:			
Aliphatic Hydrocarbons	Excellent	Excellent	Excellent
Esters	Excellent	Excellent	Excellent
Ethanols	Excellent	Excellent	Excellent
Ketones	Excellent	Excellent	Excellent
Xylene	Excellent	Excellent	Excellent
Water	Excellent	Excellent	Excellent
Linseed Oil	Excellent	Excellent	Excellent
HCl 5% (Acid)	Poor	Poor; dissolves	Excellent
Na_2CO_3 5% (Alkali)	Excellent	Excellent	Excellent
Plasticizers	Excellent	Excellent	Excellent
Migration Through Dried Layers	Excellent	Excellent	Excellent
Soap Gel Bleeding	Excellent	Excellent	Excellent
MELTING POINT (°C)/ STABILITY TO °C	NT/Fair → YR at 100+	NT/Fair → R at 100+	NT/950
LIGHTFASTNESS (*CI*/ASTM D 4302)	EX/I	EX/I	EX/I
USE IN VEHICLES			
Oil; Oil Absorption; Drying Rate; Film Properties	EX; M; AV; EX	EX; M; S; EX	×; M; A; G
Acrylic Solution	×	×	×
Acrylic Emulsion	×	×	×
Transparent Watercolor	×	×	×
Opaque Watercolor (Gouache)	×	×	×
Temperas	×	×	×
Casein	×	×	×
Encaustic	×	×	×
Frescos	×	×	×
Experimentals/Pastel/Alkyds	×/×/×	×/×/×	×/×/×
DRY REFRACTIVE INDEX	High	Medium → high	Medium
DRY CHARACTERISTICS	Dull Y	Dull RY → YBr → Y	Bright, slightly G, Y
HAZARDS	Avoid dust (iron)	Avoid dust (iron)	Avoid dust; nickel may be a sensitizer; do not heat
OTHER COMMENTS	Dense; opaque; useful pigment; origin of "Mars" uncertain	Excellent natural equivalent of Mars pigments; semi-opaque → opaque, depending on source	Useful all-round pigment

TABLE 7.1 **PIGMENTS** (*continued*)

ARTISTS' HUE	Yellow	Yellow	Yellow
COMMON NAME	**Arylide Yellow RN**	**Arylide Yellow GX**	**Arylide Yellow 5GX**
COLOUR INDEX NAME, NUMBER	PY 65 (11740)	PY 73 (11738)	PY 74LF (11741)
GENERIC NAME	2-nitro-p-anisidine-o-acetoacetanisidine	Acetoacet-o-anisidide	Acetoaceto-o-anisidine
PROPRIETARY NAME(S)	Hansa, Monoazo, Azo Arylide, Hansa RN	Hansa, Monoazo, Azo, Arylide, Hansa GX	Hansa, Monoazo, Azo, Arylide Yellow, Hansa 5GX
SYNONYM(S)			
DATES/PLACE OF DISCOVERY	Modern	Modern	Modern
CHEMICAL CLASS; CONSTITUENTS	Organic; complex organic "monoazo" compound	Organic; complex organic "monoazo" compound, AAOA coupling	Organic; complex organic "monoazo" compound, AAOA coupling
SOURCE	Synthetic organic	Synthetic organic	Synthetic organic
TYPE	L	L	L
RESISTANCE TO:			
Aliphatic Hydrocarbons	Fair	Fair	Very good
Esters	Very good	NT	Fair
Ethanols	NT	Very good .	Fair
Ketones	Poor	NT	NT
Xylene	Poor	Poor	Poor
Water	Fair	Good	Excellent
Linseed Oil	Poor	Poor	Very good
HCl 5% (Acid)	Excellent	Very good	Very good
Na₂CO₃ 5% (Alkali)	Excellent	Excellent	Very good
Plasticizers	NT	Poor	NT
Migration Through Dried Layers	Poor; bleeds	Poor; bleeds	NT
Soap Gel Bleeding	Good	NT	Slight
MELTING POINT (°C)/ STABILITY TO °C	NT/Fair to 150	264–268/Poor	293/Poor
LIGHTFASTNESS (*CI*/ASTM D 4302)	EX, G in tint/I	EX/I	VG/I
USE IN VEHICLES			
Oil; Oil Absorption; Drying Rate; Film Properties	✕; H; S; G	✕; H; S; G	✕; H; A; G
Acrylic Solution	✕	✕	✕
Acrylic Emulsion	✕	✕	✕
Transparent Watercolor	✕	✕	✕
Opaque Watercolor (Gouache)	✕	✕	✕
Temperas	✕	✕	✕
Casein	✕	✕	✕
Encaustic	✕	✕	✕
Frescos	✕	✕	✕
Experimentals/Pastel/Alkyds	✕/✕/✕	✕/✕/✕	✕/✕/✕
DRY REFRACTIVE INDEX	Low	Low	Low
DRY CHARACTERISTICS	Bright RY	Bright Y	Bright Y
HAZARDS	Avoid dust	Avoid dust	Avoid dust
OTHER COMMENTS	Paint Standard test for lightfastness only; CI lists poor resistance to solvents, water, oil; test for artists' paints before use; used in industrial oil vehicles, exterior latex paints	Paint Standard test for lightfastness only; CI lists poor resistance to solvents, oil, migration; test before use in artists' paints; used in industrial, architectural paints, printing inks, rubber	Paint Standard test for lightfastness only; CI lists fair resistance to solvents; test in vehicles first; used in industrial paints, printing inks

TABLE 7.1 **PIGMENTS** (*continued*)

ARTISTS' HUE	Yellow	Yellow	Yellow
COMMON NAME	**Diarylide Yellow HR70**	**Arylide Yellow FGL**	**Arylide Yellow 10GX**
COLOUR INDEX **NAME, NUMBER**	PY 83 (21108)	PY 97 (11767)	PY 98 (11727)
GENERIC NAME	Diazo yellow	Sulfamide azo	Arylide Yellow
PROPRIETARY NAME(S)	Various	Various	Hansa
SYNONYM(S)			
DATES/PLACE OF DISCOVERY	Modern	Modern	Modern
CHEMICAL CLASS; CONSTITUENTS	Organic; complex organic "diazo" compound	Organic; complex organic "monoazo" compound	Organic; 4-chloro-2-nitro-aniline coupled with 5-chloro-2-metho-acetoacetaniline
SOURCE	Synthetic organic	Synthetic organic	Synthetic organic
TYPE	L	L	L
RESISTANCE TO:			
Aliphatic Hydrocarbons	NT	Fair/Good	Good
Esters	NT	Fair	NT
Ethanols	Very good	Fair/Good	NT
Ketones	NT	Poor	NT
Xylene	Good	Poor	NT
Water	NT	Fair/Good	Excellent
Linseed Oil	NT	Fair	Good
HCl 5% (Acid)	NT	Good	NT
Na$_2$CO$_3$ 5% (Alkali)	Good	Good	NT
Plasticizers	NT	Poor/Fair	NT
Migration Through Dried Layers	NT	Good	NT
Soap Gel Bleeding	Good	Good	NT
MELTING POINT (°C)/ STABILITY TO °C	NT/200	NT/200	NT/NT
LIGHTFASTNESS (*CI*/ASTM D 4302)	VG/I	G/I	NT/II (oil), I (acrylic)
USE IN VEHICLES			
Oil; Oil Absorption; Drying Rate; Film Properties	✕; H; A; G	✕; H; A; G	✕; H; A; G
Acrylic Solution	NT	NT	NT
Acrylic Emulsion	✕	✕	✕
Transparent Watercolor	NT	NT	✕
Opaque Watercolor (Gouache)	NT	NT	✕
Temperas	NT	NT	✕
Casein	NT	NT	✕
Encaustic	NT	NT	✕
Frescos	NT	NT	NT
Experimentals/Pastel/Alkyds	NT/NT/NT	NT/NT/NT	NT; ✕; ✕
DRY REFRACTIVE INDEX	Low	Low	Low
DRY CHARACTERISTICS	RY	Bright Y	Bright Y
HAZARDS	Avoid dust	Avoid dust	Avoid dust
OTHER COMMENTS	Paint Standard test for lightfastness only; test before use; used in printing inks, some paints, lacquers	Poor resistance; test first; used in printing inks, acrylic emulsion paints, and watercolor paints	Paint Standard test for lightfastness only; test for solubility before use

TABLE 7.1 **PIGMENTS** *(continued)*

ARTISTS' HUE	Yellow	Yellow	Yellow
COMMON NAME	**Anthrapyrimidine Yellow**	**Isoindolinone Yellow G**	**Isoindolinone Yellow R**
COLOUR INDEX **NAME, NUMBER**	PY 108 (68420)	PY 109; n/a	PY 110; n/a
GENERIC NAME	Anthrapyrimidine	Tetrachloroisoindolinone	Tetrachloroisoindolinone
PROPRIETARY NAME(S)			
SYNONYM(S)			
DATES/PLACE OF DISCOVERY	Modern	Modern	Modern
CHEMICAL CLASS; CONSTITUENTS	Organic; anthraquinone derivative	Organic; isoindolinone derivative	Organic; isoindolinone derivative
SOURCE	Synthetic organic	Synthetic organic	Synthetic organic
TYPE	L	L	L
RESISTANCE TO:			
Aliphatic Hydrocarbons	Good	NT	NT
Esters	NT	NT	NT
Ethanols	Good	NT	NT
Ketones	NT	NT	NT
Xylene	Good	NT	NT
Water	Very good	NT	NT
Linseed Oil	NT	NT	NT
HCl 5% (Acid)	Good	NT	NT
Na$_2$CO$_3$ 5% (Alkali)	Good	NT	NT
Plasticizers	NT	NT	NT
Migration Through Dried Layers	NT	NT	NT
Soap Gel Bleeding	NT	NT	NT
MELTING POINT (°C)/ STABILITY TO °C	NT/NT	NT/Fair	NT/Fair
LIGHTFASTNESS (*CI***/ASTM D 4302)**	EX, G (tint)/I	VG/I	VG/I
USE IN VEHICLES			
Oil; Oil Absorption; Drying Rate; Film Properties	×; H; A; G	×; H; A; G	×; H; A; G
Acrylic Solution	×	NT	NT
Acrylic Emulsion	×	×	×
Transparent Watercolor	×	NT	NT
Opaque Watercolor (Gouache)	×	NT	NT
Temperas	×	NT	NT
Casein	×	NT	NT
Encaustic	×	NT	NT
Frescos	×	NT	NT
Experimentals/Pastel/Alkyds	×/×/×	NT/NT/NT	NT/NT/NT
DRY REFRACTIVE INDEX	Low	Low	Low
DRY CHARACTERISTICS	Y	GY	RY
HAZARDS	Avoid dust	Avoid dust	Avoid dust
OTHER COMMENTS	Paint Standard test for lightfastness only; test before use; used in paints, printing inks, vinyl plastics, synthetic fibers	Tested for light stability only; test before use; used in most industrial paints	Same as PY 109

TABLE 7.1 PIGMENTS *(continued)*

ARTISTS' HUE	Yellow	Yellow	Yellow
COMMON NAME	**Flavanthrone Yellow**	**Quinophthalone Yellow**	**Isoindoline Yellow**
COLOUR INDEX NAME, NUMBER	PY 112 (70600)	PY 138; n/a	PY 139; n/a
GENERIC NAME	Flavanthrone	Quinophthalone	Isoindoline
PROPRIETARY NAME(S)	Various	Various	Various
SYNONYM(S)			
DATES/PLACE OF DISCOVERY	Modern	Modern	Modern
CHEMICAL CLASS; CONSTITUENTS	Organic; anthraquinone derivative	Organic; anthraquinone derivative (?)	Organic; isoindolinone
SOURCE	Synthetic organic	Synthetic organic	Synthetic organic
TYPE	L	L	L
RESISTANCE TO:			
Aliphatic Hydrocarbons	NT	NT	NT
Esters	NT	NT	NT
Ethanols	Good	NT	NT
Ketones	Good	NT	NT
Xylene	Very good	NT	NT
Water	Good	NT	NT
Linseed Oil	Excellent (Good in oleic acid)	NT	NT
HCl 5% (Acid)	Good	NT	NT
Na$_2$CO$_3$ 5% (Alkali)	Good	NT	NT
Plasticizers	NT	NT	NT
Migration Through Dried Layers	NT	NT	NT
Soap Gel Bleeding	Good	NT	NT
MELTING POINT (°C)/ STABILITY TO °C	NT/Darkens at 260	NT/NT	NT/NT
LIGHTFASTNESS (*CI*/ASTM D 4302)	EX, G (tint)/I	NT/I	NT/I
USE IN VEHICLES			
Oil; Oil Absorption; Drying Rate; Film Properties	×; H; A; G	×; H; A; G	×; H; A; G
Acrylic Solution	×	NT	NT
Acrylic Emulsion	×	×	×
Transparent Watercolor	×	NT	NT
Opaque Watercolor (Gouache)	×	NT	NT
Temperas	×	NT	NT
Casein	×	NT	NT
Encaustic	×	NT	NT
Frescos	F	NT	NT
Experimentals/Pastel/Alkyds	G/Y/Y	NT/NT/NT	NT/NT/NT
DRY REFRACTIVE INDEX	Low	Low	Low
DRY CHARACTERISTICS	RY	Dull Y	Y
HAZARDS	Avoid dust	Avoid dust	Avoid dust
OTHER COMMENTS	Good pigment; test before use; used in paints; printing inks, vinyl, polyolefin plastics	Paint Standard test for lightfastness only; test before use	Paint Standard test for lightfastness only; test before use

TABLE 7.1 **PIGMENTS** (*continued*)

ARTISTS' HUE	Yellow	Yellow	Yellow
COMMON NAME	**Nickel Azo Yellow**	**Benzimidazolone Yellow H4G**	**Nickel Dioxine Yellow**
COLOUR INDEX NAME, NUMBER	PY 150; n/a	PY 151; n/a	PY 153; n/a
GENERIC NAME	Nickel complex Azo	Benzimidazolone	Nickel complex Azo
PROPRIETARY NAME(S)	Various	Various	Various
SYNONYM(S)			
DATES/PLACE OF DISCOVERY	Modern	Modern	Modern
CHEMICAL CLASS; CONSTITUENTS	Organic; complex nickel salts (?)	Organic; benzimidazolone	Organic; benzimidazolone
SOURCE	Synthetic organic; synthetic inorganic	Synthetic organic	Synthetic organic
TYPE	P, L	L	L
RESISTANCE TO:			
Aliphatic Hydrocarbons	NT	NT	NT
Esters	NT	NT	NT
Ethanols	NT	NT	NT
Ketones	NT	NT	NT
Xylene	NT	NT	NT
Water	NT	NT	NT
Linseed Oil	NT	NT	NT
HCl 5% (Acid)	NT	NT	NT
Na_2CO_3 5% (Alkali)	NT	NT	NT
Plasticizers	NT	NT	NT
Migration Through Dried Layers	NT	NT	NT
Soap Gel Bleeding	NT	NT	NT
MELTING POINT (°C)/ STABILITY TO °C	NT/NT	NT/NT	NT/NT
LIGHTFASTNESS (*CI*/ASTM D 4302)	NT/I	NT/I	NT/I
USE IN VEHICLES			
Oil; Oil Absorption; Drying Rate; Film Properties	×; H; A; G	×; H; A; G	×; H; A; G
Acrylic Solution	NT	NT	NT
Acrylic Emulsion	×	×	×
Transparent Watercolor	NT	NT	NT
Opaque Watercolor (Gouache)	NT	NT	NT
Temperas	NT	NT	NT
Casein	NT	NT	NT
Encaustic	NT	NT	NT
Frescos	NT	NT	NT
Experimentals/Pastel/Alkyds	NT/NT/NT	NT/NT/NT	NT/NT/NT
DRY REFRACTIVE INDEX	Low	Low	Low
DRY CHARACTERISTICS	Y	Y	Y
HAZARDS	Nickel may sensitize skin; avoid dust	Avoid dust	Nickel may sensitize skin; avoid dust
OTHER COMMENTS	Paint Standard test for lightfastness only; test before use	Paint Standard test for lightfastness only; test before use	Paint Standard test for lightfastness only; test before use

TABLE 7.1 **PIGMENTS** *(continued)*

ARTISTS' HUE	Yellow	Yellow	Yellow
COMMON NAME	**Benzimidazolone Yellow H3G**	**Benzimidazolone Yellow HLR**	**Benzimidazolone Yellow H6G**
COLOUR INDEX NAME, NUMBER	PY 154; n/a	PY 156; n/a	PY 175; n/a
GENERIC NAME	Benzimidazolone H3G	Benzimidazolone HLR	Benzimidazolone H6G
PROPRIETARY NAME(S)	Various	Various	Various
SYNONYM(S)			
DATES/PLACE OF DISCOVERY	Modern	Modern	Modern
CHEMICAL CLASS; CONSTITUENTS	Organic; benzimidazolone	Organic; benzimidazolone	Organic; benzimidazolone
SOURCE	Synthetic organic	Synthetic organic	Synthetic organic
TYPE	L	L	L
RESISTANCE TO:			
Aliphatic Hydrocarbons	NT	NT	NT
Esters	NT	NT	NT
Ethanols	NT	NT	NT
Ketones	NT	NT	NT
Xylene	NT	NT	NT
Water	NT	NT	NT
Linseed Oil	NT	NT	NT
HCl 5% (Acid)	NT	NT	NT
Na$_2$CO$_3$ 5% (Alkali)	NT	NT	NT
Plasticizers	NT	NT	NT
Migration Through Dried Layers	NT	NT	NT
Soap Gel Bleeding	NT	NT	NT
MELTING POINT (°C)/ STABILITY TO °C	NT/NT	NT/NT	NT/NT
LIGHTFASTNESS (*CI*/ASTM D 4302)	NT/I	NT/I	NT/I
USE IN VEHICLES			
Oil; Oil Absorption; Drying Rate; Film Properties	×; H; A; G	×; H; A; G	NT
Acrylic Solution	NT	NT	NT
Acrylic Emulsion	×	×	NT
Transparent Watercolor	NT	NT	NT
Opaque Watercolor (Gouache)	NT	NT	NT
Temperas	NT	NT	NT
Casein	NT	NT	NT
Encaustic	NT	NT	NT
Frescos	NT	NT	NT
Experimentals/Pastel/Alkyds	NT/NT/NT	NT/NT/NT	NT/NT/NT
DRY REFRACTIVE INDEX	Low	NT	Low
DRY CHARACTERISTICS	Y	Y	Y
HAZARDS	Nickel may sensitize skin; avoid dust	NT	NT
OTHER COMMENTS	Paint Standard test for lightfastness only; test before use		

TABLE 7.1 PIGMENTS (*continued*)

ARTISTS' HUE	Yellow	Orange	Orange
COMMON NAME	**Arylide Yellow 5GLA**	**Dinitraniline Orange (SM)**	**Cadmium-Barium Orange**
COLOUR INDEX NAME, NUMBER	n/a	PO 5 (12075)	PO 20:1 (77196/77199/77202:1)
GENERIC NAME	Hansa, mixed couplings	Dinitraniline	Cadmium-Barium Orange
PROPRIETARY NAME(S)	Various (Yellow 5GLA)	Various	Cadmium-Barium Orange
SYNONYM(S)		Azo Orange	Cadmium-Barium Orange
DATES/PLACE OF DISCOVERY	Modern	Modern	1920s
CHEMICAL CLASS; CONSTITUENTS	Organic; acetacetarylide, mixed couplings	Organic; "monoazo"	Inorganic; cadmium sulfoselenide co-precipitated with barium sulfate
SOURCE	Synthetic organic	Synthetic organic	Natural inorganic; processed mineral
TYPE	L	L	P, E
RESISTANCE TO:			
Aliphatic Hydrocarbons	NT	Fair, Poor	Excellent
Esters	NT	Poor	Excellent
Ethanols	NT	Poor	Excellent
Ketones	NT	Poor	Excellent
Xylene	NT	Poor	Excellent
Water	NT	Very good	Excellent
Linseed Oil	NT	Very good	Excellent
HCl 5% (Acid)	NT	Good	Poor; sensitive with heat
Na$_2$CO$_3$ 5% (Alkali)	NT	Good	Excellent
Plasticizers	NT	Fair, Good	Excellent
Migration Through Dried Layers	NT	Fair, Good	Excellent
Soap Gel Bleeding	NT	Fair, Good	Excellent
MELTING POINT (°C)/ STABILITY TO °C	NT/NT	302/150	NT/260
LIGHTFASTNESS (*CI*/ASTM D 4302)	NT/II (oil), I (acrylic)	F/II	EX/I
USE IN VEHICLES			
Oil; Oil Absorption; Drying Rate; Film Properties	×; H; A; G	×; H; A; G	×; M; S; G
Acrylic Solution	NT	NT	×
Acrylic Emulsion	×	×	×
Transparent Watercolor	NT	×, NT	×, sensitive to acid
Opaque Watercolor (Gouache)	NT	×, NT	×, sensitive to acid
Temperas	NT	×	×
Casein	NT	×	×
Encaustic	NT	×	×
Frescos	NT	NT	×
Experimentals/Pastel/Alkyds	NT/NT/NT	NT/×/×	NT/×/×
DRY REFRACTIVE INDEX	Low	Low	High
DRY CHARACTERISTICS	Bright Y	O	YO → RO
HAZARDS	Avoid dust	Avoid dust	Do not heat; Cd fumes toxic
OTHER COMMENTS	Paint Standard test for lightfastness only; test before use	Paint Standard test for lightfastness only; test before use; used in paints, printing inks, emulsions, alkyd enamels, lacquers, paper, cloth, linoleum, rubber, styrenes, waxes	Excellent pigment; less expensive than pure Cadmium Orange

TABLE 7.1 PIGMENTS (*continued*)

ARTISTS' HUE	Orange	Orange	Orange
COMMON NAME	**Cadmium Orange (CC)**	**Cadmium-Barium Vermilion Orange**	**Cadmium Vermilion Orange**
COLOUR INDEX **NAME, NUMBER**	PO 20 (77196/77199/77202)	PO23:1 (77201:1)	PO 23 (77201)
GENERIC NAME	Cadmium Orange	Cadmium Mercury Orange	Cadmium Mercury Orange
PROPRIETARY NAME(S)	Cadmium Orange	Various	
SYNONYM(S)	Cadmium Orange	Various	
DATES/PLACE OF DISCOVERY	1840s	Modern	Modern
CHEMICAL CLASS; CONSTITUENTS	Inorganic; concentrated cadmium sulfoselenide	Inorganic; cadmium mercury sulfide co-precipitated with barium sulfate	Inorganic; concentrated cadmium sulfide plus mercuric sulfide
SOURCE	Natural inorganic; processed mineral	Natural inorganic; processed mineral	Natural inorganic; processed mineral
TYPE	P, E (up to 15%)	P, E	P
RESISTANCE TO:			
Aliphatic Hydrocarbons	Excellent	Excellent	Excellent
Esters	Excellent	Excellent	Excellent
Ethanols	Excellent	Excellent	Excellent
Ketones	Excellent	Excellent	Excellent
Xylene	Excellent	Excellent	Excellent
Water	Excellent	Excellent	Excellent
Linseed Oil	Excellent	Excellent	Excellent
HCl 5% (Acid)	Poor; sensitive with heat	Poor; sensitive with heat	Poor; sensitive with heat
Na_2CO_3 5% (Alkali)	Excellent	Excellent	Excellent
Plasticizers	Excellent	Excellent	Excellent
Migration Through Dried Layers	Excellent	Excellent	Excellent
Soap Gel Bleeding	Excellent	Excellent	Excellent
MELTING POINT (°C)/ STABILITY TO °C	NT/260	NT/260	NT/260
LIGHTFASTNESS (*CI*/ASTM D 4302)	EX/I	EX/I	EX/I
USE IN VEHICLES			
Oil; Oil Absorption; Drying Rate; Film Properties	×; M; S; G	×; M; S; G	×; M; S; G
Acrylic Solution	×	×	×
Acrylic Emulsion	×	×	×
Transparent Watercolor	×, sensitive to acid	×, sensitive to acid	Sensitive to acid
Opaque Watercolor (Gouache)	×, sensitive to acid	×, sensitive to acid	Sensitive to acid
Temperas	×	×	×
Casein	×	×	×
Encaustic	×	×	×
Frescos	×	×	×
Experimentals/Pastel/Alkyds	NT/×/×	NT/×/×	×/×/×
DRY REFRACTIVE INDEX	High	High	High
DRY CHARACTERISTICS	YO → RO	YO → RO	YO → RO
HAZARDS	Do not heat; Cd fumes toxic	Potential: mercury; do not heat; Cd fumes toxic	Potential: mercury; do not heat, Cd fumes toxic
OTHER COMMENTS	Excellent pigment; expensive	Excellent pigment; may darken if not encased in protective binder or poorly processed (exposure to polluted atmosphere may darken mercury content)	Excellent pigment; may darken if not encased in protective binder or poorly processed (exposure to polluted atmosphere may darken mercury content)

TABLE 7.1 PIGMENTS (continued)

ARTISTS' HUE	Orange	Orange	Orange
COMMON NAME	**Benzimidazolone Orange HL**	**Perinone Orange**	**Quinacridone Gold**
COLOUR INDEX NAME, NUMBER	PO 36 (11780)	PO 43 (71105)	PO 48; n/a
GENERIC NAME	Benzimidazolone HL	Perinone	Quinacridone
PROPRIETARY NAME(S)	Various (Azo Orange)	Various	Various
SYNONYM(S)			
DATES/PLACE OF DISCOVERY	Modern	Modern	Modern
CHEMICAL CLASS; CONSTITUENTS	Organic; "monoazo" compound	Organic; anthraquinone derivative	Organic; "linear quinacridone" (unspecified derivative)
SOURCE	Synthetic organic	Synthetic organic	Synthetic organic
TYPE	L	L	L
RESISTANCE TO:			
Aliphatic Hydrocarbons	Very good	NT	NT
Esters	Fair, Good	NT	NT
Ethanols	Fair, Good	Very good	NT
Ketones	Fair	NT	NT
Xylene	Very good	Very good	NT
Water	Very good	Very good	NT
Linseed Oil	NT	Very good	NT
HCl 5% (Acid)	Very good	NT	NT
Na_2CO_3 5% (Alkali)	Very good	NT	NT
Plasticizers	NT	NT	NT
Migration Through Dried Layers	Very good	NT	NT
Soap Gel Bleeding	Very good	Very good	NT
MELTING POINT (°C)/ STABILITY TO °C	NT/G	NT/200	NT
LIGHTFASTNESS (*CI*/ASTM D 4302)	G–EX/I	NT/I	NT/I
USE IN VEHICLES			
Oil; Oil Absorption; Drying Rate; Film Properties	×; H; A; G	×; H; A; G	×; H; A; G
Acrylic Solution	G	NT	NT
Acrylic Emulsion	×	×	×
Transparent Watercolor	×	×	NT
Opaque Watercolor (Gouache)	×	×	NT
Temperas	×	×	NT
Casein	×	×	NT
Encaustic	×	×	NT
Frescos	×	×	NT
Experimentals/Pastel/Alkyds	×/×/×	×/×/×	NT/NT/×
DRY REFRACTIVE INDEX	Low	Low	Low
DRY CHARACTERISTICS	O	O	YO → O → RO
HAZARDS	Avoid dust	Avoid dust	Avoid dust
OTHER COMMENTS	Paint Standard test for lightfastness only; test for solubility before use; used in paints, printing inks, plastics	Used in paints, printing inks, vinyl, and polyolefin plastics	Paint Standard test for lightfastness only; test before use

TABLE 7.1 **PIGMENTS** (*continued*)

ARTISTS' HUE	Orange	Orange	Orange
COMMON NAME	**Quinacridone Deep Gold**	**Benzimidazolone Orange HGL**	**Benzimidazolone Orange**
COLOUR INDEX NAME, NUMBER	PO 49; n/a	PO 60; n/a	PO 62; n/a
GENERIC NAME	Quinacridone	Benzimidazolone	Benzimidazolone
PROPRIETARY NAME(S)	Various	Various (Azo Orange)	Various; Orange H5G
SYNONYM(S)			
DATES/PLACE OF DISCOVERY	Modern	Modern	Modern
CHEMICAL CLASS; CONSTITUENTS	Organic; "linear quinacridone" (unspecified derivative)	Organic; "monoazo" compound	Organic; acetoacetyl "aniline derivative"
SOURCE	Synthetic organic	Synthetic organic	Synthetic organic
TYPE	L	L	L
RESISTANCE TO:			
Aliphatic Hydrocarbons	NT	Very good	Excellent
Esters	NT	Fair, Good	NT
Ethanols	NT	Fair, Good	Excellent
Ketones	NT	Fair	Good
Xylene	NT	Very good	Good
Water	NT	Very good	Excellent
Linseed Oil	NT	NT	Excellent
HCl 5% (Acid)	NT	Very good	Excellent
Na_2CO_3 5% (Alkali)	NT	Very good	Excellent
Plasticizers	NT	NT	NT
Migration Through Dried Layers	NT	Very good	NT
Soap Gel Bleeding	NT	Very good	Good
MELTING POINT (°C)/ STABILITY TO °C	NT	NT/Good	330/about 55
LIGHTFASTNESS (*CI*/ASTM D 4302)	NT/I	G-EX/I	EX/I
USE IN VEHICLES			
Oil; Oil Absorption; Drying Rate; Film Properties	×; H; A; G	×; H; A; G	×; M; A; G
Acrylic Solution	NT	G	NT
Acrylic Emulsion	×	×	×
Transparent Watercolor	NT	×	×
Opaque Watercolor (Gouache)	NT	×	×
Temperas	NT	×	×
Casein	NT	×	×
Encaustic	NT	×	×
Frescos	NT	×	×
Experimentals/Pastel/Alkyds	NT/NT/×	×/×/×	NT/×/×
DRY REFRACTIVE INDEX	Low	Low	Medium
DRY CHARACTERISTICS			O
HAZARDS	Avoid dust	Avoid dust	Avoid dust
OTHER COMMENTS	Paint Standard test for lightfastness only; test before use	Paint Standard test for lightfastness only; test for solubility before use; used in paints, printing inks, plastics	

167

TABLE 7.1 **PIGMENTS** (*continued*)

ARTISTS' HUE	Red	Red	Red
COMMON NAME	**Naphthol, ITR**	**Naphthol, AS-TR**	**Natural Madder Lake**
COLOUR INDEX **NAME, NUMBER**	PR 5 (12490)	PR 7 (12420)	NR 9 (Natural Red 9) (75330/75420)
GENERIC NAME	Naphthol, ITR coupling	Naphthol, AS-TR coupling	Madder Lake
PROPRIETARY NAME(S)	Naphthol Carmine FB	Naphthol Crimson	Rose Madder
SYNONYM(S)			Various
DATES/PLACE OF DISCOVERY	Modern	Modern	1826
CHEMICAL CLASS; CONSTITUENTS	Organic; "monoazo"; 3-Hydroxy-2-naphthanilide	Organic; "monoazo"	Organic; ground root of *Rubia tinctorum* on alumina base
SOURCE	Synthetic organic	Synthetic organic	Natural organic
TYPE	L	L	L, E
RESISTANCE TO:			
Aliphatic Hydrocarbons	Excellent	Excellent	Good
Esters	NT	NT	NT
Ethanols	Fair	Fair	Good
Ketones	Poor	Poor	NT
Xylene	Fair	Fair	NT
Water	Excellent	Excellent	Good
Linseed Oil	Very good	Very good	Excellent
HCl 5% (Acid)	Excellent	Excellent	NT
Na$_2$CO$_3$ 5% (Alkali)	Excellent	Excellent	Poor (turns violet)
Plasticizers	NT	NT	Good
Migration Through Dried Layers	NT	NT	Good
Soap Gel Bleeding	Excellent	Excellent	Good
MELTING POINT (°C)/ STABILITY TO °C	306, decomposes/160	NT/NT	NT/300 (darkens)
LIGHTFASTNESS (*CI*/ASTM D 4302)	VG/II	EX/I	F/II (oil only)
USE IN VEHICLES			
Oil; Oil Absorption; Drying Rate; Film Properties	F; M; A; G	×; M; A; G	VG; M; A; G
Acrylic Solution	F	F	NT
Acrylic Emulsion	F	×	NT
Transparent Watercolor	NT	NT	VG
Opaque Watercolor (Gouache)	NT	NT	VG
Temperas	NT	NT	VG
Casein	NT	NT	NT
Encaustic	NT	NT	VG
Frescos	NT	NT	P
Experimentals/Pastel/Alkyds	NT/NT/NT	NT/NT/NT	NT/G/VG
DRY REFRACTIVE INDEX	Medium	Medium	Low
DRY CHARACTERISTICS	Bright BR	Bright R	YR → BR
HAZARDS	Avoid dust	Avoid dust	Avoid dust
OTHER COMMENTS	Only fair lightfastness; used in printing inks, emulsions, rubber, linoleum	Better lightfastness than PR 5	Absolute minimum lightfastness; formerly thought to be less lightfast than Alizarin crimson; useful colorant

TABLE 7.1 **PIGMENTS** *(continued)*

ARTISTS' HUE	Red	Red	Red
COMMON NAME	**Naphthol, AS-OL**	**Napthol, AS-D**	**Alizarin Crimson**
COLOUR INDEX **NAME, NUMBER**	PR 9 (12460)	PR 14 (12380)	PR 83 (58000:1)
GENERIC NAME	Naphthol Red FRLL	Napthol Red FGR	Alizarin Crimson
PROPRIETARY NAME(S)	Permanent Red FRLL	Permanent Bordeaux FGR	Various
SYNONYM(S)	Various	Various	Alizarin Crimson
DATES/PLACE OF DISCOVERY	Modern	Modern	1869; first synthesis of a natural organic colorant
CHEMICAL CLASS; CONSTITUENTS	Organic; "monoazo": same as PR 7, with a different coupling	Organic; "monoazo": same as PR 7, with a different coupling	Organic; 1:2 dihydroxy-anthraquinone on alumina base
SOURCE	Synthetic organic	Synthetic organic	Synthetic organic
TYPE	L	L	L
RESISTANCE TO:			
Aliphatic Hydrocarbons	Poor	Fair	Good
Esters	Poor	NT	NT
Ethanols	Poor	Fair	Good
Ketones	Poor	Fair	NT
Xylene	Poor	Fair	NT
Water	Good to Very good	Excellent	Good
Linseed Oil	Fair	Good	Excellent
HCl 5% (Acid)	Good	Excellent	NT
Na$_2$CO$_3$ 5% (Alkali)	Very good	Excellent	Poor (turns violet)
Plasticizers	Fair to Good	Good	Good
Migration Through Dried Layers	NT	Very good	Good
Soap Gel Bleeding	Poor	Good	Good
MELTING POINT (°C)/ STABILITY TO °C	280/150	NT/140	NT/300 (darkens)
LIGHTFASTNESS (*CI*/ASTM D 4302)	VG (full strength)/I (acrylic), II (oil)	G/II	F–P/III
USE IN VEHICLES			
Oil; Oil Absorption; Drying Rate; Film Properties	VG; H; A; G	VG; M-H; A; G	F; H; S; F
Acrylic Solution	P	P	P
Acrylic Emulsion	EX	VG	P
Transparent Watercolor	G	VG	F
Opaque Watercolor (Gouache)	G	VG	F
Temperas	NT	VG	F
Casein	G	VG	P
Encaustic	NT	VG	F
Frescos	NT (P)	VG	P
Experimentals/Pastel/Alkyds	NT/F/P	NT/F/VG	NT/F/F
DRY REFRACTIVE INDEX	Medium	Medium	Low
DRY CHARACTERISTICS	Bright YR	BR	YR → BR
HAZARDS	Avoid dust	Avoid dust	Avoid dust
OTHER COMMENTS	Poor lightfastness in tints with white; poor resistance to organic solvents; not used in exterior paints; used in printing inks, paper, linoleum	Minimum lightfastness; poor solvent resistance; not used in exterior paints; used in printing inks, latex interior paints, paper, paper coatings	Less than absolute minimum lightfastness; useful hue and character

TABLE 7.1 PIGMENTS (continued)

ARTISTS' HUE	Red	Red	Red
COMMON NAME	**Thioindigoid Red**	**Indian Red**	**Light (or English) Red Oxide**
***COLOUR INDEX* NAME, NUMBER**	PR 88 MRS (73312)	PR 101 (77491) (015/492/538)	PR 101 (77491) (015/492/538)
GENERIC NAME	Indigoid	Indian Red, bluish	Light Red Oxide, yellowish
PROPRIETARY NAME(S)	Various; Permanent Red Violet MRS	Various (Indian Red)	English Red, Spanish Red
SYNONYM(S)	Various	Light Red (Yellowish/ Bluish), Red Iron Oxide	Earth Red
DATES/PLACE OF DISCOVERY	Modern	Natural, ancient; synthetic, modern	Ancient → 1800s
CHEMICAL CLASS; CONSTITUENTS	Organic; acetic acid heated with concentrated sulfuric or chlorosulfonic acid	Inorganic; iron oxide prepared from pulverized iron ore	Inorganic; iron oxide prepared from pulverized iron ore
SOURCE	Synthetic organic	Natural inorganic; processed mineral	Natural inorganic; processed mineral
TYPE	L	P	P
RESISTANCE TO:			
Aliphatic Hydrocarbons	Excellent	Excellent	Excellent
Esters	NT	Excellent	Excellent
Ethanols	Good	Excellent	Excellent
Ketones	NT	Excellent	Excellent
Xylene	Good	Excellent	Excellent
Water	Excellent	Excellent	Excellent
Linseed Oil	Excellent	Excellent	Excellent
HCl 5% (Acid)	NT	Poor	Poor
Na₂CO₃ 5% (Alkali)	Excellent	Excellent	Excellent
Plasticizers	NT	Excellent	Excellent
Migration Through Dried Layers	NT	Excellent	Excellent
Soap Gel Bleeding	NT	Excellent	Excellent
MELTING POINT (°C)/ STABILITY TO °C	NT/175	Excellent	Excellent
LIGHTFASTNESS (*CI*/ASTM D 4302)	EX/I	EX/I	EX/I
USE IN VEHICLES			
Oil; Oil Absorption; Drying Rate; Film Properties	×; M; A; G	×; L; G; G	×; M; G; G
Acrylic Solution	×	×	×
Acrylic Emulsion	×	×	×
Transparent Watercolor	×	×	×
Opaque Watercolor (Gouache)	×	×	×
Temperas	×	×	×
Casein	NT	×	×
Encaustic	×	×	×
Frescos	NT (EX)	×	×
Experimentals/Pastel/Alkyds	NT/G/NT	×/×/×	×/×/×
DRY REFRACTIVE INDEX	Medium	High	High
DRY CHARACTERISTICS	RP	Depending on source, dull YO → YR → R → RB	Depending on source, YR → R
HAZARDS	Avoid dust	Avoid dust	Avoid dust
OTHER COMMENTS	Good new pigment; used in automobile finishes and currency inks; lightfastness rating applies only to PR 88 MRS supplied by American Hoechst Corporation	Useful hue; weak tinting strength	Useful hue

TABLE 7.1 PIGMENTS (*continued*)

ARTISTS' HUE	Red	Red	Red
COMMON NAME	**Mars Red (Red Iron Oxide)**	**Mars Violet (Violet Iron Oxide)**	**Venetian Red**
COLOUR INDEX **NAME, NUMBER**	PR 101 (77491)	PR 101 (77015)	PR 101 (77491)
GENERIC NAME	Red Iron Oxide	Violet Iron Oxide	Red Iron Oxide, yellowish
PROPRIETARY NAME(S)	Mars Red	Mars Violet	Venetian Red
SYNONYM(S)			Venetian Red
DATES/PLACE OF DISCOVERY	1800s	1800s	Natural, ancient; synthetic, modern
CHEMICAL CLASS; CONSTITUENTS	Inorganic; synthesized iron oxide plus aluminum oxide	Inorganic; synthesized iron oxide	Inorganic; synthesized iron oxide plus calcium sulfate
SOURCE	Synthetic inorganic	Synthetic inorganic	Natural inorganic, processed mineral
TYPE	P	P	P
RESISTANCE TO:			
Aliphatic Hydrocarbons	Excellent	Excellent	Excellent
Esters	Excellent	Excellent	Excellent
Ethanols	Excellent	Excellent	Excellent
Ketones	Excellent	Excellent	Excellent
Xylene	Excellent	Excellent	Excellent
Water	Excellent	Excellent	Excellent
Linseed Oil	Excellent	Excellent	Excellent
HCl 5% (Acid)	Poor	Excellent	Poor
Na_2CO_3 5% (Alkali)	Excellent	Excellent	Excellent
Plasticizers	Excellent	Excellent	Excellent
Migration Through Dried Layers	Excellent	Excellent	Excellent
Soap Gel Bleeding	Excellent	Excellent	Excellent
MELTING POINT (°C)/ STABILITY TO °C	Excellent	Excellent	Excellent
LIGHTFASTNESS (*CI***/ASTM D 4302)**	EX/I	EX/I	EX/I
USE IN VEHICLES			
Oil; Oil Absorption; Drying Rate; Film Properties	×; M; G; G	×; M; G; G	G; L; G; F
Acrylic Solution	×	×	×
Acrylic Emulsion	×	×	×
Transparent Watercolor	×	×	×
Opaque Watercolor (Gouache)	×	×	×
Temperas	×	×	×
Casein	×	×	×
Encaustic	×	×	×
Frescos	×	×	×
Experimentals/Pastel/Alkyds	×/×/×	×/×/×	×/×/×
DRY REFRACTIVE INDEX	High	High	High
DRY CHARACTERISTICS	Dull R	Dull RB	Dull YR → R (→ BR)
HAZARDS	Avoid dust	Avoid dust	Avoid dust
OTHER COMMENTS	Useful pigment; dense and heavy; more stable than natural counterpart; origin of "Mars" name uncertain	Very useful pigment; dense and heavy; origin of "Mars" name uncertain	Useful pigment; brittle films in oil have been reported

TABLE 7.1 PIGMENTS (continued)

ARTISTS' HUE	Red	Red	Red
COMMON NAME	**Light Red**	**Vermilion**	**Cadmium-Barium Red** (Light, Medium or Deep)
COLOUR INDEX **NAME, NUMBER**	PR 102 (77491/77492)	PR 106 (77766)	PR 108 (77202)
GENERIC NAME	Light Red	Mercuric sulfide	Cadmium-Barium Red (Light, Medium or Deep)
PROPRIETARY NAME(S)		Cinnabar, Chinese Red	
SYNONYM(S)		Cinnabar, Chinese Red	Cadmium Sulfoselenide, Lithopone Red
DATES/PLACE OF DISCOVERY	Ancient	Ancient	1926
CHEMICAL CLASS; CONSTITUENTS	Inorganic; calcined yellow iron oxide	Inorganic; mercuric sulfide	Inorganic; cadmium sulfide + cadmium selenide + approx. 60% barium sulfate, calcined and co-precipitated
SOURCE	Natural inorganic, processed mineral	Natural inorganic, processed mineral	Natural inorganic, processed
TYPE	P	P	P, E
RESISTANCE TO:			
Aliphatic Hydrocarbons	Excellent	Excellent	Excellent
Esters	Excellent	Excellent	Excellent
Ethanols	Excellent	Excellent	Excellent
Ketones	Excellent	Excellent	Excellent
Xylene	Excellent	Excellent	Excellent
Water	Excellent	Excellent	Excellent
Linseed Oil	Excellent	Excellent	Excellent
HCl 5% (Acid)	Poor	Excellent	Poor
Na$_2$CO$_3$ 5% (Alkali)	Excellent	Excellent	Excellent
Plasticizers	Excellent	Excellent	Excellent
Migration Through Dried Layers	Excellent	Excellent	Excellent
Soap Gel Bleeding	Excellent	Excellent	Excellent
MELTING POINT (°C)/ STABILITY TO °C	Excellent	446	—/500
LIGHTFASTNESS (*CI*/ASTM D 4302)	EX/I	EX/I but darkens if not pure or if exposed to polluted atmosphere	VG/I
USE IN VEHICLES			
Oil; Oil Absorption; Drying Rate; Film Properties	✕; M; G; G	✕; L; G; G	✕; L; G; E
Acrylic Solution	✕	NT (✕)	✕
Acrylic Emulsion	✕	✕	✕
Transparent Watercolor	✕	P	✕
Opaque Watercolor (Gouache)	✕	P	✕
Temperas	✕	P	✕
Casein	✕	P	✕
Encaustic	✕	F	✕
Frescos	✕	P	✕
Experimentals/Pastel/Alkyds	✕✕✕	NT/P/✕	✕/✕/✕
DRY REFRACTIVE INDEX	High	High	High
DRY CHARACTERISTICS	Dull YR → R	Deep R	Bright YR → RO → RB
HAZARDS	Avoid dust	Avoid dust; do not heat; metal fumes toxic	Avoid dust; do not heat— metal fumes toxic
OTHER COMMENTS	One of the best of the earth reds	Excellent hue; less pure grades may be erratic; cadmiums do not replace its special hue and physical character	Excellent hue, with variety among different manufacturers; barium co-precipitation produces strong, clean color, makes product less expensive

TABLE 7.1 PIGMENTS (continued)

ARTISTS' HUE	Red	Red	Red
COMMON NAME	**Cadmium Red** (Light, Medium or Deep)	**Naphthol AS-D**	**Cadmium Vermilion Red** (Light, Medium or Deep)
COLOUR INDEX NAME, NUMBER	PR 108:1 (77202:1)	PR 112 (12370)	PR 113 (77201)
GENERIC NAME	Cadmium Red (Light, Medium or Deep)	Naphthol Red AS-D coupling	
PROPRIETARY NAME(S)		Naphthol Red FGR, Permanent Red FGR	Cadmium Mercury Red
SYNONYM(S)	Chemically Pure (C.P.) Cadmium Red		Chinese Red, French Red
DATES/PLACE OF DISCOVERY	1893(?)–1907	Modern	Modern
CHEMICAL CLASS; CONSTITUENTS	Inorganic; cadmium sulfide + cadmium selenide, calcined and co-precipitated, concentrated but with up to 15% barium sulfate	Organic; "monoazo"; same as PR 7 with a different coupling	Inorganic; cadmium sulfide + mercury sulfide; concentrated but with up to 15% barium sulfate
SOURCE	Natural inorganic, processed	Synthetic organic	Synthetic inorganic
TYPE	P	L	P
RESISTANCE TO:			
Aliphatic Hydrocarbons	Excellent	Excellent	Excellent
Esters	Excellent	Excellent	Excellent
Ethanols	Excellent	Excellent	Excellent
Ketones	Excellent	Excellent	Excellent
Xylene	Excellent	Poor	Excellent
Water	Excellent	Excellent	Excellent
Linseed Oil	Excellent	Good	Excellent
HCl 5% (Acid)	Poor	Excellent	Poor
Na$_2$CO$_3$ 5% (Alkali)	Excellent	Excellent	Excellent
Plasticizers	Excellent	Good	Excellent
Migration Through Dried Layers	Excellent	Good	Excellent
Soap Gel Bleeding	Excellent	Good	Excellent
MELTING POINT (°C)/ STABILITY TO °C	—/500	—/180	—/260
LIGHTFASTNESS (*CI*/ASTM D 4302)	VG/I	VG/II	VG/I
USE IN VEHICLES			
Oil; Oil Absorption; Drying Rate; Film Properties	✕; L; G; E	VG; M; A; G	✕; L; G; G
Acrylic Solution	✕	NT	✕
Acrylic Emulsion	✕	VG	✕
Transparent Watercolor	✕	✕	NT
Opaque Watercolor (Gouache)	✕	✕	NT
Temperas	✕	✕	✕
Casein	✕	✕	NT
Encaustic	✕	✕	✕
Frescos	✕	NT	NT
Experimentals/Pastel/Alkyds	✕/✕/✕	NT/NT/✕	NT/NT/✕
DRY REFRACTIVE INDEX	High	Medium	High
DRY CHARACTERISTICS	Bright YR → RO → RB	Bright R → BR	YR → Deep BR
HAZARDS	Avoid dust; do not heat— metal fumes toxic	Avoid dust	Avoid dust; do not heat— metal fumes toxic; mercury
OTHER COMMENTS	Same as cadmium-barium, but more concentrated; expensive; 15% barium used for hue development and manufacturing control and is not adulteration	Moderate resistance to solvents; very good lightfastness; good hue; used in printing inks, paper and paper coating, rubber, vinyl, linoleum	Rich, deep hue; poor exterior resistance; 15% barium used for hue development and manufacturing control; less expensive than pure cadmiums

173

TABLE 7.1 PIGMENTS (continued)

ARTISTS' HUE	Red	Red	Red
COMMON NAME	**Cadmium-Barium Vermilion Red** (Light, Medium or Deep)	**Naphthol Red**	**Quinacridone Magenta**
COLOUR INDEX NAME, NUMBER	PR 113:1 (77201)	PR 119 (NA)	PR 122 (73915)
GENERIC NAME		Naphthol Red	Quinacridone Magenta Y
PROPRIETARY NAME(S)	Cadmium Mercury Lithopone Red	(Mobay R6226)	Acra Violet or Red Quinacridone Magenta
SYNONYM(S)	Chinese Red, French Red		Quinacridone Magenta
DATES/PLACE OF DISCOVERY	Modern	Modern	Modern
CHEMICAL CLASS; CONSTITUENTS	Inorganic; cadmium sulfide + mercury sulfide + approx. 60% barium sulfate	Organic; "monoazo"; same as PR 7 with a different coupling (unspecified in CI)	Organic; "linear quinacridone"; 2,9-Dimethyl derivative of cyclized 2,5 diarylaminoterephalic acid
SOURCE	Synthetic inorganic	Synthetic organic	Synthetic organic
TYPE	P, E	L	L
RESISTANCE TO:			
Aliphatic Hydrocarbons	Excellent	Unknown	Excellent
Esters	Excellent	Unknown	Excellent
Ethanols	Excellent	Unknown	Very good
Ketones	Excellent	Unknown	Very good
Xylene	Excellent	Unknown	Excellent
Water	Excellent	Unknown	Excellent
Linseed Oil	Excellent	Unknown	Excellent
HCl 5% (Acid)	Poor	Unknown	Excellent
Na$_2$CO$_3$ 5% (Alkali)	Excellent	Unknown	Excellent
Plasticizers	Excellent	Unknown	Excellent
Migration Through Dried Layers	Excellent	Unknown	Excellent
Soap Gel Bleeding	Excellent	Unknown	Excellent
MELTING POINT (°C)/ STABILITY TO °C	—/260	Unknown	—/150
LIGHTFASTNESS (*CI*/ASTM D 4302)	VG/I	NT/I	VG/I
USE IN VEHICLES			
Oil; Oil Absorption; Drying Rate; Film Properties	×; L; G; G	×; NT; NT; NT	×; M; A; G
Acrylic Solution	×	NT	NT
Acrylic Emulsion	×	×	×
Transparent Watercolor	NT	NT	×
Opaque Watercolor (Gouache)	NT	NT	×
Temperas	×	NT	×
Casein	NT	NT	×
Encaustic	×	NT	×
Frescos	NT	NT	×
Experimentals/Pastel/Alkyds	NT/NT/×	NT/NT/NT	NT/×/×
DRY REFRACTIVE INDEX	High	Medium	Medium
DRY CHARACTERISTICS	YR → Deep BR	Bright R	Bright BR
HAZARDS	Avoid dust; do not heat—metal fumes toxic; mercury	Avoid dust	Avoid dust
OTHER COMMENTS	Same as PR 113 but weaker tinting strength because of barium extender	New pigment; information still unclear	Durable pigment; weak tinting strength but useful

TABLE 7.1 PIGMENTS (continued)

ARTISTS' HUE	Red	Red	Red
COMMON NAME	**Perylene Vermilion**	**Perylene**	**Brominated Anthanthrone**
COLOUR INDEX **NAME, NUMBER**	PR 123 (71145)	PR 149 (77137)	PR 168 (58300)
GENERIC NAME	Perylene	Perylene	Brominated Anthanthrone
PROPRIETARY NAME(S)	Perylene Vermilion	Perylene Red	Brominated Anthanthrone Red
SYNONYM(S)			
DATES/PLACE OF DISCOVERY	Modern	Modern	Modern
CHEMICAL CLASS; CONSTITUENTS	Organic; "anthraquinone derivative" a perelene-tetracarboxylic anhydride condensed with p-ethoxyaniline	Organic; "anthraquinone derivative"	Organic; "anthraquinone derivative," bromated anthanthrone
SOURCE	Synthetic organic	Synthetic organic	Synthetic organic
TYPE	T, L	L	L
RESISTANCE TO:			
Aliphatic Hydrocarbons	Excellent	Very good	Excellent
Esters	NT	NT	NT
Ethanols	Excellent	Very good	Good
Ketones	Excellent	NT	Good
Xylene	Excellent	Very good (toluol)	Good
Water	Excellent	Excellent	NT
Linseed Oil	Excellent	Excellent	NT
HCl 5% (Acid)	Excellent	NT	Excellent
Na$_2$CO$_3$ 5% (Alkali)	Good	NT	Excellent
Plasticizers	Excellent	Very good	NT
Migration Through Dried Layers	Excellent	Very good	NT
Soap Gel Bleeding	Excellent	NT	NT
MELTING POINT (°C)/ STABILITY TO °C	—/150	—/200	—/NT
LIGHTFASTNESS (*CI*/ASTM D 4302)	NT/I (oil), II (acrylic)	EX/I	NT/II (oil), I (acrylic)
USE IN VEHICLES			
Oil; Oil Absorption; Drying Rate; Film Properties	✕; M; A; G	✕; M; A; G	✕; M; A; G
Acrylic Solution	NT	NT	NT
Acrylic Emulsion	VG	✕	✕
Transparent Watercolor	NT	✕	NT
Opaque Watercolor (Gouache)	NT	✕	NT
Temperas	NT	✕	NT
Casein	NT	✕	NT
Encaustic	NT	✕	NT
Frescos	NT	NT	NT
Experimentals/Pastel/Alkyds	NT/NT/NT	NT/✕/NT	NT/NT/NT
DRY REFRACTIVE INDEX	Low	Medium	Low
DRY CHARACTERISTICS	R	R	Bright YR
HAZARDS	Avoid dust	Avoid dust	Avoid dust
OTHER COMMENTS	Good hue; weak chroma in tints; used in auto paints, alkyd resin enamels, vinyl and acrylic lacquers, printing inks, plastics	Probably similar to PR 123, but is untested; Paint Standard test for lightfastness only	New, untested pigment; rated as excellent for some industrial applications; Paint Standard test for lightfastness only

175

TABLE 7.1 PIGMENTS (*continued*)

ARTISTS' HUE	Red	Red	Red
COMMON NAME	**Naphthol F3RK-70**	**Naphthol F5RK**	**Benzimidazolone Maroon**
***COLOUR INDEX* NAME, NUMBER**	PR 170 (12475)	PR 170 (12475)	PR 175 (71513)
GENERIC NAME	Naphthol Carbamide	Naphthol Carbamide	Benzimidazolone Red
PROPRIETARY NAME(S)	Hoechst F3RK-70 Naphthol Red F3RK	Hoechst F5RK Napthol Red F5RK	Benzimidazolone Maroon HFM
SYNONYM(S)			
DATES/PLACE OF DISCOVERY	Modern	Modern	Modern
CHEMICAL CLASS; CONSTITUENTS	Organic; "monoazo": same as PR 7 but with a different coupling; specified structure in CI	Organic; "monoazo": same as PR 7 but with a different coupling; specified structure in CI	Organic; "monoazo": "cyclic carbonamide"; similar to other monoazo pigments
SOURCE	Synthetic organic	Synthetic organic	Synthetic organic
TYPE	L	L	L
RESISTANCE TO:			
Aliphatic Hydrocarbons	Good	Good	Excellent
Esters	NT	NT	NT
Ethanols	Fair	Fair	Excellent
Ketones	NT	NT	Good
Xylene	Poor	Poor	Good
Water	Fair	Fair	Excellent
Linseed Oil	NT (Good)	NT (Good)	Excellent
HCl 5% (Acid)	Excellent	Excellent	Excellent
Na_2CO_3 5% (Alkali)	Good	Good	Excellent
Plasticizers	NT	NT	NT
Migration Through Dried Layers	NT	NT	NT
Soap Gel Bleeding	Good	Good	NT
MELTING POINT (°C)/ STABILITY TO °C	—/160	—/160	—/220
LIGHTFASTNESS (*CI*/ASTM D 4302)	G/II (oil), I (acrylic)	G/II	EX/I
USE IN VEHICLES			
Oil; Oil Absorption; Drying Rate; Film Properties	G; M; A; G	G; M; A; G	×; M; A; G
Acrylic Solution	NT	NT	NT
Acrylic Emulsion	×	×	×
Transparent Watercolor	NT	NT	×
Opaque Watercolor (Gouache)	NT	NT	×
Temperas	NT	NT	×
Casein	NT	NT	×
Encaustic	NT	NT	×
Frescos	NT	NT	×
Experimentals/Pastel/Alkyds	NT/NT/NT	NT/NT/NT	NT/×/×
DRY REFRACTIVE INDEX	High, medium	High, medium	Medium
DRY CHARACTERISTICS	BR	BR	R → BR
HAZARDS	Avoid dust	Avoid dust	Avoid dust
OTHER COMMENTS	Used in printing inks, lacquers, emulsion paints; solubility in organic solvents makes artist use doubtful; Paint Standard test for lightfastness only	Used in printing inks, lacquers, emulsion paints; solubility in organic solvents makes artist use doubtful; Paint Standard test for lightfastness only	Fair resistance to solvents; Paint Standard test for lightfastness only; used in inks, PVC plastics, lacquers, latex emulsion paints

TABLE 7.1 PIGMENTS (continued)

ARTISTS' HUE	Red	Red	Red
COMMON NAME	**Perylene Maroon**	**Thioindigoid Red**	**Naphthol AS**
COLOUR INDEX NAME, NUMBER	PR 179 (71130)	PR 181 (73360)	PR 188 (12467)
GENERIC NAME	Perylene	Thioindigoid	Naphthol Red HF3S
PROPRIETARY NAME(S)	Perylene Maroon		Napthol Red HF3S
SYNONYM(S)			
DATES/PLACE OF DISCOVERY	Modern	1907	Modern
CHEMICAL CLASS; CONSTITUENTS	Organic; "anthraquinone derivative" similar to PR 123, although the structure of the molecule is different	Organic; oxidized 6-chloro-4-methyl-3 (2H)-thianaph-thenone	Organic; "monoazo": same as PR7 but with a different coupling; structure specified in CI
SOURCE	Synthetic organic	Synthetic organic	Synthetic organic
TYPE	L	L	L
RESISTANCE TO:			
Aliphatic Hydrocarbons	Excellent	NT (Poor)	Excellent
Esters	NT	NT	NT
Ethanols	Excellent	NT	Good
Ketones	Good	NT	Good
Xylene	Good	NT	Good
Water	NT	NT	Excellent
Linseed Oil	NT	NT (Poor)	Excellent
HCl 5% (Acid)	Excellent	Poor (bleached)	Excellent
Na$_2$CO$_3$ 5% (Alkali)	Excellent	Poor (yellows)	Excellent
Plasticizers	NT	NT	NT
Migration Through Dried Layers	NT	NT	NT
Soap Gel Bleeding	NT	NT	Good
MELTING POINT (°C)/ STABILITY TO °C	—/—	—	—/200
LIGHTFASTNESS (*CI*/ASTM D 4302)	EX/I	NT/NR (oil), I (acrylic)	G/I
USE IN VEHICLES			
Oil; Oil Absorption; Drying Rate; Film Properties	×; L; A; G	P; NT; NT; NT	×; H; NT; NT
Acrylic Solution	NT	NT	NT
Acrylic Emulsion	×	×	×
Transparent Watercolor	NT	NT	×
Opaque Watercolor (Gouache)	NT	NT	×
Temperas	NT	NT	×
Casein	NT	NT	×
Encaustic	×	NT	×
Frescos	NT	NT	NT
Experimentals/Pastel/Alkyds	NT/NT/×	NT/NT/NT	NT/×/NT
DRY REFRACTIVE INDEX	Low		Medium
DRY CHARACTERISTICS	Dull R	Bright pink → BR	YR (orange)
HAZARDS	Avoid dust	Not documented	Avoid dust
OTHER COMMENTS	Paint Standard test for lightfastness only; test before use	Paint Standard test for lightfastness only; test before use; vat dye in textiles but poorly documented in artists' materials	Paint Standard test for lightfastness only; solvent resistance only fair; test before use; used in PVC plastics, printing inks, lacquers

177

TABLE 7.1 PIGMENTS (continued)

ARTISTS' HUE	Red	Red	Red
COMMON NAME	**Perylene Red, and Red Deep**	**Quinacridone Red**	**Quinacridone Scarlet**
COLOUR INDEX NAME, NUMBER	PR 190 (71140), PR 194 (71100)	PR 192 (NA)	PR 207 (NA)
GENERIC NAME	Perylene	Quinacridone Red Y	Quinacridone Scarlet
PROPRIETARY NAME(S)		"Acra" Red	"Acra" Scarlet
SYNONYM(S)			
DATES/PLACE OF DISCOVERY	Modern	Modern 1930s–50s	Modern 1930s–50s
CHEMICAL CLASS; CONSTITUENTS	Organic; "perylene": structure specified in CI; similar to other pigments of this family	Organic; "linear quinacridone Red Y": structure specified in CI see PR 207	Organic; "linear quinacridone": derivation of cyclized 2,5-diarylamino-terephthalic acid
SOURCE	Synthetic organic	Synthetic organic	Synthetic organic
TYPE	L	L	L
RESISTANCE TO:			
Aliphatic Hydrocarbons	Good	NT	Excellent
Esters	NT	NT	Excellent
Ethanols	Good	NT	Excellent
Ketones	NT	NT	Excellent (Good)
Xylene	Good	NT	Excellent
Water	Excellent	NT	Excellent
Linseed Oil	NT	NT	Excellent
HCl 5% (Acid)	Good	NT	Excellent
Na$_2$CO$_3$ 5% (Alkali)	Good	NT	Excellent
Plasticizers	NT	NT	Excellent
Migration Through Dried Layers	NT	NT	Excellent
Soap Gel Bleeding	NT	NT	Excellent
MELTING POINT (°C)/ STABILITY TO °C	—	—	—/300, darkens
LIGHTFASTNESS (*CI*/ASTM D 4302)	G/I	NT/I	EX/I
USE IN VEHICLES			
Oil; Oil Absorption; Drying Rate; Film Properties	×; NT; NT; NT	×; NT; NT; NT	×; M; A; G
Acrylic Solution	G	NT	×
Acrylic Emulsion	×	×	×
Transparent Watercolor	×	NT	×
Opaque Watercolor (Gouache)	×	NT	×
Temperas	×	NT	×
Casein	× (NT)	NT	×
Encaustic	NT	NT	×
Frescos	NT	NT	NT
Experimentals/Pastel/Alkyds	NT/×/G	NT/NT/NT	NT/×/×
DRY REFRACTIVE INDEX	Medium	Medium	Low
DRY CHARACTERISTICS	R	Bright YR	YR
HAZARDS	Avoid dust	Avoid dust	Avoid dust
OTHER COMMENTS	Paint Standard test for lightfastness only; test before use; used in printing inks, auto paints, vinyls	Paint Standard test for lightfastness only; test before use	High-quality pigment widely used in industry; performs well in artists' paints

TABLE 7.1 PIGMENTS (*continued*)

ARTISTS' HUE	Red	Purple	Purple
COMMON NAME	**Quinacridone Red**	**Cobalt Violet**	**Ultramarine Red**
COLOUR INDEX NAME, NUMBER	PV 19 (73900)	PV 14 (77360)	PV 15 (77007)
GENERIC NAME	Quinacridone Red y Quinacridone Violet	Cobalt Violet	Ultramarine Red
PROPRIETARY NAME(S)	"Acra" Violet		
SYNONYM(S)			
DATES/PLACE OF DISCOVERY	Modern 1930s–50s	1859	1828(?)
CHEMICAL CLASS; CONSTITUENTS	Organic; "linear quinacridone, red y": same as PR 207 with different particle size	Inorganic; calcined cobalt oxide and phosphorous oxide	Inorganic; complex silicate of sodium and aluminum with sulfur
SOURCE	Synthetic organic	Natural inorganic, processed	Synthetic inorganic
TYPE	L	P	P
RESISTANCE TO:			
Aliphatic Hydrocarbons	Excellent	Excellent	Excellent
Esters	Excellent	Excellent	Excellent
Ethanols	Excellent	Excellent	Excellent
Ketones	Excellent (Good)	Excellent	Excellent
Xylene	Excellent	Excellent	Excellent
Water	Excellent	Excellent	Excellent
Linseed Oil	Excellent	Excellent	Excellent
HCl 5% (Acid)	Excellent	Excellent	Poor
Na_2CO_3 5% (Alkali)	Excellent	Excellent	Poor, turns B
Plasticizers	Excellent	Excellent	Excellent
Migration Through Dried Layers	Excellent	Excellent	Excellent
Soap Gel Bleeding	Excellent	Excellent	Excellent
MELTING POINT (°C)/ STABILITY TO °C	—/300, darkens	—/700	
LIGHTFASTNESS (*CI*/ASTM D 4302)	EX/I	EX/I (oil only)	EX/I
USE IN VEHICLES			
Oil; Oil Absorption; Drying Rate; Film Properties	×; M; A; G	×; L; G; G	×; M; A; G
Acrylic Solution	×	×	×
Acrylic Emulsion	×	NT (P)	×
Transparent Watercolor	×	×	×
Opaque Watercolor (Gouache)	×	×	×
Temperas	×	×	×
Casein	×	×	NT
Encaustic	×	×	×
Frescos	NT	×	P
Experimentals/Pastel/Alkyds	NT/×/×	×/×/×	NT/×/×
DRY REFRACTIVE INDEX	Low	High	High in water; low in oil
DRY CHARACTERISTICS	Bright P → RP	P	P
HAZARDS	Avoid dust	Metallic cobalt is slight hazard; avoid dust	Avoid dust
OTHER COMMENTS	Same as PR 207	Widely used in many applications; weak tinter, dull chroma; *cobalt arsenate* is toxic ($CO_3(AsO_4)_2$); rarely found today, but formerly the pigment used for this hue	A weak pigment but with good chroma and lightfastness; sensitive to alkalines, acids, and some metals

TABLE 7.1 PIGMENTS (continued)

ARTISTS' HUE	Purple	Purple	Purple
COMMON NAME	**Ultramarine Violet**	**Manganese Violet**	**Quinacridone Violet**
COLOUR INDEX **NAME, NUMBER**	PV 15 (77007)	PV 16 (77742)	PV 19 (46500/73900)
GENERIC NAME	Ultramarine Red	Manganese Violet	Quinacridone Violet b
PROPRIETARY NAME(S)			"Acra" Violet
SYNONYM(S)		Mineral Violet	
DATES/PLACE OF DISCOVERY	1828(?)	1868	1930s–50s
CHEMICAL CLASS; CONSTITUENTS	Inorganic; complex silicate of sodium and aluminum with sulfur	Inorganic; manganese ammonium pyrophosphate	Organic; "linear quinacridone red b": same as PR 207 with a different particle size and configuration
SOURCE	Synthetic inorganic	Synthetic inorganic	Synthetic organic
TYPE	P	P	L
RESISTANCE TO:			
Aliphatic Hydrocarbons	Excellent	Excellent	Excellent
Esters	Excellent	Excellent	Excellent
Ethanols	Excellent	Excellent	Excellent
Ketones	Excellent	Excellent	Excellent (Good)
Xylene	Excellent	Excellent	Excellent
Water	Excellent	Excellent	Excellent
Linseed Oil	Excellent	Excellent	Excellent
HCl 5% (Acid)	Poor	Excellent	Excellent
Na$_2$CO$_3$ 5% (Alkali)	Poor, turns B	Poor, destroyed	Excellent
Plasticizers	Excellent	Excellent	Excellent
Migration Through Dried Layers	Excellent	Excellent	Excellent
Soap Gel Bleeding	Excellent	Excellent	Excellent
MELTING POINT (°C)/ STABILITY TO °C		—/"sensitive"	—/165
LIGHTFASTNESS (*CI*/ASTM D 4302)	EX/I	EX/I (oil only)	EX/I
USE IN VEHICLES			
Oil; Oil Absorption; Drying Rate; Film Properties	×; M; A; G	×; L; G; G	×; M; A; G
Acrylic Solution	×	NT	×
Acrylic Emulsion	×	P	×
Transparent Watercolor	×	×	×
Opaque Watercolor (Gouache)	×	×	×
Temperas	×	×	×
Casein	NT	NT (P?)	×
Encaustic	×	×	×
Frescos	P	P	NT
Experimentals/Pastel/Alkyds	NT/×/×	NT/×/×	NT/×/×
DRY REFRACTIVE INDEX	High in water; low in oil	Medium	Low
DRY CHARACTERISTICS	P	BP	Bright P
HAZARDS	Avoid dust	Avoid dust	Avoid dust
OTHER COMMENTS	Same as Ultramarine Red	Good hue; expensive; sensitive to alkalines	Same as PR 207

TABLE 7.1 PIGMENTS (continued)

ARTISTS' HUE	Purple	Purple	Blue
COMMON NAME	**Dioxazine Purple**	**Isoviolanthrone Violet**	**Phthalocyanine Blue**
COLOUR INDEX NAME, NUMBER	PV 23 RS (Red Shade) (51319)	PV 31 (60010)	PB 15 (74160)
GENERIC NAME	Dioxazine Violet	Isoviolanthrone	Phthalocyanine Blue (Red)
PROPRIETARY NAME(S)	Carbazole Violet	"indanthrebrilliant-violett RR, 4R"	Thalo, Phthalo, Winsor, Monastral, etc
SYNONYM(S)			
DATES/PLACE OF DISCOVERY	Modern	1909	1928–35
CHEMICAL CLASS; CONSTITUENTS	Organic; "carbazole dioxazine": a complex condensation of 3-Amino-9-ethyl-carbazole with chloranil in trichloro-benzene	Organic; "Anthraquinone derivative": dichlorobenz-anthrone treated with an alkali	Organic; copper phthalocyanine, alpha form
SOURCE	Synthetic organic	Synthetic organic	Synthetic organic
TYPE	L	L	L, E
RESISTANCE TO:			
Aliphatic Hydrocarbons	Good	NT	Fair–Good
Esters	Fair	NT	Fair–Good
Ethanols	Fair–Good	Good	Fair–Good
Ketones	Fair	Good	Fair–Good
Xylene	Fair	Very good	Fair–Good
Water	Good	Good	Fair–Good
Linseed Oil	Good	NT	Fair–Good
HCl 5% (Acid)	Good	Poor, turns G	Good
Na$_2$CO$_3$ 5% (Alkali)	Good	Poor, turns RP	Excellent
Plasticizers	Good	NT	Fair–Good
Migration Through Dried Layers	Good	NT	Fair–Good
Soap Gel Bleeding	Good	NT	Fair–Good
MELTING POINT (°C)/ STABILITY TO °C	—/150	—	—/150
LIGHTFASTNESS (*CI*/ASTM D 4302)	G–F/I (oil), II (acrylic)	NT/I	VG–EX/I
USE IN VEHICLES			
Oil; Oil Absorption; Drying Rate; Film Properties	×; M; A; G	×; M; A; G	×; M; G; E
Acrylic Solution	× (G)	NT	×
Acrylic Emulsion	VG	×	×
Transparent Watercolor	×	NT	×
Opaque Watercolor (Gouache)	×	NT	×
Temperas	×	NT	×
Casein	×	NT	×
Encaustic	NT (×?)	NT	×
Frescos	NT	NT	×(?)
Experimentals/Pastel/Alkyds	NT/×/×	NT/NT/NT	×/×/×
DRY REFRACTIVE INDEX	Low	Low	Low
DRY CHARACTERISTICS	BP	BP	Bright RB
HAZARDS	Avoid dust	Avoid dust	Copper of minor concern; avoid dust
OTHER COMMENTS	Excellent hue, tinting strength; good lightfastness; resistance to solvents requires testing before use; PV 23 BS (Blue Shade) has less lightfastness (II in oil, NR in acrylic)	Paint Standard test for lightfastness only; test before use	Most widely used blue pigment in artistic and industrial applications; must be greatly extended because of high tinting strength; Red Shade Blue more susceptible to solvents than CI 74100

TABLE 7.1 **PIGMENTS** (*continued*)

ARTISTS' HUE	Blue	Blue	Blue
COMMON NAME	**Phthalocyanine Blue**	**Indanthrone Blue**	**Prussian Blue**
COLOUR INDEX NAME, NUMBER	PB 16 (74100)	PB 22 (69810)	PB 27 (77510)
GENERIC NAME	Phthalocyanine Blue (Metal Free)	Indanthrone, Green Shade	Prussian Blue
PROPRIETARY NAME(S)	Thalo, Phthalo, Winsor, Monastral, etc.	Indanthrone	
SYNONYM(S)			Paris, Milori, Chinese
DATES/PLACE OF DISCOVERY	1928–35	1903	1704, the earliest synthetic mineral pigment
CHEMICAL CLASS; CONSTITUENTS	Organic; metal-free copper phthalocyanine	Organic; indanthrone chlorinated with sulfuryl chloride	Inorganic; ferri-ammonium ferocyanide (ferric ammonium ferrocyanide)
SOURCE	Synthetic organic	Synthetic organic	Synthetic inorganic, processed
TYPE	L, E	L	P
RESISTANCE TO:			
Aliphatic Hydrocarbons	Excellent	NT (Excellent)	Excellent
Esters	Excellent	Good	Excellent
Ethanols	Excellent	Fair (Good)	Excellent
Ketones	Excellent	Good	Excellent
Xylene	Excellent	Fair–Good	Excellent
Water	Excellent	Excellent	Excellent
Linseed Oil	Excellent	NT	Excellent
HCl 5% (Acid)	Excellent	Poor, turns $Y \rightarrow B$	Excellent
Na_2CO_3 5% (Alkali)	Excellent	Poor, turns B	Poor, bleached
Plasticizers	Excellent	NT	Excellent
Migration Through Dried Layers	Excellent	NT	Excellent
Soap Gel Bleeding	Excellent	Excellent	Excellent
MELTING POINT (°C)/ STABILITY TO °C	—/150	—/400	—/120, darkens
LIGHTFASTNESS (*CI*/ASTM D 4302)	EX/I	EX/I	G–EX/I (oil only)
USE IN VEHICLES			
Oil; Oil Absorption; Drying Rate; Film Properties	×; M; G; E	×; NT; NT; G	×; M; G; G
Acrylic Solution	×	NT	×
Acrylic Emulsion	×	×	P
Transparent Watercolor	×	×	×
Opaque Watercolor (Gouache)	×	×	×
Temperas	×	×	×
Casein	×	×	NT
Encaustic	×	×	NT (P)
Frescos	×	P	NT
Experimentals/Pastel/Alkyds	×/×/×	NT/×/×	NT/×/×
DRY REFRACTIVE INDEX	Low	Medium	High
DRY CHARACTERISTICS	Bright GB	RBG → Bright B	B
HAZARDS	Avoid dust	Avoid dust	Avoid dust
OTHER COMMENTS	Same as 74160 but with better resistance to solvents; will flocculate if not properly formulated in a paint system; will bronze if used full-strength	Paint Standard test for lightfastness only; test before use	Some dispute over name: Milori variety claimed to be more stable but Prussian name better known; widely used, reliable pigment, unstable in alkaline vehicles and high heat

TABLE 7.1 PIGMENTS (*continued*)

ARTISTS' HUE	Blue	Blue	Blue
COMMON NAME	**Cobalt Blue**	**Ultramarine Blue**	**Manganese Blue**
COLOUR INDEX **NAME, NUMBER**	PB 28 (77346)	PB 29 (77007)	PB 33 (77112)
GENERIC NAME	Cobalt Blue	Ultramarine Blue	Manganese Blue
PROPRIETARY NAME(S)	Cobalt Blue	French Ultramarine, etc	Manganese Blue, Cement Blue
SYNONYM(S)			
DATES/PLACE OF DISCOVERY	1802	Natural, 1200–1300 Artificial, 1828 (accidentally)	1935
CHEMICAL CLASS; CONSTITUENTS	Inorganic; oxides of cobalt and aluminum	Inorganic; natural: semi-precious gem, *lapis lazuli*, washed and ground. Artificial: complex silicate of sodium and aluminum with sulfur	Inorganic; barium manganate plus barium sulfate
SOURCE	Synthetic inorganic, processed	Natural inorganic, processed; synthetic inorganic, processed (artificial)	Synthetic inorganic, processed
TYPE	P	P	P
RESISTANCE TO:			
Aliphatic Hydrocarbons	Excellent	Excellent	Excellent
Esters	Excellent	Excellent	Excellent
Ethanols	Excellent	Excellent	Excellent
Ketones	Excellent	Excellent	Excellent
Xylene	Excellent	Excellent	Excellent
Water	Excellent	Excellent	Excellent
Linseed Oil	Excellent	Excellent	Excellent
HCl 5% (Acid)	Excellent	Poor, bleached	Poor, darkens
Na$_2$CO$_3$ 5% (Alkali)	Excellent	Excellent	Excellent
Plasticizers	Excellent	Excellent	Excellent
Migration Through Dried Layers	Excellent	Excellent	Excellent
Soap Gel Bleeding	Excellent	Excellent	Excellent
MELTING POINT (°C)/ STABILITY TO °C	—/900–1000	—/300	—
LIGHTFASTNESS (*CI*/ASTM D 4302)	EX/I	EX/I	EX/I
USE IN VEHICLES			
Oil; Oil Absorption; Drying Rate; Film Properties	×; L; A; G	×; M; A–S; G	×; M; G; G
Acrylic Solution	×	×	×
Acrylic Emulsion	×	×	×
Transparent Watercolor	×	×	G
Opaque Watercolor (Gouache)	×	×	G
Temperas	×	×	×
Casein	×	×	×
Encaustic	×	×	×
Frescos	×	NT, turns W in calcium ions	×
Experimentals/Pastel/Alkyds	×/×/×	×/×/×	NT/×/×
DRY REFRACTIVE INDEX	High	High	Medium
DRY CHARACTERISTICS	Dark B	Bright B	GB
HAZARDS	Cobalt content may be slight hazard; avoid dust	Avoid dust	Manganese may be a slight hazard; avoid dust
OTHER COMMENTS	Unique hue, valuable in violet mixtures due to its red cast; sometimes imitated by mixtures of ultramarine	Reliable and brilliant; *lapis* often specified in medieval paintings; weak tinting strength	Reliable, relatively weak pigment; affected by sodium and aluminum sulfates (soluble metallic salts)

TABLE 7.1   **PIGMENTS**   (*continued*)

ARTISTS' HUE	Blue	Blue	Blue
COMMON NAME	**Cerulean Blue**	**Cerulean Blue, Chromium**	**Indanthrone Blue**
COLOUR INDEX **NAME, NUMBER**	PB 35 (77368)	PB 36 (77343)	PB 60 (69800)
GENERIC NAME	Cerulean Blue	Cerulean Blue, Chromium	Indanthrone Blue, Red Shade
PROPRIETARY NAME(S)		Cobalt Aluminate	
SYNONYM(S)	Coeruleum Blue, etc		
DATES/PLACE OF DISCOVERY	1860		Modern
CHEMICAL CLASS; CONSTITUENTS	Inorganic; oxides of cobalt and tin; cobalt sulfate calcined with stannous chloride and chalk	Inorganic; oxides of cobalt and chromium	Organic; "anthraquinone derivative:" aminoanthra-quinone with potassium hydroxide and a potassium salt
SOURCE	Synthetic inorganic, processed	Synthetic inorganic, processed	Synthetic organic
TYPE	P	P	L
RESISTANCE TO:			
Aliphatic Hydrocarbons	Excellent	Excellent	Excellent
Esters	Excellent	Excellent	NT
Ethanols	Excellent	Excellent	NT
Ketones	Excellent	Excellent	NT
Xylene	Excellent	Excellent	Excellent
Water	Excellent	Excellent	Excellent
Linseed Oil	Excellent	Excellent	NT
HCl 5% (Acid)	Good, Nitric dissolves cobalt	Excellent	Excellent
Na₂CO₃ 5% (Alkali)	Excellent	Excellent	NT
Plasticizers	Excellent	Excellent	NT
Migration Through Dried Layers	Excellent	Excellent	NT
Soap Gel Bleeding	Excellent	Excellent	NT
MELTING POINT (°C)/ STABILITY TO °C	—	—/NT	—/200
LIGHTFASTNESS (*CI*/ASTM D 4302)	EX/I	EX/I	EX/I
USE IN VEHICLES			
Oil; Oil Absorption; Drying Rate; Film Properties	✕; M; A; G	✕; L; A; G	✕; M; A; G
Acrylic Solution	✕	✕	NT
Acrylic Emulsion	✕	✕	✕
Transparent Watercolor	✕	✕	NT (✕)
Opaque Watercolor (Gouache)	✕	✕	NT (✕)
Temperas	✕	✕	NT (✕)
Casein	✕	✕	NT (✕)
Encaustic	✕	✕	✕
Frescos	✕	✕	NT
Experimentals/Pastel/Alkyds	✕/✕/✕	✕/✕/✕	NT/✕/✕
DRY REFRACTIVE INDEX	Medium	High	Medium
DRY CHARACTERISTICS	Clear BG, bright	B → GB	RB
HAZARDS	Cobalt may be a slight hazard; avoid dust	Cobalt content may be a slight hazard; avoid dust	Avoid dust
OTHER COMMENTS	"Sky blue"; reliable but expensive greenish blue	A variety of Cobalt blue made with chromium, which gives it its cerulean hue	Excellent lightfastness in tints, but loses chroma when reduced too greatly; Paint Standard test for lightfastness only; test before use; expensive

TABLE 7.1 PIGMENTS (continued)

ARTISTS' HUE	Green	Green	Green
COMMON NAME	**Phthalocyanine Green**	**Green Gold**	**Chromium Oxide Green**
***COLOUR INDEX* NAME, NUMBER**	PG 7 (74260)	PG 10 (12775)	PG 17 (77288)
GENERIC NAME	Phthalocyanine Green	Nickel Azo Yellow	Chromium Oxide Green
PROPRIETARY NAME(S)	Thalo, Phthalo, Monastral, etc.		
SYNONYM(S)			
DATES/PLACE OF DISCOVERY	1935–38	1946	1862
CHEMICAL CLASS; CONSTITUENTS	Organic; chlorinated copper phthalocyanine (polychloro copper phthalocyanine)	Organic; "monoazo": nickel chelated azo, structure specified in CI	Inorganic; anhydrous chromium sesquioxide
SOURCE	Synthetic organic	Synthetic organic	Synthetic inorganic, processed
TYPE	L, E	L	P
RESISTANCE TO:			
Aliphatic Hydrocarbons	Very good	Excellent	Excellent
Esters	Very good	Good	Excellent
Ethanols	Good	Good	Excellent
Ketones	Good	Good	Excellent
Xylene	Very good	Good	Excellent
Water	Very good	Excellent	Excellent
Linseed Oil	Very good	Excellent	Excellent
HCl 5% (Acid)	Very good	Excellent	Excellent
Na$_2$CO$_3$ 5% (Alkali)	Very good	Excellent	Excellent
Plasticizers	Very good	Excellent	Excellent
Migration Through Dried Layers	Very good	Excellent	Excellent
Soap Gel Bleeding	Very good	Good	Excellent
MELTING POINT (°C)/ STABILITY TO °C	—/150	—/190	—/900–1000
LIGHTFASTNESS (*CI*/ASTM D 4302)	EX/I	EX/I	EX/I
USE IN VEHICLES			
Oil; Oil Absorption; Drying Rate; Film Properties	×; M; A; G	×; M; A; G	×; L–M; A; G
Acrylic Solution	×	×	×
Acrylic Emulsion	×	×	×
Transparent Watercolor	×	×	×
Opaque Watercolor (Gouache)	×	×	×
Temperas	×	×	×
Casein	×	×	×
Encaustic	×	×	×
Frescos	×	NT	×
Experimentals/Pastel/Alkyds	×/×/×	×/×/×	×/×/×
DRY REFRACTIVE INDEX	Low	Low	Medium
DRY CHARACTERISTICS	Bright G	YG	Dull YG → G
HAZARDS	Copper may be a slight hazard; avoid dust	Nickel may be a slight hazard; avoid dust	Chromium may be slight hazard; avoid dust
OTHER COMMENTS	Widely used for artistic and industrial applications; flocculates in some paint systems; strong tinter that must be extended	Unusual hue, very lightfast, used in auto paints and other exterior applications; weak tinter	Excellent all-round colorant; low chroma; weak tinting strength; used in plastics, emulsion paints, ceramics, printing inks for currency

TABLE 7.1 PIGMENTS (continued)

ARTISTS' HUE	Green	Green	Green
COMMON NAME	**Viridian**	**Cobalt Green**	**Green Earth**
COLOUR INDEX **NAME, NUMBER**	PG 18 (77289)	PG 19 (77335)	PG 23 (77009)
GENERIC NAME	Hydrated chromium oxide green	Cobalt Green	Green Earth
PROPRIETARY NAME(S)	Verte Emeraud, Emerald Green, Guiget's Green	Rinmann's Green, Gellert Green	Green Earth, Terre Verte
SYNONYM(S)			Terre Verte, Green Sand, Green Stone
DATES/PLACE OF DISCOVERY	1838	1780s	Roman
CHEMICAL CLASS; CONSTITUENTS	Inorganic; hydrous chromium sesquioxide	Inorganic; calcined oxides of cobalt and zinc	Inorganic; natural green earth: a clay colored by iron oxides, aluminum, potassium, and magnesium
SOURCE	Synthetic inorganic, processed	Synthetic inorganic, processed	Natural inorganic, processed
TYPE	P	P	P
RESISTANCE TO:			
Aliphatic Hydrocarbons	Excellent	Excellent	Excellent
Esters	Excellent	Excellent	Excellent
Ethanols	Excellent	Excellent	Excellent
Ketones	Excellent	Excellent	Excellent
Xylene	Excellent	Excellent	Excellent
Water	Excellent	Excellent	Excellent
Linseed Oil	Excellent	Excellent	Excellent
HCl 5% (Acid)	Excellent	Excellent	Fair
Na₂CO₃ 5% (Alkali)	Excellent	Excellent	Excellent
Plasticizers	Excellent	Excellent	Excellent
Migration Through Dried Layers	Excellent	Excellent	Excellent
Soap Gel Bleeding	Excellent	Excellent	Excellent
MELTING POINT (°C)/ STABILITY TO °C	—/250, blackens	—	—/Fair, turns BrR
LIGHTFASTNESS (*CI*/ASTM D 4302)	EX/I (oil only)	EX/I	EX/I
USE IN VEHICLES			
Oil; Oil Absorption; Drying Rate; Film Properties	×; M; A; G	×; M; A; G	×; H; S; F
Acrylic Solution	×	×	×
Acrylic Emulsion	P	×	×
Transparent Watercolor	NT	×	×
Opaque Watercolor (Gouache)	NT	×	×
Temperas	×	×	×
Casein	NT	×	×
Encaustic	×	×	×
Frescos	NT	NT	×
Experimentals/Pastel/Alkyds	NT/×/×	×/×/×	×/×/×
DRY REFRACTIVE INDEX	Low	High	Low
DRY CHARACTERISTICS	BG → G	Dull YG → BG	Dull Gray G → YG Gray
HAZARDS	Chromium may be slight hazard; avoid dust	Cobalt may be slight hazard; avoid dust	Avoid dust
OTHER COMMENTS	Not used in water-based paint systems because difficult to disperse; brighter than PG 17 but still with low chroma and weak tinting strength; widely used commercially		Weak, transparent, colorant but of unusual hue; valuable in water vehicles, where it is opaque; difficult to obtain, often imitated by mixtures; classic underpaint hue for egg temperas

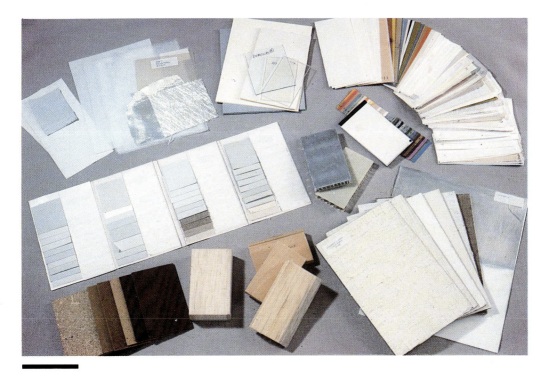

PLATE 1
Supports and Grounds (see Chapters 1 and 2)

Flexible supports, back row, left to right: polyester, polyester/cotton blend, and polypropylene, all with thermoset acrylic emulsion grounds; six different weights of thin, nonwoven polyester sheeting, pale brown cast polyester sheeting, woven fiber glass, chopped strand mat fiber glass; pale blue neutral pH corrugated cardboard, 100 percent rag mat board, foam-cored board, nonglare glass (Denglas), UF–3 and UF–4 plexiglas, fan of numerous paper samples.

Middle row, left to right: natural and synthetic fabrics, with and without grounds; aluminum honeycombed supports with (*top*) aluminum and (*bottom*) polyester skins; mat board and colored paper samples.

Rigid supports, front row, left to right: particle board, untempered hardboard, tempered hardboard, laminated maple die board, heavy- and medium-weight custom stretcher bar sections.

Stack on far right, various rigid supports with various laminated and grounds, reading from top to bottom of stack: hardboard substrate with oil on rough linen, hardboard substrate with oil on smooth linen, hardboard substrate with gesso (unsanded) on smooth linen, hardboard substrate mounted with rag paper, hardboard substrate with gesso (sanded) on smooth linen, hardboard substrate mounted with plain linen, sanded aluminum primed with acrylic emulsion gesso ground.

PLATE 2
General Materials (see Chapters 3 and 4)

Binders, front row, left to right: soya–alkyd (Reichhold 10-045), acrylic solution (Rohm and Haas Acryloid B-67 MT), acrylic emulsion (Rohm and Haas Rhoplex AC-234), polyvinyl acetate emulsion (Reichhold 10-140), ethyl silicate. *Preservative, front row far right:* Cuniphen 2778-I. *Middle row, left to right:* raw linseed oil, boiled linseed oil, cold-pressed linseed oil, alkali-refined linseed oil, linseed stand oil, safflower oil, poppyseed oil, gum arabic solution, castor oil. *Additives for acrylic emulsion binders, middle row, far right:* surfactant, two defoamers, two thickeners, dispersant, ethylene glycol. *Varnishes and driers, back row, left to right:* damar, Taubes copal painting medium, copal varnish, shellac stock, Venice turpentine, "Japan" drier, cobalt linoleate drier.

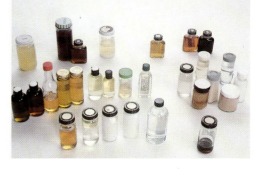

PLATE 3
General Materials (see Chapter 3)

Miscellaneous binders, resins, adhesives, front row, left to right: linseeds (flax), gum arabic, imported sheet hide glue, dextrin, methyl cellulose powder.

Back row, left to right: beeswax, microcrystalline petroleum wax, domestic granulated hide glue, mastic tears, gum damar crystals, (in the jar) alcohol-soluble nylon powder, (in front of the jar) polyterpene resin, polyvinyl acetate resin.

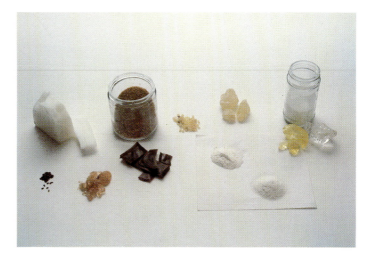

PLATE 4
Color Samples (see Chapter 7)

Front row, left to right: Blue-Wool Textile Fading Card (*top*), humidity indicator card (*bottom*), exposed Blue-Wool test panel with Textile Fading Card and black-painted aluminum covers (note the poor condition of the exposed colored pencil samples), reproduction of the visible spectrum hues.

Back row, left to right: Gray mask painted with Munsell Value 7 neutral gray acrylic emulsion paint, pigment samples, custom-made aluminum drawn-down bar and 20:1 template. *Right, top to bottom:* four different manufacturers' genuine Cobalt blue pigment in oil (1:20 in white), imitation "Cobalt blue hue" in oil (1:20 in white), genuine Cobalt blue in acrylic emulsion (1:20 in white).

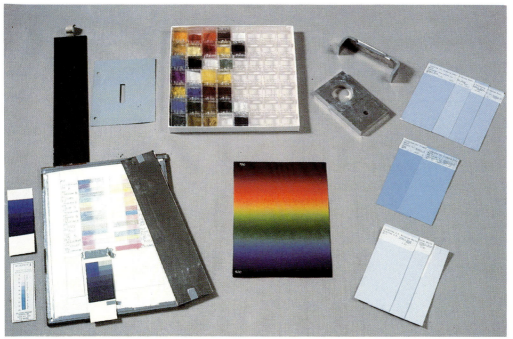

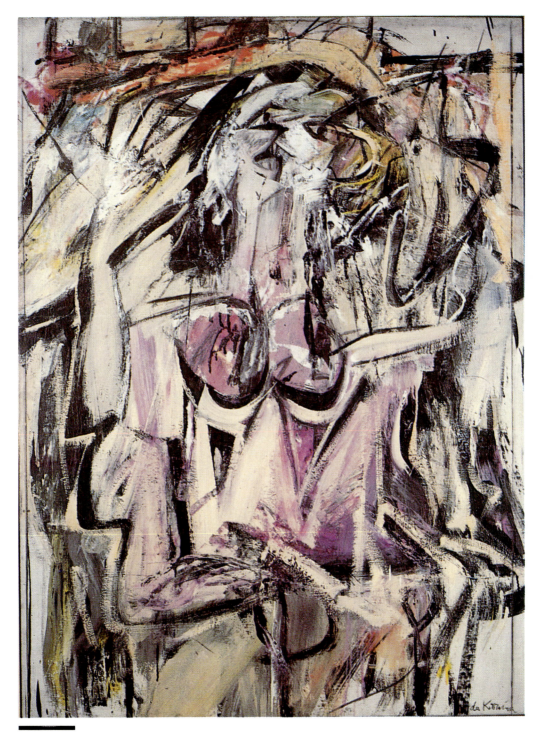

PLATE 5
Woman
Willem de Kooning (American, b. Holland 1904)
Oil on canvas, 1950, 64⅛″ × 46″
Collection Weatherspoon Gallery, UNC–Greensboro; Lena Kernodle McDuffie Memorial Gift, 1954.

An example of complex direct (and indirect) painting in oil. (See Chapter 9.)

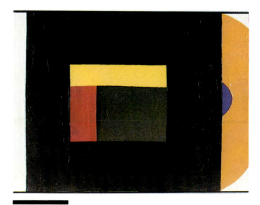

PLATE 6
Black Square Marries Orange Circle
Al Held (American)
Acrylic emulsion on paper on panel, 1965
18″ × 24″
Collection Weatherspoon Gallery
UNC–Greensboro; Dillard Collection 1965.

(See Chapter 10.)

PLATE 8
Still Life with Landscape
Christopher Stephens (American)
Egg tempera on gessoed panel, c. 1980
12″ × 9″
Courtesy of the artist.

Direct painting in egg tempera, but with translucent, shimmering applications of the paint. Limited palette, student work. (See Chapter 12.)

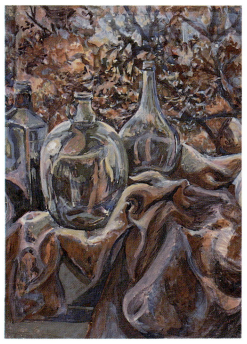

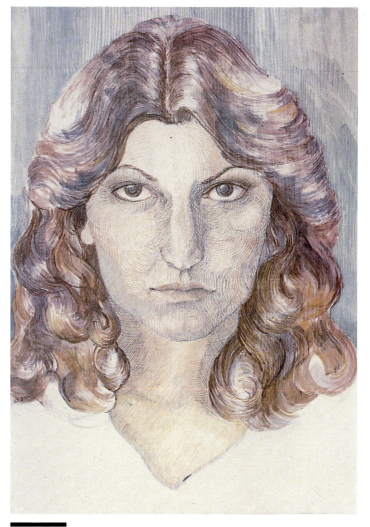

PLATE 7
Self Portrait
Cynthia Humphries (American)
Egg tempera on gessoed panel, c. 1979, 12″ × 9″
Courtesy of the artist.

Indirect building up of layers, using separated strokes of color, in the traditional style of egg tempera painting. Limited palette, student work. (See Chapter 12.)

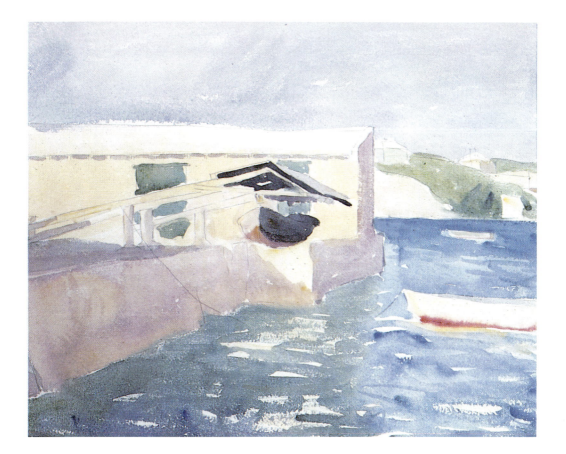

PLATE 9
***Waterfront, St. George* (Bermuda)**
George Ault (American, 1891–1948)
Watercolor on paper, 1922, 10½″ × 12³⁄₁₆″
Collection of Weatherspoon Gallery
UNC–Greensboro; Dillard Collection 1974.

(See Chapter 11.)

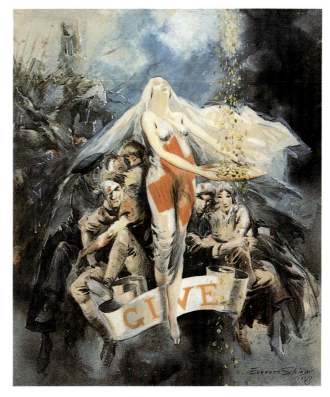

PLATE 10
***Red Cross Poster* (original work for poster)**
Everett Shinn (American, 1876–1953)
Watercolor and gouache on paper, 1918, 25″ × 21″
Collection of Weatherspoon Gallery
UNC–Greensboro
Gift of Pilot Life Insurance Company 1968.

(See Chapter 11.)

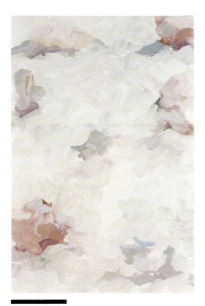

PLATE 11
Stones
Jeff Joyce (American, b. 1956)
Encaustic on panel, 1978
12″ × 9″
Collection of the author.

(See Chapter 13.)

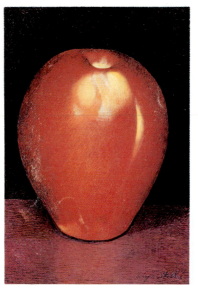

PLATE 12
Apple
Joseph Stella (American
b. Italy, 1877–1946)
Crayon on paper, n.d.
13⅛″ × 10½″
Collection of Weatherspoon
Gallery, UNC–Greensboro
Gift of Benjamin and Anne
Wortham Cone 1966.

(See Chapter 14.)

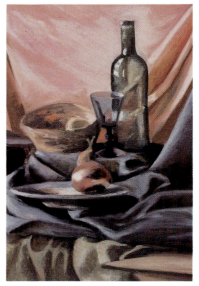

PLATE 13
Still Life
L. M. Samantha Smallwood
(American)
Oil on canvas, 1979
20″ × 16″
Collection of the author.

A student work, using a limited
oil palette of lead white, ivory
black, yellow ochre, and burnt
sienna. (See Appendix A.)

PLATE 14
Still Life
Louisa Matthiasdottir
(Icelandic, b. 1917)
Pastel on paper, 1971
19⅛″ × 25″
Collection of Weatherspoon
Gallery, UNC–Greensboro
Dillard Collection 1973.

(See Chapter 15.)

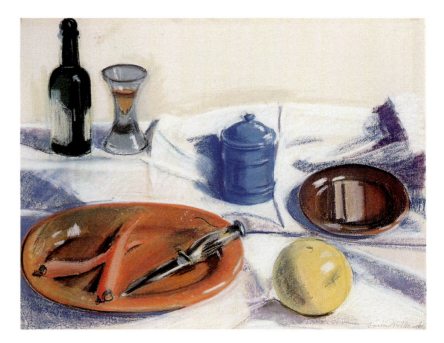

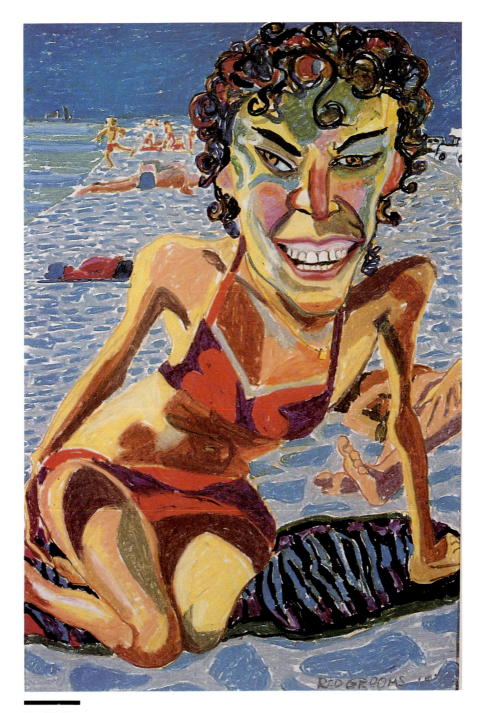

PLATE 15

Girl on Beach

Red Grooms (American, b. 1937)
Craypas (oil pastel) on paper, 1970, 35″ × 33″
Collection of Weatherspoon Gallery, UNC–Greensboro
Weatherspoon Gallery Association Purchase 1972.

(See Chapter 14.)

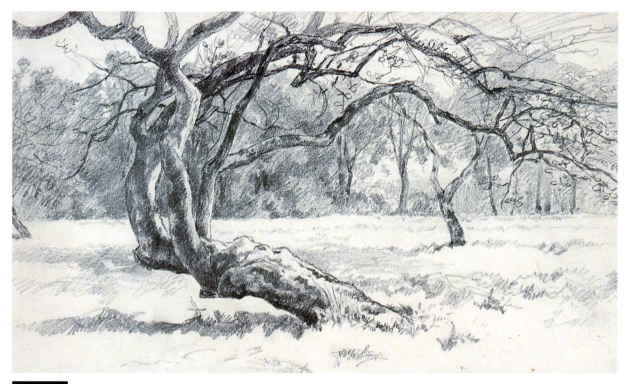

PLATE 16
Trees
H. S. Bisbing (American, 1849–1933)
Pencil on paper, n.d., 10⅛″ × 17³⁄₁₆″
Collection of Weatherspoon Gallery, UNC–Greensboro
Gift of Nelson C. White 1970.

(See Appendix B.)

PLATE 18
Maverick Landscape
Philip Guston (American, 1913–1980)
India ink on paper, 1964, 19″ × 25⅛″
Collection of Weatherspoon Gallery, UNC–Greensboro
Dillard Collection 1973.

(See Appendix B.)

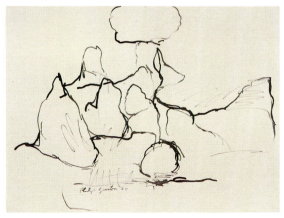

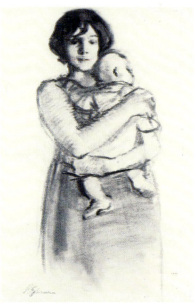

PLATE 17
Mother
Burton Silverman (American)
Charcoal on paper, n.d., 22⅞″ × 15″
Collection of Weatherspoon
Gallery, UNC–Greensboro
Dillard Collection.

(See Appendix B.)

TABLE 7.1 PIGMENTS (continued)

ARTISTS' HUE	Green	Brown	Brown
COMMON NAME	**Phthalocyanine Green**	**Mars Brown (Brown Iron Oxide)**	**Burnt Sienna**
COLOUR INDEX NAME, NUMBER	PG 36 (74265)	PBr 6 (77499)	PBr 7 (77492)
GENERIC NAME	Phthalocyanine Green	Brown Iron Oxide	Brown Iron Oxide
PROPRIETARY NAME(S)	Thalo, Monastral, etc.	Mars Brown	
SYNONYM(S)			Burnt Siena, Spanish Red, Caput Mortuum, VanDyke
DATES/PLACE OF DISCOVERY	1935–38	1800s	Prehistoric
CHEMICAL CLASS; CONSTITUENTS	Organic; brominated and chlorinated copper phthalocyanine; a derivative of phthalocyanine blue, PB 15	Inorganic; synthetic brown iron oxide or blends of synthetic iron oxides PY 42, PR 101 and PBk 11	Inorganic; calcined natural iron oxide
SOURCE	Synthetic organic	Synthetic inorganic	Natural inorganic, processed
TYPE	L, E	P	P
RESISTANCE TO:			
Aliphatic Hydrocarbons	Excellent	Excellent	Excellent
Esters	Excellent	Excellent	Excellent
Ethanols	Excellent	Excellent	Excellent
Ketones	Excellent	Excellent	Excellent
Xylene	Excellent	Excellent	Excellent
Water	Excellent	Excellent	Excellent
Linseed Oil	Excellent	Excellent	Excellent
HCl 5% (Acid)	Excellent	Poor, dissolves	Poor, dissolves
Na_2CO_3 5% (Alkali)	Excellent	Excellent	Excellent
Plasticizers	Excellent	Excellent	Excellent
Migration Through Dried Layers	Excellent	Excellent	Excellent
Soap Gel Bleeding	Excellent	Excellent	Excellent
MELTING POINT (°C)/ STABILITY TO °C	—/300	—/150	—/150
LIGHTFASTNESS (*CI*/ASTM D 4302)	EX/I	EX/I	EX/I
USE IN VEHICLES			
Oil; Oil Absorption; Drying Rate; Film Properties	×; M; A; G	×; L–M; A; E	×; L; A; G
Acrylic Solution	×	×	×
Acrylic Emulsion	×	×	×
Transparent Watercolor	×	×	×
Opaque Watercolor (Gouache)	×	×	×
Temperas	×	×	×
Casein	×	×	×
Encaustic	×	×	×
Frescos	×	×	×
Experimentals/Pastel/Alkyds	×/×/×	×/×/×	×/×/×
DRY REFRACTIVE INDEX	Low	High	High; low
DRY CHARACTERISTICS	Bright G → YG	Light Br → dark RBr	Light RBr → RBr → Dark RBr → PBr
HAZARDS	Copper may be slight hazard; avoid dust	Avoid dust	Avoid dust
OTHER COMMENTS	Excellent colorant wide industrial and artistic use; extended due to extremely high tinting strength; high chroma; flocculates in some paint systems; bronzing defect counteracted by extension in vehicles	Excellent and stable pigment; low chroma; better than the natural equivalents; origin of "Mars" name uncertain	Excellent pigment; hue depends on source and method of processing; low tinting strength; inexpensive

TABLE 7.1 **PIGMENTS** (*continued*)

ARTISTS' HUE	Brown	Brown	Brown
COMMON NAME	**Burnt Umber**	**Raw Sienna**	**Raw Umber**
COLOUR INDEX NAME, NUMBER	PBr 7 (77492/91/99)	PBr 7 (77492/91/99)	PBr 7 (77492/91/99)
GENERIC NAME	Brown Iron Oxide	Brown Iron Oxide	Brown Iron Oxide
PROPRIETARY NAME(S)			Same as Burnt Umber
SYNONYM(S)	Turkey Brown	Raw Siena	Same as Burnt Umber
DATES/PLACE OF DISCOVERY	Prehistoric	Prehistoric	Same as Burnt Umber
CHEMICAL CLASS; CONSTITUENTS	Inorganic; calcined natural iron oxide containing manganese; dioxide, alumina, and silica (trace)	Same as Burnt Sienna; (not calcined)	Same as Burnt Umber; (not calcined)
SOURCE	Natural inorganic, processed	Natural inorganic, processed	Natural inorganic, processed
TYPE	P	P	P
RESISTANCE TO:			
Aliphatic Hydrocarbons	Excellent	Excellent	Excellent
Esters	Excellent	Excellent	Excellent
Ethanols	Excellent	Excellent	Excellent
Ketones	Excellent	Excellent	Excellent
Xylene	Excellent	Excellent	Excellent
Water	Excellent	Excellent	Excellent
Linseed Oil	Excellent	Excellent	Excellent
HCl 5% (Acid)	Poor, dissolves	Poor, dissolves	Poor, dissolves
Na$_2$CO$_3$ 5% (Alkali)	Excellent	Excellent	Excellent
Plasticizers	Excellent	Excellent	Excellent
Migration Through Dried Layers	Excellent	Excellent	Excellent
Soap Gel Bleeding	Excellent	Excellent	Excellent
MELTING POINT (°C)/ STABILITY TO °C	—/150	—/150	—/150
LIGHTFASTNESS (*CI*/ASTM D 4302)	EX/I	EX/I	EX/I
USE IN VEHICLES			
Oil; Oil Absorption; Drying Rate; Film Properties	×; M; E; G	×; L; A; G	×; M; E; G
Acrylic Solution	×	×	×
Acrylic Emulsion	×	×	×
Transparent Watercolor	×	×	×
Opaque Watercolor (Gouache)	×	×	×
Temperas	×	×	×
Casein	×	×	×
Encaustic	×	×	×
Frescos	×	×	×
Experimentals/Pastel/Alkyds	×/×/×	×/×/×	×/×/×
DRY REFRACTIVE INDEX	Medium	Medium	Medium
DRY CHARACTERISTICS	Dark GBr → Dark PBr	Same as Burnt Sienna	Same as Burnt Umber
HAZARDS	Manganese may be slight hazard; avoid dust	Same as Burnt Sienna	Same as Burnt Umber
OTHER COMMENTS	Good pigment; good drier in oil; variable hue; low chroma; inexpensive; wide industrial and artistic use	Same as Burnt Sienna	Same as Burnt Umber

TABLE 7.1 **PIGMENTS** (*continued*)

ARTISTS' HUE	Black	Black	Black (Grey)
COMMON NAME	**Lamp Black**	**Carbon Black**	**Graphite**
COLOUR INDEX NAME, NUMBER	PBk 6/7 (77266)	Same as PBk 6/7	PBlk 10 (77265)
GENERIC NAME	Lamp Black/Carbon Bk		Same
PROPRIETARY NAME(S)	Carbon Black	Same as PBk 6/7	Various
SYNONYM(S)	Carbon Black	Furnace Black	Black Lead, Plumbago
DATES/PLACE OF DISCOVERY	Prehistoric	Prehistoric	Ancient, but name "graphite" coined in 1789 (from Greek: "to write")
CHEMICAL CLASS; CONSTITUENTS	Inorganic; nearly pure amorphous carbon made by burning petroleum residues such as tar or creosote	Same as PBk 6/7 (or by collecting soot from burning natural gas)	Organic; hexagonally crystalized allotrope of carbon
SOURCE	Natural inorganic, processed	Natural inorganic, processed	Natural organic; synthetic inorganic
TYPE	P	P	P, hexagonal crystal; E, sometimes, w/clay
RESISTANCE TO:			
Aliphatic Hydrocarbons	Excellent	Excellent	Not dissolved in organics
Esters	Excellent	Excellent	
Ethanols	Excellent	Excellent	
Ketones	Excellent	Excellent	
Xylene	Excellent	Excellent	
Water	Excellent	Excellent	Ok (water repellant)
Linseed Oil	Excellent	Excellent	Ok (fair)
HCl 5% (Acid)	Excellent	Excellent	Ok
Na₂CO₃ 5% (Alkali)	Excellent	Excellent	Ok
Plasticizers	Excellent	Excellent	Ok
Migration Through Dried Layers	Excellent	Excellent	Little
Soap Gel Bleeding	Excellent	Excellent	Ok
MELTING POINT (°C)/ STABILITY TO °C	—	—	—/EX
LIGHTFASTNESS (*CI*/ASTM D 4302)	EX/I	EX/I	permanent
USE IN VEHICLES			
Oil; Oil Absorption; Drying Rate; Film Properties	×; very high; VS; F–P	×; very high; VS; F–P	—; H; VS; P
Acrylic Solution	NT	NT	
Acrylic Emulsion	×	×	
Transparent Watercolor	×	×	
Opaque Watercolor (Gouache)	×	×	
Temperas	×	×	
Casein	×	×	
Encaustic	×	×	
Frescos	×	×	
Experimentals/Pastel/Alkyds	×/×/×	×/×/×	Drawing material
DRY REFRACTIVE INDEX	Medium	Medium	Medium
DRY CHARACTERISTICS	Bk ("warm")	Bk ("warm")	BrBlk ➔ Blk ➔ Grey Blk
HAZARDS	Carbon may be a slight hazard; avoid dust	Same as PBk 6/7	Dust highly toxic by inhalation
OTHER COMMENTS	Do not use in excess in oil vehicles—films slow-drying and unreliable; good hue	Same as PBk 6/7	Greasy dense black, often used as drawing material, may be combined with kaolin to regulate hardness & softness; extruded form encased in red cedar is common drawing pencil

TABLE 7.1 PIGMENTS (continued)

ARTISTS' HUE	Black	Black	White
COMMON NAME	**Ivory Black**	**Mars Black**	**Flake White**
COLOUR INDEX **NAME, NUMBER**	PBk 9 (77267)	PBk 11 (77499)	PW 1 (77597)
GENERIC NAME	Bone Black	Black Iron Oxide	White Lead (Basic Lead Carbonate)
PROPRIETARY NAME(S)		Mars Black	
SYNONYM(S)	Bone Black		Cremnitz, Silver, etc
DATES/PLACE OF DISCOVERY	Prehistoric	1800s	Ancient Greece/Roman
CHEMICAL CLASS; CONSTITUENTS	Organic/inorganic; amorphous carbon produced from charred or burnt animal bones (formerly tusks, hence name)	Inorganic; synthetic black iron oxide; ferroso ferric oxide from magnetic iron ore or from $FeSO_4$	Inorganic; basic lead carbonate; combination of lead carbonate and lead hydroxide by carbonation of lead
SOURCE	Natural inorganic, processed	Synthetic inorganic, processed	Natural inorganic, processed
TYPE	P	P	P
RESISTANCE TO:			
Aliphatic Hydrocarbons	Excellent	Excellent	Excellent
Esters	Excellent	Excellent	Excellent
Ethanols	Excellent	Excellent	Excellent
Ketones	Excellent	Excellent	Excellent
Xylene	Excellent	Excellent	Excellent
Water	Excellent	Excellent	Poor
Linseed Oil	Good	Excellent	Excellent
HCl 5% (Acid)	Excellent	Poor, dissolves	Decomposes, releases CO_2
Na₂CO₃ 5% (Alkali)	Excellent	Excellent	Excellent
Plasticizers	Excellent	Excellent	Excellent
Migration Through Dried Layers	Excellent	Excellent	Excellent
Soap Gel Bleeding	Excellent	Excellent	Excellent
MELTING POINT (°C)/ STABILITY TO °C	—/At high temp. leaves ash	—/150 → R	—/230 → R or YR
LIGHTFASTNESS (*CI*/ASTM D 4302)	EX/I	EX/I	EX/I (oil only)
USE IN VEHICLES			
Oil; Oil Absorption; Drying Rate; Film Properties	×; H; S; F–P	×; L; A; G	×; L; E; G
Acrylic Solution	×	×	NT
Acrylic Emulsion	×	×	P (NT)
Transparent Watercolor	×	×	P (NT)
Opaque Watercolor (Gouache)	×	×	P (NT)
Temperas	×	×	P (NT)
Casein	×	×	P (NT)
Encaustic	×	×	NT
Frescos	×	×	NT
Experimentals/Pastel/Alkyds	×/×/×	×/×/×	NT/NT/×
DRY REFRACTIVE INDEX	High	High	High
DRY CHARACTERISTICS	Bk ("cool")	Bk ("warm")	Warm White
HAZARDS	Carbon may be slight hazard; avoid dust	Avoid dust	Lead is toxic; avoid dust
OTHER COMMENTS	Only blue-black called "cool"; same limitations as other carbon blacks	Excellent pigment; generally better than PBk 6/7; weak tinting strength; widely used in industry; origin of "Mars" name uncertain	Well-known, ancient pigment, not used in water vehicles because of tendency to turn dark in polluted atmospheres and toxic hazard; excellent in oil

TABLE 7.1 **PIGMENTS** *(continued)*

ARTISTS' HUE	White	White
COMMON NAME	**Zinc White**	**Titanium White**
COLOUR INDEX **NAME, NUMBER**	PW 4 (77947)	PW 6 (77891)
GENERIC NAME	Zinc Oxide	Titanium Dioxide
PROPRIETARY NAME(S)	Chinese White	Titanium White, anatase or rutile
SYNONYM(S)		Titanium White
DATES/PLACE OF DISCOVERY	1751, first commercial production in 1850	1870; popular use in early 1900s
CHEMICAL CLASS; CONSTITUENTS	Inorganic; zinc oxide; calcined zinc ore which has been oxidized	Inorganic; Titanium dioxide (either rutile or anatase) with barium sulfate or zinc oxide
SOURCE	Natural inorganic, processed	Natural inorganic, processed
TYPE	P, E usually	P, E
RESISTANCE TO:		
Aliphatic Hydrocarbons	Excellent	Excellent
Esters	Excellent	Excellent
Ethanols	Excellent	Excellent
Ketones	Excellent	Excellent
Xylene	Excellent	Excellent
Water	Excellent	Excellent
Linseed Oil	Excellent	Excellent
HCl 5% (Acid)	Poor; Dissolves	Excellent
Na$_2$CO$_3$ 5% (Alkali)	Excellent	Excellent
Plasticizers	Excellent	Excellent
Migration Through Dried Layers	Excellent	Excellent
Soap Gel Bleeding	Excellent	Excellent
MELTING POINT (°C)/ STABILITY TO °C	—/At high temp → Y, if cooled, returns to W	—
LIGHTFASTNESS (*CI*/ASTM D 4302)	EX/I	EX/I
USE IN VEHICLES		
Oil; Oil Absorption; Drying Rate; Film Properties	×; H; VS; F	×; M; S; F
Acrylic Solution	×	×
Acrylic Emulsion	P (NT)	×
Transparent Watercolor	×	×
Opaque Watercolor (Gouache)	×	×
Temperas	×	×
Casein	×	×
Encaustic	×	×
Frescos	×	×
Experimentals/Pastel/Alkyds	×/×/×	×
DRY REFRACTIVE INDEX	Medium	High
DRY CHARACTERISTICS	Cool White	Cool White
HAZARDS	Zinc may be a slight hazard; avoid dust	TiO$_2$ may be slight hazard; avoid dust
OTHER COMMENTS	Excellent all-round pigment in wide use; commonly mixed with Titanium white for stability in artists' paints and to improve oil films	Excellent all-round pigment in wide use; extension improves films in oil; rutile more opaque; anatase chalks in exterior use, is bluer

TABLE 7.2
PIGMENTS OF HISTORICAL OR UNUSUAL INTEREST

COLOUR INDEX NAME/NUMBER	LIGHTFASTNESS	COMMON NAME	DESCRIPTION
PM1/77000	E	Aluminum	Al (element)
PM2/77400	E	Copper	Cu (element)
PM3/77480	E	Gold	Au (element)
PW5/77115	E	Lithopone	Heat-treated precipitated calcium carbonate
PW18/77220	E	Chalk	Inorganic calcium carbonate
PW19/77005	E	China clay	Inorganic; also known as Kaolin
PW20/77019	G	Mica	Hydrous aluminum potassium silicate; can be "micronized" to improve stability
PW21/77120	E	Blanc Fixe	Precipitated barium sulfate
PW22/77120	E	Barytes	Natural barium sulfate
PW23/77122	E	Alumina	Inorganic metallic soap
PW24/77002	E	Aluminum Hydrate	Inorganic
PW25/77231	E	Gypsum	Inorganic
PW26/77118	E	Asbestine	Inorganic; also known as talc
PW27/77811	E	Silica	Inorganic
PW27/77811	E	Diatomaceous Earth	Hydrous silica; used as a filler
PY32/77839	E	Strontium Yellow	Strontium chromate
PY36/77955	E	Zinc Yellow	Zinc chromate
PY39/77085	NT	King's Yellow	Arsenic sulfide, also known as orpiment or realgar; toxic
PY46/77577	NT	Litharge	Lead, also known as massicot; toxic
PB1/75780	P	Indigo	Dye extracted from fermented leaves of *Indigofera sumatrana*
PB30/77420	NT	Azurite	Copper carbonate + copper hydroxide; also known as Bremen blue
PB31/77437	NT	Egyptian Blue	Inorganic
PB32/77365	E	Azure Blue	Silica (crushed glass)
PB34/77450	E	Copper Blue	Copper
PV15/77007	E	Ultramarine Violet	Same as PB29, ultramarine blue
PG14/77199	E	Cadmium Green	PY37 + PB28, cadmium yellow + cobalt blue
PG16/77955	E	Zinc Green	PY36 + PB15 or PB29, zinc yellow + phthalocyanine blue or ultramarine blue
PG20/77408	F	Verdigris	Hydrated copper acetate
PG21/77410	G	Paris Green	Copper aceto-arsenite, also known as emerald green or verte emeraud; toxic

TABLE 7.2   *(continued)*
PIGMENTS OF HISTORICAL OR UNUSUAL INTEREST

COLOUR INDEX NAME/NUMBER	LIGHTFASTNESS	COMMON NAME	DESCRIPTION
PG22/77412	G	Scheele's Green	Copper
PG24/77013	E	Ultramarine Green	Same as PB29, ultramarine blue
PBk10/77265	E	Graphite	Carbon
NY3/75300	P	Tumeric	Dye from the ground root of *Curcuma longa*
NY6/75100	P	Saffron	Dye from the ground, dried stigma of *Crocus sativus* (iris)
NY9/75570	P	Quercitron Lake	Extracted dye from ground bark from *Quercus tinctoria* (oak)
NR4/75470	P-F	Cochineal	Dye from the dried bodies of the female *Coccus cacti,* 10% carminic acid; also known as carmine
*	P	Asphaltum	Tar; natural or distilled from petroleum; also sometimes called mummy
*	E	Bianco Sangiovanni	Calcium hydroxide + calcium carbonate (fresco white)
*	P	Bistre	Soot from charred beechwood
*	E	Bole	Red iron oxide or clay + iron oxide (used as the ground for gilding)
*	F-P	Cassel Earth	Earth with humus (organic matter) and bitumen (asphalt); also called Van Dyke brown or Cologne earth
*	E	Caput Mortuum	Bluish red iron oxide
*	E	Davy's Gray	Powdered slate
*	P	Dragon's Blood	Resinous exudation from fruit of *Calamus draco*
*	F-P	Gamboge	Resinous exudation from Guttifera
*	F-P	Hooker's Green	Prussian blue + gamboge
*	NT	Indian Yellow	Precipitated magnesium salt from euxanthic acid (heated cow urine)
*	P/F	Malachite	Natural basic copper carbonate
*	E	Minium	Natural or synthetic red lead oxide, also known as Minimum; toxic
*	E	Payne's Gray	PB29 + PBk6 + PY42, Ultramarine Blue + Carbon Black + Yellow Ochre
*	NT	Pumice	Complex aluminum, calcium, magnesium, iron, sodium, and potassium silicates (volcanic)
*	P	Sap Green	Dye from unripe buckthorn berries

* Pigment does not have an assigned *Colour Index* name or number.

TABLE 7.3
HAZARDOUS PIGMENTS

ARTISTS' HUE	Yellow	Yellow	Yellow	Yellow
COMMON NAME	Cadmium-Barium	Cadmium-Barium Y lt	Cadmium L, M, D	Naples Yellow
CI NAME	PY 37:1	PY 35:1	PY 37	PY 41
CI NUMBER	77199	77205:1	77199	77589/588
TYPE OF HAZARD				
Dust	×	×	×	×
Toxic Ingredient	Cadmium sulfide	Same as PY37:1	Same as PY37:1	Lead
RATING BY ROUTE OF ENTRY				
Absorption	n/a	Same as PY37:1	Same as PY37:1	Harmful
Aspiration	Harmful	Same as PY37:1	Same as PY37:1	Harmful
Ingestion	n/a	Same as PY37:1	Same as PY37:1	Toxic
Inhalation	Harmful	Same as PY37:1	Same as PY37:1	Toxic
POSSIBLE EFFECTS	Cadmium metal poisoning	Same as PY37:1	Same as PY37:1	Lead poisoning
CLASS OF HAZARD				
Severe				×
Moderate	×	Same as PY37:1	Same as PY37:1	
Mild				
Unknown	×, tests not conclusive as to toxicity of cadmium in this form	Same as PY37:1	Same as PY37:1	
CAUTIONS	Do not ingest; do not overheat	Same as PY37:1	Same as PY37:1	Do not ingest; do not overheat
OTHER COMMENTS	Hazards of cadmium pigments overstated in published accounts, but do not ignore	Same as PY37:1	Same as PY37:1	Use caution if handling this pigment in dry state

TABLE 7.3   (*continued*)
HAZARDOUS PIGMENTS

ARTISTS' HUE	Yellow	Yellow	Yellow	Yellow
COMMON NAME	Titanium Yellow	Nickel Azo Yellow	Nickel Dioxine	Chrome Yellows
CI NAME	PY 53	PY 150	PY 153	PY 34
CI NUMBER	n/a	n/a	n/a	77600
TYPE OF HAZARD				
Dust	×	×	×	×
Toxic Ingredient	Metallic nickel	Metallic nickel	Nickel	Lead chromates
RATING BY ROUTE OF ENTRY				
Absorption	n/a	n/a	Skin sensitizer	Toxic
Aspiration	Harmful	Harmful	Harmful	Toxic
Ingestion	Harmful	Harmful	Harmful	Toxic
Inhalation	Harmful	Harmful	Harmful	Toxic
POSSIBLE EFFECTS	Skin sensitizer; skin allergy	Skin sensitizer	Skin allergy	Lead poisoning
CLASS OF HAZARD				
Severe				×
Moderate	×	×	×	
Mild				
Unknown				
CAUTIONS	Avoid skin exposure; do not overheat	Avoid skin exposure, do not overheat	Avoid skin exposure; do not overheat	*Do not use these pigments*
OTHER COMMENTS				Yellow pigments of better stability & less hazard now available

TABLE 7.3 *(continued)*
HAZARDOUS PIGMENTS

ARTISTS' HUE	Orange	Orange	Orange	Orange
COMMON NAME	Cadmium Orange	Cadmium-Barium	Cadmium-Barium Vermilion	Cadmium Vermilion
CI NAME	PO 20	PO 20:1	PO 23:1	PO 23
CI NUMBER	77196/199/202	77196/199/202:1	77201:1	77201
TYPE OF HAZARD				
Dust	×	×	×	×
Toxic Ingredient	Cadmium sulfoselenide	Cadmium sulfoselenide	Cadmium metal and mercury	Cadmium metal and mercury
RATING BY ROUTE OF ENTRY				
Absorption	n/a	Same as PO 20	Harmful	Same as PO 23:1
Aspiration	Harmful	Same as PO 20	Harmful	Same as PO 23:1
Ingestion	n/a	Same as PO 20	Harmful	Same as PO 23:1
Inhalation	Harmful	Same as PO 20	Harmful	Same as PO 23:1
POSSIBLE EFFECTS	Cadmium metal poisoning	Same as PO 20	Cadmium and mercury poisoning	Same as PO 23:1
CLASS OF HAZARD		Same as PO 20		Same as PO 23:1
Severe				
Moderate	×		×	
Mild				
Unknown	×, tests not conclusive as to toxicity in this form	Same as PO 20		
CAUTIONS	Do not ingest; do not overheat	Same as PO 20	Do not ingest; do not overheat	Same as PO 23:1
OTHER COMMENTS	Hazards of cadmium pigments are overstated in published accounts, but do not ignore	Same as PO 20		

TABLE 7.3   *(continued)*
HAZARDOUS PIGMENTS

ARTISTS' HUE	Red	Red	Red	Red
COMMON NAME	Vermilion	Cadmium-Barium	Cadmium	Cadmium Vermilion
CI NAME	PR 106	PR 108	PR 108:1	PR 113
CI NUMBER	77766	77202	77202:1	77201
TYPE OF HAZARD				
Dust	×	×	×	×
Toxic Ingredient	Mercuric sulfide	Cadmium sulfoselenide	Cadmium sulfoselenide	Cadmium and mercury sulfides
RATING BY ROUTE OF ENTRY				
Absorption	Harmful/toxic	n/a	n/a	Harmful
Aspiration	Harmful	Harmful	Harmful	Toxic
Ingestion	Harmful/toxic	n/a	n/a	Toxic
Inhalation	Harmful	Harmful	Harmful	Harmful
POSSIBLE EFFECTS	Mercury poisoning	Cadmium poisoning	Cadmium poisoning	Cadmium or mercury poisoning
CLASS OF HAZARD				
Severe	×			×, mercury
Moderate	×	×	×	×, cadmium
Mild				
Unknown		×, tests not conclusive as to toxicity of cadmium in this form	×, tests not conclusive as to toxicity of cadmium in this form	
CAUTIONS	Do not ingest; do not overheat	Do not ingest; do not overheat	Do not ingest; do not overheat	Do not ingest; do not overheat
OTHER COMMENTS		Hazards of cadmium pigments overstated in published accounts, but do not ignore	Hazards of cadmium pigments overstated in published accounts, but do not ignore	

TABLE 7.3 *(continued)*
HAZARDOUS PIGMENTS

ARTISTS' HUE	Red	Purple	Purple	Blue
COMMON NAME	Cadmium-Barium Vermilion	Cobalt Violet	Manganese Violet	Phthalocyanine
CI NAME	PR 113:1	PV 14	PV 16	PB 15
CI NUMBER	77201:1	77360	77742	74160
TYPE OF HAZARD				
Dust	×	×	×	×
Toxic Ingredient	Cadmium and mercury sulfides	Cobalt oxide	Manganese metal	Copper (alpha form)
RATING BY ROUTE OF ENTRY				
Absorption	Harmful	n/a	Skin sensitizer	Harmful
Aspiration	Toxic	Harmful	Harmful	Harmful
Ingestion	Toxic	Harmful	Harmful	Harmful
Inhalation	Harmful	Harmful	Harmful	Harmful
POSSIBLE EFFECTS	Cadmium or mercury poisoning	Cobalt sensitization	Manganese sensitization	Copper sensitization
CLASS OF HAZARD				
Severe	×, mercury			
Moderate	×, cadmium			
Mild		×	×	×
Unknown				
CAUTIONS	Do not ingest; do not overheat	Do not ingest; do not overheat; avoid skin exposure	Do not ingest; do not overheat; avoid skin exposure	Do not ingest; do not overheat; avoid skin exposure
OTHER COMMENTS		Do *not* confuse with *cobalt arsenate*, $CO_3(AsO_4)_2$, which is toxic		Copper may be a slight hazard

TABLE 7.3 *(continued)*
HAZARDOUS PIGMENTS

ARTISTS' HUE	Blue	Blue	Blue	Blue
COMMON NAME	Cobalt	Manganese	Cerulean	Cerulean (Chromium)
CI NAME	PB 28	PB 33	PB 35	PB 36
CI NUMBER	77346	77112	77368	77343
TYPE OF HAZARD				
Dust	×	×	×	×
Toxic Ingredient	Cobalt oxide	Barium manganate	Cobalt oxide	Cobalt oxide
RATING BY ROUTE OF ENTRY				
Absorption	Skin sensitizer	Skin sensitizer	Skin sensitizer	Skin sensitizer
Aspiration	Harmful	Harmful	Harmful	Harmful
Ingestion	Harmful	Harmful	Harmful	Harmful
Inhalation	Harmful	Harmful	Harmful	Harmful
POSSIBLE EFFECTS	Cobalt sensitization	Manganese sensitization	Cobalt sensitization	Cobalt sensitization
CLASS OF HAZARD				
Severe				
Moderate				
Mild	×	×	×	×
Unknown				
CAUTIONS	Do not ingest; do not overheat; avoid skin exposure	Do not ingest; do not overheat; avoid skin exposure	Do not ingest; do not overheat; avoid skin exposure	Do not ingest; do not overheat; avoid skin exposure
OTHER COMMENTS				

TABLE 7.3 (continued)
HAZARDOUS PIGMENTS

ARTISTS' HUE	Green	Green	Green	Green
COMMON NAME	Phthalocyanine	Green Gold	Chromium Oxide	Cobalt Green
CI NAME	PG 7	PG 10	PG 17	PG 19
CI NUMBER	74260	12775	77288	77335
TYPE OF HAZARD				
Dust	×	×	×	×
Toxic Ingredient	Polychloro copper phthalocyanine	Nickel metal	Chromium metal	Cobalt metal
RATING BY ROUTE OF ENTRY				
Absorption	Skin sensitizer	Skin sensitizer	Skin sensitizer	Skin sensitizer
Aspiration	Harmful	Harmful	Harmful	Harmful
Ingestion	Harmful	Harmful	Harmful	Harmful
Inhalation	Harmful	Harmful	Harmful	Harmful
POSSIBLE EFFECTS	Copper sensitization	Nickel sensitization	Chromium sensitization	Cobalt sensitization
CLASS OF HAZARD				
Severe				
Moderate				
Mild	×	×	×	×
Unknown				
CAUTIONS	Do not ingest; do not overheat; avoid skin exposure	Do not ingest; do not overheat; avoid skin exposure	Do not ingest; do not overheat; avoid skin exposure	Do not ingest; do not overheat; avoid skin exposure
OTHER COMMENTS				

TABLE 7.3   *(continued)*
HAZARDOUS PIGMENTS

ARTISTS' HUE	Green	Brown	Black
COMMON NAME	Phthalocyanine	Burnt/Raw Umbers	All Carbon Blacks
CI NAME	PG 36	PBr 7	PBk 6 & PBk 7
CI NUMBER	74265	77492/491/499	77266
TYPE OF HAZARD			
Dust	×	×	×
Toxic Ingredient	Copper metal	Manganese metal	Carbon
RATING BY ROUTE OF ENTRY			
Absorption	Skin sensitizer	Skin sensitizer	Harmful
Aspiration	Harmful	Harmful	Toxic
Ingestion	Harmful	Harmful	Harmful
Inhalation	Harmful	Harmful	Toxic
POSSIBLE EFFECTS	Copper sensitization	Manganese sensitization	Carbon particles could create lung problems
CLASS OF HAZARD			
Severe			
Moderate			×
Mild	×	×	
Unknown			
CAUTIONS	Do not ingest; do not overheat; avoid skin exposure	Do not ingest; do not overheat; avoid skin exposure	Do not ingest; do not overheat; avoid skin exposure
OTHER COMMENTS			

TABLE 7.3 *(continued)*
HAZARDOUS PIGMENTS

ARTISTS' HUE	White	White	White
COMMON NAME	Flake White	Zinc White	Titanium White
CI NAME	PW 1	PW 4	PW 6
CI NUMBER	77597	77949	77891
TYPE OF HAZARD			
Dust	×	×	×
Toxic Ingredient	Lead carbonate	Zinc metal	Titanium metal
RATING BY ROUTE OF ENTRY			
Absorption	Harmful	n/a	n/a
Aspiration	Toxic	Harmful	Harmful
Ingestion	Toxic	n/a	n/a
Inhalation	Toxic	Harmful	Harmful
POSSIBLE EFFECTS	Lead poisoning	Zinc generally considered inert but can cause allergies	Titanium sensitization possible
CLASS OF HAZARD			
Severe	×		
Moderate	×		
Mild		×	×
Unknown			
CAUTIONS	Do not ingest; do not overheat; avoid skin exposure	Do not ingest; do not overheat; avoid skin exposure	Do not ingest; do not overheat; avoid skin exposure
OTHER COMMENTS			

TABLE 7.4
DRYING RATES OF PIGMENTS IN OIL

PIGMENT	FAST	AVERAGE	SLOW	VERY SLOW	HARD	BRITTLE	STRONG	FLEXIBLE	SOFT
Umbers	×				×		×		
Prussian Blue	×				×				
Phthalocyanine Blue	×				×				
Flake White	×				×		×	×	
Burnt Sienna	×				×		×		
Earth Yellows		×					×		
Cobalt Blue		×				×			
Cobalt Violet		×				×			
Synthetic Iron Oxides (Mars)		×					×		
Cobalt Green		×			×			×	
Chromium Oxide, Opaque		×			×			×	
Chromium Oxide, Transparent		×			×			×	
Naples Yellow		×					×		
Zinc Yellow		×			×	×			
Red Iron Oxides, Natural		×				×			
Green Earth			×					×	×
Cerulean Blue			×						×
Ultramarines			×		×	×			
Yellow Ochre			×				×		
Quinacridones			×						×
Dioxazine Purple			×						×
Arylide Yellow and Orange			×		×				
Ivory, Carbon, Lamp Black				×					×
Cadmiums				×			×		
Mercuric Sulfides				×			×		
Zinc White					×	×			
Alizarin Crimson				×					×

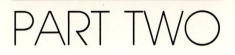

PART TWO

PAINT MANUFACTURE AND PAINTING TECHNIQUES

In Part Two, most of the paints an artist is likely to use are discussed. Making the paints, and procedures for applying both the homemade and commercial varieties, are covered. In addition, some unusual materials, such as the wax soaps and some of the mural techniques, are discussed. There is some emphasis on the traditional methods of employing these materials, since those methods have developed successfully over many years, but other application methods are also explored.

CHAPTER 8

PAINTING TECHNIQUES AND MAKING PAINTS

The beginnings of modern art can be traced far back in human history. The abstractions of human form in Egyptian wall painting certainly influenced twentieth century painting. But generally we think of the end of the nineteenth century as the beginning of the modern era. The pioneering efforts of a host of painters, notably Cézanne, Matisse, and Picasso, taught artists that the old rules of expression no longer applied, and that the restricting harness of tradition could be discarded. One result of this new way of thinking was a burst of creative energy that has produced many important works of art in this century.

Along with new ways of making paintings an idea developed that it was the concept of the work that was most important; if it were not for the idea, the work would have no meaning. This is surely undeniable, but there is something very discouraging about seeing an idea lose its meaning because the artist forgot, or ignored, the tradition of good craftsmanship. The concept is the basis for the work, but the painting expresses it; if the work deteriorates so that one's perception of it is altered, then the idea can be altered. It is possible to look at many well-known twentieth-century paintings as little as 20 years old and see that they have changed—the color has faded or changed; the collage materials have darkened, yellowed, or cracked; the paint has flaked—so much that the artists' original intention may be undiscernible. This is an irretrievable loss.

Each painting technique has a few fundamental rules for proper physical construction. Within these restrictions, which are more or less broad depending on the medium, a multitude of manipulations is possible. Outside the limits, one may find that one has produced a work that will not survive even a generation.

MAKING PAINT IN THE STUDIO

Making one's own paint was an activity engaged in by nearly every painter until the early part of the eighteenth century, when commercially made artists' paints became more widely available. Today, few artists understand the complexities of the process and, like their colleagues from the eighteenth and nineteenth centuries, rely heavily on the expertise of artists' paint makers for the quality of their paints. No one doubts that the manufacturers have a great deal of experience (some companies that began in the eighteenth century are still operating today) and that their products are superior. Still, the artist is often left to guess at some of the quality, using secondhand information. In this respect, the home manufacture of paints is a valuable experience.

Many paint-making procedures are similar; the difference between paints is in the vehicle, the liquid part of the paint. The most desirable qualities of a well-made paint include the following:

1. The even dispersion of pigment particles in the vehicle. The paints should be smooth, with each pigment particle separated from its neighbor and completely surrounded by a film of the vehicle (Figure 8.1).

2. The even consistency of texture throughout a range of hues. The paints should be characteristic of their type; a range of hues should have similar handling, textural, and drying properties.

The difficulties of making paint in the studio are related to these fundamental requirements. Without mechanical aids, the even and complete dispersion of the pigment in the vehicle is hard to attain. Manufacturers use triple-roller mills (water-cooled, high-pressure, high-speed grinders) to make excellent dispersions. With practice and experience, the basic requirements can be nearly met, though from a purely technical view homemade paints will not fully equal those made on a three-roll mill. Commercial paints are manufactured to a standard that is an average demanded by the customer—and up to 90 percent of the customers of a typical company are hobbyists, not professional artists. The advantages to artists of home-made paints are these:

1. Assurance of content. One has control over the ingredients used in the paint.

2. Clarity of hue. One can make paints far stronger than the average commercial type, with the fullest strength masstones.

3. Ability to adjust the paints according to personal needs.

There are some hazards associated with making paints which every artist should be aware of, although the precautions are standard and easily taken:

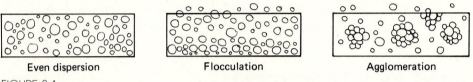

Even dispersion　　　　Flocculation　　　　Agglomeration

FIGURE 8.1
Well-Dispersed Paint, and Faults of Poorly Dispersed Paint

Left to right: Even dispersion, flocculation, agglomeration (pigment particles come in varying shapes—they are not necessarily round).

1. Pigments are fine powders that can easily be inhaled. Chronic ailments can result from inhalation of dusts—even nontoxic dusts. Wear a dust mask when handling dry pigments, and do not handle them carelessly.

2. Avoid the use of toxic pigments altogether unless the following clothing and protective devices are worn: a long-sleeved smock (used only in the studio), impermeable gloves, splash goggles, dust mask with organic mist filter. These items need be worn only until the paint paste is made, when the hazards of dusts become negligible.

3. Some vehicles can be dangerous or contain dangerous components. Wear the appropriate protective devices specified for the particular material.

It is prudent to exercise caution by knowing all the ingredients—and their potential hazards—for a particular paint, and by taking the most effective measures to protect oneself from harmful exposures. A Material Safety Data Sheet (MSDS) for each ingredient should be consulted before using that ingredient. MSDSs can be obtained from the supplier or manufacturer of the ingredient. There should be no shortcuts.

BASIC TOOLS AND MATERIALS

The following are the basic tools and materials used in the studio manufacture of artists' paints:

1. A large, sturdy table with a wooden top into which nails can be driven.

2. A slab, made of ¼-inch (6 mm) thick tempered glass or marble, of sufficiently large size to be practical—perhaps 18 inches by 24 inches (46 × 62 cm) or larger.

3. A piece of corrugated cardboard, to be used as a cushion beneath the slab. Cut it to the same size as the slab; it can be painted white, covered with white paper, or painted a neutral gray, so that the color of the paint can be better seen.

4. Four wooden cleats with double-headed nails, which are attached to the table top around the perimeter of the slab to hold it in place. Short stretcher bars will serve this purpose.

5. Medium grit (#120) Carborundum, for giving a frosted surface to the slab. Carborundum is the brand name for an abrasive wet-grinding powder.

6. A small palette knife.

7. A 6- to 8-inch (16–20 cm) long flexible steel spatula.

8. A 3- to 4-inch (8–10 cm) wide flexible steel wall scraper. This must be flexible; do not buy a cheap one that bends only where it attaches to the handle.

9. A glass muller with a flat face at least 3½ inches (9 cm) across. This is the tool used to grind the paint. When buying one of these solid glass implements, be sure there are no air bubbles near the brinding surface; they could eventually wear through and spoil the face.

10. Empty, collapsible tubes for paint, either "studio" size, about 1 by 4 inches (3 × 10 cm), or "pound" size, about 1½ by 6 inches (4 × 15 cm) for storing

the finished paint. Aluminum tubes are brittle but satisfactory; lead-tin alloy tubes should be coated with a plastic or wax film on the inside for use with sulfide pigments. Any tube used for water-based paints should have an internal coating to prevent corrosion (see Appendix D). Small capacity (2- to 4-ounce, 56–112 g) white or amber glass ointment jars with plastic caps can also be used. Plastic ointment jars will stain and are difficult to keep clean, but are satisfactory. Metal caps will rust if the paint is water-based.

11. Fabric-stretching pliers with wide jaws, for closing the filled tubes.

12. Artist-grade dry pigments.

13. A vehicle in which to grind the pigments, composed of a binder, a stabilizer, and other assorted ingredients, depending on the type of paint.

Figure 8.2 illustrates these tools and a typical paint-making setup.

PREPARING THE SLAB

The slab must be prepared with a frosty, toothy surface so that it can properly grind pigments in a vehicle. The muller and the Carborundum are used.

METHOD

1. Place the slab, with the corrugated cardboard beneath it, on the sturdy table. Cleat it in place by nailing the wooden strips to the table around the outside of the slab.

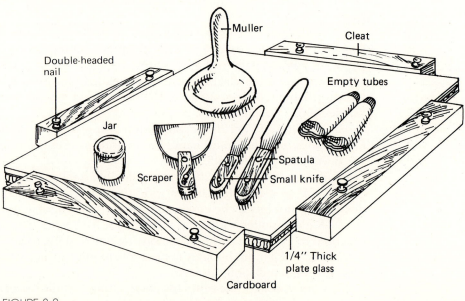

FIGURE 8.2
Paint-Making Tools and a Typical Grinding Setup

2. Put a few tablespoonsful of Carborundum on the slab and mix into a loose slurry with water and a palette knife.
3. Grind the slab with the muller in a methodical manner, using a loose-wristed, circular motion. Hold the muller with one hand low on the handle, resting more on the shoulder of the muller, and use the other hand to steady the tool. Do not exert undue downward pressure or allow the muller to skip up onto its edges. Grind patiently for about 10 to 15 minutes, or until the slab is completely and evenly frosted.
4. Scrape off and discard the slurry. Rinse the slab and muller thoroughly in water, and then wash with soap. Rinse again and allow to dry.

The slab and the muller will now have the same type of graining and texture on their respective surfaces. They are ready to grind paint.

PREDISPERSING PIGMENTS

Commercial manufacturers usually predisperse pigments in a liquid medium before grinding them into the paint vehicle. This is less important if a slow-drying vehicle like oil is used—it is sometimes unnecessary to predisperse oil paints—but crucial if a fast-drying vehicle is to be employed because the paint could dry out on the mill before it is finished. Artists who make their own paints do not generally predisperse pigments in a liquid other than the vehicle, since the quantities involved are not large and speed is not so critical. But occasionally certain pigments will be difficult to grind in the chosen vehicle without predispersion, and some techniques require that the pigments be predispersed.

The dispersion liquid is not always the same as the vehicle; it is more often the thinner for the finished paint, and is usually volatile, so that when it evaporates it leaves no residue in the paint. Any pigments that will be ground in a water-based vehicle can be predispersed in water; paints that are thinned with mineral spirits can have the pigments dispersed in mineral spirits. These two liquids cover all the paints that will be described here.

MATERIALS

1. Artist-grade dry pigments.
2. The thinner, either water or mineral spirits; use distilled water to avoid contamination of the pigment.
3. The grinding setup used for frosting the slab, including muller, spatulas, palette knives.
4. Ointment jars with plastic caps. The jars should be glass; the size depends on the volume of paste to be made. Other kinds of jars can be used, but they must be scrupulously clean. If there is any organic residue in the jar, as there might be if baby food jars are used, mold can form on the paste, spoiling it and making it unusable. As a precaution, boil the caps and jars together in water for at least half an hour.

METHOD

1. On the slab, mix the pigment and thinner together to a very stiff paste. Rub the pigment with the spatula to be sure each particle is wetted by the thinner. Use as little thinner as possible.
2. Grind the mixture with the muller until it forms a very smooth but still stiff paste. If the grinding makes the paste more liquid than stiff, spread it out in a layer to allow some of the thinner to evaporate, or add more pigment and grind again.
3. When the paste has reached a properly stiff consistency, pack it into a jar. Pick up the jar and lightly but firmly tap it on the table top, to force the paste down into the jar and drive out any air bubbles that could cause the interior of the paste to dry out. Pack the jar full to the top, and press a piece of polyethylene plastic (cut from a plastic trash can liner) over the surface of the paste. Cover tightly.

There are two possible problems to consider when predispersing pigments for grinding in oil. First, if too much thinner (mineral spirits) is used, it is possible that the resulting paint will not be like normal oil paint—its dry appearance may not resemble its wet appearance. Second, when the solvent evaporates from the film of dried oil paint, it may cause the film to shrink and crack. For these two reasons, it is probably better to predisperse pigments for oil paint in linseed oil.

If the jars used to store the predispersed paint are absolutely clean, the paste should last indefinitely. It should not be allowed to dry out; check it from time to time and moisten it with a little thinner if necessary. If the paste should dry out, remove it from the jar and grind it again. If the paste develops a mold or a strong musty odor, discard it.

In this and all subsequent paint-making operations, be sure to observe precautions regarding personal health and safety. Never underestimate potential hazards.

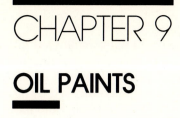

CHAPTER 9

OIL PAINTS

There obviously can be no strict adherence to all the rules about painting in oil given in this chapter. Oils are a popular and long-lived medium precisely because they are so flexible. The rules governing the use and application of oil paints can be stretched and bent. The simple exercise of common sense will allow for a broad and diverse amount of manipulation, and unhampered expressive freedom. For a discussion of painting tools and equipment, see Appendix A.

BASIC INGREDIENTS FOR HOMEMADE OIL PAINTS

The importance of making a good decision about what to include in an oil grinding vehicle cannot be overstated. Although oil paints are one of the easiest to make, a lot can go wrong with the finished product—and the defects will not show up until it is too late to do anything about them. There is latitude in the choice of ingredients, but every one of them will have an effect on the finished product.

The best advice is to use the simplest formula at first, and make written observations about the process and the character and performance of the paints that result. After some experience, you will have a basis for judging how the vehicle can be modified to fit more personal needs. At this point you may wish to experiment, while once again taking notes. If you devise a personal paint formula, it is well worth the effort to take good notes about how the formula developed so the paint can be made again. It does no good to have worked out a terrific new paint, only to realize that the formula was arrived at haphazardly and the paint cannot be duplicated. Be aware also that a complicated formula is not necessarily the best one, and that every ingredient will have an effect on the durability of the paint.

BINDERS

The most common binder for artists' oil paints is linseed oil. The cold-pressed variety is favored for its low viscosity and good wetting ability. Because it is expensive to produce and therefore expensive to buy, it is relatively rare to find it in use. Alkali-refined linseed oil is the common oil used by large- and small-scale paint makers. It is less expensive than the cold-pressed and more widely available.

Other oils that have a place in a vehicle, as a percentage of the total liquid, are those which are either less yellow or slower drying than linseed oil. They are used as modifiers for the oil vehicle, and include safflower, poppyseed, and recently some modified versions of natural soybean oil. To simplify matters, it is probably better to limit the use of these other oils to special applications and not use them in more than a 5 to 10 percent concentration of the total liquid vehicle.

DRIERS

Driers are sometimes added to the vehicle in an oil paint to produce a range of hues that have similar drying rates. On an industrial scale, the addition of such potentially damaging ingredients can be more controlled than on a small scale, so it is best to leave them out. Damar varnish has been suggested as an addition to an oil vehicle because it will impart its own rapid drying characteristics to the oil film; its reversibility is a significant problem, however, since it can make oil films less resistant to simple solvents and overpainting. It is probably best to leave varnishes and similar resins out of homemade oil paints. One suggested substitute for a drier is a faster-drying linseed oil like stand oil or sun-thickened oil as a 5 or 10 percent addition to the vehicle.

STABILIZERS

Stabilizers are the most appropriate additives to a homemade grinding vehicle. Properly used, they can give the degree of short or "buttery" consistency across a range of hues that most painters want in oil paints. Stabilizers also help to make difficult, "stringy" pigments grind into the oil a bit more easily, and help them to remain dispersed in the vehicle. Commercial producers use various inert pigments, such as aluminum stearate, alumina hydrate, and barium sulfate, as stabilizers. The small producer is more likely to use bleached white beeswax as a 1½ to 3 percent concentration in the vehicle.

PIGMENTS

Any pigment listed in Table 7.1 as suitable for oil paints can be used for the studio manufacture of oils. Some are so expensive, however, that if the cost of labor is taken into account, their use in homemade paints would be much more costly than purchasing them ready-made. Prices for dry artists' pigments fluctuate, so current price lists should be consulted in determining whether to use a pigment on this basis.

The degree of difficulty in grinding a particular pigment can also be taken into account, since extra time spent on a pigment raises the labor cost of making it into a paint. Generally speaking, the synthetic organic pigments are more difficult to grind into satisfactory oil paints because of their resistance to wetting; naturally, there are exceptions—and there are also inorganic mineral pigments that are difficult to disperse. Predispersing these pigments in mineral spirits will often make them easier to grind.

Toxicity is a factor in choosing a pigment. It is safer to eliminate those of a proven hazard, such as the lead-containing pigments, unless you are prepared to wear the necessary protective equipment. Handle all pigments in the dry state with care—do not splash them about, keep containers covered—and take all necessary precautions to guard against accidental misuse.

PREPARATION OF THE OIL VEHICLE

Assuming that the simplest vehicle will be chosen as the one for grinding, use a linseed oil and beeswax combination without any other additions. Use either cold-pressed or alkali-refined linseed oil and bleached white beeswax.

METHOD

1. Measure 7 fluid ounces (240 ml) oil into the top of a double boiler and heat very gently on a hotplate.
2. Into the heating oil break 1 ounce (28 g) of bleached white beeswax. Heat just until the wax melts completely, stirring to homogenize. Do not overheat, as this will cause the mixture to darken. Remove from the heat and allow to cool.
3. To the cooled mixture slowly add, while stirring, 24 fluid ounces (720 ml) more oil, to bring the total volume up to a quart (980 ml). The wax addition totals about 2 percent. Allow the mixture to homogenize for a day, and store it in a well-stoppered colored glass container. Use clean glass marbles to raise the level of the mixture in the bottle to the point where all air is excluded from the container (Figure 9.1). Kept this way, free from contact with air and away from light, this general purpose grinding oil will keep for quite a while. It is enough to make about 25 standard studio-size tubes of oil paint. If the least amount of oil is used to make the paint, it is possible to get more tubes out of this volume of oil.

The percentage of wax may be altered to suit a particular pigment when making this grinding oil. Some pigments can be ground into the oil without the stabilizer; others will require a bit more than the 2 percent addition. The 8 fluid ounces (240 ml) of wax–oil mixture can be stored separate from the balance of the oil, with the correct percentage of wax added only when necessary. This procedure is somewhat more difficult, since the calculations can be laborious;

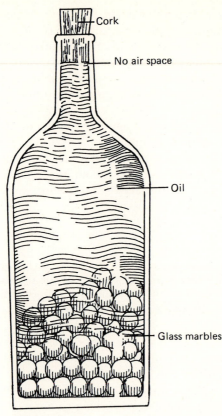

FIGURE 9.1
Glass Marbles in a Grinding Oil Storage Bottle

adding too much wax to the binder will produce a paint that does not dry to a hard film.

As the oil is removed from the storage bottle, add additional clean marbles to keep its level high and to exclude air. If a skin forms on the oil in the bottle, it has begun to dry and should be discarded. A piece of plastic wrap pressed onto the surface of the oil can help prevent skinning.

MAKING OIL PAINTS

METHOD

1. Apply a solvent-proof barrier hand cream to the hands and forearms (see Appendix D). This will prevent the absorption of mineral spirits into the skin; most will act as a barrier against mild organic solvents for about two hours of working time, but can be washed off with soap and water.

2. Set up the slab as for making the pigment pastes: on the cardboard cushion, held in place with the wooden cleats.

3. Put a volume of dry pigment in the center of the slab. The amount will depend on the size of the slab and how much paint is going to be made.

4. Add a small amount of grinding oil to the pigment and mix the two together with the spatula. Add a bit more oil and mix again. The pigment will slowly absorb the oil and begin to form a stiff paste, but do not be deceived by the crumbly nature of the mixture into adding excess oil. Remember that linseed oil is not the perfect binder; it yellows and/or darkens and grows brittle with age. Use the least amount of oil to get the job done. While adding the oil, bit by bit, rub the paste with the spatula to ensure complete wetting of the pigment particles. A very stiff paste, the consistency of cold peanut butter, should result. Remove the paste to one corner of the slab.

5. Scrape a small amount of the paste, no more than a tablespoonful, into the center of the slab.

6. Grind out the paste with the muller, using the same circular loose-wristed motion as when preparing the slab with the Carborundum. Downward pressure on the muller is not necessary; its own weight should provide the proper grinding action. Grind out the paste, working in a methodical manner, until it forms a thin film over the entire surface of the slab (Figure 9.2). Frequently scrape the sides of the muller where the paste rides up and accumulates, and grind this along with the rest. The grinding process is intended to disperse the pigment evenly in the vehicle, to be sure there is no air between the pigment particles. It is not a crushing operation—be patient.

Repeat this step until the paste is smooth and no grittiness is apparent. A drawdown with the wide scraper can be done to test the paint visually: hold the scraper at a 45° angle to a piece of white paper and draw it across a volume of the paint so a thin film is left. The film should appear smooth and without lumps of unground pigment (agglomeration) or other irregularities.

Check the consistency of the paint by gathering it all together in the center of the slab and observing its reaction to manipulation. It should retain brush marks if brushed out with a bristle brush, and it should hold its form if built to a thickness with the spatula. In other words, it should resemble commercial artists' oil paints. If the paint is too liquid, it must be reground with more pigment; return it to the paste pile and add a bit more pigment to the whole mass. If all is well, the material is oil paint. Scrape it all together and remove it to the corner of the slab opposite the pigment paste.

7. Continue in this fashion, grinding small amounts at one time, until all the paste has been made into paint. Remove the paint to the center of the slab and mix it all together with the spatula to make the general consistency

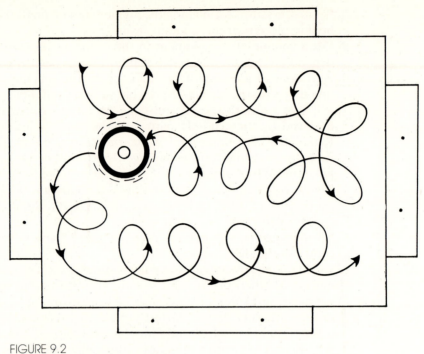

FIGURE 9.2
Grinding (Dispersion) Pattern

uniform. You may also quickly regrind the whole batch. The paint is now
ready to tube.

8. Hold the tube cap-end down. Loosen the cap to allow air to escape as the
paint is added.

9. Use the palette knife to feed the paint into the open end of the tube. Hold
the tube lightly in one hand, with the little finger cushioning the cap, and
gently but firmly tap the fist on the table top (Figure 9.3). This forces the
paint to settle into the tube, expels air from the cap end, and makes any
small air bubbles trapped in the paint rise out. Do not squeeze the tube or
bang the cap directly on the table; the result will be a burst or deformed
tube.

10. Add more paint, tapping frequently to remove trapped air, until the tube is
well packed and nearly full.

11. Place the tube flat on the slab and close the end by gently pressing on it
with the scraper. Expel a bit of paint and the remaining air by pulling the
tube out from under the spatula. Be careful not to cut the tube by pressing
too hard.

12. Fold the end of the tube two or three times, using the palette knife to get a
straight fold. Crimp the folded end with the stretching pliers.

13. Close the cap tightly and clean the outside of the tube with a rag dampened

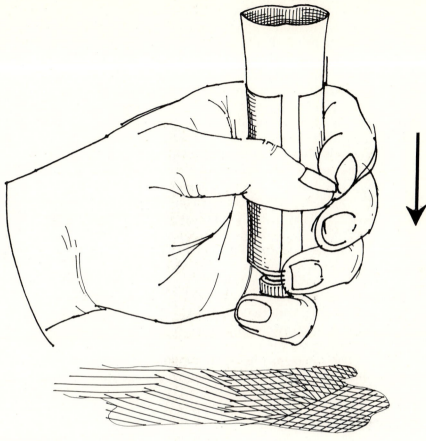

FIGURE 9.3
Packing a Tube of Paint
The little finger cushions the cap of the tube.

with mineral spirits. Label the tube with the hue, pigment, vehicle composition, and date.

14. Clean the slab, muller, and tools first with dry rags; then clean everything again, using a minimum of mineral spirits as a solvent. Wash everything with soap and water—scouring pads or scouring powder containing bleach are excellent—to clean all traces of color from the equipment. Rinse thoroughly and dry well. Once dry, the tools can be used for the next color.

15. Wash hands thoroughly, using plenty of soap (or one of the solventless handcleaning creams) and a scrub brush.

The key to the successful manufacture of oil paint—and, indeed, most other paints—is to apply a systematic method patiently. Any method of grinding that accomplishes the objective—a well-dispersed and consistent paint—is acceptable; that the method is efficient and safe is also a help.

Some paints should be placed in storage jars after grinding and before tubing, in order that they may rest and settle. This is a step commercial manufacturers include in their operation. Typically, mineral pigments can separate from the oil, in which case they are simply reground with more dry pigment. No further addition of oil is necessary. Some pigments should be allowed to rest for at least a month, some for as long as three months, before regrinding; be sure no air is present in the container.

Paints that are allowed to sit before they are tubed can be tested for defects. A well-made oil paint should not have agglomerations of undispersed pigment particles. A film of the finished paint should not show flocculation, a condition where the pigment particles clump together and rise to the surface of the film and can be rubbed off easily with a light swipe of a dry rag. Paints that flocculate usually do so due to a fault in formulation or from insufficient grinding, though the blame can also be laid to certain pigments, such as the phthalocyanines, which have a tendency to flocculate even when well dispersed.

A collapsible tube is best for the permanent storage of oil paint, but pharmaceutical ointment jars can be used. Again, remember that whenever air comes into contact with the exposed paint, the drying process will begin. If the jars are used, a polyethylene or plastic wrap, or even waxed paper, should be pressed over the surface of the paint to exclude air.

The choice of whether to modify the character or behavior of the oil vehicle should be made after personal experience with this simple, general recipe.

PAINTING TECHNIQUES

The process of oil painting is actually the application of a succession of layers. With the exception of some mixed media techniques, this process is the most complicated of all painting constructions. The way in which the layers are applied, and their composition, can affect the durability of the picture. From first to last, the layers are the support, the size, the ground, the drawing (an optional step), and the paint (and a painting medium, if one is used). In applying the paint, it is necessary to keep in mind the concept of "fat over lean." Moreover, impasto applications should be employed with caution.

THE LAYERS

The Support   The supports should be durable and stable. If it is attached to an auxiliary support, fabric should be stretched well in the recommended manner. Paper supports should be heavy enough to carry their own weight plus the weight of the paint, or else should be mounted on a rigid auxiliary support; lightweight papers should be matted when the picture is finished (see Chapter 17). Panels should be rigid and correctly braced.

The Size   Oil binders dry by oxidation and are destructive to susceptible supports. The size itself should be nondestructive; it must not be a shiny coating, but a sealer. It should be correctly formulated and applied.

The Ground   Grounds generally must be white and provide tooth, absorbency, or roughness, or some agreeable combination of the three so that the oil paint can adhere. An oil ground must be separated from the support by a size; the so-called "acrylic emulsion gessoes" are a size-and-ground combination and do not need a size to separate them from the support. The size and the ground together are sometimes referred to as the *primer,* or *priming;* preparing the support with a size and a ground is sometimes called priming the support. The ground may have a middle-value oil wash applied to it.

The Drawing   After the support has been prepared, a drawing can be made, in order to find the placement of the shapes and forms in the work. This step is not always necessary, and depends largely on the style, intention, or approach of the artist. Drawings are usually executed in soft pencil or vine charcoal or, on a gesso panel, in black ink, watercolor, or egg tempera, and then corrected or emphasized in oil paint thinned with mineral spirits to a very dilute consistency. After fixing the drawing with the dilute paint, excess dust from charcoal or chalk drawings should be removed from the surface by flicking with a rag; excess charcoal dust in particular can muddy color mixtures in subsequent overpainting.

THE APPLICATION OF PAINT

The paint itself can be applied in one layer or in several layers. The two techniques create quite different effects.

Direct Painting   A painting can be completed in one layer of paint, in one sitting, in a style called *alla prima* (Italian for "at the first"). In this approach, called "direct painting," the broadest shapes and hues are put on in a loose, very general way, with dilute paint. Application is by brush, rag, or any other tool. Definition is kept to a minimum, with a sense of the entire composition becoming the main objective. The painting is finished with daubs of paint the artist intends to leave as final statements—without further manipulation. This approach is obviously subject to variation, and circumstances will more often than not prevent the artist from completing a work in a completely pure "direct" manner.

Direct painting is difficult because it forces the artist to make quick and definite decisions about the progress of the work while being open to change, and because all the issues of painting—color, shape, mass, placement, composition, and so on—must be handled simultaneously.

Indirect Painting   Indirect painting is usually thought of as the traditional way, since its slow and deliberate method has a long history. Indirect painting was probably a necessity in the early days of pure oil painting; slow-drying oils and resins and the damp, cool northern European climate did not combine to provide a quick-drying and easy painting system.

In this method, considerably more complex in intention and effect than the direct method, layers of opaque and transparent paint are applied in succession. Theoretically, the color effects are made by *glazes*—transparent layers of darker colors applied over lighter colors—and *scumbles*—transparent layers of lighter colors applied over darker colors—so that the colors in the upper layers alter the appearance of those in the lower layers. Color resulting from this type of application has a greater luminosity than can be achieved in purely opaque direct painting, because light is not only reflected from the surface of the paint films but also travels through them and is refracted, while being reflected from the lower films. Thus, a strong orange hue can be softened and made to appear cooler by glazing over it a transparent blue; a cool, dark blue can be made warmer and lighter by scumbling over it a light orange hue.

The usual procedure is to first make a loose drawing on the ground. Then, using one or two colors plus a fast-drying, low oil content white (flake white), the composition is laid out in thin, fluid paint. The thinner is mineral spirits or gum turpentine, and in neither case should so much thinner be used that paint becomes like a watercolor glaze; this could cause adhesion problems later. Make the paint about the consistency of cream. The value range is established but kept lighter than is intended for the final picture and the drawing, if any, is made as sharp and precise as possible. Sharpness of delineation and lightness of tone are necessary in the monochrome because glazing and scumbling will lower value and chroma, and somewhat obscure details. The so-called underpainting, or *grisalle* (gray painting), is then allowed to dry for two or three days.

When the underpainting has dried, local and tonal color can be applied by glazing and scumbling. These effects can be applied by any means that suits the artist. Any combination of technical procedures and applications can be used to strengthen, clarify, or refine the underpainting. Big changes are not often made, but are possible if opaque painting is employed. Final applications of opaque paint are made, in the direct manner, to bring the painting to its conclusion. "Wet-into-wet" painting is possible (opaque or transparent paint applied to still-wet glazes and scumbles), as are many other manipulative effects that serve the purpose of the work. The idea of the work should always take precedence over the technical procedures, which are merely the means to express the idea.

"FAT OVER LEAN"

Whatever technique the artist uses when painting in oil, the traditional rule of "fat over lean" should be observed. "Fat," or more oily paint, must always be applied over "lean," or less oily paint. This is because thin oil paint applied over a glossy, oily underpainting may not adhere to the underpainting; the overpainting will also dry more quickly and is then liable to crack. The oily underpainting will develop a skin as the paint dries from the top down (unlike paints which dry by evaporation of a solvent or thinner), so that it appears to be dry. But underneath the skin the wet paint is still expanding and contracting. In conjunction with this rule, use pigments which are low oil absorbers in the underpainting (see Chapter

7, Table 7.1), which is the reason the white pigment of choice for underpainting in oil is lead white. Pigments that absorb a great deal of oil should be used only in the final layers of a complex indirect painting.

IMPASTO

Impasto, or thick, rough strokes of paint, must be applied with care when painting in oil. Impasto is most safely used when scattered throughout the painting in combination with thinner passages, rather than as a continuous layer. A thick layer of impasto may crack, sometimes through to the ground; this cracking can even lead to the detachment of portions of the paint from the picture.

PAINTING MEDIUMS

Painting mediums are used in oil painting (and other forms) to extend the color without diluting its chroma, to change the brushing or application characteristics of the tube paint, or to make the paint into a transparent glaze or scumble without giving up its oil content. Numerous proprietary materials made by every commercial paint maker can satisfy the demands of the marketplace; an artist will find that there is little need for most of these concoctions, and those few that are absolutely necessary are easily homemade. In some of the other heavy-bodied paints the addition of various materials to the paint film will not much affect the performance of the paint. But in oil paints, as versatile and flexible as they may be, such additions can be disastrous if not carefully controlled. It is advisable strictly to limit their use.

Glazing mediums are necessary for those who wish to paint indirectly and, as usual, recipes for them can be found in every book on the techniques of oil painting. The requirements of the artist should dictate the ingredients. Generally recipes contain advice to use at least three materials: an oil, a thinner, and a varnish. Damar varnish is the usually recommended varnish, gum turpentine the thinner, and a partially polymerized linseed oil—stand oil or sun-thickened oil—the oil.

Since the technique of glazing is simple but the physical makeup of an oil painting is complex (Figure 9.4), the addition of a complicated glaze medium to the structure of the work can be damaging. Damar and other varnishes are particularly susceptible to being redissolved by applications of fresh paint containing the varnish's solvent, and to being unintentionally removed during future cleaning or restoration. It is far better to use a simple glaze medium that does not contain a varnish, with perhaps the following ingredients: 1 part mineral spirits and 2 parts linseed stand oil or sun-thickened linseed oil.

A glaze medium is mixed to a soupy consistency with the tube paint, so that the applied film is thin and transparent. It can be applied with a soft brush, a rag, or other tool, to the painting on an easel—or, to avoid drips, to the painting laid horizontally on a table. Some practice, experience, patience, and a fairly good idea of the intended result are necessary to develop the technique.

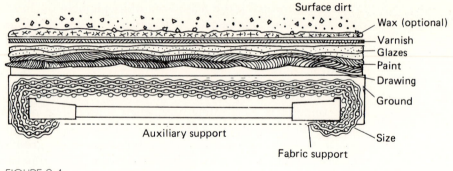

FIGURE 9.4
Cross-Section of an Oil Painting

Typical of other heavy-bodied paints.

Glaze mediums do not dry quickly, and additions of driers are sometimes recommended. Driers in oil paint can cause structural damage and should therefore be avoided; use a pigment, such as a metallic umber, which acts as a drier for linseed oil. When painting in oil, accept slow drying as an attribute of the medium—convenience and speed are not the point, and can be found in other techniques anyway.

In any event, it is best to use as little medium as possible. The point is to avoid yellowing or darkening, both of which can be traced to excess oil. It is possible to use no glaze medium, in fact, with a completely dry underpainting. Most tubed oil paints contain the proper proportion of oil to pigment, so mechanically spreading the paint into a thin film, using a rag or a stiff-bristled brush, can also work very well.

SAVING OIL PAINT

Oil paint placed on a palette will develop a dry outer skin as it begins the drying process. Skinned-over oil paint that has begun to dry will lose its adhesive and binding properties; breaking the skin and thinning the paint with a medium or diluent will not restore these properties. The paint should be scraped off the palette and discarded.

Here are some tricks for saving paint left over from a day's work: (1) Transfer the blobs of paint to a strip of glass and immerse it in water; (2) press plastic wrap closely over each bit of paint to exclude air; (3) cover the palette with plastic wrap and put it in a freezer. But these tricks may be more trouble than they are worth—especially since artists soon learn to judge the amount of paint they need for an average day's painting.

PAINTING OVER OLD OIL PAINTINGS

The practice of painting a new picture over an old one can work, and is economical with some kinds of painting, but it is not advisable with oil paints. Even with laborious scraping and sanding to remove thick strokes of paint, the old image will eventually appear beneath the new; oil paint films gradually become more transparent—they saponify, especially if painted with lead-containing pigments —as they age. *Saponification,* or turning to soap, produces an effect known as *pentimento,* and can be seen in many thinly painted early works where the artist evidently had a change of mind about the placement of a form or made corrections in drawing. Even a dry old oil painting may not provide enough tooth or absorbency to allow fresh oil paint to adhere properly.

COMMERCIAL OIL PAINTS

Professional-grade oil paints, the best of each manufacturer's line, are made for full-time professional artists. They usually contain the finest ingredients (that is, those ingredients which can be identified), and are well labeled. There is in fact little difference among the best products of the top manufacturers, since oil paints are relatively inexpensive to make. Everyone uses the best materials they can get for their best paints because good and continuing reputations are founded on this quality. What causes one artist to prefer one brand over another is usually an intangible, based on a preference for a certain texture, color range, or other subjective quality. These high-quality materials are sometimes expensive.

Student-grade paints, particularly in oil, differ only in two respects: The pigment content is less concentrated than in the professional grades, or is extended more than is necessary for proper color development (thus cheapening the product while also making it less expensive); and substitute pigments or pigment mixtures are often used in place of the more expensive genuine pigments. In the first instance, one must use more paint in order to have the same tinting strength, say, than with the professional version of the paint. In the second case, it would be impossible to get the same purple by mixing a cadmium red medium with a substituted "cobalt blue hue," a "variety of ultramarine," or a "mixture of phthalocyanine and ultramarine with white" as one would get using the genuine cobalt pigment.

It seems not worth the aggravation of attempting subtle color mixtures, nor is it worth the extra paint needed when using an adulterated, excessively extended pigment, to purchase student-grade materials. Student-grade paints are made for the 90 percent of the art materials market which is composed of hobbyists and "Sunday painters," not for professionals or serious students who are engaged in a professional course of study. Buy the professional grade of all paints: high price is not a guarantee of first-rate quality in a particular company's line, but at least there is some assurance of getting good value for the money.

THE CARE OF OIL PAINTINGS

A finished oil painting—most paintings, in fact—must receive a final coating of a protective varnish. The biggest problem with oil paintings is that they can take a long time to dry. Usually a picture of "average" thickness will require from three months to a year of drying before it can be varnished: very thin paint will take less time, and thicker paint will take longer. During this time the picture should be stored in a dust-free environment, since dirt deposited on the surface before it has received a protective coat cannot be removed without possible harm to the painting. Neither can unvarnished oil paintings be easily or completely cleaned. If the painting must leave the studio before it is varnished, put on a thin coat of a diluted retouch varnish as a temporary protection. Notify the client that the picture will be given its final varnish at a later date. Set the date, and be sure to follow through on the promise.

CHAPTER 10

SYNTHETICS

The synthetic paints make use of binders made from resins synthetically derived from petroleum. These resins are twentieth-century industrial innovations adapted to artists' materials. The artists' materials market is very small; the principal research and development of these resins is still conducted by the producers of the raw materials, who have relatively specific industrial applications as their motivation. Only a few manufacturers of artists' materials have the financial resources and expertise to develop the synthetic resins with specific art products as the end result. Most of the development has involved an attempt to improve on the performance and durability of traditional media, or to provide new effects not usually possible with the traditional paint systems—principally oils. Even after nearly 50 years of continuous use and development, during which time certain of the synthetic paints have become very popular, we should really consider them experimental systems. Fifty years is not a very long time when measured against the history of art.

The synthetics are by no means a replacement for other kinds of paints, although certain aspects of their performance—drying time, clarity, flexibility, or convenience—can be seen as definite improvements. These materials should be thought of as separate and distinct entities, with individual sets of problems and possibilities.

See Chapter 17 for instructions on the care of paintings made with synthetics. Paintings of acrylic solution and alkyd should be varnished; acrylic emulsion paintings should be protected with an acrylic solution varnish.

ACRYLIC SOLUTION PAINTS

BINDER

The binder for the acrylic solution paints is an acrylic resin—a solution of polymers, the principal monomer being an ester of acrylic acid. There are over 25 different acrylic solutions produced by Rohm and Haas, the main supplier, only a couple of which are dissolved in a solvent considered safe for normal artistic use without adding the burden of restricting and uncomfortable protective equipment. Acryloid B-67MT is supplied as a solution of 45 percent solids in mineral spirits and is compatible with alkyds and alkyd-oil mixtures, aliphatic hydrocarbon solvents, and other paint system liquids. Its main industrial use is for plastic coating, or for inks and lacquers. The binder is a rapid drier, and forms films that are clear, nonyellowing, reasonably flexible, and adhesive.

The binder comes as a rather heavy syrup. It is sometimes necessary to thin it a bit in order to be able to grind a paint easily by hand. Mineral spirits can be used for this purpose. It is not necessary to add more than 1 or 2 parts by volume of mineral spirits to 20 parts of the resin solution.

PIGMENTS

All the pigments compatible with acrylic solution resins, listed in Table 7.1, can be used with these paints. Generally, all pigments that can be used in oil are used in acrylic solution paints. Do not use the toxic pigments in the dry state.

PREPARATION OF THE VEHICLE

Other than a slight thinning, if necessary, no further preparation is needed. The procedures, materials, and methods for making these paints are exactly the same as for making oil paints, although, obviously, the vehicle is different. It is advisable to predisperse the pigments in mineral spirits, since speed is important when making these paints. Too much time spent trying to get a pigment well dispersed in the acrylic syrup may leave a hopelessly gummed-up slab and muller. Although the paints are simple to make, this problem can be significant if the artist is attempting to make large volumes of it. The solvent, mineral spirits, is volatile enough so that the paints begin to assume their tube consistency almost as soon as they are ground. They must be placed in air-free storage (tubes or jars) immediately. Of course, you can grind the paints to liquid, with an excess of solvent in the vehicle, and then allow them to reach the proper viscosity before packaging them.

PAINTING TECHNIQUES

The same tools, brushes, and other equipment and accessories used in oil painting can be used with the acrylic solution paints. The techniques used in preparing the surface and applying the paint varies slightly from those used when working with oils.

SUPPORTS AND GROUNDS

All the grounds so far discussed (oil, glue gesso, and acrylic emulsion) can be used with the acrylic solution paints; the paint's adhesion is very good. Lack of flexibility can be a problem, however, so the best supports would seem to be rigid, or flexible supports mounted on a rigid backing.

Since there is no problem with the oxidation of the acrylic resin affecting the integrity or durability of the support—as there is with linseed oil—it is possible to use these paints on unprimed supports. The support itself should be stable and white. Morris Louis's veil paintings of the 1950s—strikingly brilliant, thin transparent washes of Magna (acrylic solution) paints on unprimed cotton duck—are an excellent example of this technique. Of course the support (or any ground applied to it) can have a middle-tone wash of the paint applied to it.

THE APPLICATION OF PAINT

The acrylic solution paints behave very much like oil paints, and can be manipulated for a comparable range of effects. They have a slightly different brushing quality from oils, and may not seem quite as viscous. The dried paint films are more transparent than linseed oil's and are not yellow, so the colors seem more saturated and brilliant. Thickly painted passages of the paints will normally take less than two days to dry.

One difficulty with acrylic solution paints is that the films remain soluble in mineral spirits or gum turpentine after drying. This characteristic poses problems in overpainting, because subsequent applications of paint can dissolve and muddy the underpainting. To overcome this problem, it is necessary to isolate the underpainting with a retouch varnish made of an acrylic solution that is not soluble in mineral spirits. Acryloid A-21 is soluble in n-butyl alcohol and forms a tough film good for this purpose, but exercise caution: n-butyl alcohol should be considered flammable and harmful (its vapors can be very irritating). Once the isolating varnish is dry, overpainting will not lift previously painted layers.

COMMERCIAL BRANDS

Bocour Artists Colors, Inc., makes the best-known version of an acrylic solution paint, called Magna, which has been on the market since about 1946. This gives it the distinction of being one of the first commercially available synthetic paints. The Magna paints are offered in a good range of colors, although not nearly as extensive as the range found in oil paints, in the usual collapsible tubes. There is also a proprietary isolating varnish, two painting mediums—glossy and matte—and a gel medium for making the paints very viscous. The Magna paints are oil-miscible, but mixing them with oil paints will contribute the faults of oil—slow drying, yellowing, eventual embrittlement—unless the mixtures contain a preponderance of the acrylic resin.

Maimeri, an Italian company, has had its Restoration Paints marketed in this country by Conservation Materials, Ltd., and Charvoz-Carsen. These paints are ground in a "resinous gum," with "completely volatile solvents." From the description of their use and performance, it can be deduced that, although they may not be strictly acrylic resins, they perform the same way. The color range is rather limited to those pigments that have a certifiable degree of lightfastness (certified by Maimeri, that is); the solvent is mineral spirits or gum turpentine (see Appendix D).

ALKYD PAINTS

BINDERS AND PIGMENTS

Alkyd resins, as explained in Chapter 3, are made by reacting a polybasic acid with a polyhydric alcohol and an oil or a fatty acid. Typical combinations might include phthalic anhydride (the polybasic acid), ethylene glycol or glycerine (the polyhydric alcohols), and soybean, linseed, or safflower oils (the fatty acids or oils). These resins have had industrial applications in coatings technology for a long while—housepaints, deck paints, automobile paints—but only recently have they found use in durable artists' materials. The alkyds used for artists' paints are called "long-oil alkyds" because they have more than 60 percent oil content, usually in the range of 60 to 70 percent, depending on the type of oil. The oil content is essential if the alkyd binder is to form a stable, tough film because the alkyd resin by itself is considered too brittle. Curiously, artists and artist's paint makers called these oil-extended binders "oil-modified alkyds," but the raw materials manufacturers call them "unmodified alkyds." They also produce alkyds that have rosin or phenol-formaldehyde additions—for better hardness and water resistance—which are not for artists' paints, and these they call "modified alkyds."

Alkyd binders come from the manufacturer already prepared as a paint vehicle, at about 50 to 70 percent solids content. The solvent preferred for artists' paints is mineral spirits. A variety of alkyds modified by soybean, linseed, or safflower oil, reduced with mineral spirits, is available from Reichhold Chemicals (see Appendix D) under the trade name Beckosol. The 10-000 series, unmodified long-oil alkyds, are best for artists' paints. Two that may be used for homemade artists' paints are Beckosol 10-045, P-296-70, 65 percent soybean oil, reduced in mineral spirits, and Beckosol 10-051, P-381-70, 65 percent linseed oil, reduced in mineral spirits.

Another additive, appropriate for manufacture on a commercial scale but not feasible for homemade paints, is a drier. These are used with commercial artists' paints to ensure a relatively consistent drying rate among a range of colors, but cannot normally be added in such minute quantities as required for home production. A 1 to 2 percent wax stabilizer can be incorporated into the vehicle using the method given for oil paints.

The pigments appropriate for oil paints can be used for alkyd paints.

PREPARATION OF THE VEHICLE AND THE PAINT

Use the method given for oil paints if a wax stabilizer is desired. The binder as it comes from the supplier might have to be thinned slightly. Use a very small amount of mineral spirits—no more than 1 part in 20 of the alkyd binder.

The methods, materials, and procedures for making oil paints are the same for alkyd paints as well. The pigments can be predispersed in mineral spirits, but the vehicle does not dry out as quickly as the acrylic solution vehicle. The oil content of the vehicle slows the drying process.

PAINTING TECHNIQUES

The tools, brushes, and other equipment used with oils are used with alkyd paints. Painting techniques are very much like those used with oils.

SUPPORTS AND GROUNDS

The supports and grounds used for oil paints are appropriate for alkyd paints. Oxidation of the alkyd resin seems not to affect the durability of the support, so that unprimed, white supports (mounted papers or museum boards, for instance) can be used. A middle-tone wash of alkyd color can be used to modify the color of the support or the ground.

THE APPLICATION OF PAINT

The performance of alkyd paints is so similar to that of oil paints that the artist can easily use oil painting procedures. Alkyd paints will dry more quickly than oil, usually overnight; different colors will dry at different rates in homemade versions of the paint. Glazing and other indirect techniques can be used without waiting as long as one has to wait with traditional oil paints. Wet-into-wet techniques can be used for direct effects. The paints are nonyellowing (but linseed-oil-modified alkyds *do* yellow), and resemble dried oil paint more closely than acrylic solution paints. Oil paints can be judiciously mixed with alkyds to slow drying time or alter viscosity; too much oil paint can make the alkyd colors yellow as the oil ages.

COMMERCIAL PRODUCTS

Winsor & Newton and a small company in California, PDQ Artists' Paints (see Appendix D), both market an alkyd resin-based paint. It remains to be seen whether either manufacturer will make significant progress in the marketplace. The principal difficulty seems to be a misconception about the nature of the product—the name "alkyd" may not inspire distrust, but it certainly is not attracting customers. It may be helpful to think of these paints as oils, for that is really what they are if they contain more than 50 percent oil in the binder. Check the label on a can of oil-based deck paint sometime—industrial paints are better labeled for contents than artists' paints—and see how much alkyd resin is in the vehicle. Another problem with the artists' alkyds is that they are expensive (Winsor & Newton has to import them), although PDQ's paint is not so far out of line with good-quality oils. Finally, there has been a problem with formulation, leading some of the colors to dry erratically. This problem is apparently being quickly solved by Winsor & Newton.

A number of auxiliary materials are offered with the commercial brands of alkyds, which can also be used with oil paints. Winsor & Newton makes Liquin, a thin, translucent gel; Oleopasto, a stiff, translucent gel; and Win-Gel, a clear gel. All these mediums are more *thixotropic* than the paints—they are stiff, but flow easily when brushed out. The mediums can be mixed with the paints to produce impasto or glaze effects with little risk of cracking and yellowing, according to the manufacturer. When mixed with oils, the mediums will speed drying.

ACRYLIC EMULSION PAINTS

BINDERS

Artists' paints based on acrylic emulsion binders are by far the most popular of the synthetics, mainly because of their convenient and easy cleanup, but also because of their versatility and flexibility. The binder is an acrylic resin emulsified with water; of the more than 30 Rhoplex emulsions made by Rohm and Haas, Rhoplex AC-34 seems to be the most popular. When a thin film of the translucent, milky white liquid is painted out, it dries rapidly as the water evaporates to a relatively clear, tough, water-resistant layer. The dried films are not as clear as oil, acrylic solution, or alkyd films, but they are nonyellowing and do not get brittle as they age.

The formulation of an acrylic emulsion vehicle is the most complex of all the synthetic vehicles. The vehicle does not have to be a straight acrylic emulsion, but can contain other kinds of emulsions in addition: combinations of acrylic emulsions, acrylic plus polyvinyl acetate emulsions, or even two different AEs plus a PVAE, depending on the specific requirements of the manufacturer. The terms "co-polymer" (two polymers) and "ter-polymer" (three polymers) seen on some labels make reference to this practice.

In addition to the varieties of binders, a commercial vehicle can contain some or all of the following ingredients:

Dispersants and surfactants: improve the wetting of the pigments by the vehicle and inhibit pigment flocculation
Defoamers: inhibit foaming of the vehicle
Preservatives: prevent the growth of molds
Glycols: provide freeze-thaw stability and flexibility
Thickeners: increase the viscosity of the vehicle
pH balancers: adjust the alkalinity of the emulsion

These additives are let into the emulsion in precise proportions, depending on the pigment type being dispersed. Deviation from rather standard formulas can produce bad paints, which can "rock up" in the tube, or emulsions that "break," or separate.

PIGMENTS

Pigments cannot be loaded into the vehicle to the extent that they can in other paints, because of the character of the emulsion (particles suspended in a liquid). It is for this reason, combined with the translucent rather than transparent nature of the film itself, that colors in oil, alkyd, or acrylic solution vehicles may seem richer and higher in chroma than the same colors in acrylic emulsion paints. (When the acrylic emulsion paints dry, their chroma can approach that of oil paints.) Furthermore, some pigments cannot be used in the acrylic emulsion because of their inability to form stable paints. Titanium white, for instance, is the only white pigment used with acrylic emulsion vehicles. A typical pigment list for a line of acrylic emulsion paints might contain the following colors:

Reds:	Quinacridone reds
	Cadmium reds
	Naphthol reds
	Iron oxide reds
Oranges:	Cadmium orange
Yellows:	Cadmium yellows
	Arylide (Hansa) yellows
	Iron oxide yellows
Greens:	Phthalocyanine green
	Chromium oxide opaque
Blues:	Phthalocyanine blue
	Ultramarine blue
	Cerulean blue
	Cobalt blue
Purples:	Quinacridone violets
Blacks:	Ivory black
	Mars black or Iron oxide black
Whites:	Titanium white

PREPARATION OF THE VEHICLE AND THE PAINT

Because of the difficulties of adding small but precise volumes of a large number of important ingredients, there can be no assurance that acrylic emulsion vehicles put together in a studio will perform as expected. The precision necessary is possible only if large volumes of vehicle are being prepared, and even then lack of experience will often lead to a poor result. If the paint made under such circumstances does not exhibit immediate defects, it may show effects of early deterioration—flocculation, for instance—after a work is completed. For this reason, recipes or instructions for making acrylic emulsion paints must be adjusted individually for each pigment, and the kind of latitude possible in making other paints is not permissible here if one wishes to be assured of good quality.

A basic acrylic emulsion vehicle (which should not be assumed to be suitable for all pigments) *might* contain the following ingredients:

Binder:	1180 parts
	Rhoplex AC-34, 5 gallons (19.4 l); 93.70% of the vehicle

Glycol: 64 parts
Propylene glycol, used to slow the drying time of the vehicle, 1 quart (480 ml); 5% of the vehicle

Thickener: 16 parts
Methocel (Dow Chemical), 4 fl. oz. (120 ml); 1.25% of the vehicle

Surfactant: 1 part
Nacconal NRSF (Allied Chemical), a wetting agent, ⅛ fl. oz. (3.75 ml); 0.05% of the vehicle

Use 1 gallon (3.8 l) of the binder, and stir in the glycol. Add this mixture to the remaining 4 gallons (15.2 l) of binder. Add the thickener while stirring until the mixture is uniform and smooth. Mix the wetting agent with some water and add it to the emulsion while stirring. Making this large amount of vehicle can present storage problems; make smaller amounts using the recommended percentages of the various ingredients.

This vehicle does not contain pH balancers to counteract the extreme alkalinity of the binder, nor does it contain preservatives, dispersants, or defoamers. The pigments are mixed into the vehicle on a slab, using only a palette knife. The paints will dry too quickly with the heat of the friction caused by grinding with a glass muller. Store the finished paints in glass jars with plastic covers. Using pigments predispersed in water will help in getting a good dispersion, but do not be discouraged by paints that do not resemble commercial quality products; this is not a commercial product.

Artists who wish to experiment with acrylic emulsion paints are urged to contact the chemistry departments of the major suppliers of coatings emulsions —Borden Chemical, Rohm and Haas, and Union Carbide—for suggested formulations. Literature on artists' materials containing recipes should be consulted with healthy skepticism. As remarkable as they are, the acrylic (and vinyl) emulsion paints are not cure-alls for every painting problem, nor are they miracle paints that can be stretched beyond limits—and the limits are only now becoming known. Much of the published literature is occasionally overly enthusiastic.

PAINTING TECHNIQUES

TOOLS AND BRUSHES

Brushes and tools used in oil painting can be used with the acrylic emulsion paints, provided they are kept scrupulously clean. If the paint dries in the bristles, it is nearly impossible to remove without using strong solvents that can damage the brush. Brushes in use should be kept in a jar of water near the palette, and promptly and thoroughly washed with warm water and mild soap when the day's painting is over. Bristle brushes can soften and lose their snap and spring with prolonged soaking in water; some artists prefer to use the newer nylon filament brushes, which retain their lively feel.

The conventional wooden palette is difficult to use, since the paint dries rapidly. A plate glass palette is much easier to keep clean. And it should be kept clean during the painting session—dried bits of paint can interfere with clean color mixtures.

The usual assortment of scrapers, painting and palette knives and containers that accompany conventional oil painting are also used with the acrylic emulsion paints. Keep in mind, however, that water can cause metal knives and containers to rust. Plastic knives and glass or plastic jars, with plastic caps, can be substituted.

SUPPORTS AND GROUNDS

Because of the very adhesive and flexible nature of the binder, acrylic emulsion paints can be used on a great variety of supports. Among these are rigid panels such as aluminum, plywood, and hardboards, interior plaster and plasterboard walls; rag cardboard and paper and the usual fabric supports can also be used. The supports should be stable and durable.

Although the paint is adhesive enough to stick to plain support surfaces, a ground should be used to provide an evenly toothy and absorbent, and white, surface. An acrylic emulsion "gesso" primer is the recommended ground—it may be washed with a neutral or colored middle tone. Neither acrylic emulsion grounds nor paints should be applied over oil-painted surfaces—oil grounds or old oil paintings. The bond between these two different types of films may not be sufficiently stable to ensure the work's survival.

THE APPLICATION OF PAINT

Painting methods are flexible. The effects of direct and indirect painting can be used with results comparable to those in oil paint, the major difference being that the drying time for the paint is quick—about 20 minutes for an "average" layer—and ideas can be developed or changed sooner. In fact, the drying time may be too fast for those used to working wet-into-wet in oil. Two suggestions— use a very light misty spray of water to keep the paint film wet, or mix a retarder gel with the paint to make it dry slower. Traditional water-thinned paints—transparent and opaque watercolors, and temperas— can be imitated in this medium, although the actual characteristics and appearance of the original material cannot be duplicated.

When thinning the acrylic emulsion paints to imitate other water techniques, be careful not to use too much water. As with oil painting, it is possible to overthin the binder. The result is in a paint that lacks enough binder to hold the pigment to the support. Mix a little of the gloss or matte medium into the paint to improve the adhesion of the thinned-out color.

Unlike with oil paint, the rule of "fat over lean" need not be observed in acrylic emulsion painting techniques. The paint merely loses its water content through evaporation—the acrylic resin coalesces into a porous, continuous film

—and there is little oxidation or polymerization. It is therefore possible to develop a wider range of texture effects with the paint, using the various auxiliary mediums and additional inert additives.

The development of collage is perhaps most easily accomplished with the acrylic emulsion paints. *Collage,* the technique of making a composition by gluing various materials not normally associated with each other—bits of paper, newspaper or magazine fragments, colored fabrics—to a picture surface, can be successful here because of the strongly adhesive and durably flexible nature of the binder. Other inert materials such as sand, sawdust, pieces of wood, and so forth, can also be added to the paint films, but these additions should be judicious.

All the materials to be added to acrylic emulsion paintings should be known to be pure and clean, and as durable as the paints themselves. The known durability of the paints will not keep materials like newsprint from disintegrating and perhaps altering the original color or compositional intention of the work. Also consider the weight of the additions being made to the painting: an abundance of sand or wood scraps will certainly be too heavy for a canvas or linen support. Well-braced rigid supports are best for mixed media collage compositions that contain built-up layers of different materials or materials that are unusually heavy.

To be sure that the added materials will adhere to the support, coat them well with the gloss or gel mediums described below. Powdery materials (sand, sawdust) should be mixed with a little medium to ensure adhesion; coat both sides of added papers or fabrics before sticking them onto the painting, then give them a further overcoating to be sure they are stuck down well.

Of course, the development of a personal technique will dictate the direction of experiments with collage and mixed media. It is only necessary to continue to try many different approaches, and to bear in mind that most artists are concerned with producing a permanent record of their activities.

AUXILIARY MATERIALS

The auxiliary mediums and other additives that come with most lines of acrylic emulsion paints are used to alter the working properties of the straight paint. Some are very effective glues.

Gloss Mediums   These are slightly thickened emulsions that can be added to the paint to increase its brilliance and transparency. They are useful in achieving interesting glaze effects, and can also be used as a collage adhesive. Matte mediums are less transparent, have poorer adhesive properties, and show a flat finish when dry.

Gel Mediums   These are very thick versions of the emulsion, with about the same body as the tube paints. The gels are added to the paints for the same glaze effects one gets with the gloss and matte mediums, but with considerably greater textural or impasto possibilities. Adding a gel medium to the paint reduces its tinting strength and somewhat lengthens the drying time. The gels are also excellent adhesives.

Modeling Paste This is a combination of the emulsion with inert bulk fillers, such as marble dust. The paste can produce thickly textured areas of impasto which should be built up in layers, and can even be carved when it dries. Its use should be restricted to rigid supports, since it can be quite brittle; adding a little of the gel medium to it will increase its flexibility.

Retarder This jellylike mixture in a tube can be mixed sparingly with the paint to slow drying. Too much retarder may inhibit drying altogether, and produce soft, easily damaged paint films.

Varnishes Acrylic emulsion varnishes are available in matte and gloss finishes; they should be used only as an integral part of the painting, not as a final coating. It is now generally recognized that dried acrylic emulsion films are quite porous to water and susceptible to accumulations of dust and dirt. An emulsion varnish will *not* provide surface protection for the work; furthermore, it is not removable with simple solvents.

COMMERCIAL PRODUCTS

In the early 1950s, Permanent Pigments introduced the first commercial line of acrylic emulsion paints under the name Liquitex; Binney and Smith, Inc., now owns the company, and both the oil paints and acrylic emulsions are called Liquitex. Other popular brands are sold by Grumbacher (Hyplar), Utrecht Linens (New Temp), Bocour (Aquatec), Martin/F. Weber (Permalba), and Hunt (Speedball). The major European manufacturers, Winsor & Newton and George Rowney, are also beginning to market their acrylic emulsion paints here. A host of other manufacturers, large and small, foreign and domestic, have saturated the market with this profitable material (see Appendix D). All the paints are water-thinned, come in collapsible plastic or metal tubes and plastic jars (in a slightly thinner consistency than the tubed paint), and are accompanied by a large variety of related mediums and modifiers. In the early years, some of the binders exhibited erratic behavior—separation, uncontrolled drying—but most commercial preparations are now considered reliable.

The only caution concerning the use of these materials is one that has been offered in earlier writings, and still seems prudent now: Brands should not be indiscriminately mixed, for each may use a slightly different formula for its product (see Appendix D).

POLYVINYL ACETATE EMULSION PAINTS

Polyvinyl acetate emulsions, familiar as the common "white glue" used as a household adhesive and recommended as a size, have been used in artists' paints. They can occur as a co-polymer with acrylic emulsions, and have been used alone in some experimental applications. The published literature does not supply conclusive information about the durability of paints made solely with PVA emulsions.

Lefranc et Bourgeois has marketed Flashe, a water-thinned "vinylic" paint that behaves quite like traditional gouache, although it is not re-soluble in water once it dries. The term "vinylic" refers to the source of all acrylic resins, the vinyl group, and does not indicate that this paint is a vinyl emulsion or an acrylic emulsion. Its use should be restricted to applications where permanence is not expected until there is independent confirmation of the manufacturer's claim for its performance (see Appendix D).

POLYVINYL ACETATE SOLUTION PAINTS

There have been experiments conducted using the straight PVA resin dissolved in solvents such as alcohol or toluene. Aside from the potential health and safety hazards associated with the solvents, the resins themselves form soft and easily damaged paint films without considerable modification. Independent testing of paints using PVA resins is not conclusive, and early claims for their excellence—not entirely unwarranted—should be taken with caution.

A NOTE ON THE STUDIO MANUFACTURE OF SYNTHETIC PAINTS

Artists who wish to experiment with the synthetic binders by preparing their own paints from the raw materials should contact manufacturers of the ingredients for advice. Artists' paint manufacturers hold their formulas as trade secrets and will not divulge them; raw materials chemists who specialize in coatings formulation can offer suggestions, but not guarantees—and their recommendations are often for relatively short-lived industrial applications.

The mechanical procedures discussed in this section can be used, but you should not expect to be able to make a completely reliable and durable paint. The vehicles for synthetic paints are notoriously complicated, and published recipes are relatively vague about proportions—including the recipes suggested here. These difficulties point to the inadvisability of making one's own synthetic paints. With 40 years of experience behind them, commercial producers of artists' paints can offer products of high quality and proven durability.

A summary of the available synthetic resins is given in Table 10.1, which follows.

TABLE 10.1
SYNTHETIC RESINS

SOLUTION BINDERS	SOLVENT	MANUFACTURER	COMMENTS
Acryloid B-67MT	Mineral spirits	Rohm and Haas	Retains solubility in mineral spirits; isolating varnish should be used; compatible with oil binders but not with natural resin varnishes (damar).
Acryloid B-67	VM&P Naphtha	Rohm and Haas	
Acryloid F-10	Mineral spirits	Rohm and Haas	Eventually loses solubility; compatible with oil binders but not with natural resin varnishes.
Elvacite 2044	Gum turpentine	Du Pont	Comes in powder form, must be dissolved in gum turpentine (1 part resin to 2 parts solvent, by volume); compatible with oil binders but not with natural resin varnishes.

ALKYD BINDERS	SOLVENT	MANUFACTURER	COMMENTS
Beckosol 10-045	Mineral spirits	Reichhold	65% soybean oil; compatible with all components of oil paint systems.
Beckosol 10-051	Mineral spirits	Reichhold	65% linseed oil; compatible with all components of oil paint systems.

EMULSION BINDERS	THINNER	MANUFACTURER	COMMENTS
Rhoplex AC-34	Water	Rohm and Haas	Most widely used in commercial products, with other additives.
Rhoplex AC-33	Water	Rohm and Haas	

CHAPTER 11

WATER-THINNED PAINTS

Paints thinned with water have a long history. From the earliest times, artists decorated surfaces with pigments bound in adhesive gums from animal and vegetable sources. The expressive possibilities of water media cover the widest possible range, from the extremely controlled calligraphy of medieval manuscript illumination to the freer, more spontaneous styles associated with twentieth-century art.

The most readily apparent characteristic of water paints is that they dry very quickly. This is the reason why many artists like to use them as a sketching medium to work out ideas in advance, before proceeding to a more involved technique. Of course, watercolor paints need not be thought of as a medium to be used solely for quick studies. Many of the most important works by modern masters such as Klee were executed in watercolors.

Water paints can also be thinned to a very dilute and fluid state, allowing them to be brushed out in a freely flowing style without suffering any appreciable loss in binding capacity. Very thin applications of water paints can be controlled for tight, descriptive work. In fact, the binders for water paints are relatively weak, and the material should not be applied in thick, impasto layers. Impasto applications of watercolors will crack or separate from the support.

Watercolors are normally matted for storage, but can also be kept in a portfolio (stored flat) without matting if the pictures are interleaved with a neutral barrier paper. For exhibition, matting and framing behind glazing is necessary (see Chapter 17). Gouache paintings require the same care, in storage and exhibition. For size paintings, varnishing is optional if the work is exhibited behind glass. Casein paintings can be varnished, matted, and framed.

TRANSPARENT WATERCOLOR

This familiar and popular medium is sometimes called by the French term *aquarelle,* to distinguish it from opaque techniques. The most common name for transparent watercolor is simply watercolor, not a wholly descriptive term, but a generally acceptable one.

BINDER AND PIGMENTS

The primary binder for transparent watercolor is gum acacia, or gum arabic, a slightly acidic water-soluble gum exuded from the acacia tree.

Commercial watercolor vehicles are often blends of several materials in addition to the binder gum; wheat starch binders are added (dextrin), as well as preservatives (usually less than 1 percent by volume), thickeners, plasticizers, and wetting agents.

The only appropriate additive for a homemade watercolor vehicle is a plasticizer. Glycerine, for instance, will increase the elasticity of the rather brittle binder and allow dried paints to redissolve more easily. Glycerine is easily obtained from a pharmacy.

Most of the pigments used in oil painting can be used in transparent watercolor, except those which are susceptible to atmospheric impurities. For example, Lead white and Naples yellow should not be used in their dry state in any case because of their toxicity. Poorly processed grades of Vermilion, which contains mercuric sulfide, can darken in watercolor. Naturally transparent pigments—the Arylide (Hansa) yellows, the Quinacridone reds and violets, Manganese blue, Viridian green—work particularly well in this medium.

PREPARATION OF THE VEHICLE AND THE PAINT

It is suggested that, in preparing the vehicle, you make only enough for one working session, since the solution does not store well. Because of the laborious, even tedious grinding necessary for the production of a fine transparent watercolor, however, it may be simpler to purchase the paints. If you are up to the task, though, your patience will be rewarded.

MATERIALS FOR MAKING THE VEHICLE

1. 2 parts by volume gum arabic.
2. 4 parts by volume boiling distilled water.
3. 1 part (or less) by volume glycerine.
4. A small pot.
5. Fine-mesh cheesecloth.
6. Very clean glass jar with cover.

METHOD

1. Put the gum in the small pot and pour the hot distilled water over it. Stir to hasten the solution.
2. Stir in the glycerine.
3. Allow the solution to cool a short time before straining it through the cheesecloth into the clean jar.

When you are making the paint, small adjustments of the pigment-to-binder ratio are often necessary for different pigments. Experience is the best guide, but start with a 1 to 1 mixture, by volume, and work from there.

MATERIALS FOR MAKING THE PAINT

1. The vehicle.
2. Dry artists' pigments used in watercolors.
3. A grinding setup.
4. Small containers for the finished paints. The paints are made in cake form: purchase a small enameled steel watercolor palette with depressions for each color (plastic palettes will stain). Or you may use very small wide-mouthed ointment jars.

METHOD

1. Prepare the binder.
2. Predisperse each pigment in distilled water or in the binder to the consistency of tubed oil paints. A drop of denatured ethyl alcohol added to the dry pigments just before dispersal in the water will act as a wetting agent and allow easier dispersal of the powder. Organic pigments resist wetting.
3. Using a stiff spatula, rub the predispersed pigment into a fine, smooth paste with some of the binder. Do this on the slab.
4. Grind the paste, completely and thoroughly, into a very smooth liquid paste. This is the most difficult part of the process. As the water evaporates, the paints gum up and become difficult to grind. Add distilled water (a plastic sprayer can be used to mist water over the paint) if this should happen, and continue grinding. Do not add more binder. The paint must be ground to the finest possible degree so that it does not appear to be gritty when washed on paper in a thin, transparent layer. Make test washes to observe the progress of the grinding. A strong dose of patience is required.
5. Allow the finished paint to dry a bit to a pasty consistency before filling the containers. The paint will harden into a cake that can be reliquified by the application of a little water.
6. Clean the tools thoroughly with soap and water before proceeding to the next color.

PAINTING TECHNIQUES

TOOLS AND BRUSHES

Watercolor palettes, with small indentations for holding the paints and larger spaces for mixing, are found in art supply stores; a simple china plate will also serve. Palettes specifically designed for watercolors often come with sets of the paints, and are made of plastic or painted metal. Some palettes have folding covers to protect unused paints.

At least two jars for water are necessary: one for clean water used for mixing with the paint, and one to hold water for rinsing the brushes. Plastic jars with covers are best for working outdoors. Distilled water is recommended for use in areas with hard water, since it does not contain dissolved mineral salts that could affect the spreading of the paints. Most artists, however, will find local tap water sufficiently soft.

The brush of choice for most watercolorists is the "pure" red sable (see Appendix A). The hair is especially soft but springy, and the brushes can hold a great deal of color but still make an exquisitely fine point. Sable brushes are very expensive, but other brushes cannot perform in the same way. It is not usually necessary to purchase more than two or three sables of various sizes.

A fat, soft "mop," made of squirrel or badger hair, will also be helpful. The hair of these brushes is floppy, and they will not hold a fine point or edge, but they do hold a lot of water and paint and are indispensable for laying down washes over large areas. All brushes should be thoroughly rinsed and washed with mild soap and tepid water after use; keep the brushes in a box with a few mothballs if they are to be stored for a long time.

SUPPORTS AND GROUNDS

Transparent watercolors are most commonly painted on paper, but thin fabrics such as silk, and other supports such as vellum, parchment, gessoed panels, and ivory have been used. Watercolor papers should be composed of 100 percent cotton or linen rag. Linen is preferred because its individual fibers are longer and stronger than those of cotton, but linen rag papers are rare today. (For a more complete discussion of papers in general, see Appendix B.)

The surface of a watercolor paper is important. It should be evenly absorbent and sized during its manufacture to prevent uncontrolled spreading and bleeding of the paint. Plain drawing papers may not be sized; one method of sizing papers is given in Chapter 2. The surface texture of a watercolor paper is controlled by the manufacturer. Most fine papers come with three distinct surfaces: rough (sometimes called "not" or "not pressed"), cold pressed (a medium finish), and hot pressed (a smooth finish). An artist's preference for one type of finish over another is personal, although traditionally the rougher surfaces have found favor because they impart a lively variation to the appearance of the picture.

Generally the heavier-weight watercolor papers are preferred because light-weight papers will wrinkle in an unpleasant way when flooded with water. Lighter papers can be used, however, if they are stretched in a rigid drawing board. Two procedures are available; the choice depends on whether the edges are to be preserved.

METHOD A: TO PRESERVE THE EDGES OF THE PAGE

1. Dampen the paper on both sides by spraying with water, soaking the paper in a tub of water, or liberally sponging on the water.
2. Lay the damp paper on a sturdy drawing board and flatten it out. Pin it down all around the perimeter using thumbtacks or pushpins with long, thin shafts. As the paper dries, it will shrink tight. When the painting is finished, remove the tacks—the pinholes will hardly show (Figure 11.1).

METHOD B: WITHOUT PRESERVING THE EDGES OF THE PAGE

1. Use the procedure as in method A, but use light or heavy staples to attach the paper to the board. This is quicker and more convenient than pinning, but will certainly mutilate the edges of the paper if care is not used.
2. Follow the procedure in method A, but use brown paper wrapping tape (the kind that has a water-soluble glue backing). Tape down the edges of the paper, overlapping about ¼ inch (6 mm) of it. The tape may not stick securely at first—keep pressing down on it. When the picture is finished, peel away the tape after carefully dampening it to loosen the glue, or merely cut the picture loose with a sharp blade. This method will most certainly destroy the deckle edge of a fine paper. Under no circumstances should

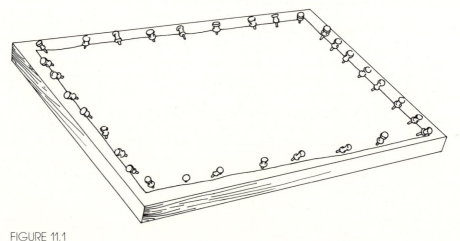

FIGURE 11.1
Stretching Paper

With pins, to preserve the edges of the page.

masking tape be used; its adhesive can stain the paper and migrate into the image, and it will not stick easily to wet paper (Figure 11.2).

Some artists prefer to forego the inconvenience of the stretching paper by using commercially available blocks of watercolor papers. A number of sheets of paper are held together in a block by adhesive applied around its edges. When the picture is finished, a thin knife can be inserted between the sheet and the rest of the block to separate it.

Naturally, other papers can be used, as suits the artist. Rag matboard and some of the many varieties of Oriental papers may be attractive, depending on one's intentions. Since the fibrous surface of the paper plays a part in holding the paint on the support, papers with glazed or shiny surfaces should be avoided.

It is the white color of the support that allows the development of a value scheme in transparent watercolor—the white shows through the transparent paint—so grounds are not necessary. If you are painting on a panel, try a glue gesso ground; it is very white and very absorbent.

THE APPLICATION OF PAINT

Technical styles of transparent watercolor painting can vary tremendously, according to the wishes of the painter. An artist can do a careful line drawing in full detail, over which pale washes are slowly built up to achieve the desired value range and depth of color. For those whose drawing of forms needs attention, this method is desirable at first, since it is difficult to go back and make corrections

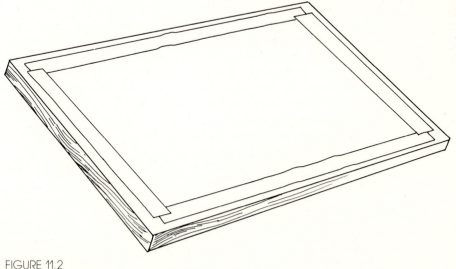

FIGURE 11.2
Stretching Paper
With tape, without preserving the edges of the page.

without the changes in the picture becoming obvious. On the other hand, it is perfectly feasible to use a direct painting method, without any preliminary drawing. In this manner the image is given life quickly and broadly, and then refined with a few touches here and there.

In any case, keep in mind that transparent watercolor has a luminosity and lightness unlike other techniques. This is due partly to the transparency of the binder, partly to the fact that the pigments are so finely ground, and partly to the fact that often the paper is more of a binder for the pigments than the gum itself. Overmixing can easily lead to a muddying of the color or an unpleasant opacity. Removal of unwanted passages of very fluid paint can sometimes be accomplished by blotting with a tissue; dried areas of paint can be lightened, but not entirely removed, by scrubbing the area with a bristle brush or a toothbrush dampened with water, followed by blotting.

If the artist wishes to plan ahead to leave areas of the painting white, for highlights or accents, masking is appropriate. Use small pieces of plain masking tape, one of the proprietary masking fluids, or rubber cement. These can be painted over freely; when the picture is dry, they are removed by peeling or rubbing with a dry cloth. Some artists use a very sharp knife to pick or scrape out tiny highlights—but only heavier papers with considerable surface texture are able to stand this manipulation without it becoming obvious.

COMMERCIAL PRODUCTS

The best lines of most paint manufacturer's watercolors are well-made products; mechanical production is less tedious than hand production, and the formulas are simple and rather standardized. Preference for one brand over another is more often related to the form in which the paint comes—tubes, pans, or cakes—or to some specific handling characteristic or color range. Look for those professional grades of transparent watercolors that are fully labeled for both pigment and vehicle content.

By contrast, student-grade watercolors and hobby sets are usually variable in quality. They may contain fillers that lessen the tinting strength of the colorants; extra binding agents of questionable value and durability; substituted pigments bearing the name of a real pigment but only imitating that pigment's hue. Or they may not be labeled at all and contain colorants not found in the best lines and that may be impermanent. Take no chances with commercial brands of watercolors; buy only the well-labeled professional grades.

Commercial producers of watercolors market a variety of auxiliary mediums to go with their products. These can be viewed as unnecessary—one of the virtues of the medium is that it is so simple—but interesting adjuncts. Winsor & Newton, for example, sells the following mediums for transparent watercolor: Aquapasto (for giving impasto effects), gum arabic (for increasing gloss), Gum Water (containing plant oils, to increase gloss, transparency, and wetting), Ox Gall (the traditional wetting agent formerly used in commercial and homemade watercolors), Size (gelatin-based, for sizing paper), Raising Preparation (a "pigmented, highly bodied" paste that can be remoistened and made sticky with one's breath, used for "illumination"), two mediums (for improving flow and brilliance), and a Water Matt Gold Size (a pigmented base like the traditional bole used for gilding metallic leaf).

OPAQUE WATERCOLOR

Gouache is the name of the technique of painting with an opaque watercolor made with the same binder used in transparent watercolor. Like "watercolor," "gouache" is not really a descriptive term, but it is generally accepted as the name of a paint. The pigmentation of opaque watercolors is the same as for transparent watercolors, but the paints are made opaque by the addition of precipitated chalk to the vehicle. Because extremely fine grinding is not necessary to produce a good gouache paint that covers well and can be applied smoothly, it is more easily homemade than its transparent cousin.

PREPARATION OF THE PAINT

Since this is such an easy paint to make, good recordkeeping about the amounts of binder to pigment used for each color will ensure that you can reproduce successful mixtures. Custom colors can easily be prepared.

The paints can be ground to a more liquid consistency than ultimately desired, then allowed to thicken by evaporation of the water before putting them in the container. Spreading the paint out on a smooth, nonabsorbent surface will speed the process. A clean pane of glass works well.

Test the paints by rubbing a well-dried (overnight) test patch with a soft, dry cloth. Properly bound paints should not rub off, but may stain the cloth slightly. Paints with too little binder will crumble or crack, or rub off entirely.

MATERIALS

1. Vehicle—the same as that suggested for transparent watercolor. Because these paints are more liquid, they can be more susceptible to attack by microorganisms so a preservative may be appropriate. Use Cuniphen 2778-I (0.5 percent by weight of the vehicle) if the volume of vehicle being made makes precise calculations possible.
2. Artist-grade dry pigments—the same as those used in transparent watercolor.
3. Precipitated chalk; whiting, a coarser natural chalk, can be substituted.
4. A grinding setup.
5. Containers for the finished paint. The paint is liquid; use small, collapsible tubes, ointment jars, or sterilized baby food jars.

METHOD

1. Prepare the vehicle, using distilled water as the diluent.
2. Mix each pigment with the precipitated chalk in a separate container. For good opacity, mix about 1 part pigment with 1 part chalk.
3. Predispersing the pigment and chalk is not necessary, but may facilitate grinding.
4. Rub the pigment and chalk (paste or powder) into a smooth paste with some of the vehicle, using a stiff spatula. Each pigment will absorb a different amount of the vehicle, but as a general starting point begin with approximately 3 parts pigment to 1 part vehicle, by volume. Adjust for each color as necessary.
5. Grind the mixture with the muller to a smooth and somewhat liquid consistency. Fill the containers and cap tightly.
6. Clean the equipment thoroughly before proceeding to the next color.

PAINTING TECHNIQUES

Red sable watercolor brushes work well with gouache. Since the paint can be applied in relatively thicker layers than transparent watercolor, some artists also like to use bristle brushes.

SUPPORTS AND GROUNDS

Paper is the usual support for gouache painting, although the paint will work equally well on glue-gessoed panels and rag matboards. Since opaque watercolor is not dependent on the white of the support for light values, the support can be given a middle-tone tint of color—either gouache or watercolor can be used for making the tint wash.

THE APPLICATION OF PAINT

Painting processes are the same as for other water media, except that the paint can be built to a thicker film. This does not mean a film the thickness of an oil impasto, but rather one that can hold and retain brushstrokes and small areas of delicate impasto. Any defect that might occur because of a film that is too thick will show up as soon as the paint is thoroughly dry. Areas that have crumbled or cracked can be reworked by scraping and painting over; the paint is more easily resoluble with water than transparent watercolor, which stains the support with hand-to-remove color.

Opaque watercolor is well suited to many variations in the transparency and opacity of applied layers; a watercolor wash for the middle tone can be combined with transparent watercolor passages in the body of the work. Furthermore, opaque watercolor can be combined with other media like pastel, ink, and charcoal for successful mixed-media effects. Bear in mind that gouache tends to dry lighter in value than it appears when wet (the chalk content is translucent when wet but opaque when dry). This can alter the result. Also, be on the lookout for the dominance of technical manipulations over conceptual matters. The idea of using mixed-media approaches can easily run away with the idea that supports the work. In an opaque watercolor and mixed-media painting, gouache should be the dominant technique, and all the other manipulations and additions should be subordinate.

COMMERCIAL BRANDS

A number of manufacturers produce ready-made opaque watercolors. These brands are often labeled "designer's gouache," indicating that their primary use is for applications where permanence may not be a requirement (designers do their work for reproduction, not posterity, although there are many who now wish the paints were more durable). The brighter colors in these lines have been observed to fade completely in less than a year of exposure to sunlight. Use only those commercial opaque watercolors labeled with the generic name of the pigment content; avoid proprietary color names. These paints have notoriously poor labels concerning vehicle content.

SIZE PAINTS

Size paints are sometimes called *distemper* paints. This phrase refers to the "tempering" of the pigments with the binder or vehicle, and can rightly be applied to almost any kind of paint. The name of egg tempera paints grows out of this usage, which can be misleading if one thinks of the entirely impermanent variety of "poster temperas" in use today.

True size paints are water-thinned paints made of artists' pigments dispersed in warm hide glue. These are very quick drying and particularly suited to decorative effects. Their use ranges over the centuries from Egyptian and Far Eastern wall decoration to the small, marvelously luminous paintings of Bonnard.

BINDER AND PIGMENTS

Standard-strength hide glue size is the binder. The pigments used in watercolors can be used in size paints. The same cautions about toxic and reactive pigments apply.

PREPARATION OF THE PAINT

This paint is easy to make. Because it does not keep well, it should be made fresh for each painting session. If you are making a large volume of paint, it may be possible to use either Cuniphen 2778-I or sodium benzoate in 0.5 percent or 5 percent solutions of the vehicle, respectively. The use of preservatives can be hazardous, however, and should be avoided whenever possible.

MATERIALS

1. Hide glue vehicle. Water is the diluent.
2. Artist-grade dry pigments.
3. A grinding setup.
4. Small containers for the finished paint. Screw-top containers are not necessary.

METHOD

1. Prepare the vehicle. Keep it warm, but not steaming.
2. Predisperse the pigments in distilled water, or tap water if the local water is soft.
3. Disperse about 3 parts pigment paste in about 1 part warm vehicle, by volume. Place the paint in storage containers.
4. Clean the equipment before proceeding to the next color.

The paints can be made opaque by the addition of about 1 part precipitated chalk to 1 part of the vehicle. The binder is then added to the pigment paste as in step 3.

The finished paints can be made somewhat less soluble when they dry by adding a couple of drops of an acrylic emulsion matte medium to the thinner. Do not add the emulsion to the paints, but rather to the thinner used in the painting process.

PAINTING TECHNIQUES

Either hair or bristle brushes can be used with size paints. Hair brushes include sable, "camel," and squirrel.

SUPPORTS AND GROUNDS

The paint is rather brittle: Flexible supports should not be used unless they are mounted on a rigid substrate. Any ground except an oil ground will accept size paint; acrylic emulsion gessoes may not be absorbent enough, however. Museum boards and very stiff papers do not require a ground. Glue-gesso grounds can be particularly attractive when used with this technique with chalk added, because the paint then becomes like a colored gesso; sizing the ground is not necessary.

THE APPLICATION OF PAINT

The paint can be thinned with a great deal of water, but take care not to thin the lower layers of the painting too much. The upper layers should not contain stronger glue than the lower layers, as this could cause the upper layers to crack. A problem with painting a number of successive layers in this medium is that the water content of the fresh paint can sometimes dissolve and lift the underpainting. Adding a drop of acrylic emulsion matte medium to the thinner, water, can lessen the effect or prevent it from occurring.

CASEIN

Casein is a protein derived from the dried curds of skim milk, a natural emulsion containing a small amount of butterfat suspended in water. The skim milk is allowed to sour, or made to sour by adding a weak acid or an enzyme (rennet); the resulting curds are separated from the whey, allowed to dry, and ground up into a white powder. Casein powder can be obtained from chemical supply houses like Fisher Scientific (see Appendix D). Always use the freshest powder available; aged casein will not make a very strong or reliable solution.

The casein powder is dissolved in water with the assistance of an alkaline emulsifier—ammonium carbonate, a crystalline powder that is available from the local pharmacy. Concentrated clear ammonia water—also available in large pharmacies—can be used instead of the ammonium carbonate, but be sure that it is the clear, not the cloudy, variety.

All the pigments used in the other water paints can be used in casein.

PREPARATION OF THE VEHICLE AND THE PAINT

MATERIALS FOR MAKING THE VEHICLE

1. 2 parts by volume of casein powder, the freshest available.
2. 1 part by volume ammonium carbonate crystals or concentrated ammonia water. *Caution:* Ammonia is harmful; concentrated exposures to skin can be corrosive, and inhalation of the vapors or ingestion can be severely irritating or fatal. Wear eye protection and gloves, and use with care. Local exhaust ventilation is recommended.
3. 16 parts distilled water, divided equally between two containers.
4. Wooden kitchen spoon.
5. A large glass, heavy plastic, enameled steel, or glazed ceramic bowl in which to mix the solution. Do not use plain metal containers to make or store the casein; they can react with the solution.

METHOD

1. To 2 parts by volume of the casein powder, slowly add 8 parts by volume of water. Add a little water at a time, stirring with the wooden spoon, to first make a thick, then thin, paste. This method, as opposed to adding the casein to the water, will help prevent the formation of lumps. Stir thoroughly to make the solution smooth.
2. With a little of the remaining water, mix 1 part by volume of the ammonium carbonate crystals into a smooth paste. Add the paste to the casein and water mixture and stir. Or add the concentrated ammonia water—1 part by volume—to the solution, and stir. *Caution:* do not inhale the vapors or handle the paste with unprotected hands.
3. Allow the solution to rest for at least an hour, or until there is no more odor of ammonia. Stir in the remaining 8 parts of water. This is the vehicle, a

clear, syrupy solution. Store it in a plastic-topped plastic or glass jar until ready to use.

Some writers recommend that the casein syrup be heated to drive off the excess ammonia gas. Heating will certainly shorten the preparation time, but to do so requires more equipment: (1) a large enameled steel double boiler, (2) a hotplate, (3) a candy thermometer. Follow steps 1 and 2 under "Method," and put the casein and water solution in the top portion of the double boiler. Gently heat it on the hotplate. Then proceed as follows:

1. Prepare the ammonium carbonate paste or the ammonia water and add it to the casein and water. Because of the heat there will be considerable foaming of the mixture, which is the reason the enameled steel double boiler must be very large. Add the remaining 8 parts of water.
2. Continue to heat the mixture until it reaches a temperature of approximately 180° F (82° C). Keep it at this temperature—do not allow it to get hotter or cooler—for at least half an hour, or until there is no odor of ammonia from the mixture. Stir continuously.
3. Cool the solution quickly by placing the top of the double boiler in a bucket or sink filled with icewater. Stir until the solution is completely cooled.

It is advisable to make only small amounts of casein at one time and to use it promptly, although the solution can be stored in a cool place (but not refrigerated) for about a week before it spoils. The life of the solution can be somewhat prolonged by the addition of a preservative, if you care to make the calculations: 5 percent sodium benzoate by weight of the solution, or 0.5 percent of Cuniphen 2778-I by weight. Add the preservative after step 3. Unless you are making a large stock of casein for multiple uses (paint binder, gesso adhesive, general adhesive), it is generally not worth the bother to measure such small amounts.

To make a glue gesso using casein as the binder, mix a volume of chalk and pigment filler equal to that of the casein solution prepared above. Combine them as instructed in Chapter 2. Dilute this mixture with more water until the gesso reaches a brushable consistency. Casein gesso does not gel when it cools, and does not have to be reheated; it is somewhat harder than hide glue gesso; it is more water resistant than hide glue gesso.

MATERIALS FOR MAKING THE PAINT

1. The vehicle described above.
2. A grinding setup.
3. Artist-grade dry pigments.
4. Small containers for storing the finished paints. Ointment jars with plastic caps or baby food jars that have been sterilized will work well.

METHOD

1. Predisperse each pigment in distilled water. Place each pigment and water paste in its own storage container.

2. Place a small volume of each paste on a palette. It is helpful to use an enameled steel palette or a plastic watercolor palette that has individual depressions to hold the paint. Or use small individual plastic or ceramic ink bowls, one for each color. Add a volume of casein solution equal to the volume of the paste to each color. Mix thoroughly to make the paint.
3. You can grind the pigments directly into the casein solution. Make only enough for one day's painting, because the solution will not keep well.

PAINTING TECHNIQUES

Hair or bristle brushes can be used. Water is the thinner. Be sure to use plenty of water and keep the brushes moist: dried casein paint is difficult to remove from brushes. The palette is glass, enameled steel, or ceramic.

SUPPORTS AND GROUNDS

All supports used for other water-thinned paints can be used for casein painting: rag papers and museum board, panels, fabrics or thin papers mounted on a rigid auxiliary substrate. Heavy rag papers can be used without mounting.

Casein gesso or hide glue gesso can be used as a ground, although no ground is necessary for white rag papers and museum boards. The ground need not be sized. A middle tone of color can be washed onto the ground with diluted casein paint or watercolor.

THE APPLICATION OF PAINT

Casein can be used in thin washes like the other water paints, or opaquely. It can also be built up to a bit of an impasto. Since casein is not easily resoluble in water once it dries, its paint layers dry water resistant and overpainting is not a problem. Corrections can be made easily, and watercolor-like glazes can be applied over heavily painted areas without lifting the underpainting. Paints that have dried on the palette should be scraped off and discarded, and any paint not used by the end of the day should be discarded.

To make the paints even more water resistant, add a drop or two of acrylic emulsion matte medium to the thinning water.

MIXED TECHNIQUES

Casein can also act as an emulsifier; that is, the casein syrup can be used to emulsify other oily, waxy, or resinous materials into mixtures that are thinned with water but dry water resistant (see Chapter 12).

The usual procedure is to mix 1 part by volume of the casein syrup with 1 part by volume of the other ingredient. Examples include the following:

Linseed stand oil: This produces a paint that can yellow considerably.
Damar varnish (5 pound cut): This vehicle dries quickly and can crack and/or yellow.

Venice turpentine: This gives a paint that dries quickly with a good gloss, and one that will not show brushstrokes.

Saponified wax, also called wax soap (see Chapter 14): This paint dries quickly with a matte surface, but has films that can be soft if too much wax is used.

Once the vehicle has been assembled, the pigment and water paste is mixed into it to produce the paints. If more waxy, oily, or resinous material than casein syrup is used in the emulsion, water can no longer be used as the thinner: use mineral spirits instead.

To make oil paints that dry very rapidly, first make a selection of casein paints as outlined above. Then, using a palette knife, mix 1 part by volume of each casein color with 1 volume of oil color straight from the tube. These casein and oil paints can be thinned with the casein syrup, or with one of the mixed emulsions mentioned above. Casein-oil paints are particularly useful where one wishes to introduce crisp highlights and lights into wet oil paint. Straight casein paints can also be used, very thinly, as a fast-drying underpainting for oil paints.

COMMERCIAL BRANDS

Casein paints can be bought in tubes from one or two manufacturers in this country: Shiva, distributed by Standard Brands, is one (see Appendix D). Because pure casein spoils, these paints have an abundance of preservatives in them, or they are solutions of casein containing other ingredients to prevent hardening or putrefying. Be sure to purchase the freshest tubes available: ask the retailer or write the manufacturer for an explanation of the code usually found imprinted in the tube crimp. Make a test of each color to be sure it is stable.

Casein-based housepaints are not made for artistic purposes, and should not be used with expectations of durability.

CHAPTER 12

TEMPERAS

Tempera paints employ a vehicle that is thinned with water but upon drying becomes water-resistant, making the paint somewhat like casein and placing it somewhere between pure water paints and oil paints. In fact, before the development of the technique of pure oil painting as a separate process, during the sixteenth century, egg tempera was the prevalent easel painting technique. Much of the religious panel painting done between the twelfth and fifteenth centuries was executed in this delicate and subtle process, which is capable of highly detailed and complex development. Since the sixteenth century, tempera painting has enjoyed sporadic revivals. Several modern painters—Ben Shahn, Andrew Wyeth, and Robert Vickery, for instance—have helped to rekindle an interest in the technique.

The binder in egg tempera painting is an emulsion—a suspension of a resinous, oily, fatty, or waxy material in a watery material. This type of suspension is called an oil-in-water emulsion, and is like milk with its suspended component of butterfat. There are also "water-in-oil" emulsions, an example of which is butter (it has a small component of aqueous material) or a mixture of oil paints and casein. The two different materials are held in suspension with the assistance of a third ingredient, the emulsifier. Simple natural emulsions are found in fig tree sap (a latexlike suspension mentioned in archaic paint-making recipes) and eggs.

THE CARE OF TEMPERA PAINTINGS

A dilute picture varnish can be applied to the painting, but varnishing can emphasize the contrast between opaque and glazed areas (by changing the refractive index of the binder), and reworked or overworked areas can show up in an undesirable way. It is sometimes advisable to frame egg tempera paintings behind glass. Egg-oil emulsion paintings should receive the same care as pure egg tempera works. See Chapter 17.

255

PURE EGG TEMPERA

BINDER AND PIGMENTS

Egg yolks contain a fatty material called "egg oil," a watery material, albumen (which is the greater part of the white of an egg), and an emulsifier called lecithin. Lecithin is an efficient natural emulsifier often found in processed foods; albumen is also an emulsifying agent, but its major contribution to the system is that it coagulates under heat and light, giving the binder a tough, flexible, and relatively insoluble character (observe a frying egg to see how rapidly albumen coagulates; try washing a plate that has had dried egg sitting on it for a day to see how tough a film it makes).

All the pigments usable in the water paints can be used in egg tempera.

PREPARATION OF THE VEHICLE AND THE PAINT

The egg vehicle does not keep and should be made fresh for each session. Some writers recommend adding a preservative (a few drops of white vinegar, or sodium benzoate). But the preservative may cause the emulsion to separate if it is not precisely calculated. Refrigeration of the vehicle is not advised.

MATERIALS FOR MAKING THE VEHICLE

1. A fresh raw chicken egg.
2. Distilled water. Normally, local soft water can be used (hard water should not be used), but to be on the safe side, use distilled water.
3. A small glass jar, or a paper cup.

METHOD

1. Crack the egg and separate the yolk from the white by passing it from half-shell to half-shell, or by using an egg separator (Figure 12.1). Discard the white, or save it to make meringues.

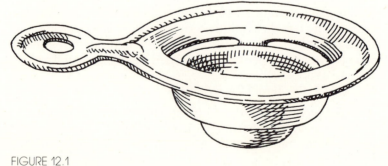

FIGURE 12.1
Egg Separator

The white slides through the slots in the sides; the yolk is held in the center depression.

2. Dry the yolk by rolling it gently on a towel, or by passing it gently from hand to hand, wiping each hand clean on a towel between passes (Figure 12.2).

3. Pick up the yolk by grasping its skin between forefinger and thumb and hold it over a small, clean glass jar or cup (Figure 12.3). With a sharp knife, puncture the sac and allow the yolk to run out into the jar. Excess yolk can be squeezed out with the fingers. Discard the yolk sac.

4. Mix a little distilled water with the yolk. This is the vehicle, which, as noted, should be made fresh for each day's painting.

It is possible to grind the dry pigments directly into the vehicle, skipping the pigment and water paste step. Leftover paint must be discarded at the end of the workday.

Each pigment will require slightly more or less than an equal volume of vehicle to make a satisfactory paint. To test the resulting film, paint a thin strip, diluted with water as in normal applications, onto a piece of glass. After the paint dries overnight, you should be able to peel the strip off the glass with a razor blade in one continuous ribbon. Paint that crumbles or powders needs more binder. A well-made egg tempera paint should not stain a dry white cloth that is gently rubbed against some dried paint.

MATERIALS FOR MAKING THE PAINT

1. The egg vehicle.
2. Artist-grade dry pigments.
3. A grinding setup.
4. Small containers to hold the finished paint.

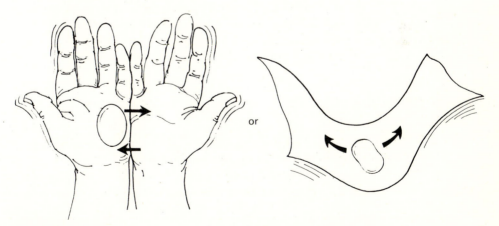

FIGURE 12.2
Drying the Yolk

Left: Passing the yolk from hand to hand.
Right: Rolling the yolk in a towel.

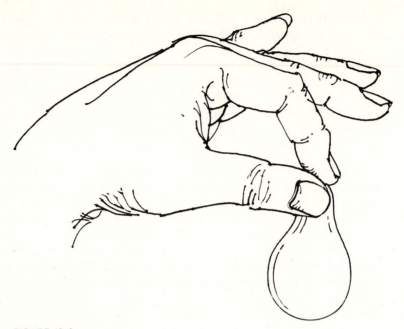

FIGURE 12.3
Picking up the Yolk

METHOD

1. Prepare a pigment and water paste with each pigment, using distilled water as the diluent, to the consistency of tubed oil paints.
2. For each color, mix approximately 1 volume of pigment paste with 1 volume of egg yolk. The combination can be done directly on the palette, or separate jars can be used for each color. Watercolor palettes with depressions around the mixing surface are good for storing the prepared paints.

PAINTING TECHNIQUES

For classical painting techniques, a fine-tipped red sable brush can produce very fine lines and subtle cross-hatchings. Other, larger hair and bristle brushes can be used for broader and more robust effects.

A fine sharp knife blade is handy to have for scraping out errors; the technique is translucent, not opaque, and errors are hard to cover up.

SUPPORTS AND GROUNDS

Although egg tempera is a relatively flexible medium compared to many of the water paints, it is rather brittle when compared to oil paints. The support therefore should be rigid; if paper or a fine fabric support is preferred, mount one on a panel. Mounted papers and museum boards do not need a ground. A glue-gesso panel, with its brilliantly white and absorbent ground, is the traditional support system. Finishing the gesso ground off to an eggshell surface is important if the artist wishes to emphasize the delicate linear quality of the medium. The ground should be perfectly smooth.

THE APPLICATION OF PAINT

Painting methods will naturally vary according to the needs of the artist, but to appreciate the subtlety of the medium, you should try at least one painting in the classical style. In this well-documented method, all the ideas—the drawing, values, shapes, forms, content—are worked out in advance in a drawing on paper. Because it is difficult to remove unwanted passages from a tempera painting, you should make the preliminary drawing as complete and "correct" as possible.

Transfer the outlines of the drawing to the panel. This can be done by using a proportional grid system or by using graphite transfer paper, a thin paper coated on one side with a film of graphite dust. Do not use ordinary carbon paper; the ink will bleed through the paint layers. Once you have transferred the contours of the forms, develop a monochromatic or dichromatic underpainting with thin, gradually built up layers of paint. Thin the paint with plenty of water so that it resembles a watercolor wash: With the correct proportion of binder to pigment, the vehicle will hold properly despite a great deal of thinning.

The underpainting need not be entirely monochromatic, but can have varying shades of neutralized color. In the traditional approach, areas of flesh tones are underpainted in a greenish hue (specifically, green earth pigment) to emphasize cool shadows and contrast with the warm, local color of the flesh. It is possible to develop an underpainting composed entirely of hues complementary to those that will be applied later in glazes.

Overpainting is applied in thin, small, translucent strokes of cross-hatching or parallel hatching which describe the direction of turning in the form. The idea here is to build up layers of strokes that do not completely obscure the underpainting but use it, in combination with the cross-contour hatching, to model the lights and darks of the forms. This technique was developed because it is difficult to make smooth blends of color in egg tempera, especially when blending one color into another. Imagine artists' delight when pure oil painting finally evolved!

It is particularly important at this stage to keep the paint translucent, not opaque. Be sure to thin it with plenty of water. To avoid opaque blobs of paint at the beginning or end of each stroke, try the following method: Load the brush with a full charge of thinned paint, then squeeze out about half with the fingers; or wipe the loaded brush on a tissue to partly discharge the paint. Do not scrub the paint on in a back-and-forth, housepainting style; use single strokes of paint in one direction. When painting over fresh strokes, wait a few seconds for the previous layer to dry.

Of course, this approach takes a great deal of planning and control in the application process, and may not be entirely suitable to more modern, expressionist methods. Any other application technique can be used, as long as the special character of the paint is retained. Egg tempera should be applied well thinned, so as to produce translucent films. It is not an opaque technique, but opaque effects can be achieved by building up layers of translucent applications.

Finished egg tempera paintings, dried for a week or more in a normal environment, harden somewhat as the egg coagulates into a tough film. The painting can then be polished with a soft cotton cloth or nylon stocking to bring out its unique low surface sheen. The friction of polishing will harden the painting surface and provide a little protection against superficial dust and scratches. While the paint is water-resistant, it is *not* waterproof. Do not expose it to excessive moisture.

EGG-OIL EMULSIONS

Egg-oil emulsion paints can be considered an intermediate step between pure egg tempera and pure oil painting. In this variation, the character of the egg medium is considerably altered by the addition of linseed stand oil, sun-thickened linseed oil, alkali-refined or cold-pressed linseed oil, damar or other natural resinous varnishes, or wax soaps. A whole egg is used as the emulsifier of the oily and aqueous ingredients.

Depending on the materials in the vehicle and their proportions, the egg-oil emulsion paints can take on some of the aspects of an oil paint while retaining the qualities of a pure egg tempera; the paint still dries quickly but can be blended more easily, and it can be painted on with slightly more impasto than the pure egg tempera.

PREPARATION OF THE VEHICLE AND THE PAINT

MATERIALS FOR MAKING THE VEHICLE

1. A sterilized tall glass bottle.
2. A fresh raw chicken egg.
3. Distilled water.
4. A measure equal in volume to that of the whole egg of any one, or a combination, of the following ingredients: linseed stand oil, sun-thickened linseed oil, alkali-refined linseed oil, cold-pressed linseed oil, damar varnish (5 pound cut), Venice turpentine, saponified beeswax (see Chapter 14).

METHOD

1. Chip a hole in the top of the egg and put its entire contents in the tall glass bottle. Cap the bottle and shake it vigorously to mix up the egg.
2. Fill the eggshell with the oily ingredients. Various combinations of two or

more of the ingredients can be used, as long as the total volume is equal to that of the eggshell. Put the oily materials into the bottle with the egg and shake again to mix them together.

3. To the egg-oil mixture, add one or two eggshellsful of distilled water. Shake vigorously to emulsify the oil and water mixture. This is the vehicle.

Following the procedures outlined under "Pure Egg Tempera," combine the egg-oil emulsion with dry artists' pigments or with pigment and water pastes.

The egg-oil emulsion vehicle will keep far longer than pure egg binders, provided it is stored in a cool place (but not refrigerated). Do not use preservatives. Egg-oil emulsions begin to smell strongly as they deteriorate, and no longer can make a good, adherent paint. Discard the spoiled emulsion. Do not use a bottle in which an egg-oil emulsion has spoiled without first resterilizing it by boiling. Ordinary tap water or eggs that are not fresh can produce emulsions that do not dry properly. Be sure all the ingredients are pure and fresh.

The yolk alone can be used to make an egg-oil emulsion, but then precise measurement of the ingredients becomes more difficult. Furthermore, the excellent emulsifying capacity of the egg white is missing from an emulsion made only with the yolk.

If the amount of water in the emulsion is decreased, the resulting paint will be more like a fast-drying oil paint. Egg-oil emulsion paints made with the normal proportion of water can be thinned with water, but these paints made with little or no water must be thinned only with the emulsion. The emulsion is good, but not perfect, and may separate in the jar during manufacture of the paints, or during the painting process. Shake the bottle vigorously from time to time to be sure the mixture is thorough and stable.

Paints can be tested for proper pigment-to-binder proportions in the same way as pure egg tempera paints are tested.

PAINTING TECHNIQUES

Bristle brushes can be used with egg-oil paints, for the quality of the paint invites a more vigorous application, and the paint is able to show the brushstrokes off with more character than pure egg tempera. Of course, hair brushes can be used with equally pleasing results.

SUPPORTS AND GROUNDS

Egg-oil emulsion paints work well on the same supports and grounds used for pure egg tempera. Some artists may be inclined to think that because the emulsion contains oily materials it must be more flexible, but this is not necessarily so. Egg-oil emulsion temperas can crack as easily as pure egg temperas when used on flexible supports, especially if the layers of applied paint are of varying thicknesses. Mount flexible supports to rigid auxiliary supports to be sure the paint will not crack.

THE APPLICATION OF PAINT

Procedures used in painting with pure egg tempera can be used with the egg-oil emulsion paints. Because the paint seems to have more body, a freer, less precise style may be attractive. Thin the paints with water or the emulsion; they dry more quickly than pure oil paint but more slowly than pure egg tempera, depending on the type of oily ingredients used. Allow the paints to dry to touch before painting over fresh underpainting.

Pure oil paints can be incorporated into the emulsion paints to produce an egg-oil paint that can make a thicker impasto. Squeeze paints straight from the tube, in proportions varying from 1 part oil paint to 1 part egg-oil paint, to 1 part oil paint to 2 or 3 parts egg-oil paint. Paints in the 1 to 2 ratio can be thinned with plain emulsion—not water. Paints containing larger proportions of oil paint should be thinned with mineral spirits. Remember also that by adding oil paint to the egg-oil emulsion, you can easily lose the special characteristics of the egg paint. If this is the case, be sure to follow all the rules of oil painting, especially with regard to painting oilier layers over less oily layers.

MIXED TECHNIQUES

Like casein paints, pure egg tempera or egg-oil tempera paints can be used in the final stages of oil painting to introduce crisp, fast-drying highlights and accent touches into still-wet oil glazes. Egg temperas can also be used as a fast-drying underpainting material for oil paints. The underpainting must be kept very thin and be painted on a very lean ground (if it is an oil ground) in order that it not interfere with the adhesion of the oil paint. Execute the underpainting broadly and rapidly; errors can be wiped out with a damp rag. The overpainting in oil should be done in glazes to retain the visual character of the underpainting. If an egg-oil emulsion is used for the underpainting, the glaze medium in the oil paint should contain the same ingredients found in the emulsion; use the medium sparely. Finishing touches of opaque oil paint are applied on top of the glazed areas. Application of the touches can be into wet glaze, or on top of dried glaze. If the opaque touches are in egg tempera or egg-oil emulsion tempera, they should be applied to the wet oil glazes to become incorporated into the paint. These paints could crack if applied to dried glazes that contain much oil because of the continuous movement of the oily layer.

The same caution suggested for other mixed techniques holds true here. Mixed techniques in egg tempera and egg-oil emulsion tempera should be attempted by painters who have a firm grasp of what they want from the painting. The work should be executed with dispatch, in two or three more or less transparent layers, without a great deal of manipulation. Those who wish to apply thicker, more varying layers of paint, or who wish to apply many more layers of paint in a typical oil painting manner, should stay with pure oil painting.

COMMERCIAL BRANDS

George Rowney (English) and Sennelier (French) both market a tubed egg tempera in this country (see Appendix D). Because of the necessity of having a paint that will store well—sitting on a dealer's shelf—these are egg-oil emulsion paints, although they can be thinned with water and used like pure egg temperas. Be sure to purchase by generic pigment name, and buy the freshest of the dealer's stock.

CHAPTER 13

ENCAUSTIC

Encaustic is a hot wax painting process in which the wax-bound paints are fused together and adhered to the ground with heat applied from an external source. The process was probably developed by the ancient Greeks, and the name is derived from the Greek *enkaustikos,* "to burn in," referring to the final step. The Egyptian Fayum period sarcophagus portraits dating from the second century A.D., purportedly created by Greek painters, have remained remarkably well preserved—a testament to the durability of this medium—and are outstanding examples of a highly refined technique.

Although the process itself is simple, the equipment required to make the pictures in the past was bulky and awkward. Consequently, the use of the encaustic method declined as less involved processes were developed. During the beginning of this century, when electric heating devices became more common and easy to move about, the technique was occasionally revived. Even though it is not as popular as other, more familiar, easel painting techniques, mainly because of its apparent inconvenience, encaustic now enjoys a considerable reputation. Jasper Johns is probably the best-known modern proponent of encaustic painting.

Finished encaustic paintings need not be varnished with resinous finishes; the usual solvents, mineral spirits or gum turpentine, can soften the wax. The paintings can be displayed with a polished surface alone, or with a thin coat of a wax paste (see Chapter 14) for some surface protection. For the best protection, framing the painting behind glass is recommended. Avoid extremes of heat and cold, to prevent softening or cracking of the picture. Large encaustic works should be heavily framed (see Chapter 17).

BINDER AND PIGMENTS

The binder for encaustic is simply melted, bleached white beeswax. It is combined with up to 25 percent of a resinous or oily component which acts as a hardener for the relatively soft vehicle. The vehicle is mixed with dry artists' pigments to make the paint. Such simplicity of formulation, along with the use of a very stable binder, produces a paint that is known for its high durability. In comparison with oil painting, for example, the pictures do not yellow or darken with age, because the oil content is very low and the wax is colorless. And because the wax binder is virtually inert, the pictures are very resistant to chemical changes, atmospheric moisture, and other forms of decay. The only threat to encaustics is extreme heat, which could cause the paints to melt, and extreme cold, which can make the paintings brittle and subject to mechanical damage if jarred or moved carelessly.

All the pigments used in oil painting are suitable for encaustic. The pigments must be finely pulverized. Do not handle toxic pigments without proper safety precautions.

PREPARATION OF THE VEHICLE AND THE PAINT

Repeated heating and cooling of the solid cakes of encaustic paint may eventually cause the oily or resinous content to break down; they are the culprits in a deteriorating encaustic painting. If the encaustics are going to be used only occasionally, you can prolong their storage life by not adding these ingredients to the paint until you are ready to work. Follow the suggested method for making the paints, but eliminate step 2 in the preparation of the vehicle. Make the cakes *without* the oily or resinous content. When you are ready to paint, rub the cakes on the palette to form puddles of color, and then add a small amount of the prepared liquid ingredients.

MATERIALS FOR MAKING THE VEHICLE

1. Bleached white beeswax.
2. The oily or resinous ingredients: oil—linseed stand oil; or resin: 3 parts 5 pound cut damar plus 1 part Venice turpentine.
3. Small enameled steel saucepan, or a medium-sized tin can.
4. A hotplate.

METHOD

1. Break the beeswax into small pieces. (Freeze it and then wrap it in a cloth and smack it with a hammer, and it can be broken up quite easily.) Place it in the small saucepan or the tin can. Heat it gently on the hotplate until it just melts. Do not heat it to the point where it begins smoking. Exercise caution. Hot wax can cause severe burns.
2. Remove the melted wax from the heat and stir in the oily or resinous ingredients. The proportion of the added ingredients should not exceed 25 percent of the volume of the wax. Consider the wax to be 4 parts by volume (you could have volume level markings on the inside of the can or pan): add 1 part by volume of the oily or resinous mixture.

Small tin cans—tunafish cans are excellent—or those individual foil ''boats'' used for baking potatoes can be used for making and storing the color cakes described here. The individual containers can be placed directly on the palette and the colors melted in them. The only problem with using the cans as both storage and painting containers is that the various colors can be contaminated with one another during the painting process.

The thinner and solvent for encaustic is mineral spirits. This liquid can be used to predisperse the pigments prior to mixing them with the wax vehicle, a particularly helpful procedure when dealing with gritty pigments. *Caution:* Mineral spirits is flammable.

MATERIALS FOR MAKING THE PAINT

1. The vehicle.
2. Artist-grade dry pigments.
3. A muffin tin, containing as few as six depressions or as many as a dozen, depending on the number of colors being made.
4. A hotplate.
5. A spatula or stiff palette knife.

METHOD

1. Heat the muffin tin on the hotplate. Place dry pigments in the depressions in the tin, a different color for each depression. Be careful not to mix the pigments inadvertently—or make deliberate custom mixtures, as desired. The tin should be warm, not hot.
2. Reheat the vehicle until it just melts. Pour some of the vehicle into one of the depressions, and use the spatula to mix the wax and pigment thoroughly. The consistency of the mixture should be very smooth, without lumps of agglomerated pigment particles, and about the viscosity of a thin tubed oil paint.
3. If the wax in the saucepan has begun to solidify, gently reheat it. Continue pouring and mixing each individual color until all the pigments have been mixed into paint.
4. Allow the cakes of color to cool and solidify. They can be popped out of the tin and wrapped in paper for storage, or stored in the tin. For use in painting, they are simply rubbed on the heated palette (see the section below on tools and brushes) to make a puddle of liquid paint.

PAINTING TECHNIQUES

TOOLS AND BRUSHES

Bristle brushes are used for painting in encaustic; hair brushes will not stand up to the abuse of the process. Only natural bristle brushes should be used—plastic bristles will melt—and they need not be the best quality, since good brushes are as quickly ruined as cheap brushes.

The major pieces of equipment are the palette and the burning-in tool. The ancient Greeks used a container of burning charcoal covered by a flat metal plate. Today, use a hotplate with variable temperature controls, topped with a hollow steel box. The box can be welded from scrap steel: The top surface should be at least ¼ inch (6 mm) thick, while the sides and bottom can be thinner. A useful size is about 18 by 24 by 2 inches thick (46 × 61 × 5 cm); the hollow box form allows for an air space within the palette that helps to distribute the heat evenly.

Manufactured palettes can be purchased from specialty suppliers. The palettes are made of aluminum with built-in thermostatically controlled electric heating elements, with depressions in the surface to hold the paints, and they can be quite expensive. The least expensive alternative to both palettes described above is an electric frying pan made of aluminum, the kind with a thermostat in its handle; these can usually be found in junk stores and can be adapted for use by the artist. Their only drawback is that they are quite small. *Caution:* Do not use the frying pan for cooking food after using it as an encaustic palette (Figure 13.1).

The other big piece of equipment is the burning-in lamp. Any heat lamp can be made to work if the heat emitted by the bulb is enough to melt the wax—but be sure that the lamp will melt the entire thickness of the paint layers, not just the top layer. Better than a simple heat lamp is an electric coil, mounted around a ceramic heatproof core that has a screw-mount base. These can be screwed into a ceramic heatproof socket and put into a bowl reflector (Figure 13.2). Be sure that none of the elements is flammable—some ordinary light sockets have cardboard insulating material that can ignite, and most have plastic parts that can melt—and that the whole apparatus can be held safely by a handle.

SUPPORTS AND GROUNDS

Although the addition of the oily or resinous component to the vehicle makes the wax binder a bit more flexible, the normal proportions given above do not make the paints flexible enough to use on unmounted paper or fabric supports. A rigid panel, correctly braced at the back, is the best support for an encaustic painting.

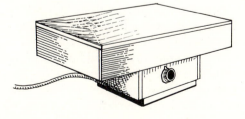 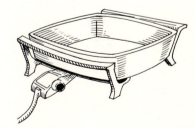

FIGURE 13.1
Encaustic Palettes

Left: Welded steel box on top of a hotplate.
Right: Electric frying pan with rheostat.

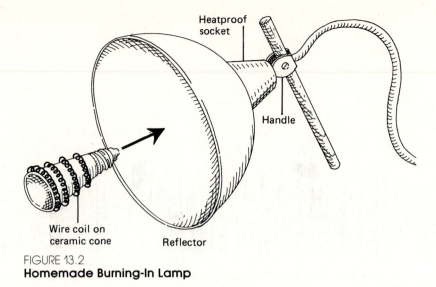

FIGURE 13.2
Homemade Burning-In Lamp

Papers, fabrics, and museum boards can be used as supports if they are mounted on a rigid panel. Adding a larger amount of oil to the vehicle could make the paint usable on a flexible support, but then you run the risk of producing a painting that will yellow badly (the wax is transparent), or one that dries very slowly. It may be possible to substitute one of the acrylic solution binders (Acryloid B-67MT) for the linseed stand oil, to limit yellowing.

The preferred ground for encaustic is glue gesso, because it is absorbent enough to allow firm attachment of the paint layers when they are fused and burned-in when the painting is finished. Acrylic emulsion grounds may work if they are sufficiently roughened by sanding with a medium-grit sandpaper, but they can be fairly unabsorbent grounds.

THE PAINTING AND BURNING-IN PROCESS

Set the box palette on top of the hotplate and preheat it to about 200° F (93° C). If the temperature control on the hotplate does not indicate degrees, simply heat the palette to the point where it easily melts a sample of one of the color cakes. Lower the temperature and keep it steady at about 150–175° F (65–79° C), or at a temperature where the color sample stays liquid but does not bubble, smoke, or burn. When the palette has reached the proper temperature, rub the various color cakes to form discrete puddles of color, or set individual containers of the wax colors on the palette and wait until the contents have melted. Add the oily or resinous content if necessary. Place two cans of the thinner—mineral spirits—near, but not on, the palette.

You can then use any standard painting technique, except that, because the paint dries (cools) very quickly, you should work more rapidly to get the paint to the picture before it hardens in the brush. Put the palette close to the work. You can use wet-into-wet techniques by holding the heating lamp close to the work with a free hand. Subtle glaze effects can be obtained by thinning the paint with mineral spirits and rubbing it on briskly. Rinse the brushes frequently to keep color mixtures clean.

This technique seems especially suited to impasto and various kinds of knife painting, although you should be careful not to overdo it; too thick an application of the paint may crack. The paint is already endowed with an impasto "look." You can work on the painting indefinitely, since removal of unwanted areas is easy; heat the surface and scrape away the paint.

Brushes and knives can be cleaned by warming them on the palette and then wiping them on a rag. After rinsing in mineral spirits, they can be washed like other brushes. Although clean brushes will ensure clean paints, going to a great deal of trouble to get them perfectly clean may not matter in the long run—the heat of the palette can reduce some brushes to stubble in short order.

Burning-in is accomplished by laying the picture flat on a table and passing the heat lamp back and forth across the painting, about 4 to 6 inches (10–15 cm) from its surface. Heat the picture until all the paint softens and fuses, the layers to each other and the whole structure to the ground. Do not overheat so that the paint bubbles or burns, although this procedure can be controlled so the effects one artist might call defects another will find desirable. In fact, if the surface is heated to the proper temperature, pigments seem to float around within the vehicle. What happens is that heavier, denser pigments sink, and lighter pigments rise to the surface. Organic pigments, usually light and fluffy, are likely to float up through heavier metallic or earth pigments in a characteristic pattern. Some degree of practice is necessary to control the burning-in process.

When the initial burning-in is finished, further touches and corrections can be made, and then the painting can be given a final burning-in. At this point, some artists will spray the surface of the painting with mineral spirits and ignite it, or use a blowtorch to finish off the surface. These practices are not recommended: In the first case there is the danger of explosion or fire, and in the second case you can vaporize the heavy metallic pigments into toxic metal fumes.

After the final burning-in, the painting will have a soft matte surface. After a few days, it can be polished with a cotton cloth to harden the surface and produce a semi-gloss finish.

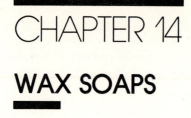

CHAPTER 14

WAX SOAPS

Two kinds of saponified wax pastes can be prepared as modifiers for different kinds of paints, as the waxy ingredient in casein or egg-oil emulsions, and as a protective coating for finished paintings. Wax soaps are quite soft, and they never harden sufficiently to be used alone as binders for paints. Excessive use of wax soaps, or their commercially made counterparts, can be disastrous for paint films, leaving them vulnerable to mechanical damage.

Slightly modified pigmented wax soaps can be made into crayons or oil pastels, in imitation of the commercial products.

WAX-WATER EMULSION

This wax soap can be used as an addition to oil paints to obtain interesting glazing and impasto effects; to avoid soft paint films, do not use more than 1 part of the paste to 2 parts of oil paint straight from the tube. Mix the materials thoroughly on the palette; thin the paint with mineral spirits or gum turpentine, as usual. To use the soap as an ingredient in emulsions, simply add it at the appropriate time during the preparation of the emulsion.

As a surface wax for protecting paintings, the soap can be applied only when the painting is thoroughly dried. Apply the wax with a bristle brush or a rag, spreading it thinly on the surface. Before it hardens, polish it with a soft rag to be sure the film is thin and even (the heat of friction helps to spread the wax). After the water has evaporated from the emulsion, polish the wax again to harden the surface—it will become transparent and give the surface a pleasing semi-gloss finish. Do not use this wax on water-soluble paints.

MATERIALS

1. Bleached white beeswax.
2. Distilled water.
3. Ammonium carbonate crystals.
4. A large enameled steel saucepan. Foaming occurs in this process, so use a large pan to make a small amount of emulsion.
5. A hotplate.
6. Covered glass jar for storage.

METHOD

1. Place 2 parts by volume of the beeswax and 16 parts by volume of the distilled water in the saucepan. Heat on the hotplate, over low heat, until the wax melts.
2. Mix 1 part by volume of the ammonium carbonate with a little water to make a thin paste, and stir it into the wax-water mixture. Exercise caution. Do not allow the ammonium carbonate to touch the skin, and do not breathe the vapor. The ammonium carbonate helps the emulsification, and causes a great deal of foaming. If the mixture begins to overflow the saucepan, remove it from the heat until the foam subsides.
3. Stir the mixture and continue to heat it gently until all traces of the ammonia odor have disappeared. A creamy white emulsion will have formed. It can be thinned out with a little more distilled water, or stored as a paste.
4. While the emulsion is still warm, pour and scrape it into the glass jar. It will keep indefinitely, if tightly covered.

WAX PASTE

This soap can be used in exactly the same ways as the wax-water emulsion. As a surface wax, it can be applied over any kind of paint that will not be harmed by contact with mineral spirits.

MATERIALS

1. Bleached white beeswax.
2. Mineral spirits.
3. Enameled steel saucepan.
4. A hotplate.
5. Covered glass jar for storage.

METHOD

1. Place 1 part by volume of the beeswax and 3 parts by volume of the mineral spirits in the saucepan.

2. Heat gently on the hot plate. *Caution:* Mineral spirits is flammable. Do not allow any mineral spirits to spill onto the hotplate heating element.

3. When the wax has melted into solution with the mineral spirits, remove the mixture from the heat and stir it until it cools. It will form a very soft paste.

4. Spoon the paste into the glass jar, where it will keep indefinitely if covered tightly.

COMMERCIAL PRODUCTS

Grumbacher's Zec and Gel and Dorland's Wax Medium are examples of manufactured wax soaps that can be used like the homemade pastes (see Appendix D). These are not entirely pure soaps, however, and can contain such ingredients as linseed oils, varnish resins, other kinds of waxes (petroleum and fossil waxes), and colloidal silica, which can significantly affect handling, drying, and sometimes the durability of the paints. They are also more expensive than the homemade variety. Use all wax soaps with caution.

WAX AND OIL CRAYONS

A growing interest in using alternative or nontraditional paints—such as paint in stick form—has led to increasing use of products like wax crayons and oil crayons (also called oil pastels). You can easily make these in the studio and be assured of a higher quality product.

WAX CRAYONS

To make crayons in the traditional stick form, use a mold into which the molten wax pigment mixture is poured. The mold can be made out of any material that can be separated easily from the crayon once the wax has hardened; plasticene (a nondrying clay) or heavy-gauge aluminum foil will work. Make as many molds of a handy size as needed.

Use the materials and follow the method given for encaustic paints (see Chapter 13), being very careful to get a smooth, semi-liquid paste that can be poured into the molds. Since pure beeswax produces a relatively soft and sticky crayon, you may wish to add a small amount of paraffin (petroleum wax) to the mixture; this may produce harder crayons. But be careful not to add too much, since paraffin is not considered very durable as an art material. Grinding the pigments on a slab with a small amount of mineral spirits will ensure a smooth, grit-free crayon. Pour the pigment wax paste into the molds and let them cool. Remove the crayons and wrap them in paper, if desired.

For some artists, making molds is too much trouble—and the product is not perfectly uniform like the commercial sticks. Dispense with the molds and make large encaustic cakes: Use them like crayons.

OIL CRAYONS

To make these crayons, use the same method outlined for wax crayons. Grind the pigments first in a small amount of mineral spirits, very stiffly. Melt the wax and stir in a small amount of alkali-refined linseed oil or linseed stand oil—1 part oil to 3 parts wax. Then add the pigment paste and proceed as with wax crayons. You may have to make adjustments until you find exactly the right proportions, but keep the oil content to the minimum. Too much oil will prevent the hardening of the wax.

CRAYON PAINTING TECHNIQUES

Heavy rag paper or museum board can be used for crayon work if the layers of paint are kept thin. For thicker applications use a panel support, or mount the paper on a rigid substrate. These materials can be brittle in heavy applications, so unmounted flexible supports should not be used.

The application of these materials is more like a drawing action, since filing the "dry" paint against the textured surface of the support deposits a layer of material. After application, these paints can be brushed over and thinned into washes with mineral spirits. Interesting and subtle effects can result, much like those in encaustic. Heavy impasto will be of doubtful durability in these paints, however.

COMMERCIAL PRODUCTS

Most of the commercial incarnations of wax and oil crayons are labeled so poorly —the contents of the vehicle or binder is not revealed and the colorants are called by proprietary, not generic, names—that it is impossible to be sure of their durability. Lightfastness tests show that several brands have good to excellent durability in light for some colors (though the same colors in other brands have failed the test), but this test does not account for the durability of the vehicle. Furthermore, manufacturers frequently change formulas for these products, so it is worthless to recommend specific brands. The formulas may be different from week to week. Artists wishing to use the commercial products should conduct their own tests for lightfastness with these materials. Wax crayons for children are not permanent art materials—they have not passed any lightfastness tests and were not designed to—and should not be used for permanent work.

CHAPTER 15

PASTEL

Pastel, like the oil and wax crayons, is sometimes thought of as primarily a drawing medium because the material is applied dry. Since it uses color, however, it is proper to think of it as a painting medium. It is, in fact, the purest of the painting techniques in that the sticks of color are composed mostly of pigment, with very little vehicle added.

Although chalks dug from the ground and mixtures of colored clays with weak binders have been used since prehistoric times, the development of true pastel as a separate and distinct painting medium dates only from around the beginning of the eighteenth century. Red, white, and black chalks were used as accent hues in Renaissance drawings, and there are some works in full color dating from the early seventeenth century, but the technique was not fully realized until about a hundred years later.

Artists such as Jean-Étienne Liotard, Maurice Quentin de la Tour, and Jean-Baptiste-Siméon Chardin were early practitioners who refined pastel painting into a highly sophisticated medium for portraiture. Édouard Manet, Pierre-Auguste Renoir, and most notably Edgar Degas exploited other possibilities of expression in pastel, producing less slickly finished works in favor of more spirited, loose constructions. Degas's work in pastel can stand by itself, apart from his other, equally formidable work, as a monumental achievement. He experimented more than any other artist before him, and stretched the limits of pastel far beyond its established boundaries.

Although most artists prefer to purchase their pastels ready-made, the items are easy to make. Artist-grade pigments are simply combined with the binder; the lighter tints of the various hues are made by combining a white pigment or inert filler with the full-strength colors. As in all the other paint-making processes, you can make up special colors that are not available commercially; it is easy to make very large pastel sticks if you wish to work with big sweeps of color.

Artist-grade dry pigments used for the water paints are appropriate for pastel. Avoid the toxic pigments, especially since you are apt to inhale the dust during the painting process.

During and after the painting process, fixative is sprayed on, so that the particles will not be brushed off. Fixative can be made in the studio too.

Pastels are usually matted and framed behind glass for exhibition. For storage, they should at least be matted to protect their fragile surfaces. See Chapter 17.

PREPARATION OF THE BINDERS

Good pastel binders can be made of gum acacia, gum Tragacanth (the traditional pastel binder), or methyl cellulose. Each of the three ingredients requires a slightly different method of preparation, and each in turn is made as a stock solution to be diluted further for making the pastels.

MATERIALS FOR THE THREE METHODS

1. The binder.
2. Distilled water.
3. One large, clean glass jar with cover, and 5 smaller clean glass jars with covers.

METHOD: GUM ACACIA (GUM ARABIC)

1. Combine 1 part by volume of powdered or lump gum with 2 parts by volume of boiling distilled water.
2. Remove from the heat, and stir to dissolve the gum.
3. Allow the solution to cool, then strain it through some fine-mesh cheesecloth into the large glass jar. This solution will keep for a few days in a cool place. It may be refrigerated if necessary, but will have to be warmed before use. A preservative can be used, but is not necessary if all the vehicle is to be used at once to make a complete set of colors.

METHOD: GUM TRAGACANTH

1. Put 1 part of the powdered gum into a clean glass bottle and moisten it with a very little bit of denatured ethyl alcohol or grain alcohol. Add 25 to 35 parts of distilled water, cap the bottle, and shake the mixture.
2. Allow the solution to sit overnight, by which time it will have formed a gel—a colloidal solution. Warm the gel in a water bath (place the bottle in a pot of water on a hotplate) to complete the solution.
3. Work the warmed solution through a cheesecloth strainer into a clean glass jar. The solution will keep as long as the gum Acacia, but need not be refrigerated. Preservatives are not necessary.

METHOD: METHYL CELLULOSE

1. Mix 1 part by volume methyl cellulose powder with 24 parts by volume of cold distilled water. Cap the jar and shake; a thick solution will form within minutes.
2. Add a small amount of distilled water to thin the solution to a syrupy state. No preservative is necessary; the solution will keep a long time and need not be refrigerated.

VEHICLE STRENGTHS

All of these solutions are stock vehicles that can be used full strength to make the pastels, but for some pigments they are far too strong and will make sticks that are too hard to use easily. Whichever binder is used, reduce the vehicle to five different strengths with additional distilled water, as follows:

1. Divide the stock solution in half. Label the reserved stock #1.
2. To the second part of #1, add 2 parts water. Divide it in half again and label the reserved portion #2.
3. To the second part of #2, add 2 parts water. Divide it in half again and label the reserved portion #3.
4. To the second part of #3, add 2 parts water. Divide it in half again and label the reserved portion #4.
5. To the second part of #4, add 2 parts water. Label it #5.

The pastel chalks are made with these various strengths of vehicles. Since identically named pigments can vary in texture and particle size from supplier to supplier, it is difficult to give precise instructions as to which strength of binder is appropriate for which pigment. On the whole, the stock solution, #1, is rarely needed. The weakest vehicles, #4 and #5, will generally bind the organic pigments sufficiently, although some varieties will need #2. Vehicles #2 and #3 will bind the natural and manufactured mineral pigments, although some need only #5 or, in a few cases, water alone. It is a simple matter to make a test stick: Take notes to remember how the color was made.

MAKING PASTELS

A surprisingly small volume of pigment will make quite a large number of sticks, depending of course on the pigment being used. For instance, 2 ounces (60 ml) of arylide (Hansa) yellow, a relatively inexpensive pigment, can be reduced with about 4 ounces (120 ml) of precipitated chalk without losing any of the chroma of the straight pigment. This volume of pigment (6 ounces, or 180 ml) can be made into 10 to 15 sticks of full-strength pastel, not counting any reductions with white to make the tints. If a stick of bright yellow pastel purchased in an art supply store costs, on the average, about 50 cents to a dollar (or more depending on the pigment), you can readily see the savings involved in making your own pastel sticks.

MATERIALS

1. A mortar and pestle. It is easier to mix the pigments with this equipment than with a grinding setup, because you are making a rather dry dough instead of a liquid. Large porcelain or ceramic mortars and pestles can be obtained from restaurant supply houses or chemicals suppliers.
2. The vehicles.
3. Artist-grade dry pigments. For the white pastels, use titanium or zinc white, or plain precipitated chalk or whiting. For the filler, used to make light tints, use whiting (calcium carbonate) to produce harder chalks, and precipitated chalk or kaolin (China clay) to produce softer chalks. Barium sulfate can also be used for the filler.
4. Newspapers and trays for drying the sticks. Cover a hardboard panel with several layers of newsprint.

Make the white pastel first, as it will be used to reduce the full-strength colors to tints. Make a rather large volume of the white.

METHOD

1. Place a volume of dry pigment in the mortar. If the pigment is a fine powder, which it should be, proceed to step 2. If the pigment is somewhat coarse, pound and grind with the pestle to separate the lumps.
2. Add a bit of the selected vehicle. Grind the mixture, and add some more vehicle. Continue grinding and adding small amounts of vehicle until the mixture is a smooth, doughy paste. It should be very smooth and of the consistency of bread dough, or a slightly moist lump of clay.
3. Remove the dough from the mortar and divide it in half. Reserve half to make tints; to keep it moist while the white sticks are being made, place it in a bowl and cover the bowl with a cloth dampened with water.
4. Separate the dough into smaller lumps and use the flat of the palm to roll each out into a stick about 3/8 inch (1 cm) in diameter and 3 inches (7.5 cm) in length, or whatever diameter and length stick is desired. If you want a stick with smooth and regular contours, use a piece of stiff cardboard or a small block of wood to roll out the sticks.
5. Put the sticks of white pastel on a layer of newsprint, on a tray, and set them aside to dry. They may be dried near a source of gentle heat, but too rapid drying may cause them to crack. If you are making a test stick to check the vehicle strength, set the tray in the sun or on a radiator.
6. To make full-strength colored sticks, select a pigment and repeat steps 1 through 5. Reserve half of the full-strength dough, as in step 3.
7. To make a half-strength tint of a full-strength color, combine the colored dough with an equal portion of the reserved white dough. Mix them to-

gether thoroughly so that there are no streaks of color evident. Divide the mixture in two and reserve half as in step 3. Make the half-strength sticks as in steps 4 and 5.

8. To make quarter-strength sticks, combine an equal portion of the white dough with the reserved half-strength dough. Reserve half as in step 3.

9. Continue as above, making weaker and weaker tints if desired, until the white dough is no longer tinted by the remaining colored dough. Usually three or four reductions are enough, although some of the stronger pigments can be reduced by as much as 80 or 90 percent before they no longer have a coloring effect on the white dough.

10. Clean up all the equipment with soap and water, and proceed to the next color. If you have made a huge batch of white dough, begin with a new colored dough; otherwise, make some more white first.

Some sticks will form a surface crust when dry. Simply scrub the stick on a rough surface to break through the crust.

White pastels can be made of one single kind of pigment, or a combination of the pigment and a chalk filler, or a single chalk filler, or a combination of chalk fillers, depending on the desired consistency of the resulting chalk. Kaolin and precipitated chalk will produce smoother chalk sticks; blanc fixe, a precipitated barium sulfate, will produce smoother sticks; natural calcium carbonate, whiting, will produce harder or coarser chalks. Likewise, the selection of the variety of filler chalk will affect the consistency of any colored pigments that are added to it to make tints. The possibilities are endless.

Although the operation is very simple, it is wise to take written notes of the ingredients used and their proportions when making pastels—it is wise to take notes when making paints in any case, but perhaps more important when making pastels. Such a variety of combinations can be made that it would be impossible to duplicate successful results without some written record of the recipe.

PAINTING TECHNIQUES

TOOLS

Ordinarily, no tools other than fingers (used for blending) are necessary for painting in pastels. Some artists prefer to use a rolled paper stump or chamois cloth for blending, rather than fingers. Short-bristled brushes are useful for scrubbing off mistakes, especially when the pastel has been built into a thickness; a small sharp knife blade can also be used, as can a kneaded rubber or vinyl eraser.

SUPPORTS AND GROUNDS

Any permanent, toothy support can be used for pastel, although too rough a surface might not work well, and fabric supports will not work unless they are mounted. Mounted fabrics can have a very thin ground applied—so as not to obscure the weave—and some smooth-surfaced supports, like hardboards, should have a toothy ground.

Papers made especially for pastel are available; they have a textured coating applied to the surface which is ideal for pastel painting. It is easy to make your own pastel papers, using ground pumice powder or other rough, powdery material and a little thin glue.

METHOD

1. Thin 1 part of a PVA emulsion glue (any white glue will do) with 10 parts of water, and brush it liberally over the surface of a stretched paper.
2. Sprinkle the powder evenly over the surface of the paper.
3. Pick up the support, holding it horizontally and face up, and give it a good shaking back and forth and side to side—as though you were flouring a greased baking pan—to distribute the powder evenly.
4. Tilt the support and shake off any excess powder that has not stuck to the glue.
5. Allow the glue to dry.

Colored papers can also be used for pastel supports, but they should be pigmented or dyed with permanent colorants, and should be made of permanent, acid-free materials. Better: Give a rag paper support a thin, even wash of watercolor paint.

THE APPLICATION OF PASTELS

The same rule applies here as in other techniques. The use of the material is governed by an artist's needs. Most artists try to avoid overblending pastel in a careless manner, which can result in a smudged or blurry appearance. Separated strokes of color can blend optically with one another to produce mixtures of hues, and layers of color that do not obscure each other can be built up in this way. Once the tooth of the support has been completely filled in by applications of the chalk, subsequent layers of color will not adhere well unless the ground is reexposed. A slight impasto is possible, but heavier applications will eventually fall off the support, especially if the picture is roughly handled.

Mixed techniques with pastel are attractive: combined with water-thinned paints, they can produce exciting images; they can also be combined successfully with the temperas, casein, oil, acrylic solution, acrylic emulsion, and alkyd paints. As with any other mixed technique, you should have some idea of which medium will be dominant and which will be used for accents or supporting touches.

FIXATIVES

A fixative is applied as a final weak film and is used to adhere the particles of pastel to each other, and somewhat to the support, to prevent their being jarred loose or falling off. A fixative must be sprayed on; it is not applied as a measurable layer or coating. Too heavy an application of fixative can change the refractive index of the paints, causing a drastic change in the look of the work—and the idea—thus rendering those passages painted with opaque strokes transparent and darker. Fixatives can be applied during the painting process, too, in order to prevent movement of painted layers as further applications of color are made.

The choice of fixative is important. It should be weak in strength, as colorless as possible, and very fast-drying. Commercial spray fixatives in art supply stores are usually solutions of acrylic or vinyl resins in alcohol, mineral spirits, toluene, or combinations of these solvents. They should be used with caution, especially if the label indicates the presence of toluene, for most of the solvent vapors are harmful, if not toxic. An organic vapor mask should be worn when spraying fixatives, or good cross-ventilation of air should be provided.

PREPARATION OF HOMEMADE FIXATIVES

Homemade fixatives are a less expensive alternative to the commercial brands. The shellac solution described in Chapter 5 can be used. For those who might object to the slight yellowing shellac can cause—it is really negligible in the dilution suggested for fixatives—try the following alternatives.

METHOD: ACRYLIC SOLUTION

1. Dilute 10 parts Acryloid B-67MT with 40 parts of its solvent, mineral spirits.
2. To increase the rate of evaporation, add 1 part toluene, but exercise caution. Toluene is toxic and extremely flammable.
3. Spray to apply, and use the recommended protective devices.

METHOD: POLYVINYL ACETATE SOLUTION

1. Dissolve 1 part of PVA resin in 10 parts ethyl alcohol. If the PVA is in large chunks, it will take as long as 24 hours to dissolve (alcohol is not the best solvent for PVA, but is the safest); if it is powdered, the solution will form in less time.
2. Spray to apply, and agitate from time to time to keep the PVA in solution.
3. Excersise caution: Alcohol is harmful and flammable. Use the recommended protective devices.

SPRAY EQUIPMENT

Since fixatives should be sprayed, not brushed, consider the equipment available for spraying. The old-fashioned mouth atomizer (Figure 15.1) works well, but places the user very close to potentially harmful spray mists. An alternative to this is the commercial spray solutions, a self-contained solution of resin and solvent with an inert propellant. These can become expensive if a large volume of spray is being used; in addition, the pressure in the can is reduced with use, so that the final bursts of spray are more like spurts of globs than mists.

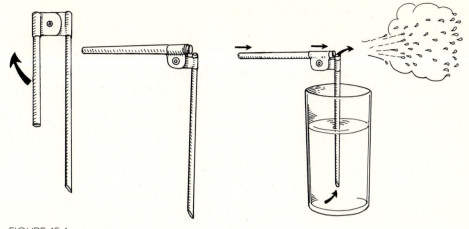

FIGURE 15.1
How a Mouth Atomizer Works

   Another alternative is to use one of the small devices that have a container of inert propellant attached to a reservoir into which anything that can be sprayed is placed—one only need replace the can of propellant when it runs out. The best alternative is a compressed-air sprayer or an electric sprayer—especially if you want to do spray varnishing too. See the section on spray varnishing in Chapter 17 for a further discussion of spray devices.

CHAPTER 16

MURAL TECHNIQUES

Mural painting is distinct from easel painting in several ways. Murals are usually executed for architectural spaces—rooms, public halls, walls, floors, ceilings, and exterior walls—and thus must be planned to fit the design requirements of the particular space. Because the paintings must usually be viewable from all angles, they must be free from surface glare and reflections or other elements that could interfere with the perception of the work. The paintings usually cover a relatively large expanse, and although murals need not be complicated—full of figures in involved situations—they sometimes are. The total impact of the design and composition must transcend intricacies in specific areas. Murals present an added set of technical difficulties related to permanence. Public spaces, and even some private ones, have hard-to-control environments, and the technique chosen should be able to withstand more than the usual stresses to which an easel painting is exposed. Finally, murals intended for exterior exposure must not be vulnerable to even more stressful exposures: wind, rain, strong and variable ultraviolet light, heat, cold, and the abrasive action of windblown dust, dirt, and pollutants.

Most contemporary interior mural paintings are not done in the traditional *fresco buono* (affresco) method because of the rather delicate nature of the painting's surface. Instead, *secco* techniques are sometimes used, although it is more convenient, less expensive, and relatively less technically involved to choose one of the easel painting techniques: acrylic or vinyl emulsion, acrylic solution, alkyds, casein, or one of the temperas. Exterior murals must be done in more resistant techniques, depending on the nature of the exposure: mosaic, colored cements, glazed ceramics, porcelain enameled steel, acrylic emulsions, or the silicate paints.

PLANNING

Unless you are free to do anything—in your own home, for instance—it is usually necessary to work with others on a mural project. The client, other artists, artisans, interior designers, and the architects are ordinarily consulted during the

282

planning of new construction; engineers and landscape architects might have to be included for the planning of exterior decorations. At the very least, the client must be satisfied if you are doing work in an existing structure. It is therefore essential that everyone involved have an understanding of the work, and that all are capable of working together.

A series of studies—drawings or color work—is generally the beginning point. These studies should be done to scale, so that their appropriateness to the setting can be judged, and they should take into account the surroundings and the viewer's distance from the work. After the studies have been approved, they can be scaled up by means of the grid system (Figure 16.1) to a full-size cartoon and transferred to the surface being decorated. Any of the intermediate steps—site selection, and wall, ceiling, or floor surface preparation—between the acceptance of the design and the execution of the work will depend on the type of technique chosen.

INTERIOR MURAL PAINTS

Fresco is the Italian word for "fresh," and it properly refers to mural paintings executed on fresh wet lime plaster; sometimes the term *buono fresco* (*fresco buono*) or *buona fresco* is used to distinguish the fresh technique from *secco,* painting on dry lime plaster, and *mezzo,* painting on half-dry lime plaster.

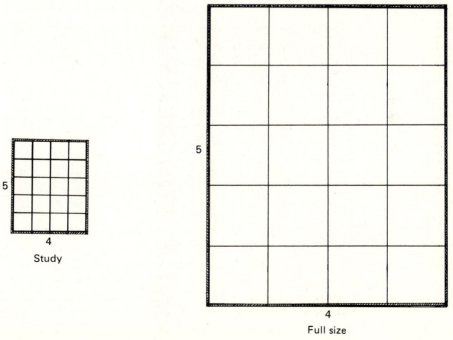

Study

Full size

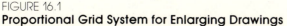

FIGURE 16.1
Proportional Grid System for Enlarging Drawings

FRESCO

The fresco technique of interior and exterior wall painting has its beginnings in the eastern Mediterranean Minoan civilization. Wall decorations in India date from 200 B.C. During the Renaissance, some of the masterpieces of Western art were executed in Italy, and it is there that we can see frescoes from all periods since Roman times. Giotto, Massacio, Fra Angelico, Piero della Francesca, Michelangelo, and Raphael were masters of the technique, and their work exemplifies the classical and traditional approaches to fresco.

As explained in Chapter 3, fresco is a catalytic medium. That is, dry pigments predispersed in plain water are brushed onto and absorbed into the plaster-coated wall. They become part of the wall, which undergoes a complex chemical change to convert back to its original form while locking the pigments within its matrix. Only those pigments which are resistant to an alkaline binder (or, in the case of exterior application, an alkaline binder and an acidic environment) are used in fresco, which rather limits the palette.

The actual procedures for painting in fresco are simple. It is the preparation that is expensive, and time-consuming. Artisans competent in wall construction and plastering must be hired if the artist cannot do the work, and they must understand the special nature of fresco plaster. Often apprentices or assistant artists are needed to help in the execution of the work.

THE SITE

When planning a fresco, the artist must consider the interior spaces and architectural embellishments. Aspects such as lighting, the viewpoint of the audience, the size of the work, and the scale of the space present problems. For interior spaces, it should be pointed out to the client that polluted city atmospheres may shorten the life of a fresco, since the pigments are not protected by a covering film or layer of vehicle. An enclosed and controlled environment is best for fresco, although planners in the countryside, where the air is fresher, may not need to worry so much about this problem.

Exterior sites are much more difficult, exposed as they are not only to pollutants, but to wind, rain, and dust. A protected courtyard wall, a wall with a slight divergence from the vertical, or walls with protective overhangs might be made to work, but one should not make claims for the life of the painting.

PREPARING THE WALL

If you can start with new construction and have a fresco wall built from scratch, so much the better. It is more usual to have to build up the wall over existing construction. The wall must be absorbent and toothy, to provide a key for the plaster, and its structure must not contain any impurities that can later leach out and discolor the painting. New constructions and renovations should be done well in advance of the painting, to allow the structure to settle. Cracking is almost inevitable in both cases, and repairs should be made to the wall, not to the live plaster ground.

Exterior Walls   The fresco plaster cannot be applied over concrete or cement substrates; dissolved mineral salts will effloresce through the coatings. Smooth wooden walls, rarely encountered outdoors, and other wooden structures should have an exterior lattice of fir or spruce applied, to which a wire screen lath can be nailed as a key for the plaster (Figure 16.2).

Brick walls are excellent, provided they are carefully prepared. The cement mortar between the bricks should be pointed and repaired, with all loose particles removed and replaced. Any soft or crumbly bricks must be cut out and replaced, as must bricks that show efflorescence, mold, or any surface growths. Smooth and even brick walls should be given a tooth by going over the entire surface with a hammer and chisel to chip, score, and texture the surface. The entire wall must then be washed repeatedly with clear water: Wash twice while scrubbing to remove loose particles (use a stiff bristle floor brush), then rinse twice.

Interior Walls   Ideally, there should be an air space between an interior wall that backs onto an exterior exposure; the inside of the exterior wall should be coated

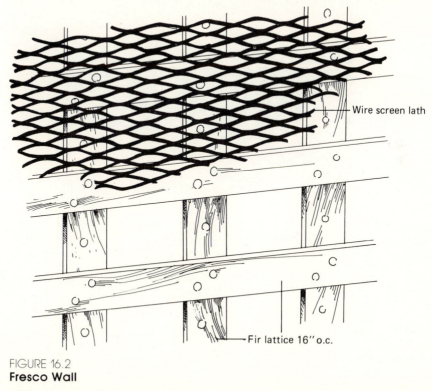

Wire screen lath

Fir lattice 16" o.c.

FIGURE 16.2
Fresco Wall

Lattice support with wire screen lath.

thoroughly with a waterproof asphalt-based paint. The space provides an insulating pocket of dead air—it is even better if the space can be filled with fiberglass or foam insulation—and the coating prevents atmospheric moisture from affecting the lime plaster wall. Walls that back on other interior spaces do not necessarily need the insulating space.

New or old plaster and plasterboard walls should be removed. It is best to build the lime plaster on a stud framing with lattice or wire screen lath attached (Figure 16.3). To save the mess of tearing down a wall, you can build a stud wall in front of, and slightly separated from, existing interior walls. Standard construction techniques should be used to ensure that the wall is sound. There should be both sills and top plates, and the studs should be spaced at 16 inches on center (46 cm). Although it need not be a bearing wall, supporting the ceiling above, bearing wall construction will be sounder than any shortcuts. Allow this kind of new construction to settle before plastering.

SUPPORT, GROUND, AND BINDER

The plaster, or mortar, for fresco is the support, the ground, and the binder for the painting. It must be prepared with particular care, of the purest and cleanest

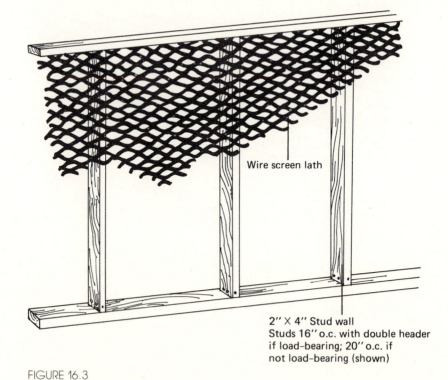

Wire screen lath

2″ × 4″ Stud wall
Studs 16″ o.c. with double header
if load-bearing; 20″ o.c. if
not load-bearing (shown)

FIGURE 16.3
Fresco Wall

Stud framing with wire screen lath.

ingredients, to prevent any problems as it dries and ages. The plaster is applied in three or four coats of varying composition, with the last coat being richest in lime. The different coatings of lime plaster, in order of application, are the following:

1. The rough coat. Also called the rough-cast or scratch coat and, in Italian, *trullisatio* or *trusilar*.
2. The brown coat. In Italian, *arricciato* or *arriccio*.
3. The sand coat. In Italian, *arenato*. This coating is sometimes left out.
4. The painting coat. In Italian, *intonaco*.

Slaked Lime   The plaster binder for all of these coats is made from a base of roasted calcium carbonate, called, variously, quick lime, calcium oxide, or high-calcium lime. This caustic alkali may be found in building supply stores: Take care that it is the purest available, and that it does not contain clays, gypsum, mica, or metallic salts that can later cause efflorescence. It should be bought in powder form and handled with caution: Quick lime is caustic and can cause burns once it is mixed with water.

The calcium oxide is converted to lime putty for the mortar by a process called *slaking*. Water is mixed with the calcium oxide powder, and the mixture is allowed to age. Since the character and performance of slaked lime improves with age, the time needed to prepare and cure it sufficiently is the principal drawback in making a proper fresco ground. It can take as long as two years for the slaked lime to age to a good consistency, and the best slaked lime has been allowed to age for 25 years or more. You may be able to locate a ready commercial source for slaked lime; be sure, however, that the substance is made of the purest calcium oxide.

To make the slaked lime putty, follow these steps:

MATERIALS

1. Quick lime (calcium oxide).
2. Clean soft water, with no dissolved mineral or metallic salts, and a garden hose.
3. A large wooden trough (Figure 16.4).
4. A garden hoe or a masonry hoe (Figure 16.5).
5. A large wooden box with lid for storing the lime (Figure 16.6).
6. Gravel.
7. An ordinary shovel.

METHOD

1. Out of doors, mix the quick lime in the wooden trough with enough water to make a loose paste. Using the hoe, mix carefully and thoroughly, and avoid splashing the caustic mixture.
2. Dig a pit in the ground, below the frost line, and lay down a base of gravel. The gravel provides drainage at the bottom of the hole and is essential: it should be about 6 inches (150 cm) deep.
3. Construct a wooden box big enough to hold all the lime and lower it into the hole. Shovel the lime and water mixture into the box, spray it with

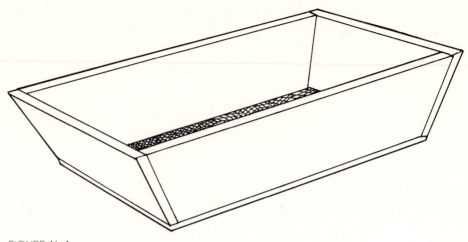

FIGURE 16.4
Wooden Trough

For mixing slaked lime putty.

water, cover it with the wooden lid, and shovel earth over the cover. As it ages, the lime may be stirred from time to time. Eventually it will develop into a putty that is malleable and perfect as a binder for the mortar.

Additives to the Lime   To strengthen the wall, the different coatings of lime plaster are reinforced by diminishing amounts of filler materials; the lower layers

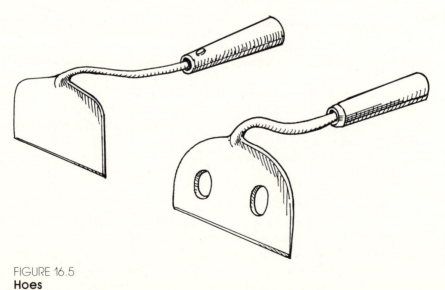

FIGURE 16.5
Hoes

Left: ordinary garden hoe.
Right: preferred masonry hoe (note holes).

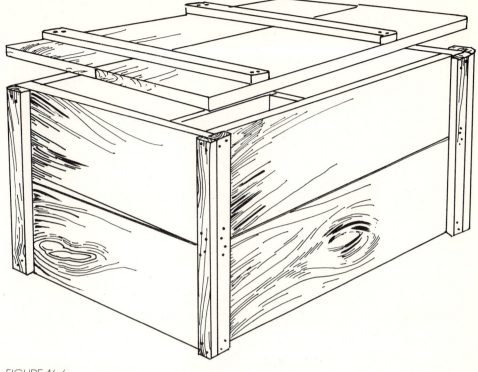

FIGURE 16.6
Wooden Box with Lid

Buried in the ground and used to store the slaked lime.

have more filler in proportion to lime, while the upper layers are richer in lime. Likewise, the lower layers of plaster should contain coarser filler, and the upper layers, finer filler. Filler materials include the following, arranged in order from coarse to fine:

> *Crushed brick, crushed unglazed clay tile, or coarse sand:* The average particle size should be about $\frac{1}{16}$ to $\frac{1}{8}$ inch (1.5–3 mm) in diameter.
> *Coarse marble meal:* The average particle size should be about $\frac{1}{32}$ to $\frac{1}{16}$ inch (0.75–1.5 mm) in diameter.
> *Fine sand or marble dust.*

None of the filler materials should have any impurities that could cause efflorescence. The sand should be river sand, not beach sand (which can contain dissolved salts), and it should be thoroughly washed. The brick and tile pieces and the marble meal and dust should also be thoroughly washed.

To wash the coarse fillers, spread them on a screen outdoors and rinse with water from a hose. The screen should be fine enough to prevent the filler from being washed away. Rinse several times, and spread the material out on a clean tarpaulin to dry. Store it in bags indoors where it will not pick up any organic impurities from the ground.

To wash finer filler such as sand and marble meal or dust, stir it in a bucket into a very loose slurry with water. Allow it to settle, and pour off the water. Repeat this procedure until the water is absolutely clear. Spread the filler out to dry; store in bags indoors.

When it is mixed with the lime putty, the filler must be not only very clean but completely dry. A film of water around the particles of sand, for example, could prevent the complete integration of the putty with the sand.

As noted earlier, the proportion of coarse aggregate to fine adhesive materials in the mortar decreases with successive layers, producing a sound construction analogous to that of an oil painting ("fat over lean").

THE ROUGH COAT

1. 1 part lime putty.
2. 3 parts filler. Use crushed brick, crushed unglazed clay tile, or marble meal.

THE BROWN COAT

1. 1 part lime putty.
2. 3 parts filler. Use coarse sand.

THE SAND COAT

1. 1 part lime putty.
2. 2 parts filler. Use fine sand or marble dust.

THE PAINTING COAT

1. 1 part lime putty.
2. 1 part filler. Use fine sand or marble dust.

Application of the Lime Plaster   To make a proper mixture of the ingredients, they should first be combined while they are dry. Use a wooden trough and a hoe to make the initial mix, and make sure that the various materials are fully incorporated with one another.

When the cover is removed from the lime pit and the putty is exposed, you will often find that a crust has formed on the surface of the putty. Scrape off the crust and remove bits and pieces of it before mixing with the filler, by straining it through a screen. Hoe the strained putty with the filler thoroughly to make a dry mixture in which there are no lumps or separate agglomerations of one or the other material.

After the dry mixture is made, add a little water and hoe again. Keep adding water a little at a time until the mortar reaches a plastic consistency that can be troweled onto the wall.

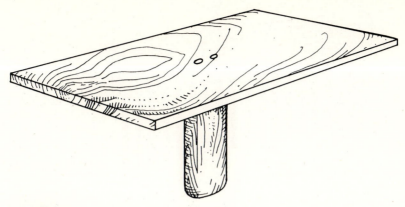

FIGURE 16.7
Mortar Board

MATERIALS

1. Clean, well-aged lime putty.
2. A hose and a source of clean water.
3. The various fillers.
4. Wooden mixing trough and hoe.
5. Buckets for measuring the ingredients.
6. A mortarboard for holding the mortar (Figure 16.7).
7. A trowel for throwing the mortar, about 4 by 10 inches (10×25 cm) with a handle. The size will be determined by the area of wall to be covered (Figure 16.8).
8. A perfectly straight length of 2 by 4 (5×10 cm) lumber, the length determined by the size of the wall.
9. A metal comb for scoring the plaster (Figure 16.9).
10. A wide, soft-bristled plastering brush (Figure 16.10).

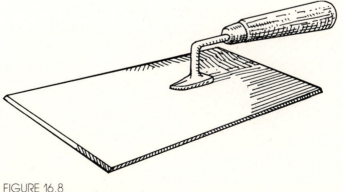

FIGURE 16.8
Plaster-Throwing Trowel

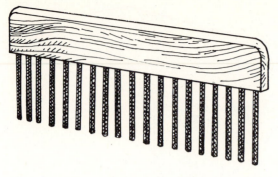

FIGURE 16.9
Metal Comb for Keying the Plaster

11. A wooden float for smoothing the surface of the mortar, about 6 by 12 inches (15 × 30 cm) (Figure 16.11).
12. A metal float for polishing the mortar, a tool somewhat like a spackle knife used for sheetrock work (Figure 16.12).

The application of each coating of lime plaster should proceed once the previously laid layer has set, but before the surface has dried to a crust. A crust will normally form within 6 to 10 hours of application, depending on the relative humidity of the environment. If you will not be able to apply the next coating before a crust forms, provide a mechanical key for the new layer by applying the lower coat roughly or by scratching a key into it with the metal comb.

Before the initial application of the rough coat, and between each succeeding application of the other coatings, the wall should be thoroughly wetted with water, either by brushing it on with the plastering brush or by liberally spraying it with the hose. Allow the water to soak into and disappear from the surface of the wall before applying the mortar.

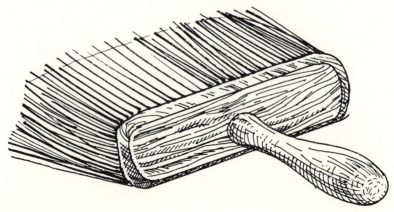

FIGURE 16.10
Plastering Brush

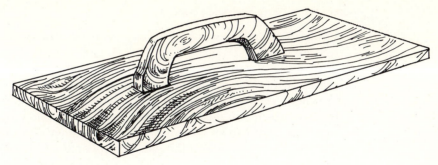

FIGURE 16.11
Wooden Plaster Float

METHOD: THE ROUGH COAT

1. If the wall is brick, soak it thoroughly with water. Allow the water to soak into the wall.

2. If the wall is a stud wall with wooden lath, soak the lath as in step 1.

3. If the wall is a stud wall with a wire screen lath, there is no need to soak it.

4. Mix the rough coat's dry ingredients in the wooden trough, and then add enough clean water to make a stiff paste. Mix thoroughly.

5. Beginning at the bottom of the wall and working toward the top, use the trowel to throw the mortar at the wall from a distance of about a foot or two (30–60 cm) and at a slight angle to the wall. The mortar is slapped on from this distance, to force it into the mechanical key and to rid it of air bubbles; the angle of application will keep bits of the mortar from splattering back into your face.

6. Build the rough coat to a thickness of about ¾ inch (1.8 cm).

7. Level the surface of the wall with the length of straight lumber, but do not make the surface too smooth. Scratch the wall with the metal comb in an allover random pattern to provide a key for the next layer.

8. Spray the wall with water before the plaster sets. It will set in about 20 to 30 minutes.

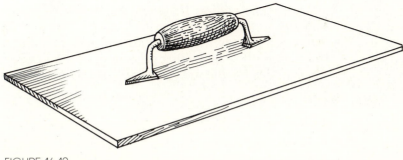

FIGURE 16.12
Metal Plaster Float

METHOD: THE BROWN COAT

1. While the rough coat is setting, clean out the trough and mix the brown coat materials.
2. Wait until the standing water on the wall has disappeared, but begin application of the brown coat before the wall dries out. It is possible, but not absolutely necessary, to apply the brown coat in two steps: in a thin, even layer of brown coat mixture thinned with water, followed immediately by a richer layer of brown coat of normal consistency. The application of two layers will ensure better adhesion. Trowel on the brown coat(s) evenly and smoothly.
3. Build the brown coat to a thickness of between ½ and ¾ inch (1.2–1.8 cm). Some accounts recommend that the thickness of the rough coat and the brown coat combined be 1 inch (2.5 cm); others say they can be of equal thickness, for a combined total of 1½ inches (3.75 cm). Experience indicates that thinner walls, and thinner layers within the wall, present fewer adhesion problems; on the other hand, thicker walls can be more stable.
4. It should not be necessary to level the brown coat with the straight edge. Scratch it with the metal comb, as before, to give it a key.
5. Spray the wall with water after the plaster sets, but before the crust forms.

METHOD: THE SAND COAT

1. While the brown coat is setting, clean out the trough and mix the sand coat materials.
2. Wait until the standing water on the wall has disappeared, but begin application of the sand coat before the wall dries out. The sand coat may also be applied in two steps like the brown coat. Trowel the mortar on evenly and smoothly.
3. Build the sand coat to a thickness of between ⅜ and ½ inch (9 mm–1.25 cm).
4. Before the wall sets, give it a smooth finish with the wooden float; lightly splatter the wall with the plastering brush dipped in water. Dip the float in water to keep it from sticking to the wall, and scrub it over the sand coat with a circular motion, holding it flat against the wall, until the surface is smooth.
5. You can allow the wall to dry before you apply the painting coat, since there is usually some further preparatory work to be done before painting can begin. Spray the wall with water before proceeding with the painting coat.

METHOD: THE PAINTING COAT

1. Fresco paints will be absorbed into and held by the lime only when the painting coat is fresh and damp. Therefore, only as much painting coat as can be covered by a day's painting (say, 6 to 10 hours) can be applied at one

time. Any unpainted areas of the painting coat must be cut out of the wall at the end of the day, and a new application of fresh lime made before the next painting session.

2. Spray the sand coat with several applications of water.
3. Mix the painting coat ingredients in a clean trough.
4. After the water has been absorbed into the plaster, trowel on the painting coat to a thickness of no more than ⅛ inch (3 mm). Cover only those areas of the design surface that can be painted in one day.
5. Finish the painting coat surface with a wet wooden float. To make a finer surface, polish the mortar with the metal float using the circular motion and holding the float flat against the wall, as with the wooden float. After the painting coat has been finished off, the painting can begin.

PREPARATORY CARTOONS

Only the most accomplished and self-assured artists can use an improvisational approach to painting in fresco. So much energy and expense goes into preparing the wall that few are willing to risk spoiling the effort; large or obvious mistakes cannot be painted over with any guarantee of success. The prudent artist will prepare sketches, drawings, and tonal studies of the project, all subject to approval by the client, and a final color sketch showing the artist's conception in its final form, in scale with the surface to be covered. For the color sketch, it is wise to use a water-thinned paint and only those pigments that can be used in fresco.

Since approval for the idea must be obtained before the project can begin, the sketch should be ready before the wall is built. The final small-scale color study is enlarged by means of the proportional grid system into a full-size line drawing that looks like outline drawings in a children's coloring book—hence the name *cartoon*. Brown wrapping paper, white butcher's paper, or smaller pieces of paper taped together can be used for the cartoon (Figure 16.13). The cartoon need not include every detail of the composition, but it should show all the major design elements and their proper placement within the picture. Charcoal, conté crayon, or soft pencil can be used to make the cartoon drawing, and when it is finished the whole picture can be divided with heavier lines into sections to estimate what will take a day to paint (Figure 16.14).

The lines of the drawing are then gone over with a pounce wheel (Figure 16.15), which pierces the paper at regular intervals. An ordinary finishing nail or large pin can be used for this, but the pounce wheel will perforate the paper easily and is the easiest tool to use. The effect is to produce a stencil that can be transferred to the wall.

When the cartoon is finished and perforated, it is hung over the damp painting coat of the wall by means of tape or small tacks through its upper edge. A cheesecloth bag full of crushed charcoal is then pounced against the drawing: The charcoal dust will go through the perforations and be deposited on the wall. This leaves a faint outline of the cartoon—a dotted line—which is a guide to the painting that will follow.

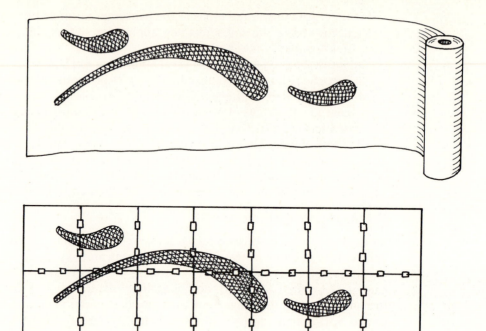

FIGURE 16.13
Cartoons: Alternative Methods

Top: Large roll of paper.
Bottom: Small pages taped together.

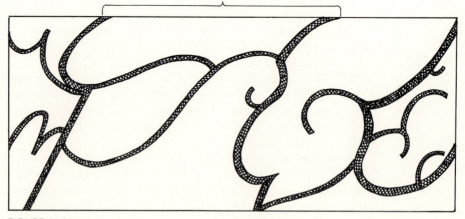

One day's work

FIGURE 16.14
Division of Cartoon into Sections for Daily Painting

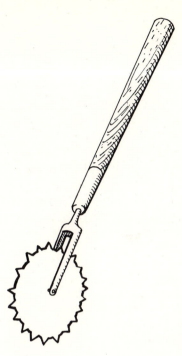

FIGURE 16.15
Pounce Wheel

If the wall cannot be completely covered in one day's painting, then the entire wall is not covered with the painting coat. By the same reckoning, the entire cartoon will not have to be transferred—only those sections that are going to be painted. Some artists prefer to see the whole idea at once as it is developed, and this is difficult if the wall is so large that it canot be painted in a day. A way around this problem is to pounce the cartoon onto the sand coat before the painting coat is applied. Excess charcoal should be dusted off the sand coat before applying the painting coat, so as not to interfere with the adhesion of the painting coat.

If the cartoon is transferred to the painting coat, transfer only those sections marked on the cartoon as suitable for a day's painting. Try to make these divisions as inconspicuous as possible, perhaps running the dividing line along edges of shapes: a line through a large flat area of color will make it very difficult to match color mixtures during the painting—especially from one day to the next.

PIGMENTS AND HOMEMADE FRESCO PAINTS

The lime plaster is an alkaline ground. Since it is also the binder for the paint, it becomes intimately mixed with the pigments. Therefore, only those pigments resistant to alkaline systems can be used in fresco. A palette can consist of as little as one pigment from each hue section below, depending on the intentions of the artist or the requirements of the design.

Reds: Indian red
Light red oxide (English red)
Mars red
Naphthol AS-TR red (PR7)
Venetian red
Cadmium reds, but test first for resistance to the lime
Quinacridone magenta, scarlet, and red

Oranges: Cadmium orange, but test first
Benzimidazolone orange (PO62)
(Oranges can be mixed from reds and yellows.)

Yellows: Raw sienna
Mars yellow
Yellow ochre
Arylide (Hansa) yellow
Cadmium yellows, but test first
Titanium yellow

Greens: Chromium oxide, opaque
Viridian (chromium oxide, hydrous)
Green earth
Cobalt green
Green gold
Light green oxide
Phthalocyanine green

Blues: Cobalt blue
Both varieties of Cerulean blue
Ultramarine blue, but it can turn white in the presence of calcium
Phthalocyanine blue, alpha form (PB15/74160). 74100 may bronze: see the pigment list, Table 7.1.

Purples: Mars violet
Cobalt violet, cobalt oxide variety, but test first
Ioxazine purple
Quinacridone violet
(Purples can be mixed.)

Browns: Mars brown
Burnt sienna
Raw umber
(Browns can be mixed.)

Blacks: Ivory black
Mars black
Carbon black

Whites: Titanium white
Zinc oxide
Slaked lime putty
Bianco Sangiovanni—Saint John's White—the traditional white fresco pigment

Bianco Sangiovanni can be made in the studio. The method is as follows:

1. Form small cakes of aged slaked lime, and allow them to dry completely.
2. Crush the cakes and grind them on a slab with a muller and some distilled water into a paste. Form cakes and allow them to dry completely. Repeat the process until the cakes will no longer hold together in a solid lump.
3. Grind the cakes with water into a loose paste to make the white paint.

Although this list of pigments is rather limited by comparison to those in other mediums, it is still quite large. To avoid having to make too many choices, you can use a palette consisting of a few basic low-chroma hues at first. Brighter colors can be harder to control in a massive composition.

MATERIALS FOR MAKING FRESCO PAINTS

1. Distilled water
2. Artist-grade dry pigments
3. A grinding setup
4. Glass or plastic jars with plastic screw-on covers

METHOD

1. Grind each pigment separately in distilled water to a creamy consistency rather like sour cream.
2. Store the paints in the jars. Pour a bit of distilled water over the top of the creamy pastes to keep them from drying out.

PAINTING TECHNIQUES

Tools and Brushes Both bristle and hair brushes can be used for fresco. Because of the scale of most frescoes, it is advisable to have a supply of large brushes with longer hairs and bristles than are employed in easel painting. The plasterer's brush can be used for wetting the wall and making washes.

Palette and painting knives can be used for mixing large batches of paint; a plastic palette knife is helpful for making the cuts when removing a section of the painting coat that cannot be painted in one day. A putty knife is handy for helping in the removal of painting coats, and can also be used for mixing large batches of color.

Mix the colors in various glass or ceramic containers—jars, cups, and so on—that can be cleaned out or easily discarded.

A water sprayer filled with distilled water can be used to wet colors on the palette to keep them from drying too quickly, and also to spray the wall.

The Application of Paint If all the ideas of the composition are worked out beforehand, the artist should be able to begin work immediately after the wall has been completed and the cartoon transferred. Artists who are inclined to change their approach to the work in midstream must be able to do so within the time limits imposed by the drying lime plaster. Painters with a clear idea of the intent and arrangement of the work can probably make small adjustments as they go along, but it is certainly easier, and far less nervewracking, to have a well-thought-out plan of action to rely on.

To begin, allow the painting coat to dry out for about half an hour, until it is set to a consistency that will hold the indentation left by a fingertip pressed gently into it. There should be no water standing on the surface of the wall. Transfer the cartoon by pouncing. Start the painting at the top of the wall and work down, to avoid splashing finished areas with drips and splatters. Proceed as you would with transparent watercolor, by washing on transparent tones of color over broad, general areas. This approach will unify the composition from the beginning, but it is by no means a rule.

Allow washed-over areas of paint to sink into the plaster before applying overpainting. Overpainting can proceed with additional washes of thin color, leaving the bare wall as the white or highlight areas, and gradually deepen the color tones until the final effect is reached. Or more direct applications of color can be made by mixing paints—color with color or colors with white—separate from the painting.

When white admixtures are made with color, the result is somewhat like what occurs in gouache: The mixtures appear translucent when they are wet, but dry much lighter. This effect should be taken into account. The lightening of the tone is more apparent with the lime putty white and Bianco Sangiovanni than with the titanium white.

Bianco Sangiovanni is oxidized lime putty, which is why it no longer has a binding effect. But the lime putty white is the pure slaked lime used to make the wall; it acts not only as a pigment but also as a binder. When lime putty whites are used, either alone or in mixtures with color, it is possible to build up a slight impasto. This most emphatically does not mean the impasto used in oil painting.

As the painting continues, try to resolve the image quickly and conclusively. Again, as in transparent watercolor, areas that are worked over excessively tend to lose vitality and luminosity. Furthermore, remember you are working on a damp ground that can be disturbed by too much brush activity. It is helpful to keep the color harmonies simple and broad at first—using complementary colors for shadow areas, for instance, rather than going immediately to darks and lights—reserving the detail touches and small corrections for the end of the painting. Final accents of straight color and whites or light colors can be applied only when the complete idea is realized.

When the painting coat begins to dry out, painting must stop for the day. Paint that seems to go on dry, as though it were being drawn rapidly from the brush (as paint sometimes goes on an unsized glue-gesso ground), is a sign that the plaster is drying out. The drying out can be delayed for a while by spraying the wall with a bit of distilled water, but paint must not be applied to the dried surface, for it will not stick.

Any areas that have not been painted must be cut out of the wall. Score the edge of the cut along a line in the design that is inconspicuous—a contour separating two distinct color areas, for instance—so that the painting can begin the next day without delays caused by having to attempt a color match; dividing a large, flat area of color will pose numerous problems. Use the plastic palette knife or putty knife to make the cut deep enough to penetrate the painting coat completely, and slightly undercut the line to provide a key for the next day's application of fresh plaster (Figure 16.16). Scrape away the excess painting coat with the putty knife. When replastering the next day, wet the edges of the cut with a liberal spray of distilled water, so the new plaster will adhere to the old. Put on the new mortar carefully, to avoid splashing the painting.

Corrections in the painting, if kept to small areas, can be made in paints like egg tempera or casein, or with a variation of the *fresco buono* technique called *secco* (discussed in more detail in next section).

METHOD: SECCO PAINT

1. Make a lime water by mixing 1 part of slaked lime putty with 4 parts distilled water. Allow the lime putty to settle and drain off the water. Allow the drained water to settle again.
2. Grind fresco pigments in the settled lime water. Make corrections to large areas of the wall by cutting out that section of the wall, replastering, and repainting; some writers recommend cutting out the sand coat along with the painting coat, and reapplying both. Corrections to large areas should be made within 24 hours of the original plastering.

As the wall continues to dry, the paint will become slightly lighter in tone. The wall will take a month, at least, to dry completely, depending on the relative humidity of the surroundings. When making small corrections in a different medium, it is advisable to wait until the wall is completely dry so that color matches can be more accurate.

The cycle of damp and dry conditions in the atmosphere may produce cracks in the wall, but should not cause deterioration of the painting. The greatest dangers to the life of a fresco are related to pollution and efflorescence.

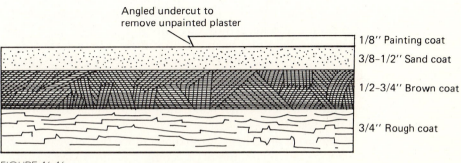

Angled undercut to remove unpainted plaster

1/8″ Painting coat
3/8-1/2″ Sand coat
1/2-3/4″ Brown coat
3/4″ Rough coat

FIGURE 16.16
Undercutting to Remove Unpainted Plaster

SECCO

Secco is the Italian word for "dry," and refers to the process of painting on a dry lime plaster wall. Technically, there is no such thing as *fresco secco,* since this phrase is a contradiction in terms, but the phrase is often used.

Secco can be executed in any number of different kinds of paints on a fresco wall, the principal difference between it and *fresco buono* being that the paint has its own binder and sits attached to the surface of the wall. In *fresco buono,* the wall is the binder and the pigments become a part of it, making for a more durable structure; *secco* techniques, subject to greater stresses than relatively smaller easel paintings, can suffer a proportionately greater number of defects.

A technique that perhaps gives rise to the notion of a *fresco secco* is the following: A regular fresco wall is built up to the sand coat layer. Instead of a painting coat finish, the wall is given three or four coats of a dilute lime putty paint—slaked lime putty diluted with distilled water to the viscosity of a latex house paint. Each coat is applied as soon as the preceding coat is set but not bone dry. The paints are made by grinding the pigments in lime water and applied to the wall using the fresco painting process. Although the effect is like fresco, the pigments lie on the surface of the wall and are quite likely to chip or flake off as the wall ages, or if moisture penetrates the wall.

Other paints can be used on a dry fresco wall: egg tempera, egg-oil emulsion tempera, casein, and size paints. All these paints should be thinned well with water and built up slowly—heavy applications of impasto will fail. Acrylic emulsion paints can be applied to a fresco wall, also thinned and slowly built up, and they can produce more opaque effects and greater impasto with less chance of failure.

Acrylic solution and alkyd paints can be used for secco painting, but the work will rapidly begin to lose the special optical quality of a mural paint: rather dry-looking, light and somewhat narrow value ranges, minimum surface irregularities, little surface reflection. If the paint is applied as it should be, in layers containing the correct proportion of binder to pigment, these paints will soon develop a reflective surface. Because the fresco surface is absorbent—but not necessarily evenly absorbent—the painting can end up with a disagreeably uneven appearance, which to be corrected must be varnished. And of course the problem is compounded by varnishing.

Oil paints have also been used for interior murals, but, again, the fresco wall is unevenly absorbent and can produce a spotty effect. The optical and technical characteristics of oil paint are not compatible with the desired effect of a mural paint. Furthermore, oil paints present complicated technical problems—yellowing, embrittlement—that make their use in such a scale on a plain wall formidable and ill-advised.

When artist and client agree that a more reflective and robust paint is suitable, *marouflage,* the technique of attaching a painted fabric support to a wall with an adhesive, can help reduce the drawbacks outlined above. The painter's task is simplified a bit—the artist can do the work in the studio, without the assistants needed for fresco work—but the installation can be complicated. If the wall is large, a good bond between the fabric and the wall may be hard to achieve. The use of white lead in oil, the traditional adhesive for marouflage, will guarantee a good bond but will also make the work difficult, if not impossible, to remove from the wall if conservation problems appear. The white lead adhesive will also deteriorate beneath the fabric, if the wall is subject to damp and dry cycles, producing cracks and tears in paint and fabric. An alternative to marouflage is to execute the paintings on standard supports, rigid or flexible, and then to attach them independently to the wall. Of course, the work is no longer a mural, but just a very large picture.

FRESCO PANELS

If the problems of working at the site cannot be surmounted or if there are logistical difficulties, fresco paintings can be done on small panels which are then attached to interior walls. Lumber stock 1½ by 2 inches (3.75 × 5 cm) is nailed together to form a framework for the structure, with the 1½ inch (3.75 cm) dimension forming its depth. The rear of each corner should be braced with angle irons, in order to keep the panels square. A wire screen lath is then nailed to the rear of the frame, and cross-bracing added to large frames; the cross-bracing is behind the lath. The fresco wall is then built within the frame and brought flush with the front of the wooden surrounds (Figure 16.17). The painting proceeds as in the classical technique.

Fresco panels are excellent practice for those who are unfamiliar with the technique. As finished products they are also good, although if the panels are large, they can be very heavy and thus may be difficult to install. Steel hangers should be attached to the upper perimeter of the panel. These are then hung on steel rails built into the wall. Such custom work can be expensive, but perhaps no more so than any other mural process.

EXTERIOR MURAL PAINTS

The problems of durability and resistance to mechanical damage are magnified when the mural is exposed to outside atmosphere. Even in relatively pollution-free environments, exterior mural paints are subjected to abnormal stresses; intense exposure to ultraviolet light and windborne particles are especially destructive. If glossy paints are used, adhesion of the ground and paint to the support is made difficult if there are any openings, however tiny, through which water vapor can penetrate.

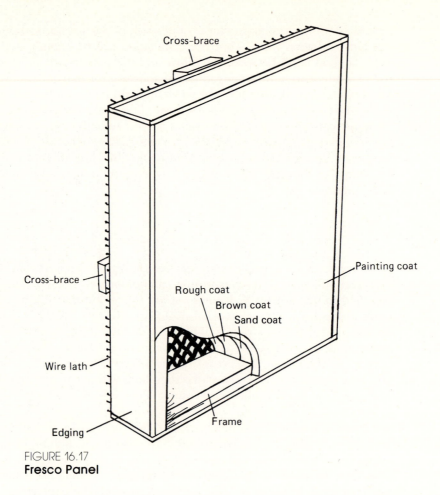

Cross-brace

Cross-brace

Painting coat

Rough coat

Brown coat

Sand coat

Wire lath

Edging

Frame

FIGURE 16.17
Fresco Panel

THE SITE

If possible, the site and its orientation should be given major consideration. A wall facing northeast will not only be out of the direct rays of the sun but will be sheltered from the prevailing winds. Overhangs or parapets will provide some protection from rain; particularly choice sites are cloisters or other galleries open to the outside but sheltered by a covered walkway. Since moisture is the biggest problem, apart from exposure to ultraviolet light, try to arrange the execution of the mural in late spring, when dry weather is more constant and predictable.

THE WALL

A plain brick wall may be used for an exterior mural, provided it is thoroughly gone over to remove any broken or crumbly bricks, bricks with surface efflores-cence, mold, old paint, other organic growths, and any crumbly mortar. A solution of 1 part household bleach to 3 parts water can be used to eliminate mold and mildew. The wall should be scoured with a wire brush and thoroughly washed with water, and all the mortar repointed and brick repaired.

The artist can paint directly on the brick if he or she does not mind the textural interference the brick and mortar will cause. The wall should be primed with at least two coats of a PVA emulsion adhesive—1 part adhesive to 5 parts water—to buffer against the alkaline constituents present in all masonry walls, to lessen the absorbency of the surface, to make it more evenly absorbent, and to isolate the wall from the painting as far as possible. It is not wise to attempt to seal the surface completely, since blistering of applied paints can easily occur; the PVA emulsion is porous, and at the recommended dilution it will allow water vapor to be absorbed and expelled from the brick.

A less textured surface can be applied to a brick wall, which gives it something of the character of a plaster wall. A cement mixture containing proportions of Portland cement (a hydraulic cement made of pulverized hydraulic calcium silicates), fine clean river sand, and slaked lime putty can be troweled on the wall in two layers, flattened and smoothed, primed, and painted. The mixture is called *stucco*. Two kinds of stucco can be made, one for hard brick or concrete walls and one for soft brick or concrete.

MATERIALS FOR MAKING HARD STUCCO

1. The same tools used for making and applying a fresco lime plaster (pp. 287, 291–292).
2. Clean water.
3. Very clean, washed river sand.
4. White Portland cement.

METHOD

1. Mix 1 part dry Portland cement with 3 parts dry sand. Mix enough for two coats; reserve half.
2. Add enough water to half the mixture, a little at a time, while thoroughly hoeing, until the stucco reaches a puttylike state. Reserve the second half, in its dry state, for the second coat.
3. Chisel a key onto the support if there is an insufficient texture to hold the stucco; most hard walls will need to be chiseled. Spray the wall with water until it is soaked, and wait until there is no standing water on its surface.
4. Apply the first coat with a trowel or wooden float, starting at the bottom and working up, to a thickness of about ¼ inch (6 mm). When it has set, but before it has dried, scratch it all over to give it a key.
5. Apply the second coat when the first coat is dry, using the wood float to get a smooth surface, to the same thickness as the first coat. A light spray of water can be given to the first coat before the second is applied; do not apply the second coat to standing water.

MATERIALS FOR MAKING SOFT STUCCO

1. The same materials and equipment as for the hard stucco.
2. Slaked lime putty.

METHOD

1. Mix 1 part dry white Portland cement, 1 part slaked lime putty, and 5 parts dry sand. Mix enough for two coats; reserve half.
2. Add enough water to half the mixture, a little at a time, while thoroughly hoeing, until the stucco reaches a puttylike state. Reserve the second half of the dry mixture for the second coat.
3. A key need not be chiseled onto the support, but it should be given an application of PVA adhesive—1 part adhesive to 5 parts water. One coat should be enough. Allow the primer to dry.
4. Apply the first and second coats of soft stucco as in the instructions for hard stucco.

Whether the stucco is hard or soft, avoid applying either when there is danger of frost. If there is any crumbled or powdery areas in the stucco when it has dried, they must be cut out and replaced.

PIGMENTS

Pigments chosen for outdoor application must have the highest lightfastness rating. They must also be resistant to alkaline supports, grounds, and vehicles, and to acidic atmospheres. The palette is slightly more limited than for indoor frescoes.

Reds:	Red iron oxides (Mars, burnt sienna)
	Thioindigoid red (PR88)
	Quinacridone red and scarlet
Oranges:	(Oranges can be mixed from reds and yellows.)
Yellows:	Titanium yellow
	Yellow iron oxides (Mars, raw sienna, yellow ochre)
Greens:	Phthalocyanine green (PG7)
	Green gold
	Chromium oxide green, opaque
	Light green oxide
Blues:	Phthalocyanine blue, alpha type (PB15/74160)
	Cerulean blue
	Cobalt blue
	Manganese blue
Purples:	Quinacridone violet
	Mars violet
	(Purples are easily mixed.)

  Browns: Brown iron oxides
  Blacks: Mars black
  Whites: Titanium white, rutile (nonchalking) type

SYNTHETIC EMULSION PAINTS

Acrylic emulsion paints can be used for exterior mural decoration. Industrial varieties will not have the durability equal to those made by artists' paint manufacturers. Claims of "high performance exterior paints" mean that they may last as long as seven to ten years, hardly high performance where artists' expectations are concerned. There is no reason to adopt a fatalistic attitude about this situation, however. Spend the money and use the best artists' paint for exterior murals; do not mix brands.

The paint can be applied over a PVA emulsion priming, without the application of a ground, but it is better to have a white reflective surface if the colors are to be fully developed. An acrylic polymer emulsion gesso ground, or a thin layer of acrylic emulsion titanium white paint, can be applied to the PVA emulsion priming. A stucco surface made with white Portland cement may be white enough so that a ground is not needed. To protect the paints from ground moisture, which will rise by capillary action, start the painting at least 2 feet (60 cm) above ground level.

Preliminary sketches, color studies, and cartoons should be developed as in fresco painting. The wall can be squared up with chalk snap lines, and the cartoon can be pounced onto the surface. Use hair and bristle brushes to paint; if the wall is large, choose large brushes. The paint can be applied straight but will penetrate the wall better if it is thinned with up to 4 parts of clean water for the first coat. In order to maintain coherence in the design, it will be necessary to work the image as broadly as possible at first, reserving the details for later application. A slight impasto can be built up, but remember that projections from the plane of the wall will collect a surprising amount of dirt.

The porous synthetic emulsion paints should not be varnished in exterior applications: A sealed surface can develop blisters that will eventually crack open, and the varnish will be degraded quickly by ultraviolet light—it can bloom or craze over its surface and obliterate the image. A glaze of acrylic emulsion matte medium, thinned 2 to 1 with water, can be applied over the work and will provide some protection for a limited time. The mediums have been known to bloom on excessive exposure to moist atmospheres, however, and they probably should not be used. Any bloom that occurs in the paint films themselves may be overpowered by the colorants present. But again, so much depends on the exposure conditions that predictions for durability are not reliable.

EXPERIMENTAL EXTERIOR PAINTS (SILICATE PAINTS)

The silicate paints, first developed in the nineteenth century in Germany and perfected by the chemist Adolf Wilhelm Keim, are based on solubilized sodium, potassium, or lithium silicate. The potassium silicate paints that Keim developed (from earlier work with sodium silicates by von Fuchs) were further improved in the 1930s. These paints were ultimately developed as industrial coatings, primarily "zinc-rich" paints for protecting equipment and structures outdoors. They are used mainly on nonabsorbent substrates, as distinct from the normally absorbent bases for mural paints.

A great deal of speculation about the durability of the silicate paints has been generated in literature on artists' materials; Mayer and Wehlte offer more or less cautious endorsements of the medium. Conservators and paint chemists who deal with artists' paints are a bit more cautious in their opinions, and some have condemned the technique as not as durable as once thought. The paints have been in use only for about 40 years in varying conditions of exposure, and they were certainly not developed specifically for artist use, so it is reasonable that any recommendations are provisional.

The chemical process by which silicon ester binders work is essentially catalytic—that is, the binder, containing ethyl silicates and ethyl alcohol, remains stable and inert until a catalyst, a mixture of water and hydrochloric acid, is added. When the catalyst is added, a reaction occurs which causes the alcohol to evaporate and the silica to form a colloidal gel. The reaction is not reversible and cannot be inhibited once the catalyst is added. When the binder is exposed in thin films outdoors, atmospheric moisture and continuing reactions within the colloidal silica contribute to the gel's further reduction to pure silica. Pure silica is the dioxide form of silicon, a nonmetallic element occurring in nature in both amorphous and crystalline forms, especially in quartz and agate rocks. In other words, the binder is reduced once again to its natural form, and in doing so will lock within its crystalline matrix pigments which are dispersed in it.

Although the silica forms a layer, its film is very porous—even more porous than those made by the emulsion paints. The paints on a porous wall look like those applied in a fresco technique, which is to say that the vehicle is nearly undetectable and what one sees is the wall and the color. The films, therefore, are subject to mechanical wear and tear, and can be scraped off by abrasion or worn off by abrasive particles such as might be blown against the surface by wind.

Survival of the paints depends on the nonreactive characteristics of the inert silica and the resistance of the pigments. The problem with the fresco technique as applied outdoors is that the substrate (the lime plaster wall) can react with modern acidic atmospheres and deteriorate; if the silicate binders are as inert as claimed, they ought not to react even under such extreme conditions of atmospheric pollution as are often found in urban areas. Unfortunately, it is too early to tell about the survival rate of paintings in the silicate binder. Only the actual passage of time will indicate the durability of murals painted with the silicates.

Nevertheless, those who wish to try the technique can use one of the methods recommended by Union Carbide's Coatings Materials Division (Old Ridgebury Road, Danbury, CT 06817) in publication F-41629C, "Ethyl Silicates." This paint is used in industrial applications and may not be suitable for artistic use.

Remember that the manufacturer cannot accept responsibility for the use or potential misuse of its products, and assumes no legal liability for such use. All the silicate paints and their derivatives discussed in this chapter should be considered experimental materials until such time as controlled, scientific testing is conducted to determine their durability and performance characteristics as artists' materials.

PIGMENTS

The pigments used for silicate painting are all those recommended for fresco, as they must be resistant to the alkali ground, white Portland cement.

PREPARATION OF THE VEHICLE

There are three methods for preparing the vehicle; they use the same materials.

Caution: The materials can be dangerous.

MATERIALS

1. Ethyl silicate 40. *Caution:* Ethyl silicate 40 is flammable (flash point is 90° F, 32° C) and harmful. Do not breathe the vapors; use with cross-ventilation and wear a vapor mask.
2. Ethyl alcohol in 80 percent solution. *Caution:* Ethyl alcohol is flammable. Do not breathe the vapors. To make an 80 percent solution of ethyol alcohol, reduce 80 parts of 100 percent ethanol with 20 parts of distilled water. "Ever Clear" grain alcohol is 90 percent ethanol, and available in some liquor stores.
3. Hydrochloric acid in 0.3 percent solution. *Caution:* Hydrochloric acid is dangerous. Wear splash goggles, acidproof gloves, and either an air-supplied respirator or an organic vapor mask; it is recommended that a fume hood or direct local exhaust be used when handling HCl. To make 0.3 percent solution, reduce 1 part of chemically pure HCl with 120 parts distilled water in a glass container: *Add the acid to the water.* Store the solution in an amber-colored glass bottle; HCl deteriorates in light.
4. Distilled water.
5. A wide-mouthed glass jar with a plastic cover.

METHOD A

1. Mix 80 parts of the ethyl silicate with 18 parts ethyl alcohol and 2 parts 0.3 percent HCl, in that order, in the glass jar. Allow to stand, covered, for 8 to 12 hours.
2. Add 5 parts distilled water.

This solution should be used within 8 hours of mixing, although Mayer reports that 2 hours is enough of a wait and may be better. It has a higher silica content than the solution described in method B. After the binder is made and the pigments combined with it, it will slowly begin to thicken as the reaction begins.

This thickening cannot be stopped, nor can it be delayed by thinning the binder; if the paints made with the silicate vehicle thicken to a point where they cannot be brushed out in thin layers, they must be discarded.

METHOD B

1. Mix 15 parts ethyl silicate, 8 parts 80 percent ethyl alcohol, and 2 parts 0.03 percent HCl (dilute 1 part of the 0.3 percent solution of HCl with 10 parts distilled water), in that order, in the glass jar.
2. Allow to stand, covered, for 8 to 12 hours.

This solution may be used after the first rest period, without further additions of distilled water. It has less silica content than the solution made by method A.

METHOD C

An experimental variety of ethyl silicate made by Union Carbide, called UCAR Silicate ESP-X, is available for evaluation. It is called a "one-package system" because no additions need be made to the solution to activate the hydrolysis. Once the pigments are added and the vehicle exposed to air, however, the solution will begin to gel. Once complete gelation has occurred and the paints can no longer be brushed out into thin layers, the solution should be discarded.

HOMEMADE SILICATE PAINTS

Making the paints is the most difficult aspect of the process. The pigments must be combined with the vehicle directly before painting, but the binder is highly volatile, making grinding on a slab an unsatisfactory method of dispersion. Again, three methods are suggested.

METHOD A

Use a deep, narrow mortar—a deep and narrow mortar will inhibit rapid evaporation—and a pestle to disperse the pigment.

METHOD B

1. Place the vehicle in a can.
2. Sprinkle in the pigment while stirring vigorously with a stick or wooden spoon. The consistency of the paint should be that of a smooth syrup.
3. Cover the can and discard the stick.

METHOD C

1. Use a jeweler's tumbler, or gem polisher, to approximate the method by which lacquer and enamel paints and inks are made. The tumbler is a small container laid horizontally on two rollers; the rollers are attached to a motor by a belt, which turns the rollers and so the container. The device is also called a ball or pebble mill because the machine used to make inks and

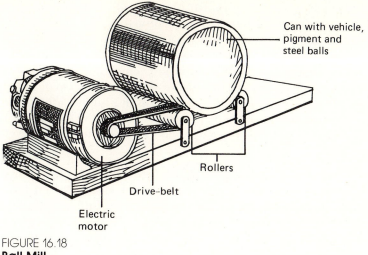

FIGURE 16.18
Ball Mill

Converted from a jeweler's tumbler, used for dispersing pigments.

lacquers holds small steel balls, natural stone pebbles or ceramic pebbles that tumble about, dispersing the pigment in the vehicle (Figure 16.18).

2. Jeweler's tumblers usually have rubber or plastic containers. Replace them with a can with a tight-fitting cover, or a heavy glass jar with a tight-fitting screw-on cap.

3. Using ⅜ to ½ inch (3–6 mm) diameter stainless steel ball bearings, fill the container half-full of the ball bearings. Add the pigment and vehicle, and tumble for about 5 minutes.

4. Strain the paint through a funnel lined with cheesecloth into a glass jar. Tightly cap the jar.

5. Clean both the tumbler and the ball bearings immediately with alcohol.

For all methods, use approximately these proportions of vehicle to pigment, by volume: 80 parts vehicle, 3 to 5 parts pigment. (Remember that pigments can vary tremendously in volume-to-weight ratios; by weight, the proportions are 10 parts vehicle, 3 to 5 parts pigment.) A small proportion of the pigment volume can be replaced by "micronized" mica (hydrous potassium aluminum silicate) to improve the stability of the mixture. The mica flakes will hold the pigments in suspension in the vehicle.

OTHER TYPES OF SILICATE PAINT

This variety of silicate vehicle described so far—ethyl silicate—is the one most often discussed in relation to fine arts painting. Some others deserve investigation for their potential application. Samples are available from E. I. Du Pont de Nemours and Company, Inc. (see Appendix D).

Polysilicate 48 Solution, Technical   This is a lithium silicate which is dispersed in an aqueous and therefore nonflammable vehicle. Du Pont recommends it as an excellent binder in inorganic coatings on concrete, glass, and aluminum; it can be loaded with more pigment than the ethyl silicates; it is not sensitive to moisture; and as an additive to PVA emulsion vehicles, it will improve hardness. It is toxic by ingestion and irritating to the skin and eyes. Avoid skin and eye contact by wearing gloves and goggles, and wash thoroughly after handling.

Preparation of the vehicle is simple. Open the container. Disperse pigments in the same manner as recommended for the ethyl silicates; paint before gellation occurs.

Potassium Silicate, Electronics Grade #200   This is a hydroscopic mixture of potassium carbonate and pure silica sand, supercooled to form potassium silicate glass. The potassium silicate glass is then dissolved in hot water to form a clear solution. As the water content of the solution evaporates on application—the reaction can be speeded up by heating the solution or films of the solution—the usual gellation and eventual film forming occurs. Du Pont recommends it as an excellent binder in mortars and as a binder for roofing granules, but makes no recommendations specifically regarding paint coatings. The material, however, seems to meet all the requirements for paint application if used like the ethyl or lithium silicates: in thin films on porous cement walls. *Caution:* The solutions are alkaline, and may irritate the skin; the dried flakes of the potassium silicate glass are capable of causing eye injury. Avoid skin and eye contact by wearing goggles and gloves, and wash thoroughly after handling.

Preparation of the vehicle, dispersion of pigments, and use are the same as recommended for the ethyl silicates.

Ludox Colloidal Silica, HS-40%   This is a water-based colloidal dispersion of silica particles that has many industrial applications: high-temperature binder for refractory cements, paper and film coatings, antisoil coatings, adhesion promoter, wetting promoter, reinforcing agent for latex emulsion coatings and adhesives, and a binder for pigments and decorative coatings on bricks. Other proprietary forms of colloidal silica are used extensively in artist's paint manufacturing as reinforcing agents and wetting promoters, primarily in the acrylic emulsion paints. Ludox is unlike the other silicates mentioned in that it does not have a crystalline structure: The silica particles are spheres, dispersed in an alkaline medium (not as alkaline as the other silicates), and the film-forming capability is achieved by the fact that the particles repel each other in the alkaline medium—they are given a negative electric charge by the medium. Gellation occurs, as in the other silicates, when the water evaporates from the vehicle; gellation of Ludox can also occur if the pH is altered, or if a water-miscible organic solvent is added.

Caution: Ludox HS-40% is alkaline and can cause some skin irritation. Avoid skin and eye contact by wearing goggles and gloves, and wash thoroughly after handling.

Warning: The dried silica particles can cause pneumoconiosis, a lung disease. Do not spray the liquid; the use of a fine-particle respirator is recommended.

Preparation of the vehicle, dispersion of pigments, and use are the same as recommended for the ethyl silicates.

SILICATE PAINTING TECHNIQUES

Tools and Brushes   Long bristle and hair brushes can be used. The binder is hard on brushes, so use medium-quality rather than expensive ones. The various containers used to hold the made-up paint should be disposable—cans or glass jars are best—since once the pain is exposed to the air, it begins its irreversible drying process. Any leftover paint should be discarded at the end of the day's work, certainly within 8 hours.

Two separate containers holding amounts of vehicle should be on the site: One is used to store brushes when they are not in use—do not allow the paint to dry on the brushes. The other can be used to thin the paint. Do not thin the paint too much, and do not attempt to thin a paint that has begun to gel.

At the end of the working day, clean all tools with alcohol before washing them out with soapy water.

Supports and Grounds   Stucco surfaces, bonded to brick or concrete, are the best for the silicon ester paints. Prepare them as for painting in acrylic emulsion paints, applying a hard stucco to hard brick or concrete and a soft stucco to crumbly brick or concrete. The substrate should be cleaned prior to the application of the stucco.

Application of Paint   The vehicle and a supply of fresh paint should be made each day. The vehicle can be put together the night before if the ES40 is being used; combine pigments and vehicle the day the paints are to be used.

Two methods are suggested. (1) The paint may be applied in thin glazes, as in the fresco or watercolor processes; or (2) the paint may be applied more opaquely, with glazes over the opaque films.

The frescolike applications using paint that has been thinned with the plain uncolored vehicle seem to work well, provided the paint is ground well enough so that flocculation or streaking does not occur If the grinding method used does not give a good, smooth paint, it is better to use the more substantial application.

To apply the paint more opaquely, do not thin it with the clear vehicle. Glazing, if desired, should be done so that thinner paint overlies thicker paint, in order to ensure adhesion. "Thicker paint," incidentally, means as thick as opaque watercolor, not as thick as oil paint.

In both methods, it is necessary to wait a few minutes for lower layers of paint to set before applying glazes or overpainting. Thin films will dry in about one hour; complete curing of the paints, and the binder's conversion to pure silica dioxide, will take several weeks, depending on the moisture content of the atmosphere.

The vapors produced by the ES vehicles should be considered harmful, and the vehicles themselves are flammable. If they are applied outdoors, there should be enough air movement to prevent the inhalation of too great a concentration of vapors. Indoors, it is recommended that air-supplied respirators be worn. Keep all containers and tools away from flame or sparks.

SILICATE PANELS

Smaller panels for practice or the production of portable silicate paintings can be made the same way such panels are made for fresco. Use a hard stucco built up on a wire screen lath that has been attached to a supporting wooden frame (Figure 16.17).

OTHER EXTERIOR MURAL TECHNIQUES

Although these are not painting methods, the following mural techniques are particularly appropriate for exterior use. In outdoor applications, it seems, any paint is destined to fail sooner or later, and these techniques offer a reasonable alternative where more durable media are sought.

SGRAFFITO

This method is more adaptable to flat, two-dimensional designs than it is to free-flowing, naturalistic, or spatial compositions. It basically consists of a two-, three-, or even four-layer wall built of different colored mortars, through which is scratched a design that reveals the different layers; it is like the ancient Chinese technique of colored lacquer carving. The design can be bold and graphic, utilizing planes of color, or essentially linear. The name of the process comes from the Italian *sgraffiare,* meaning "to scratch." The technique itself dates at least from the thirteenth century.

The wall is built of stucco plaster, made with white Portland cement, clean sand, and slaked lime putty (if needed). A rough coat is first applied to the keyed wall, to a thickness of about ½ to ¾ inch (1.25–1.85 cm). Before it is set, a thin film of color is applied to it using the fresco technique. When this layer has dried, a second coat of stucco is applied to a thickness of about 2 inches (5 cm). This layer may also be colored. When the second layer is set, but before it dries, it is incised to reveal the lower layer; any tool that can incise or cut away the top layer of the wall is used. Only pigments usable in fresco—that is, alkaline-proof pigments—can be used. As in fresco, only sections of the wall that can be completed in a day can be worked at one time.

To use more than two colors, more layers of this cement must be applied and individually colored, but the total thickness of the wall should not exceed 2½ inches (6.25 cm). Since the process then becomes more complex, smaller sections must be worked individually so there is time to complete each one before the cement dries.

Sgraffito can be combined with other graphic techniques using paint, although there is the problem of durability if the mural is outdoors.

MOSAIC

Mosaic uses small units of variously colored materials, set in a mortar, which together form a design. The technique dates at least from about 1750 B.C. in Babylon, although it reached its height during the Byzantine Empire, A.D. 476–1453. Simple designs, subordinate to the surrounding architectural elements, can be executed in mosaic, but some remarkably naturalistic works have also been done, particularly by the Byzantines. Mosaic is used on floors, walls, ceilings, and even in small framed supports. Interesting modern examples of mosaic can be seen in some New York City subway stations, where they have survived nearly 50 years of exposure to filthy environments.

The mosaic units are called *tesserae,* from the Latin word for both the technique and the units, *tessellatus.* They can be pieces of colored stone, marble, glazed or plain ceramic tile, or glass. Other materials can be used indoors, but only these will be impervious to outdoor conditions. Colored glass is of particular interest, since when it is fractured the broken side (as opposed to the smooth front and back) present a sparkling, very reflective surface. The tesserae are most often cut into regular pieces about ¼ to ⅜ inch (6–9 mm) on a side and perhaps as thick. Stones, naturally, will vary in size, and there is no rule today which says that the units must all be of the same size or even of the same shape.

There are two ways of setting the tesserae: placing them directly into damp mortar on the wall, or presetting them before applying them to the wall. As in all mural techniques, a complete plan of action should be worked out in advance. Simple mosaics, or those in which the artist wishes to improvise without a plan, can be carried out directly; those who wish to design a more complex picture will prefer presetting the tesserae.

Presetting is carried out in the following way. Shallow trays are constructed of plywood with wooden surrounds (Figure 16.19) and filled to a depth of about $1/16$ inch (3 mm) with fine sand. The tesserae are laid in the sand face up, with a distance of about $1/8$ inch (6 mm), more or less, between each unit. The sand keeps the tesserae from moving around. Once the tray is full and the design approved, a piece of muslin soaked in a water-soluble glue (or heavy paper brushed with the glue) is pressed and smoothed over the design, with care taken to be sure each tesserae is in contact with the cloth. The whole is allowed to dry, and then lifted and set into place in the damp mortar. A stucco or fresco wall can be used, and it can be white, gray, or some color that fits with the design. The entire design can be laid out in advance this way, using a large warehouse floor, for example, then cut into sections, carried to the site, and applied to the wall, much like the installation of bathroom tile.

Before the wall has set, the tesserae must be pushed into the mortar using a flat wooden block and a hammer; they are not set too evenly, as some surface varia-

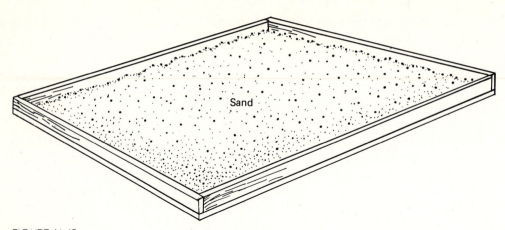

FIGURE 16.19
Layout Tray for Mosaic Tesserae

Filled with a thin layer of fine sand.

tion is desirable, but deeply enough to become securely held by the mortar. When the wall has set and dried, the muslin is gone over with a damp sponge to loosen the adhesive and the cloth is stripped from the wall. The work is inspected for defects; loose tesserae can be knocked out and reset.

Another method of presetting, used less often, has the artist glue the tesserae face down on a paper or cloth support. This then is carried to the site and installed as described above. The difficulty with this method is that one must work in reverse, although artists who do much printmaking will be used to working with reversed images.

PORCELAIN ENAMEL

Porcelain enamel uses colored *frits* fused by high heat to a metal substrate, forming a glossy, glasslike impervious surface. Frits resemble powdered glass, but also contain in addition to the colorant a flux (to lower the melting point of the frit) and a refractory (a material that balances the flux and stabilizes the mixture). They are made by melting the ingredients together, cooling them, and milling them into a powder. Frits are sold through enameling materials suppliers. The color of the dry frits is not always an indication of the final color after the frits are fired. Cloisonné is an example of a delicate form of porcelain enamel in which the colored shapes are separated by thin brass or copper wires. Some old street signs and modern stove surfaces are made of pocelain-enameled metal.

Anyone with a ceramics kiln that is capable of reaching a temperature of at least 2000° F (1082° C) can produce these products, although it is sometimes more convenient to send the material to a professional enameler for fusing. Suppliers sell iron or steel sheets of various sizes onto both sides of which has been fused a base coat of cobalt oxide—in black or gray—and a second coat of opaque

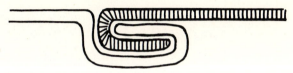

FIGURE 16.20
Interlocking Flanges for Metal Panels

white of tin oxide or titanium dioxide. The artist then applies the frit, thinning the colored paste with water as desired, or mixing the powdered colored frit into a paste with water and then thinning it. The paste is allowed to dry to an even, powdery layer and then fired to fuse the color to the base. Since each color should be fired to a specific temperature in the neighborhood of 1450–1550° F (about 815° C), it is usually necessary to refire after each application of a different frit. This complication can be frustrating if one must wait for the work to be returned from the enameler's, or if the workers in the factory do not have a clear understanding of the artistic purposes of the work.

The major difficulty with the standard application procedure is that the powdery layer of frit, once dry, cannot be overpainted to make corrections without disturbing or muddying the underpainted layer. It is also difficult to build up layers of colors in the free-flowing, brushy technique that today's artists might prefer. If the frits are ground in a watercolor vehicle composed of gum Acacia, water, and glycerine, this difficulty is lessened. As an added benefit, the colors will appear more like they will after firing. The binder will be destroyed in the firing long before the frits are fused into enamel layers.

Aluminum, copper, steel, or iron sheets, prepared with the base coat of cobalt and a white ground and of various sizes, can be had from suppliers. If they are custom-designed with interlocking flanges (Figure 16.20), it is possible to put together large works from several smaller components panels. Because very large panels may warp during firing, it is better to work with several smaller panels, even though it is impossible to avoid the visual disruption caused by the divisions between them. The panels can be hung on an exterior wall using special clips—a standard construction procedure today. Consult an architectural engineer about the various methods employed.

If colorants that are permanent in strong light exposures are used, the enameled panels will be as durable as mosaic tiles. Their only susceptibility is to scratches, chips, and cracks that could develop as the result of mechanical stresses to the metal substrates caused by temperature changes. Cracks or chips can allow moisture to come into contact with the metal interior, leading to rusting or oxidation, which in turn can cause the enamel to blister or powder. Enameled metal panels installed in exterior situations should be inspected frequently for these defects, especially at the edges. They must be repaired immediately by painting or removal and refiring.

PART THREE

PICTURE PROTECTION AND RESTORATION

Part Three examines various means of protecting finished works of art: varnishing and other surface protection, matting and framing, and storage. There is also a section on the documentation of works of art, and a brief discussion of the general problems encountered by conservators and restorers in preserving objects.

CHAPTER 17

PICTURE PROTECTION

All pictures, well-crafted or not, will inevitably suffer deterioration as a result of exposure to atmospheric conditions, ultraviolet light, or the vicissitudes of age-ing. Mishandling, improper storage, or other forms of negligence can also con-tribute to the untimely demise of a work of art. It is possible to slow the deterio-ration of the work by careful framing and matting, proper surface protection, and good storage and display conditions.

VARNISHING

A final varnish is a protective surface coating. It should be clear, nonyellowing, and elastic enough to absorb the movements of the support and paint layers without cracking. The varnish coating should be reversible: Even the cleanest of storage or display conditions will not prevent the eventual accumulation of dirt on the picture's surface; some loss of transparency, yellowing, and embrittlement are also inevitable over the course of many years. The coating should be remov-able with mild solvents that will not harm the paint layers beneath it. Finally, the varnish should have an appropriate degree of surface reflectivity for the work; too glossy a varnish will make the work hard to see, and too matte a surface will not provide good protection for the work.

Some types of paintings do not require, or traditionally receive, a varnish coating. These include the water-thinned paints (opaque and transparent water-color, size), casein, the egg and egg-oil emulsion temperas, encaustics, and pastels. Usually the water paints are matted and framed behind glass. The tempera paints can be varnished, but this often changes the refractive index of the paint and alters the appearance of the picture; simple polishing of the temperas is recom-mended. Encaustic paintings are usually polished to a semi-gloss finish with a soft cloth and do not require varnishing, but they can be given a coat of paste wax soap. Pastels are never varnished; they are given a light spray of a weak fixative merely to hold the pigment particles in place. Murals, indoors or out, are not usually varnished either.

Paintings in oil, acrylic emulsion, acrylic solution, and alkyd vehicles should be varnished. The acrylic emulsion, acrylic solution, and alkyd paints can be varnished as soon as they are completely dry, usually within a few days or at most a week. Oil paintings must be allowed to dry thoroughly before they are varnished. A painting of "average" thickness will dry in about six months, and thicker paintings will take a year or longer, all depending on the conditions in which the paintings are stored. Because oil paintings dry from the top layer down toward the support, a dry surface does not mean that the painting is completely dry. If the artist suspects that an oil painting is not dry enough to support a final varnish coating without causing it to crack, an application of a light retouch varnish will provide temporary protection.

A simple solution varnish such as damar or mastic in gum turpentine is the usual finish for oil paintings, although it has been established that damar grows brittle and yellows as it ages far more rapidly than the newer acrylic solution or ketone resin varnishes. Liquitex's Soluvar, a solution of n-butyl methacrylate and iso-butyl methacrylate resins in mineral spirits, and Winsor & Newton's Artist's Picture Varnish or Griffin Picture Varnish, a ketone resin solution in mineral spirits, represent newer synthetic alternatives to the traditional varnish coatings. Most commercial preparations are supplied in liquid and spray can form, and can be had in, or adjusted to, gloss or semi-gloss finishes. For a summary of surface coatings for various types of pictures, see Table 17.1.

MATERIALS AND METHODS

Varnishing should be done in a warm room on a dry day. Atmospheric humidity can contribute to the formation of bloom behind the varnish film. *Bloom* is a whitish or cloudy haze that obscures the image and is generally believed to be caused by moisture trapped beneath the varnish; warm, dry conditions will help prevent bloom.

The room in which the varnishing is to be done should be swept or vacuumed to lessen the possibility that airborne dust will settle on the freshly varnished surface. Sweep or vacuum the night before varnishing day, to allow dust left—there is always some dust left hanging in the air—to settle. All tools used in varnishing should also be very clean, and free of water moisture.

MATERIALS

1. A 2½- to 3-inch (6–8 cm) wide bristle brush. Special varnishing brushes which have fairly long bristles of mixed varieties and which taper to a very thin edge are available. They have short, comfortable handles. Ordinary artists' bristle brushes can be used to varnish small works, but they will not hold a substantial amount of varnish.

TABLE 17.1
VARNISHES AND COATINGS FOR PICTURES

COMMON NAME	Damar	Mastic	Sandarac	Shellac
TYPE	Natural resin	Natural resin	Natural resin	Natural resin
APPLICATION			Not recommended	
Oils	✕	✕		
Acrylic Solutions				
Acrylic Emulsions				
Alkyds	✕			
Water-thinned				
Temperas	✕			
Encaustics	✕			
Pastel (fixative)				Fixative only
Murals (surface coatings not recommended)				
METHOD OF APPLICATION				
Brush	✕	✕		
Hand-rub				
Spray	✕	✕		✕, fixative only
CAUTIONS				
Ventilation	✕	✕		✕
Goggles	✕	✕		✕
Respirator	✕, poor ventilation	✕, poor ventilation		✕, poor ventilation
Gloves				
Coveralls	✕	✕		
REVERSIBILITY	G; over time becomes F	G; over time becomes F		G
SOLVENT	Gum turpentine and stronger	Alcohol and stronger		Alcohol
DURABILITY				
Interior	EX	G		G
Exterior	P	P		P
Rigid Support	EX	EX		EX
Flexible Support	G	F–P		P
RESISTANCE TO				
Water	G	F		P
Acid	F	F		F
Alkali	F	F		F
Pollutants	G	F		F
Ultraviolet Light	P	P		P
Mechanical Damage	P	P		P
Oxidation	P	P		P
POSSIBLE DEFECTS	Bloom, cracking, mechanical damage	Bloom, cracking, mechanical damage		Severe yellowing, bloom, darkening
ESTIMATED LIFE	20 years, in ideal conditions	Less than 20 years in ideal conditions		Short life
OTHER COMMENTS	Not considered a reliable surface coating	Less reliable than damar	Not recommended	Use as a fixative only when better synthetics not available

Note: EX = excellent; G = good; F = fair; P = poor; NT = not tested.

TABLE 17.1 *(continued)*
VARNISHES AND COATINGS FOR PICTURES

COMMON NAME	Bleached white beeswax	Acrylic solution	Vinyl solution
TYPE	Natural wax	Synthetic resin	Synthetic resin
APPLICATION			Not recommended
Oils	×, after varnish	×	
Acrylic Solutions	×, after varnish	×	
Acrylic Emulsions		×	
Alkyds	×, after varnish	×	
Water-thinned	×	×, thinly	
Temperas	×	×, thinly	
Encaustics	×	×, very thinly	
Pastel (fixative)		×, weak dilution	
Murals (surface coatings not recommended)	×, surface protection for murals		
METHOD OF APPLICATION			
Brush	×, if paste	×	
Hand-rub	×, preferred		
Spray	×, dilute paste	×	
CAUTIONS			
Ventilation	Only if sprayed	×	
Goggles	Only if sprayed	×	
Respirator	Only if sprayed	×, if sprayed	
Gloves			
Coveralls	Only if sprayed	×, if sprayed	
REVERSIBILITY	G	G	
SOLVENT	Mineral spirits	Mineral spirits	
DURABILITY			
Interior	EX	EX	
Exterior	G	F	
Rigid Support	EX	EX	
Flexible Support	G	G–EX	
RESISTANCE TO			
Water	EX	G–EX	
Acid	F	G	
Alkali	G	G	
Pollutants	EX	G	
Ultraviolet Light	EX	F–G	
Mechanical Damage	F	G	
Oxidation	EX	G–EX	
POSSIBLE DEFECTS	Melts or sags (heat) brittle (cold), easily scratched	May craze	
ESTIMATED LIFE	More than 20 years in ideal conditions	More than 20 years in ideal conditions	
OTHER COMMENTS	Excellent surface coating over a varnish	Reliable surface coating if correct resin used; most commercial products reliable	Vinyl solution solvents hazardous

TABLE 17.1 *(continued)*
VARNISHES AND COATINGS FOR PICTURES

COMMON NAME	Ketone resin	Silicone	Petroleum microcrystalline
TYPE	Synthetic resin	Synthetic resin	Synthetic wax
APPLICATION			
Oils	×	×	×
Acrylic Solutions	×	×	×
Acrylic Emulsions	×	×	×
Alkyds	×	×	×
Water-thinned			×
Temperas	×		×
Encaustics			×
Pastel (fixative)			
Murals (surface coatings not recommended)			×
METHOD OF APPLICATION			
Brush	×		×, diluted
Hand-rub	×		×, preferred
Spray	×	×, only	×, very diluted
CAUTIONS			
Ventilation	×, if sprayed	×	×, if sprayed
Goggles	×, if sprayed	×	×, if sprayed
Respirator	×, poor ventilation	×	×, poor ventilation
Gloves		×	
Coveralls	×, if sprayed	×	×, if sprayed
REVERSIBILITY	Surface G; over time becomes F	NT	G
SOLVENT	Mineral spirits	Trichlorotrifluoroethane Caution	Mineral spirits
DURABILITY			
Interior	EX	NT	EX
Exterior	F	NT	G
Rigid Support	EX	NT	EX
Flexible Support	EX	NT	G
RESISTANCE TO			
Water	G	NT	EX
Acid	F	NT	F
Alkali	F	NT	F
Pollutants	G	NT	G
Ultraviolet Light	EX	NT	G
Mechanical Damage	G	NT	F–G
Oxidation	G–EX	NT	EX
POSSIBLE DEFECTS	Slight craze if mechanically damaged	Untested	Very soft films; easily damaged
ESTIMATED LIFE	More than 20 years	Unknown	More than 20 years in ideal conditions
OTHER COMMENTS	Tested by manufacturer; seems reliable	Expensive; tested only by producer; developed for conservators	Adhesive wax for conservation; possible use as surface coating over varnishes with hardener

2. A cup or a can to hold the working varnish.
3. Clean white cotton rags.
4. A kneaded eraser and a soft-hair dusting brush.
5. The varnish thinner.
6. The varnish, in the correct dilution with its thinner.

Ordinarily, the heavy, syrupy condition of the varnish as it is sold or home-made is too thick to be manipulated easily into a thin, even film. A dilution of 3 or 4 parts thinner to 1 part varnish will usually produce a solution that is more workable. You may have to experiment with various proportions in order to find the correct dilution. Consider applying 2 or 3 thin coats of varnish rather than one thick coat. This is a rule of thumb every housepainter understands.

METHOD

1. Lay the painting flat, face up, on a table. Position it so that light can be seen reflected from its surface. This positioning will enable you to determine if the picture has received an even coating of varnish.
2. If the picture is thoroughly dry, dust it gently with the soft-hair brush. The kneaded eraser can be used to pick up particles of dirt not removed by dusting.
3. Further surface dirt can be removed by gently wiping the painting with a clean white rag slightly dampened with mineral spirits. Be particularly careful with oil paintings less than one year old or those with delicate glazed passages, and also be on the lookout when cleaning acrylic solution paintings. Check the rag frequently for traces of color. Color on the rag can show a number of conditions: the painting is not thoroughly dry; the paints have been thinned too much, without additions of a painting or glaze medium, so that they are underbound; or the manufacturer of the paint had a formulation problem with a particular pigment that is known to flocculate.
4. Pour some varnish solution into the cup or can. This is the working varnish and should be kept separate from the stock supply. Close the stock bottle and put it away to avoid confusing solutions.
5. Load the varnish brush, then discharge it against the inside of the container so that it holds a minimum amount of varnish. A dripping brush is too full.
6. Begin application at one corner of the painting. Cover a small patch at a time, say two or three brush widths. Brush on each patch first in one direction, then in a direction perpendicular to the first. Feather the edges of each patch so you can blend into the next area. Work quickly, but avoid a sloppy application, so that the surface receives as thin and even coating as possible.
7. Working quickly and deliberately, since the varnish will set rather quickly, proceed in a systematic way across the surface of the painting. Check the work against the light from time to time to be sure that all parts of the

surface are receiving an equally thin coating. Brushstrokes should not be evident because most varnishes level out quite readily; if they are, a featherlight pass with the tip of the brush will remove them.

8. After the entire painting has been varnished, allow it to sit for about 10 minutes before removing it from the table. If it is lifted to a vertical position too soon, the varnish may sag or run. After 10 minutes, the painting can be removed from the table and leaned against a wall, face in, to finish drying. Dust in the air cannot settle on the surface of a painting leaning face-in against a wall, but be careful not to stir up any dust on the floor in the vicinity of the painting.

9. Discard any working varnish left in the cup or can. Working varnish should be considered contaminated and should not be returned to the stock bottle.

10. The next day, when the varnish is dry, check to see if there are any sunken-in areas, where the varnish has been absorbed into the picture and the surface looks dull and flat. Revarnish the entire picture to remove these patches. It may be necessary to give the picture two or three thin coats of varnish in order to even out the appearance of the surface.

When using the acrylic solution, ketone resin, or silicone varnishes, be aware that these can dry more quickly than damar or mastic solutions.

A semi-gloss or matte surface finish may be appropriate for a particular work. Commercial varnishes with these finishes are available from various manufacturers, or you may apply a very thin beeswax coating to the surface of a glossy varnish. Use the beeswax and water emulsion or the beeswax and mineral spirits paste, depending on the solubility of the paint layers, described in Chapter 14. Apply the paste to a completely dry varnish with a stiff brush or soft cotton cloth pad. The wax can be warmed slightly to help it spread; use a short, circular motion to apply the paste with the pad, and be sure that the film is very thin and even. When the wax coating has hardened, it can be polished to a low sheen with a clean cotton cloth or nylon stocking. A wax coating on the surface of a picture is likely to attract dust, and can be easily scratched or damaged. The wax is more easily removed and replaced in case of damage, however, than the varnish coating, and it also provides some protection for the varnish.

A reminder: Acrylic emulsion paintings should *not* be varnished with glossy or matte varnish mediums supplied as auxiliaries for the paints. These films cannot be easily removed or separated from the paint films, and they are as porous and susceptible to damage as the paint films. Use an acrylic solution varnish to coat these paintings.

SPRAY VARNISHING

Spraying a varnish coating can be more efficient, particularly if a large number of works are to be varnished at one time. The technique is significantly different from brushing, and requires practice. Furthermore, spray varnishing can be a health and fire hazard, because large amounts of resin and solvent are put into the air in a fine particle and vapor mist. Appropriate ventilation is a must, preferably direct forced-air. A powerful window fan with explosion-proof grounding, correctly placed to draw out the offending mists can work (Figure 17.1), but the artist should also wear an organic vapor respirator, eye protection, gloves, and a long-sleeved smock or overalls.

Three types of apparatus can be used for spray varnishing:

1. Small spray packs that have a reservoir for the varnish and an attached, replaceable propellant can. These operate like the traditional mouth atomizers, by external mixing, and are suitable for small pictures and the application of fixatives (Figure 17.2). As the propellant runs out and the pressure decreases, these devices can begin to spit out globs of varnish in an erratic manner, giving an unsatisfactory finish to the work. Be sure to have replacement cans of propellant handy.

2. Electric compressors. The most common type of electric spray compressor has no reservoir for compressed air, but usually provides a fairly steady pressure for spraying medium- and large-size works. These work on the principle of external mixing, like the spray packs.

Another type of electric sprayer does not work by compressed air or with external mixing, but by an internal mixing mechanism that operates by centrifugal force: A rapidly spinning plate at the end of a hollow rod picks up the liquid, draws it up the inside of the rod, and hurls it out of the nozzle in a fine spray. These sprayers are designed for use with water-based, nonflammable mixtures, but with caution can be used with varnishes thinned with mineral spirits. Do not use them to spray lacquers or any solution containing solvents stronger than mineral spirits.

3. Electric compressors with large air tanks for holding a reserve of pressurized air are powerful enough to spray large amounts of varnish for a sustained period. The air reservoir ensures even pressure; the pressure lines should have an oil trap

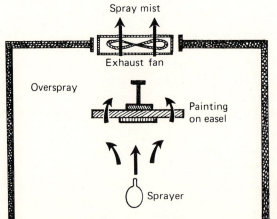

FIGURE 17.1
Spray Varnishing Setup
Note: Overspray exhausts to rear.

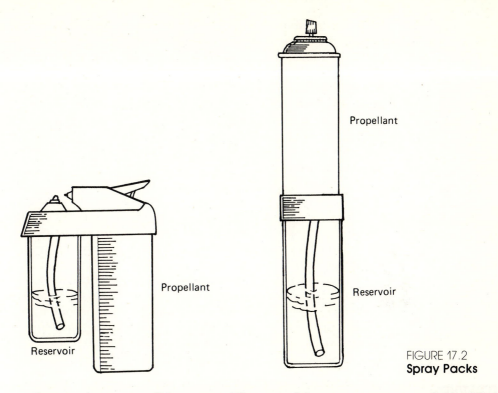

Propellant

Propellant

Reservoir

Reservoir

FIGURE 17.2
Spray Packs

to keep moisture out of the system. The cost of these compressors can be justified only if the artist has a huge amount of work to varnish or if there is another use for the tool (such as for airbrush painting) (Figure 17.3).

The preparation of the work for spray varnishing is the same as the preliminary work done for varnishing with a brush. The work to be varnished is not

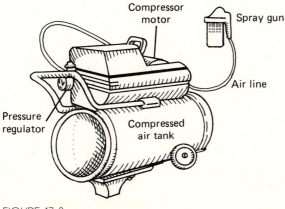

Compressor motor

Spray gun

Air line

Pressure regulator

Compressed air tank

FIGURE 17.3
Electric Sprayer: Compressor and Air Tank Reservoir
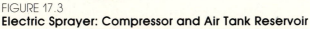

placed on a table, however, but hung vertically on a wall or easel. Mask the surrounding area with brown paper or plastic sheeting to protect it from over-spray. Position the setup so that overspray is drawn out of the room by the exhaust system, either to the rear of the setup or to the side.

A sprayed varnish must be diluted more than a brushed varnish, and thus will contain more thinner. Test various dilutions before spraying to find the proper mix for the varnish being used. Because of the dilution with the thinner, a sprayed-on varnish will dry more quickly than a brushed-on varnish. Usually two or three coats, with sufficient drying time in between, are necessary to achieve a satisfactory finish.

Test the spray device on scrap paper before proceeding to the work to see what kind of spray pattern is produced, and to discover how far from the surface you must hold the gun in order to produce a thin, even film. Holding the spray gun too close to work will cause the varnish to puddle, sag, drip, or run. The optimum distance is about 8 to 12 inches (20–30 cm), depending on the force of the spray and the pattern.

Start spraying at the top. Spray off one edge of the work and spray all the way across the top, off the other side. The return stroke should overlap the previous stroke by about half. Be sure to carry each stroke beyond the edge of the work in order not to form a puddle. Keep the gun moving, and your hand at a constant distance from the surface of the painting. Proceed back and forth across the work, depositing a thin film of varnish, until the entire surface is covered.

FIXATIVES

Fixatives are applied to pastel paintings, and also to charcoal or graphite drawings if desired, to hold the particles of colorant immobile. A fixative must be applied as a very light, dilute spray so that it does not form a layer or film; carelessly applied fixatives can completely alter the apearance of the picture by changing the refractive index of the pigments.

Prepared fixatives can be purchased in spray cans. There are two types: workable fixatives, which allow the relatively easy erasure and further application of the media, and nonworkable fixatives, which are harder to work over. Exercise caution when using commercial fixatives, as they can contain solvents that are fire and health hazards. Or use one of the homemade fixatives suggested in Chapters 5 and 15. Use caution with these fixatives too.

Clean conditions and surroundings are essential when you apply fixatives. Since spraying solvents and resins can be a hazard, be sure to follow the precautions given under the application of spray varnishes.

Lay the work face up on a table top or the floor. Hold the spray device vertically over the piece so that it will operate properly, and discharge the fixative so that it floats down to settle on the surface of the work. This method is preferable to spraying against the work hung vertically, since the force of the spray is often enough to dislodge the particles of colorant. One light coat of fixative should be enough to hold the particles in place.

Pastel painters who apply intermediate touches of fixative as they work on their paintings, in order to prevent smearing as they overpaint with successive layers of pastel, may find that the particles are fairly well fixed by the time the painting is finished. In this case, a final fix can be applied to the work hanging vertically, using the same procedure as for spray varnishing (but do not apply a thick coating of fixative!). This is a more convenient form of application.

MATTING

A *mat* is the most popular protective housing for works of art on paper. It provides some protection for the work, in storage and while on exhibit, and it can also be an esthetic addition to the work.

In the past decade, high-quality mat boards have become widely available. Boards made of 100 percent rag fibers (usually cotton) or purified lignin-free and acid-free wood pulp, treated with an alkaline buffer to absorb atmospheric acidity, can be obtained in many art supply stores or by mail order (see Appendix D). These materials are often called "acid-free" or "museum-quality" mat boards. To be truly high-quality materials, they should contain an extra reserve buffer of the alkaline material—say, calcium carbonate or magnesium carbonate—that has been incorporated during manufacture, and they must not contain lignin.

Colored paper-covered pasteboard has long been found in framing shops, where an appeal to the customer's taste may take precedence over a concern for longevity. These boards can be distinguished from high-quality mat boards by looking at the core of the material. It is usually white or cream-colored, contrasting with the paper covering. These boards are of low quality and deteriorate rapidly, and their failure can damage the work of art. Several manufacturers offer colored mat boards of acid-free construction in which the color is a pigment, not a dye, and which can be identified by observing the color of the core. The coloring is continuous throughout the thickness of the board—there is no paper covering. The color selection in these products is relatively limited, but quite adequate for most needs. Be sure that the manufacturer certifies the contents of the board as being of museum quality—do not rely on the word of the retail salesperson.

Museum board comes in varying thicknesses, or plys: 2, 4, 6, or 8 ply boards are the most common. Each ply is approximately $1/16$ inch (1.5 mm) thick. The boards are also available in two common sizes: 30 by 40 inches (75 × 100 cm), and 40 by 60 inches (100 × 150 cm). It is generally wise to use the thicker boards for larger works.

PREPARING AND CUTTING MATS

In handling the art work, measuring, cutting, and hinging, cleanliness is essential for a professional-looking product. Hands should be thoroughly washed, and the job done in a clean environment. Any pencil marks or light smudges on the visible portions of the mat must be erased with a vinyl eraser, which should not harm the surface of a good-quality rag mat board. Ordinary pink rubber erasers can be too abrasive. If there are any eraser crumbs, dust them away from the work area with a soft dust brush. This sort of cleanup should be done before the work is placed in the mat.

Be sure that all cutting blades are very sharp. Dull blades will tear, not cut.

MATERIALS FOR CUTTING AND HINGING MATS

1. Mat cutter. There are a number of options here, depending on cost. Most of these tools hold a sharp blade of either 45 or 60°, enabling the framer to cut a beveled opening in the mat board; the Dexter mat cutter is an example of this tool. Some mat cutters not only hold the blade at an angle, but also provide a runner guide that ensures a perfectly straight cut and a heavy pressure bar to hold the mat stable while it is being cut. The Keeton Cutter or C & H Mat Cutter are examples. The more work the tool does, and the more precise its operation, the more expensive it is. Only the sharpest blades should be used for cutting mat board. Be sure to have an ample supply of replacement blades for the cutter.

2. Mat knife. This simple tool, also called a utility knife, consists of a metal handle holding a rather heavy single-edged blade. It is used for cutting the boards to size, but can also be used for cutting levels if you have a very steady hand (Figure 17.4).

3. Marking gauge. This is a carpenter's tool like a sliding T-square, used for making repeat measurements of a set distance. The tool consists of a shaft divided like a ruler into $1/16$-inch (1 mm) markings fitted with an adjustable sliding stop that can be fixed at any measurement with a thumbscrew. One end of the shaft has a holder into which a pencil can be inserted (Figure 17.5).

4. A steel T-square and a steel ruler. Both should be marked with divisions every $1/16$ inch (1 mm).

5. Hinging and hanging tape. There are presently no pressure-sensitive tapes (masking tapes, cellophane tapes) which are recommended for this job. The adhesives in these tapes tend to dry out over time, cannot be removed safely without strong solvents, and can stain or discolor the work and the

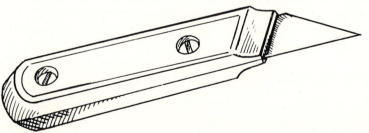

FIGURE 17.4
Mat Knife

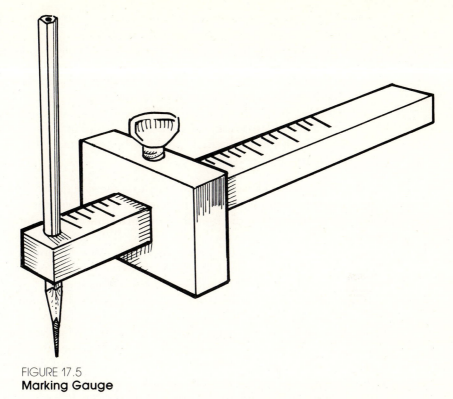

FIGURE 17.5
Marking Gauge

Converted to a mat-marking tool by removing the scratch pin and replacing it with a pencil.

mat. A thin linen tape using a water-soluble adhesive is available in various widths in some art supply shops or framing studios, or through mail order (see Appendix D). This type of tape is strong and stable, and the glue is easily reversible. Some conservators object to its use because it can be too strong for the work and because its sharp edges can damage fragile papers. It is, however, excellent for hinging the backboard of the mat to the window.

Small patches made from water-cut Japanese rice or mulberry papers are an alternative to using the linen tape. Buy archival Japanese papers from conservation suppliers to be sure of getting a quality material. Japanese paper is favored because it is long-fibered and therefore both strong and flexible. Hinges are made by moistening the paper with a small brush dipped in distilled water, and then gently separating the fibers along a straight edge; tearing or cutting the paper is not recommended because both can shorten the fibers and reduce the strength of the hinge. The hinges are attached to the mat and the work using a cooked starch paste or methyl cellulose paste, both of which are reversible water-thinned glues.

6. A bone folder or smooth, short plastic rod. This is used to fold the hinges, and to smooth tiny surface defects in the mat.

7. Very fine sandpaper or garnet paper. Used to clean up ragged cuts.

8. A vinyl plastic eraser. An eraser is handy for removing light smudges and stray pencil marks. The vinyl erasers are gentle and do not leave crumbs.

9. A soft dust brush, the kind used in drafting.

10. An HB pencil. A hard pencil like this will leave only faint marks on the mat, which are easy to erase. A hard pencil can also make depressions in the mat; if you have a heavy hand, it would be better to use a 4B pencil even though the marks will be darker.

A traditional mat is like a book, hinged along the side or top, whichever is longer. The front has a window opening through which the work is viewed. The back is solid, and provides support for the work. Most important, the window separates the work from the glazing used in the frame. If the art work has a border then the window mat can overlap the paper around its edges to hold it down securely (a T-hinge is used for hanging). If the image extends to the edges of the paper, the window should not overlap the work (a V-hinge is used).

The width of the border around the window is determined by convention or esthetics. Large works might require a large border 3 to 6 inches (7.5–15 cm) in width; a small work may require a narrow border. Whatever the choice, it is the usual practice to make the top and two side borders the same dimensions and the bottom border slightly larger—for instance, the top and sides might be 3 inches (7.5 cm) wide, and the bottom 4 inches (10 cm) wide. These proportions provide a visual balance to the look of the work. If all the borders are the same width, the visual impression can be that the work is sliding off the bottom of the mat. Naturally, this convention is ignored if the needs of the work dictate a different arrangement.

In the example below, a drawing 10 inches high and 8 inches wide (25 × 20 cm) on a piece of paper 12 by 10 inches (30 × 25 cm) is matted using 4-ply rag mat board.

METHOD FOR CUTTING THE MAT

1. Measure the image. Here, the image is 10 by 8 inches (25 × 20 cm), and since there is plenty of extra paper around the image, the mat will be used to cover the paper to within ⅛ inch (3 mm) of the edge. Adding ¼ inch (6 mm) to each of the image's dimensions (2 times ⅛) gives the size of the opening for the window: 10¼ by 8¼ inches (25.6 × 20.6 cm).

2. Determine what border widths are satisfactory for the image. In this example, let 3 inches (7.5 cm) for the sides and top and 4 inches (10 cm) for the bottom be appropriate. Add 7 inches (17.5 cm) to the height of the window opening (3 + 4) and 6 inches (15 cm) to the width of the window opening (3 + 3) to give the outside dimensions of the mat: 17¼ by 14¼ inches (42.1 × 35.6 cm). Try it; it's not as complicated as it sounds.

3. Cut two pieces of the 4-ply museum board to exactly the dimensions determined in step 2. Use the T-square to be sure that all markings on the board are square and true. Use a padding of scrap mat board beneath the good pieces to preserve the knife blade. Be sure that the mat knife is very sharp. One piece of mat board will be the backboard; set it aside in a clean place.

4. Use the marking gauge to mark the borders of the window mat on the back side of the mat. Set the stop at 3 inches (7.5 cm) and mark the top and sides, then at 4 inches (10 cm) for the bottom. Hold the stop firmly against the edge of the board and press down lightly with the pencil end of the gauge. Slide the gauge along the board and a line 3 inches (or 4 inches) from the edge of the board will be inscribed, parallel to the edge. With practice, it is not necessary to inscribe the full length of each line; mark just the corners where the lines intersect.

5. Cut out the window. If you are using the hand-held type of mat cutter, first check the blades to be sure they are sharp. Guide the tool carefully along a straight edge held firmly against the marking lines. A mat-cutting machine will have a weighted bar to hold the work firmly, and a sliding track to make sure the cut is straight. Set the blade depth adjustment so the blade will extend about $1/16$ inch (1.5 mm) below the cut to be sure of making a clean cut with no ragged edges. Also allow each cut to extend about $1/16$ inch (1.5 mm) beyond each corner mark to be sure the corners are fully and cleanly cut through. Although it is possible to cut window mats with 90° angle edges, it is more common to use beveled edges. A bevel is cleaner looking and does not allow the mat to cast a shadow on the image; the bevel can be 30°, 45°, or 60°.

6. Set the scrap piece from the window aside and check the edges and corners of the cut for ragged bits of torn mat. If there are any, a gentle pass with the fine garnet paper will smooth them out. Turn the mat over to the front side and lightly burnish the inside edges of the window with the bone folder or plastic rod: this will prevent any sharp edges from damaging the work of art.

7. Lay the window mat face down and place the backboard beside it. Since the longest part of the mat in this example is the side, the two pieces will be hinged together like a book. (If the longest edge were the top, the two would be hinged there.) Cut a length of linen tape just slightly shorter than the length of the side, moisten it, and assemble the mat. When the adhesive dries, fold the mat closed. Set it aside in a clean place (Figure 17.6).

T-HINGE METHOD

A T-hinge is used to hang works whose edges are covered by the window mat.

1. Lay the work face down on a clean surface, and prepare the hinging materials. To make the hinge, use either water-cut archival-quality Japa-

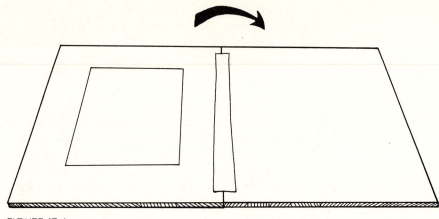

FIGURE 17.6
Assembling the Mat

nese paper or the linen tape; the Japanese paper is preferred. Each hinge consists of two pieces of paper or tape, one smaller than the other. The smaller is attached to the back of the art work and forms the stem of the T. The larger piece forms the crosspiece of the T.

2. Prepare the smaller tabs first. For a work of the size in the example, there need be only two hinges. Larger works may require more, depending also on the weight of the work. Lay the small tabs on a blotter or absorbent piece of scrap paper and apply cold archival-quality methyl cellulose glue (the consistency of heavy cream) to half the width of the tab. When the blotter has absorbed excess moisture from the tabs (a few seconds), place them in position on the back of the work, on the top edge, close to the corners. Overlap the edge of the work with enough of the tab to ensure that it will hold the work securely. Allow the adhesive to dry; this may take more than an hour.

3. Position the work on the backboard so it is properly located beneath the window, and hold it in place with a light weight cushioned with clean blotting paper or clean scrap paper; or use a clean finger. If the work is on heavy paper, a weight will not be needed. Open the window.

4. Prepare the larger crosspiece tabs of the hinges. These should be longer and wider than the smaller tabs. Apply adhesive to the entire surface of the tabs. Place them over the loose ends of the smaller tabs to stick them to the backboard. The large tabs should be centered over the smaller tabs and at a distance from the top edge of the work that is at least equal to the thickness of the work. A correctly hung work will hang freely on the tabs, allowing it to expand and contract as it reacts to changes in the atmosphere, but will be held securely in the mat. When the adhesive dries, close the mat (Figure 17.7).

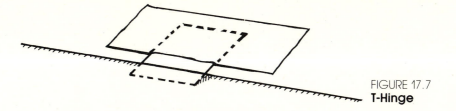

FIGURE 17.7
T-Hinge

V-HINGE METHOD

If the image extends to the edges of the page, it is necessary to "float" the work in the window mat so that the window does not cover the edges of the work. An inverted V-hinge, like a modified and reinforced stamp-hanging hinge, is employed here.

1. Cut the mat as before, being sure to make the window large enough that it does not cover any edge of the work. Assemble the mat.
2. Position the work in the window of the closed mat. Lightly weight it in place if it is so fragile that it will shift.
3. Open the mat. With a pencil, carefully mark on the backboard the position of the upper two corners of the work. Remove the weight, if used, and turn the work over so that the upper corners of the work are now above the pencil marks. Weight it in place. Erase the pencil marks.
4. Prepare two small and two larger tabs as for a T-hinge. Apply adhesive to the entire surface of each of the smaller tabs. Immediately position the tabs on the back of the art work, near the corners, and stick them to both the work and the backboard. About half of each hinge should be attached to the back of the work, and half to the backboard.
5. Apply adhesive to the entire surface of each of the larger crosspiece tabs. Place the crosspieces over the part of the hinges which are attached to the backboard, with the top edge of each just a bit away from the edge of the work. The crosspiece should not show when the work is viewed from the front. Allow the adhesive to dry.
6. When the tabs have dried, turn the picture right side up, pivoting it on the hinges, and close the mat (Figure 17.8).

Using water-cut, feathered-edged rice paper for the hinges may seem like an unnecessary bother because of the added task of making the adhesive to attach them, but they are far superior in strength and gentleness to the linen tape. If the art work is on a heavy, strong piece of paper, however, the disadvantages of linen tape are less worrisome and it can be used for making the hinges.

Matted works that are not to be immediately framed need protection from possible damage—the open window of a mat will not protect the surface of the work from harm. A slip sheet of acid-free glassine, a stable, smooth-surfaced, semi-opaque paper, can be placed between the surface of the work and the window opening. The matted work should then be stored flat, in a closed port-

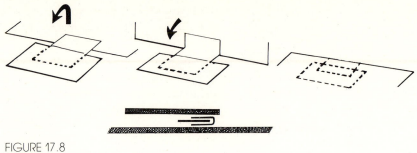

FIGURE 17.8
V-Hinge

folio or print storage box until it is framed. The work can also be slipped into an envelope made of Mylar, a clear form of polyester sheeting for storage; Mylar is stable in light, but to keep the encapsulated matted work in a portfolio, use an uncoated, archival Mylar.

DOUBLE MATS

Pastels and works with high impasto present a special problem for the framer. The surfaces are either very sensitive to damage (pastel) or are so thick that they will extend above the plane of a single mat (impasto). A double mat is one solution; it can be made of 8-ply museum board, or two 4-ply or 6-ply mats glued together.

If you use an 8-ply board, proceed as outlined in the section on mat cutting; be sure that the cutting blades are stiff enough to do the job without wandering off the marked lines—thick mat board has a way of causing thin blades to wander. If you are using built-up 4- or 6-ply boards, follow the procedure outlined here.

METHOD

1. Cut three pieces of museum board exactly the same size. One will be the backboard, two will be glued together to form the double-thick window mat.

2. Use either of these two methods to attach the double window boards together: glue or double-faced tape.

   a. Brush a PVA emulsion glue on the face of one of the window boards. Be sure the coating of glue is thin, even, and covers the board to its edges. Position the second window board on top of the glue-covered board, being absolutely sure that the edges align perfectly. Use gentle pressure all over the surface of the board to make sure they have adhered to each other. Clean up the edges to catch any drops of glue that have squeezed out. Cover the boards with a clean sheet of paper and then a piece of hardboard, and weight them down until the glue has dried thoroughly. Go to step 3.

b. This method uses double-faced polyester transparent tape from 3M (product #4I5; see Appendix D). Testing has shown that this tape has good ageing properties. This tape can not be used on the art work itself, but it is good for this purpose. No other pressure-sensitive tapes should be used. Since you cannot tape the boards together and then cut the window out with any assurance of accuracy, it will be necessary to cut the window openings in each board separately. There is opportunity to experiment with various configurations: both bevels aligned so that it appears there is only one; separated bevels; a regular bevel on one mat and a 90° cut on the other (Figure 17.9). Those who do not have a great deal of experience cutting mats or those who are using a hand-held mat cutter will find that trying to make two cuts appear as one is extremely difficult. Cut the mats, align them, and check the appearance. Remove the top mat. On the back of the top mat, place strips of the double-faced tape around the perimeter of the board, about 1/16 inch (1.5 mm) from the edge, and around the inside perimeter of the window, about 1/16 inch (1.5 mm) from the edge. Peel off the protective film on the back of the tape, and carefully align the two boards; press on them to be sure they stick together.

3. Proceed with the window cutting as instructed, if the glue method has been used. Be sure that the blades being used in the mat cutter are extremely sharp, and that they are stiff enough to prevent them from wandering off the guidelines.

4. Assemble the window mat and backboard as before and hang the work with T-hinges or V-hinges, as required (Figure 17.10).

SINK MATS

A sink mat is an alternative to double matting and is especially useful for mounting works with high impasto or those that are in general thicker than an ordinary sheet of paper. Works done on thin hardboard, canvas board, or museum board can be mounted in sink mats with ease.

A sink mat is constructed of 4- or 6-ply museum board like a standard mat, except that the space around the work is built up to the thickness of the work with filler boards. The filler boards support the heavy work, which would otherwise put a strain on the hinges used to hold it in the mat. The window board of a sink mat is attached to the built-up filler boards.

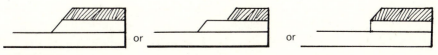

FIGURE 17.9
Beveling Choices for Double Mats

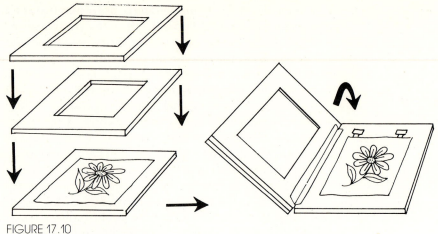

FIGURE 17.10
Assembly of a Double Mat

METHOD

1. Cut two pieces of museum board to a size appropriate for the proportions of the work.
2. Cut the window opening in one piece. Since works cannot be floated in a sink mat, the window edges should overlap the edges of the work by about ⅛ inch (3 mm) on each side.
3. Make enough T-hinges to support the work comfortably. Attach the smaller stem tabs to the back of the work, leaving at least half the tabs showing and free of adhesive.
4. Position the work on the backboard, place the window over the work, and adjust the location of the work and the window. Gently weight the work, if necessary, and remove the window and set it aside.
5. Attach the work to the backboard by gluing the crosspiece tabs over the smaller stem tabs to form the T-hinges.
6. Figure out the number of thicknesses of mat board that will be needed to equal the thickness of the work.
7. Cut a strip of mat board that will fit the right side of the backboard, extending flush along the side of the board from top to bottom, and just a hair from the right edge of the work (about 1 mm). Be sure the filler is exactly flush with all edges of the backboard and does not touch the work. Cut as many other strips as are needed to achieve the correct thickness of the filler to the same size as the first strip.
8. Use either PVA emulsion glue or double-faced polyester tape to assemble the strips into a block. Place the block in position and attach it to the backboard. Be careful to check the alignment of the block with all edges of the backboard.
9. Use the methods in steps 7 and 8 to assemble and attach a filler block for the left side of the mat. The filler block should not touch the work.

10. The bottom filler is assembled in the same manner as the side fillers, and is attached to the backboard below the work and between the two side fillers. It should be flush with the bottom of the backboard and the insides of the two side fillers, and the same distance away from the work as the other fillers.

11. The top filler does not support the work. It is constructed in the same manner as the others, but is narrow enough so that it does not cover the hinges. It should be flush with the insides of the side fillers and the top edge of the backboard.

12. When all the fillers have been put in place, attach the window board to the top of the filler boards along the longest side of the mat. Use wide linen tape.

13. Insert the work and close the mat. If you wish to remove the work from the mat, open it and tilt it until the work slips out. If you want to avoid the possibility of dropping the work, use this method to make a lifting tab: Glue a length of rice paper to the inside of the backboard, where it will be hidden by the work; it should be long enough to extend out from underneath the work when the object is put in place. Do not glue the free-hanging end of the paper, and use only enough glue on the other end to ensure a firm attachment. The length of paper will be hidden under the window mat, and can be used to lift the work out of the sink (Figure 17.11).

SINK MOUNT

It is occasionally desirable to mount a work of art on a backboard but forego the use of a window mat, which can disrupt the visual impact of the work. In this arrangement, the work hangs freely from the backboard, which provides a visual border around the work, and the whole is placed in a frame. It is not recommended that a work be mounted this way for storage (unless the work is framed in storage) because it is necessary to have protection for the front of the work. A spacer in the rabbet of the frame keeps the work from coming into contact with the glazing material.

Without the added rigidity of the window mat, the backboard is likely to buckle in the frame. Six- or 8-ply museum board should be used. In addition to the 8-ply mount, insert a piece of ⅛ inch (3 mm) thick hardboard cut to size behind the backboard. In the frame, the backboard of the work should be isolated from the hardboard by a barrier paper; acid-free glassine with an added alkaline buffer will work, or use two-ply buffered mat board.

Determine the position of the art work on the backboard. Use V-hinges for hanging the work. Assemble the frame. Insert the glazing into the frame rabbet. A product called Frame-Space, made of a clear plastic, which can slip onto the edges of the glazing and simultaneously act as a spacer to keep the work from touching the glazing, can be used (see Appendix D). Or attach the spacers, made of thin strips of museum board the same color as the backboard, to the inside of the rabbet. They should provide between ⅛ and ½ inch (3–12 mm) of space

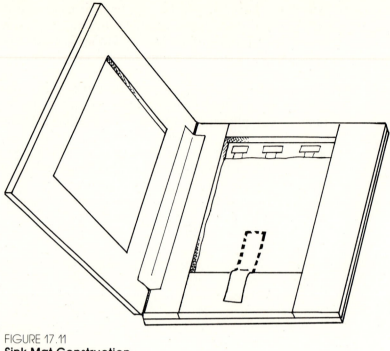

FIGURE 17.11
Sink Mat Construction

With optional sling.

between the glazing and the surface of the free-hanging work, depending on the depth of the frame (see the section on framing for details and illustrations).

FRAMING

A frame provides additional protection for works of art, and can also be considered a visual "stop" for the edges of the image. It is especially necessary to frame works that will be handled a great deal, or those that will be moved to exhibitions. The more substantial the frame, the more protection it will give the work.

STRIP FRAME

A strip frame is often used for temporary exhibition purposes or in storage situations. This construction consists of little more than thin strips of wood tacked around the perimeter of the painting with small brads (Figure 17.12). Sometimes the wood is left plain, sometimes it is varnished or painted, and sometimes it is stained and has a decorative beading at the front edge.

Lightweight strip framing can be attractive if done well, but it has several disadvantages. If the painting is the least bit out of square, strip framing will often

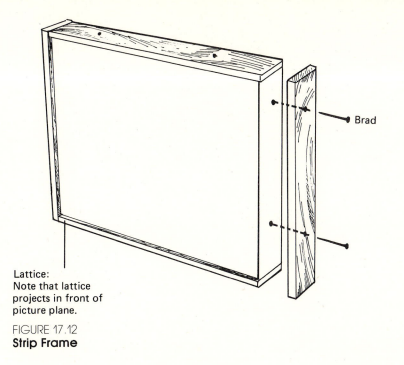

Lattice:
Note that lattice
projects in front of
picture plane.

Brad

FIGURE 17.12
Strip Frame

emphasize rather than hide the problem. The method of attaching the strips to the frame, by hammering brads into the stretchers or strainer, can damage the painting or the chassis. Because there is little room at the back edge of the strips for hanging apparatus, screw eyes or strap hangers must be attached to the chassis; this arrangement can put undue strain on the painting. Finally, the strips do not offer any protection for the front edge of the painting.

BOX FRAME

The box frame is the preferred and standard method of framing paintings and matted works on paper. It consists of a rigid framework of wood or metal constructed with 45° angle mitered corners. The inside of the frame has a rabbet, usually about ¼ inch (6 mm) deep, to hold the work (Figure 17.13). A frame is constructed to provide an independent structure in which the picture can be protectively suspended.

A table saw, for making the rabbet in the frame stock, and a miter box, for cutting the 45° mitered corners, are the major pieces of equipment needed to make frames. If you do not have a table saw, it is often possible to convince a local mill or lumberyard to rabbet the frame stock to the required dimensions. Hardwoods like maple or oak are recommended because of their strength, although semi-hard woods like poplar are easier to work with. It is easier and more convenient, but also more expensive, to purchase ready-made frame stock. Few

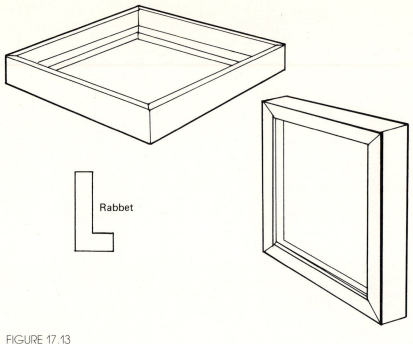

Rabbet

FIGURE 17.13
Box Frame
45° mitered corners, rabbet.

frame shops will sell their stock at retail, but several distributors of stock that have established thriving and reliable mail-order businesses (see Appendix D). These concerns will supply a wide variety of styles, in different woods and metals (mostly aluminum), and even chop the frames—that is, cut the components to the correct size for the work in question, with mitered corners. The artist then need only assemble and finish the frames.

MATERIALS FOR CONSTRUCTING THE FRAME

1. Table saw.
2. Miter box.
3. Corner clamps (two). Used for holding the assembled joints until the glue has set.
4. Carpenter's square, for checking corners.
5. A small drill. When working with hardwoods, it is necessary to drill pilot holes for the nails. Soft or semi-hard woods can be nailed without drilling the pilot holes. A thin, sharp awl might work here; a small brad, the diameter of the ones being used for the frame, chucked into an inexpensive hand-operated drill, will also work.

6. Nail set. This is for setting the brads below the level of the wood. If very small finishing nails are used, another nail will work as a nail set.

7. Tack hammer.

8. A selection of small brads and finishing nails.

9. A screwdriver.

10. An accurate tape measure.

11. A brad pusher. This device consists of a sliding sleeve enclosing a magnet; a brad is held in the sleeve by the magnet, and the tool is used for pushing brads into the frame.

12. Strong wood glue. The yellow aliphatic carpenter's wood glues are far superior in this application to the white PVA emulsion glues.

13. Brass or steel mending plates, drilled to accept screws. These are sometimes called Z plates, for their configuration (Figure 17.14), and can be fabricated or purchased. They are used to hold unmatted works in the frame. A proprietary product called All-Flex (See Appendix D) can be used for this purpose.

14. Putty for filling nail holes. Putty, or spackle, can be painted to match the color of the frame, or one can buy putties to match different color woods.

15. Shellac. The white residue left from making shellac fixative is good for sealing the insides of the frames.

16. Cork cushions. Cut a wine bottle cork in half lengthwise, then make ⅛ inch (3 mm) slices of the halves so that small discs are left. These are used between the painting and the inside of the rabbet, for works that are not matted (Figure 17.15).

17. Brown paper, to be used as a dust barrier on the rear of framed, matted works. It is not archival—not used in museums—but does not come into contact with the matted work. If you are concerned about this, use an archival glassine or tissue as a dust barrier.

18. Braided steel picture wire, of a gauge appropriate to the weight of the

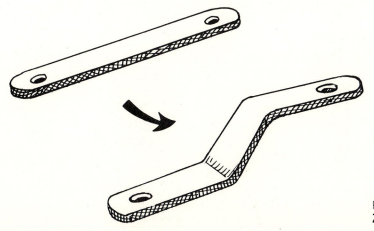

FIGURE 17.14
Z Plate

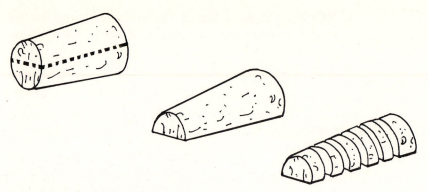

FIGURE 17.15
Making Cork Cushions

work. This wire is good, but can embrittle with age; heavy-gauge copper wire is better—it is more malleable—but also more expensive. Fishing line is not recommended.

19. Screw eyes or strap hangers. Screw eyes can put a strain on the frame and split the wood. Hangers are small metal plates with one or two screw holes and a freely moving metal loop. They are more secure hanging devices that do not put too great a strain on the frame members (Figure 17.16).

20. A thin, sharp awl.

21. Glazing. For works that are framed behind glass, use singleweight window glass. Glass does not provide much protection from ultraviolet light, however. Acrylic sheets from Rohm and Haas, Plexiglass UF-3 and UF-4, shield works from up to 95 percent of UV radiation, at the slight cost of some illumination. These sheets can also have a slight yellow cast. Plastic

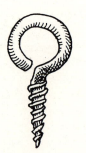

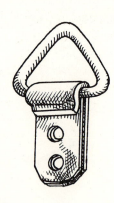

Screw eye   Strap hanger

FIGURE 17.16
Screw Eye (*left*) and Strap Hanger (*right*)

glazing is lighter in weight than glass, and much less liable to break—particular advantages if the work is to be shipped. But plastics are easily scratched, and can develop strong static electrical charges—so strong that pastel and charcoal can be drawn right off the surface of the work. Plastics can be treated and cleaned with antistatic solutions to relieve the electrical charge, but very delicate works should be put behind regular glass. Partial filtering of ultraviolet can be obtained from styrene plastic glazing such as KSH-UVF from Westfall Framing (see Appendix D), but this product is recommended only for temporary use. Nonglare glass is not recommended because, for it to work, it must be pressed against the surface of the work. A product called Denglas is clear and need not be placed directly against the surface of the work. It is expensive, but also provides some ultraviolet filtering (see Appendix D).

CUTTING THE FRAME

Select a frame profile appropriate for the work. Take into consideration the style of the art: An ornate, carved and gilded frame might be acceptable when placed around a nineteenth-century painting but might look silly with a nonrepresentational work. There are hundreds of frame profiles to choose from (Figure 17.17 shows some examples).

Whether the art work is matted or on stretched fabric or panel, the procedure for cutting the frame is identical except for the amount of space to be added (see step 1). Instructions for the two types of assembly of the frame follow the directions for cutting.

METHOD FOR CUTTING THE FRAME

1. Measure the work. If the work is on a stretched fabric or panel, add ¼ inch (6 mm) to each dimension to allow a ⅛-inch (3 mm) space between the inside rail of the frame and the outside edge of the work. If the work

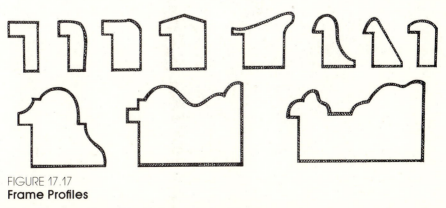

FIGURE 17.17
Frame Profiles

Note: The size of the rabbet is the same in all these examples.

is matted, add ⅛ inch (3 mm) to each dimension. These spaces will allow the work to move within, and independently of, the frame. If, for example, a painting on linen measured 16 by 20 inches (15 × 51 cm), the inside dimensions of the frame would then be 16¼ by 20¼ inches (15.6 × 51.6 cm).

2. Measure and cut the frame stock. Measure accurately and mark all cutting lines to be sure of getting a precise 45° angle; be sure to measure from the inside of the rabbet, not the outside of the frame. Check the miter box for accuracy, and see that the back saw is very sharp. The cuts should be clean and smooth—any slightly ragged edges can be smoothed with fine sandpaper or garnet paper.

3. Use the corner clamps to assemble two adjacent sides of the frame, and check the joint for accuracy. Separate the joint slightly and coat the end of one rail with glue. Reassemble the joint and close the clamp tightly. Wipe away any glue that has oozed out of the joint. Allow the glue to set. Check one corner, or all four, by laying out the frame members and using the carpenter's square. Then, use a strap clamp—or a homemade version of one—to assemble and glue the entire frame at once (Figure 17.18).

4. If necessary, drill pilot holes for the finishing nails. Make the holes slightly smaller than the diameter of the nails. At least two nails should be used in each joint, though a large or heavy frame might require as many as four or five. Insert the nails at a slight angle to the sides of the frame to draw the joint tight. Countersink the nails and set the assembly aside to dry (Figure 17.19).

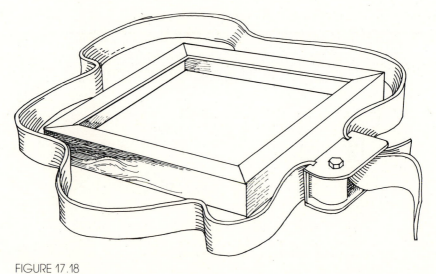

FIGURE 17.18
Strap Clamp

Tighten the bolt to wind up the strap.

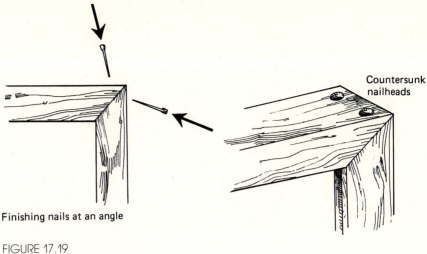

Countersunk
nailheads

Finishing nails at an angle

FIGURE 17.19
Nailing the Frame Corners

Left: Nails angled to prevent corner separation.
Right: Countersink the nailheads.

5. Assemble the other two sides of the frame, using steps 3 and 4, unless the strap clamp has been used. When both corners are dry, assemble the complete frame in the same manner. Lay the frame flat in a safe place until all the glued joints are completely dry.
6. Inspect the frame corners for open joints, cracks, or splits. Small openings or cracks can be filled with putty. Fill the nail holes with putty.
7. Unfinished stock should be sanded smooth, using a sanding block to ensure that all corners and edges will remain sharp and square. An electric orbital sander is good for this, but use a piece of museum board beneath the sandpaper to keep the device from rounding off edges and corners. The outside of the frame can be painted, or given a coat of polyurethane varnish, or rubbed with linseed oil and then waxes, or merely waxed—use a good quality paste wax. Shellac or varnish the rabbet, but do not paint or wax it.

METHOD FOR ASSEMBLING THE FRAME: MATTED WORKS

1. Lay the completed frame face down on a clean surface.
2. Clean the glazing. Acrylic or styrene glazing should be cleaned with a plastic cleaner and a soft, lint-free cotton cloth to avoid scratching the surface. Glass can be cleaned with a glass cleaner. Newspapers make excellent lint-free glass cleaners (but do not use on plastic glazing). Cheaper than a commercial glass cleaner is a very mild solution of ammonia and water. Mix 1 part household ammonia with 20 parts water and use in a sprayer.

Caution: Ammonia can be a health hazard; do not breathe the vapors; label the sprayer carefully. Lay the glazing in the frame.

3. If the work is to be floated without a window mat, now is the time to insert the spacers. Very thin wooden strips, at least ¼ inch (6 mm) thick and as wide as the rabbet—generally ¼ inch (6 mm)—may be tacked to the inside of the rabbet with small brads. They may be finished the same as the frame, in order to be as inconspicuous as possible. The spacer will keep the work from touching the inside of the glazing. Thick museum board, the same color as the backboard, can also be used; nail it in place. The spacers should be removable—they should not be glued in place (Figure 17.20). Frame-space, made by Frame-Tek, can also be used as a spacer between the backboard and the glazing, (see Appendix D).

4. Place the work in the frame. If the work is floated, stand the frame upright to keep the free-hanging edge of the work from swinging out and touching the glass. It may be necessary to do this anyway, if the surface of the work is too dusty and fragile. Insert a stiffening backboard behind the matted work. The backboard should be the same size as the mat backboard, and made of archival materials: another piece of museum board, archival corrugated cardboard (see Appendix D)—but never ordinary corrugated cardboard!—archival foam-core board, or a sandwich of ⅛ inch (3 mm) thick tempered hardboard faced with an archival barrier paper (Figure 17.21).

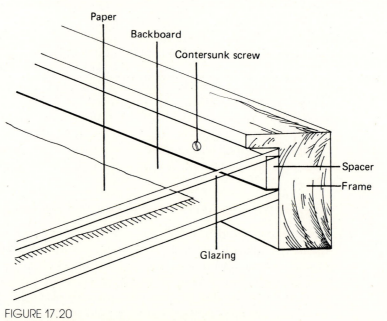

FIGURE 17.20
Frame Spacer for Floating Unmatted Works

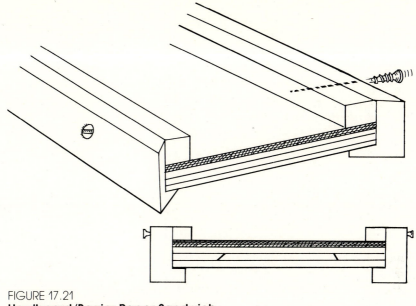

FIGURE 17.21
Hardboard/Barrier Paper Sandwich

Used as a stiffener for very large works, whether matted or floated.

5. If the work is not floated, but is in a regular mat, use the brad pusher to insert the brads into the rabbet to hold the work into the frame. Gently press down on the back of the work with one hand and guide the brads in at a slight downward angle. Space the brads every 2 inches (5 cm) around the edge of the work, with extra brads close to each corner.

6. The back of the frame should be covered to keep out dust; the covering will also slow the picture's reaction to atmospheric stresses. Cut a sheet of brown wrapping paper larger than the back of the frame. Wet the paper with a damp sponge or a light spray of water. Lay a thin bead of glue around the back edge of the frame. Place the paper over the frame and stretch it tight. When the glue dries, trim the excess paper off with a sharp razor blade to make a neat edge; as the paper dries, it will stretch tight.

7. Attach the hanging hardware to the frame. As a rule of thumb, the screw eyes or strap hangers can be placed at a point about one-third the distance from the top to the bottom of the frame. This will alow the frame to hang away from the wall at a slight angle (Figure 17.22).

8. Attach the hanging wire. Stretch the wire taut between the two hanging points—it will stretch a little more when the work is hung, so it is important that it be tight as possible. (This is when screw eyes reveal themselves to be inferior to strap hangers: When the wire is stretched, screw eyes can split the frame.) Use a lock twist on the wire to keep it from slipping off the hangers (Figure 17.23).

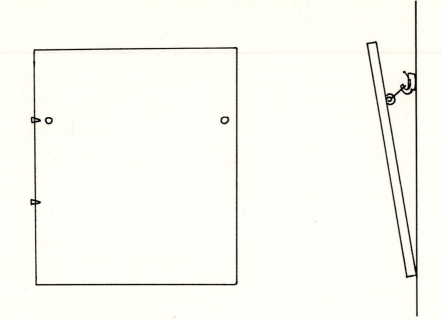

FIGURE 17.22
Attaching the Hanging Wire

Left: One-third of the distance down from the top of the frame.
Right: Wire correctly placed allows the work to angle forward to lessen reflection.

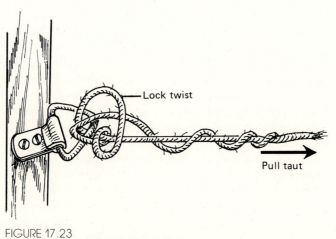

FIGURE 17.23
Lock Twist for the Hanging Wire

METHOD FOR ASSEMBLING THE FRAME: WORKS ON STRETCHED FABRIC AND PANELS

1. Lay the frame down on a clean surface.
2. Attach a dust cover to the back of the picture if it is a stretched fabric on a chassis. The cover should be made of stiff cardboard or foam-core board —it will prevent dirt and dust from settling in the rear of the picture between the chassis and the back of the fabric, and it will also prevent mechanical damage to the rear of the work. Cut the cover about ½ inch (1.25 cm) smaller than the dimensions of the work, and attach it to the back of the chassis with flathead screws and countersunk washers (Figure 17.24). Fome-Cor (Monsanto) is available in ³/₁₆, ¹/₈, and ³/₈ inch (4.5, 6, 18 mm) thicknesses.
3. Place the work in the frame. Notice the space between the inside of the rabbet and the edge of the work. This space can be filled with a shock-absorbing material, for which the little half-discs of cork are used. Using the blade of the screwdriver, jam the discs into the space between the frame and the picture at even intervals (Figure 17.25).

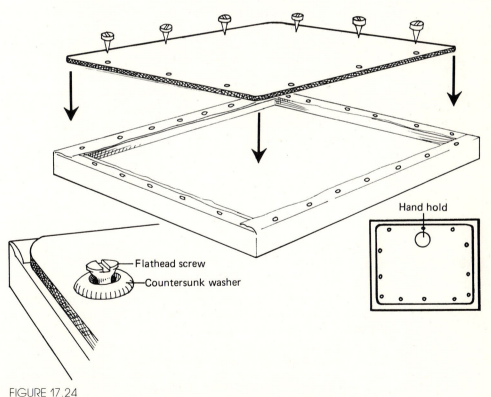

Hand hold

Flathead screw

Countersunk washer

FIGURE 17.24
Dust Cover for the Back of a Stretched Fabric Support

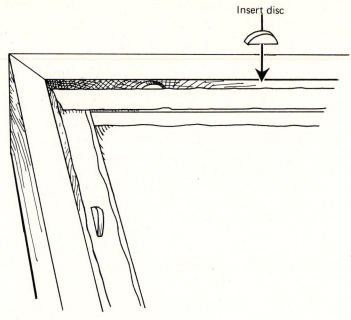

Insert disc

FIGURE 17.25
Inserting the Cork Cushions

4. Attach the mending plates to the back of the frame, using flathead or panhead wood screws. The plates should be bent down in the Z shape so that they exert pressure on the back of the work to hold it in the frame. There should be no need to use screws to hold the plates to the back of the work—the pressure of the plates against the chassis should be sufficient—but there is no harm done if screws must be used, as long as care is taken with their installation. Use at least two plates on each side of the frame (Figure 17.26).

5. Attach the hanging hardware and wire to the back of the frame.

LABELING THE WORK

Pictures should have a descriptive label attached to the back of the dust cover or frame, never directly to the work itself. The label should provide complete identification of the artist and the work. The label is a record of the picture and can be a help to those who might, in the future, have to clean or repair it.

The label should have the following minimal information about the work:

1. The artist's name. Some artists provide address and telephone number.
2. The title, date, and dimensions of the work (height preceding width).
3. A complete listing of the materials used in the work, including brand names.

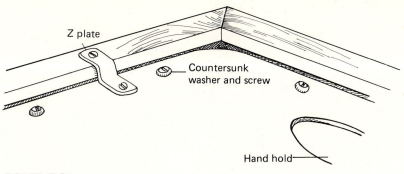

Z plate

Countersunk
washer and screw

Hand hold

FIGURE 17.26
Attachment of the Z Plates

The type of support, ground, paint(s) and other ingredients in the paint layers, and the kind of varnish or surface coating should be given.

Here is a sample label including the information listed above:*

IMPORTANT TECHNICAL DATA · KEEP WITH ARTWORK
MAY ASSIST CONSERVATORS IN CASE OF DAMAGE OR FUTURE CLEANING

ARTIST:	DATE:
TITLE:	I.D.#:
	DIMENSIONS:

MATERIALS AND METHODS (BRAND NAMES, FORMULATIONS, ETC.)

SUPPORT: SURFACE COATING/VARNISH:
PRIMING:
GROUND:
DESIGN LAYER: MEDIA/ADHESIVES/ETC.   DESIRED FINISH
                                            ☐ NONE   ☐ SEMIGLOSS
                                            ☐ MATTE   ☐ GLOSS

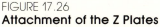 **waac** western association of art conservators   THIS INFORMATION HAS BEEN PROVIDED BY THE ARTIST IN COOPERATION WITH THE WESTERN ASSOCIATION OF ART CONSERVATORS 5905 WILSHIRE BLVD. LOS ANGELES, CA. 90036 (213) 937-4250

CAUTION: DO NOT AFFIX TO REVERSE OF ORIGINAL FABRIC OR PAPER

---

* Reproduced by permission of the Western Association of Art Conservators.

STORAGE

Clean and controlled storage conditions make it possible to keep work in good shape for immediate exhibition or sale. Museum facilities are beyond the capacity of most artists, and except for rare, valuable, or exceedingly delicate objects, they are not really necessary. A spacious closet, or the corner of a studio set aside exclusively for storage, can be made into a suitable area if certain basic requirements are met.

CLEANLINESS

It is essential that the storage space be clean, and kept that way. Dust and dirt in the air can settle on surfaces and eventually cause damage. Flies, moths, and other insects can damage works. If the storage is in an open area such as the corner of a studio, the objects should be covered. Have a regular program of vacuuming— better than sweeping—and dusting.

LIGHT

Many works are sensitive to continued exposure to light, which can cause fading, chroma, or color changes in pigments, or otherwise degrade the picture and its support. The storage area, therefore, should have minimal lighting, preferably low wattage incandescent lights or dim north daylight.

Oil paintings, as usual, are the exception. Linseed oil has a tendency to yellow as its ages, and yellowing seems to be accelerated when the paintings are kept in the dark. Oil paintings should therefore be exposed to a minimum amount of diffuse natural light. The yellowing caused by the dark is reversible: Just expose the picture to some sunlight or other natural daylight for a few days.

Works that are on exhibit need to be given a rest once in a while. Sensitive paintings should not be continuously exhibited but rotated, on a regular basis, with those in storage.

HEAT AND HUMIDITY

It is not so much high or low heat or humidity that causes damage to works of art; it is the constant changes in these two atmospheric qualities—which act always in concert—that cause the damage. Rapid change in relative humidity and temperature can cause a support or paint layer to crack, especially if the work is ageing and brittle. Even relatively slow changes in atmospheric conditions, because they occur on a cyclical schedule, can stress an object.

Museums strive to keep both exhibition and storage spaces at a stable temperature and relative humidity. The optimum values can vary, according to the type of object, but the normal range for temperature is 65–70° F (18–21° C) and for relative humidity, 55–70 percent moisture.

Without completely separate storage facilities, insulated, heated, humidified or dehumidified, and monitored, an individual artist cannot hope to meet these ideal conditions. But an artist can choose a more or less stable environment—say, an interior closet away from radiators and forced-air heating registers—and provide at least a good environment for the work. Temperature can be monitored with a simple thermometer, and relative humidity can be kept track of with humidity indicator strips from Multiform Dessicants (see Appendix D).

STORING PAINTINGS

Paintings on fabric or panels should be stored off the floor in racks, standing vertically on one edge. In an ideal situation each painting has a separate compartment, so that paintings of different sizes can be stored without damaging one another. Practically speaking, this arrangement is often impossibly expensive or inconvenient. Place a large stiff piece of corrugated cardboard between each painting (Figure 17.27). The idea is to keep each painting physically separated from the others.

Paintings on fabrics that have been removed from their chassis can be stored by thumbtacking them at the upper edges to large pieces of corrugated cardboard. The paintings are easily handled in this manner, and can be stood in the racks with the rest of the work (Figure 17.28).

To protect the surfaces of the paintings in the racks, attach a dust cover. Cut a piece of brown wrapping paper large enough to cover the work and thumbtack it

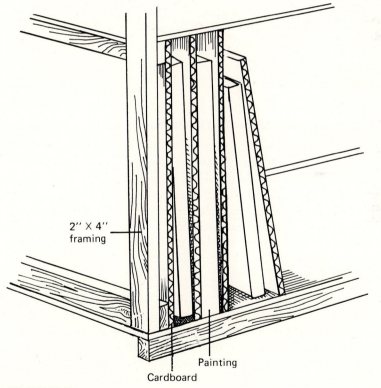

2″ × 4″
framing

Painting

Cardboard

FIGURE 17.27
Painting Storage Rack

Cardboard spacers between paintings.

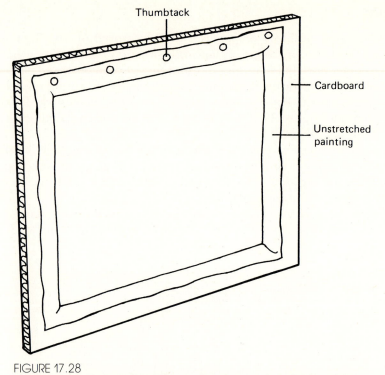

FIGURE 17.28
Storing Unstretched Painting by Pinning to Cardboard Sheet

to the back of the chassis. Fold it over the top edge of the chassis and allow it to hang freely in front of the work (Figure 17.29).

Paintings on fabric should never, as a general rule, be rolled, either for storing or for shipping. Whether the works are rolled face-in or face-out, this practice places great stress on painted films, no matter how thin or flexible the films may appear.

STORING WORKS ON PAPER

Art or paper supports are usually fragile or susceptible to mechanical damage, and so should be carefully stored. Matting all paper works will certainly provide a measure of safety, and a slip sheet of archival glassine placed between the window opening and the surface of the work will keep dust and dirt from touching the surface. As a further precaution, a covering flap cut from museum board can be hinged to the mat and folded over the front of the window (Figure 17.30).

The matted works should be stored flat, in a portfolio. Arrange the pictures in the portfolio so that they cannot damage each other, and limit the number of works in one stack. Hinged portfolios can place a strain on a large stack of matted objects by squeezing them along the edge of the portfolio's hinge. Better and

Brown paper

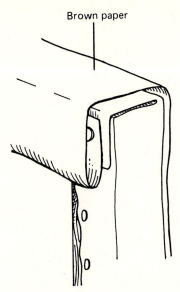

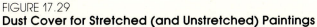

FIGURE 17.29
Dust Cover for Stretched (and Unstretched) Paintings

safer, though more expensive, are specially made print and drawing storage boxes constructed of archival buffered board (Figure 17.31). When these close, they do not exert any pressure on the objects inside. The boxes can be homemade using linen tape and 8-ply museum board; line the box with glassine or Mylar to act as a moisture barrier. Commercial varieties come in an array of standard sizes (see Appendix D), and some come with clasps and carrying handles so they can double as portfolios as well as storage containers.

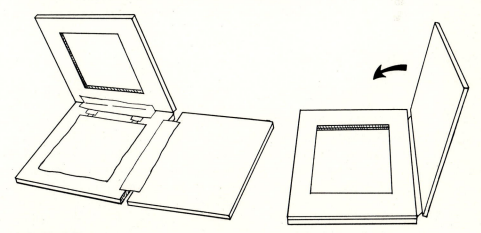

FIGURE 17.30
Dust Cover/Rigid Facing for Matted Works

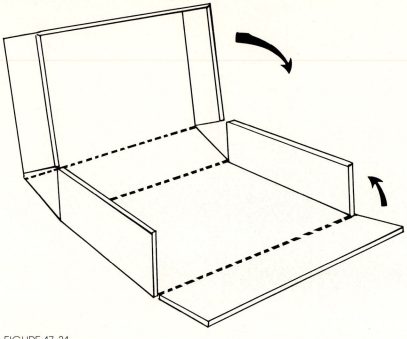

FIGURE 17.31
Print Storage Box

For works on paper.

Large shallow-drawered print storage cabinets can be used to store drawings or other works on paper that have not been matted. Do not overfill the drawers, and be sure to place a slip sheet between each work and the next (Figure 17.32).

Works on paper should never be rolled, either for shipping or storage.

PHOTOGRAPHING PICTURES

Having a record of your work is important, and keeping a file of color slides or prints or black and white prints is a valuable aid in documentation. For insurance purposes, proving the condition of a work prior to damage is essential. When you are making initial contacts with clients, agents, dealers, galleries, or employers, having a high-quality photographic portfolio can be an advantage; final judgments about an artist's work are usually made from the actual object, but first impressions more often come from viewing a photographic portfolio.

If you have a basic understanding of the operation of a 35 mm single-lens reflex camera and a light meter, making prints or slides of your work is not difficult. Because it is not a difficult process, artists can overlook details; this may be one reason why some artists seem to be satisfied with less than acceptable

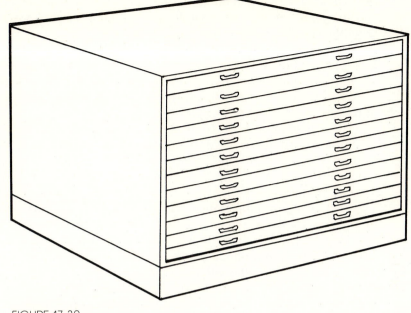

FIGURE 17.32
Print Storage Cabinet

For works on paper, matted or unmatted.

reproductions of their work. Once you see that a photograph of a painting, while not a perfect replica of the color, can be better than you thought, you may begin to pay more attention to how that good photograph was made. Many artists needlessly hire professional photographers to do work they can learn to do as well, at much less cost. You should keep in mind that the photography of works of art is a mechanical process not dependent on an outside esthetic. The art provides the esthetic, and the photograph must merely reproduce it as perfectly as possible. There is an art to good photography too, but it need not operate when you are photographing your work.

EQUIPMENT

The following selection of equipment is the minimum needed for the job.

The camera should be, as noted, a 35 mm single-lens reflex, with adjustable aperture and shutter speed. In most cases a normal 50 mm focal-length lens is all that is needed, although a telephoto lens or a 2× magnifying extension that fits between the lens and camera body is useful for making detailed closeups of a portion of a picture. Other camera sizes can be used if you want greater resolution of the image: 5 × 7, 8 × 10, or 11 × 14 formats are possible. These cameras, and the film, can be very expensive. The 35 mm format is most commonly used because few people expect to see perfect resolution, and they would rather make the final judgment based on the actual work anyway. For the highest quality color and sharpness—if you were publishing a catalog of your work, for instance—a large format camera is recommended.

A cable release screws into the shutter release button, allowing you to make a shot without touching the camera body. On long exposures, a cable release is useful in preventing any movement of the camera from spoiling the picture.

A professional tripod with adjustable legs and center post prevents movement of the camera during long exposures.

Tripod light stands are adjustable in height; attached bowl reflectors accept photoflood or tungsten photography lamps. Although it is possible to make good pictures using daylight, the amount and quality (color rendering) of the light can be extremely variable. For more consistent results, you can develop an operating scheme, using artificial light, that can become almost automatic after a while. Tungsten and photoflood lamps both put out a constant light in a predetermined strength and color rendering quality, although the strength deteriorates with time and the light output diminishes. The tungsten lamps should be rated at 3200° K and the photoflood lamps at 3400° K, abbreviated 3200 K and 3400 K. The figures refer to the color temperature of the light in degrees Kelvin (an absolute measure of temperature). Since these lamps are not very costly, it is advisable to have fresh lamps on hand; after about five hours of use, their output will diminish noticeably. Use the worn-out lamps as auxiliary lighting in the painting studio.

Many 35 mm cameras today have through-the-lens metering systems, which can be useful though not very accurate. For more precise results, a simple hand-held light meter is recommended.

Color filters are used to balance the color of the film to match the light being used to illuminate the picture. The filters are not expensive and are easily screwed onto the front of most lenses; some lenses may require a special mounting ring. Consult Table 17.2 to see which filters might be necessary. In any case, conditions can be arranged so that color filters are unnecessary. Pictures that have highly reflective surfaces can be difficult to light and photograph without picking up specular reflection (appearing as glaring whitish areas on the picture). Polarizing filters, which screw to the front of a lens, can eliminate most of the glare. They do not alter the color of the reproduction, but they do lower the amount of light reaching the film, making longer exposures necessary.

Finally, you will need a carpenter's level and an accurate tape measure.

FILMS

The selection of Kodak films shown in Table 17.2 can be used to make color slides or color prints, or black and white prints, with a 35 mm camera. Note the film speed, shown by the ASA/ISO number (American Standards Association/ International Organization for Standardization)—the lower the number, the more light required or the longer the exposure to make a good photograph. Also

TABLE 17.2
35 mm COLOR SLIDE AND PRINT FILMS

FILM	TYPE	LIGHT SOURCE	DAYLIGHT	PHOTOFLOODS (3400 K)	TUNGSTEN (3200 K)
Kodacolor II	Prints	Daylight, blue flash, or electronic flash	80* No filter†	25 80B	20 80A
Ektacolor Professional (short exposure)	Prints	Daylight, blue flash, or electronic flash	100 No filter	32 80B	25 80
Kodachrome II Professional A	Slides	Photoflood 3400 K	25 85	40 No filter	32 82A
High Speed Ektachrome Tungsten EHB	Slides	Tungsten 3200 K	80 85B	100 81A	125 No filter
Kodak Ektachrome 50 Professional	Slides	Tungsten 3200 K	40 85B	40 81A	50 No filter
Plus-X Tri-X	B&W prints B&W prints	The color temperature of the light source does not affect the performance of black and white films.			

* ISO film speed.
† Filter.

note the filters that may be required, depending on the light source. A complete listing of films for 35 mm cameras, and other camera sizes, can be found in the Eastman Kodak publication *Kodak Color Dataguide,* available in most camera stores.

Always check the data sheet supplied as a package insert with each film, since the ISO speed can be different from the assumed speed, depending on the factory batch. The data sheet will give the corrected speed for that roll of film.

Color films should be stored under refrigeration as a general rule, although most films are not that sensitive to heat. Refrigeration will extend the life of the film. Put the film in a plastic bag and store in a refrigerator to be sure of its stability; allow the film to come to room temperature before using—remove it from the refrigerator about two hours prior to use.

COLOR CONTROL

Also in the *Kodak Color Dataguide* are two pages of interest to artists who wish to control the color rendering of their prints. Color slides can be processed only to the level of quality at which they were photographed—the printer cannot adjust for photographer error—but prints can be adjusted if the Gray Scale and Color Control Patch standards are used. The Gray Scale is for value adjustment, the Color Control Patches for color.

For the first exposure of each roll of film, take a photograph of a picture with the *Dataguide*'s Gray Card, Gray Scale, and Color Control Patches placed in front of it, in the same lighting used on the picture. These control standards can then be used by the printer to adjust the color balance of the prints made from that roll, ensuring better color rendition and thus better color reproduction.

PRINTING

All Kodak color films can be processed by Kodak or by local laboratories. If you have a working relationship with a local printer, it is possible to get better prints than you can get from a mass processor like Kodak. Remember, though, that with slides, what is photographed is what is printed: No adjustments or improvements can be made.

Be patient with the printer. Only the artist really knows how the prints should look in comparison to the actual work. It probably will be necessary to go back to the laboratory the first few times until the desired quality is achieved. Usually the Color Control Patches and Gray Scales will help a great deal.

MAKING THE REPRODUCTION

Assuming that you will make the photographs inside under artificial light, the most convenient arrangement is to set aside a corner of the studio for photography. You can block off the windows with shades to prevent daylight from spoiling the color balance of the film; or you can photograph the works at night.

Not all pictures fit the 35 mm format perfectly. There is always some background showing around the edges of the slide or print image, a condition that can be distracting to someone looking at the reproduction. Masking the image, by cropping the print or by using an opaque silver or black slide-masking tape, can be tedious and time-consuming. Instead, make the background behind the subject as plain and nonreflective as possible. The best solution can be chosen from these alternatives:

1. Paint the wall against which the works are to be photographed with a flat black latex housepaint.

2. Buy a large roll of flat black photographic paper. The paper comes in widths up to about 12 feet (3.6 m) and can cover large areas of the background.

3. Use a large piece of black velvet to cover the wall behind the picture. Black velvet will absorb nearly all light striking it, and is the least reflective of the background coverings suggested here.

The black background will make masking the slide or cropping the print unnecessary.

Some device should be provided for holding the work perfectly vertical and level while it is being photographed. You can set up an ordinary painting easel to do the job, or remove the vertical member from an adjustable easel and attach it to the wall. Paint the easel with flat black latex paint. It is possible simply to put nails in the wall to hold the work, although getting the work level in this case is sometimes a bother. Be sure to allow plenty of room on either side of the picture-holding area for a variety of lighting arrangements (Figure 17.33).

Every artist develops a method of photographing art work, and there are so many variables in possible conditions (lighting, film type, and so on) that there can be no single perfect method. Nevertheless, it is helpful to consider a representative case: making a color slide of a painting, in an indoor studio, using artificial light. The film is Kodak's Ektachrome 50 (tungsten) ISO speed 50; 3200 K lamps are used. No filter is required.

1. Set the painting up on the easel. If the work is framed behind glass, remove it from the frame; photographs made through glass may show specular reflections from the glass, or reflections of the camera and photographer. Use the carpenter's level to make sure the picture is perfectly level and exactly vertical. For proper illumination of the object, it is necessary to get an even wash of light across its surface. Since the lighting will be from either side of the work, place it on the easel so that its narrowest dimension is vertical (Figure 17.34).

2. Attach the camera to the tripod and adjust it to a vertical position to conform to the arrangement of the picture. Place the tripod and camera on

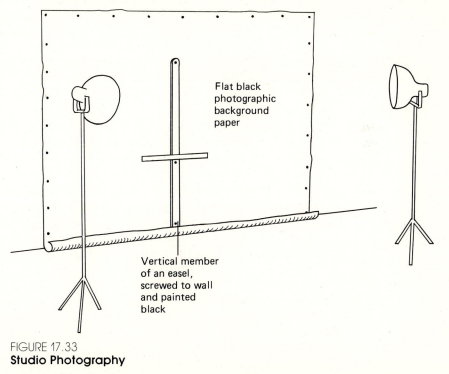

Flat black photographic background paper

Vertical member of an easel, screwed to wall and painted black

FIGURE 17.33
Studio Photography

A typical setup for making prints or slides. More than two lights may be necessary.

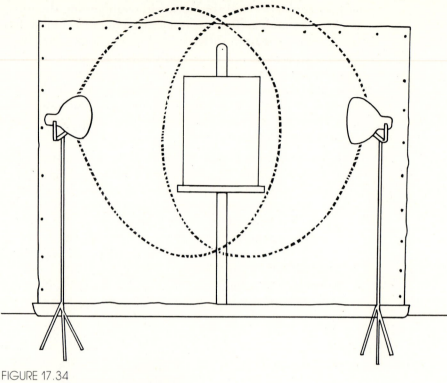

FIGURE 17.34
Arranging the Work for Lighting

On the easel, the painting's narrow dimension is vertical for the most even lighting.

a line with the exact center of the picture, far enough away from it so that the image fills the viewfinder of the camera comfortably. The plane of the back of the camera must be parallel to the plane of the picture to avoid distortion at the edges of the reproduction known as *parallax* (when straight vertical or horizontal lines appear to curve). Adjust the height of the camera so that the lens points directly at the center of the picture. You can do this visually, but to be more accurate, and to avoid parallax, make this quick calculation: divide the height of the picture by 2 and add the distance measured from the bottom of the picture to the floor. This total will give the required height of the center of the camera lens (Figure 17.35).

3. Position the light stands to either side of the painting, one on each side and each about the same distance away from it. They should be placed so that they are at an angle of 45° to the line running from the center of the picture to the camera, and their height should be the same as that of the camera (Figure 17.36).

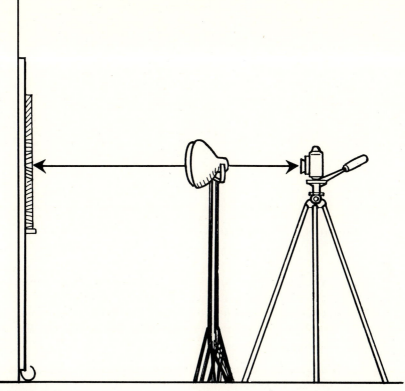

FIGURE 17.35
Orientation

Vertical and horizontal orientation of camera-to-picture to avoid parallax.

4. Turn on the lights and check to see that the picture is evenly lit. Use the light meter to take a number of readings of the light reflected off the picture at various points on its surface. Adjust the distance of the lights from the picture accordingly, to get an evenly lit picture.

5. Use the meter to figure the f-stop setting for the camera. Set the meter at ISO 50 (the speed of the film) and take readings at several points on the picture's surface. Since most pictures have both dark and light areas, and therefore are not equally reflective at all points across their surfaces, average the readings. It will be helpful to take a reading in the same light from the Kodak Gray Card, held close to the picture's surface. In both cases, hold the meter not more than 6 inches (15 cm) from the surface of the card or picture, and do not allow any cast shadows to interfere with the reading. Choose the setting indicated by the meter that allows the f-stop to be set as small as possible with the shutter speed set a $1/10$ of a second or faster. A

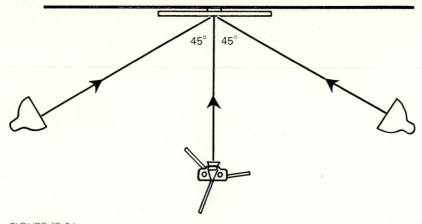

FIGURE 17.36
Position of Light Stands and Camera Relative to the Picture
Camera 90° perpendicular to picture; lights each 45° to the perpendicular.

very small aperture will allow you to record very fine details, but too slow a shutter speed may throw off the color balance of the film.

6. Check the camera to be sure the ISO setting matches that of the film. Adjust the f-stop and shutter speed according to the meter reading. Focus carefully and shoot.

Photographers commonly bracket exposures by taking two more shots with the aperture set a half-stop higher and a half-stop lower than the original setting. Some photographers suggest two additional exposures a full stop higher and lower than the original, for a total of 5 exposures. Bracketing will ensure at least one acceptable reproduction of the picture, and possibly a few.

If taking so many shots of each picture seems like an awful expenditure of film—you can get only 7 theoretically perfect slides from a 36-exposure roll—consider this: It is more trouble to set up the studio to reshoot a set of slides because an entire roll was either under- or overexposed. Furthermore, when shooting in this manner, you get 5 slides of each picture, and it is always helpful to have an extra set. Shooting slides or prints from the original picture is often preferable to having copies made from the slide (copies from a color negative are usually acceptable—that is, after all, how the original print was made—but having duplicate negatives is also desirable).

LABELING SLIDES AND PRINTS

When the slides have been returned from the processor, label them immediately. The information on the label should include the following:

1. Artist's name.
2. Title of the work.

3. Date of the work.
4. Dimensions of the work, height preceding width.
5. Medium or technique.
6. An indication of the top of the work, so the viewer can orient the slide correctly in a projector.
7. A notice of copyright, if desired.

The same information should be put on a label stuck on the back of a print. Do not write on the back of the actual print.

STORING SLIDES AND PRINTS

Light will fade most color photographic reproductions. Store prints and slides in the dark. Mylar polyester slide sheets with small pockets for individual slides, with three-hold margins for insertion into three-ring binders, are good, and the slide can be looked at without being handled. Polyester envelopes for prints are also available, with the three-hole margins.

The three-ring binders can be kept in a box with other records about the work, to keep them from getting dusty. All this is just a matter of organization; once a system is established, none of it is difficult or time-consuming.

TRANSPORTING ART WORKS

The more a work of art is handled, the more likely it is that damage can occur. Transporting a work can be significantly hazardous unless the work is properly protected.

ASSEMBLING THE CRATE

Crates must be custom-built to accommodate the individual works properly, but the carpentry involved is no more complicated than that used to make strainers or bracing for panels.

A crate is essentially a suspension system in which the picture floats, so it must be made slightly larger in every dimension than the work it is to hold, in order to make room for the added packing materials. As a rule, add 4 inches (10 cm) to length, 4 inches (10 cm) to width, and 4 to 5 inches (10–13 cm) to the depth of the work, to arrive at the interior dimensions of the crate. Thus a painting 16 by 20 by 2 inches thick ($40 \times 50 \times 5$ cm) will require a crate with interior measurements of 20 by 24 by 6 inches ($50 \times 60 \times 15$ cm). Remember to take into account the thickness of the wood when calculating the dimensions of the lumber for purchase.

MATERIALS

1. Handsaw.
2. Hammer.

3. Slotted screwdriver.
4. Carpenter's square.
5. Staple gun.
6. Electric drill with bits. The drill bits should have the same diameter as the shaft of the flathead wood screws used to fasten the top of the crate.
7. Plywood ½ or ¾ inch (1.25–1.89 cm) thick. Plywood forms the flat sides of the crate; thinner plywood can be used for small crates, but thicker plywood should be used for large crates.
8. White pine, yellow pine, or fir boards. The boards are nominally 1 inch (2.5 cm) thick, but usually measure about ¾ inch (1.89 cm) thick. They come in various widths—2, 3, 4, 6 inches—and since they are used to build the collar of the crate, choose the width equal to the correct depth for the crate. Also obtain some lengths of 1- by 3-inch (2.5 × 5 cm) boards to use for bracing the flat sides of the crate, and for battens inside the crate.
9. A strong carpenter's wood glue.
10. Masking tape.
11. A selection of flathead wood screws and countersink washers.
12. A selection of flathead nails. Longer nails can be used to assemble the collar of the crate. Shorter nails are used to attach the bracing to the plywood sides, and the plywood to the bottom of the crate.
13. Cushioning materials. These are used to float the work in the crate, and should be light, strong, and bulky but compressible. The choices include Bubble-pak, cells of air sealed in plastic, available in rolls, forming a strong and lightweight cushioning; Kimpak, multilayered paper packing that is strong and soft; foam lining used as cushioning under wall-to-wall carpeting, an open-cell foam, thin and soft, and relatively inexpensive.
14. Brown wrapping paper.
15. Waterproofing materials, for making the interior of the crate water-resistant. Some writers advise against the use of plastic, since it can trap moisture and cause condensation inside the crate, but plastic is acceptable if the wrapping is not airtight. Thin plastic sheets can be obtained in rolls. A water-resistant paper for lining crates is available from Glas-Kraft or a local paper distributor (see Appendix D). It is a laminate of paper and a water-resistant core material.
16. Corrugated cardboard (inexpensive) or Fome-Cor (expensive).

METHOD

1. Cut the wood for the collar and sides to the proper dimensions.
2. Assemble the collar using nails through butt joints. For very secure joints, use glue.
3. Attach the bottom of the crate to the collar with nails. Glue if desired.
4. Put the top of the crate in place and drill holes for the screws. Attach the top with flathead wood screws and countersunk washer. Mark the top of

the crate and the collar at each screw head so that the top of the crate can be realigned properly.

5. If the crate is large enough to require bracing, cut and attach bracing struts with nails—and glue, if desired.

6. Disassemble the crate and carefully check the interior for protruding nails or splinters. Remove by filing them down or cutting them off.

PACKING THE CRATE

Before packing the picture, check to see that it is snug in the frame, and that there are no loose wires, hanging apparatus, or other dangling parts that could damage the work. The wire should be removed or taped down. Cover glass—but not acrylic or styrene—with closely spaced strips of masking tape to hold it in case it breaks (Figure 17.37).

1. Line the inside of the crate with the waterproof paper or the plastic sheeting. Cut two pieces to fit the top and bottom covers and one long strip to fit around the inside of the collar. Use glue or short staples to attach the liner—be sure the staples are completely flush with the inside of the crate.

2. Cut corrugated cardboard to fit the bottom of the crate.

3. Wrap the painting in brown paper to protect it from dust. Use masking tape to hold the paper.

4. Make pads for the corners of the painting. Use either Kimpak or foam carpet padding cut into long strips and rolled into tubes. Fold the pads

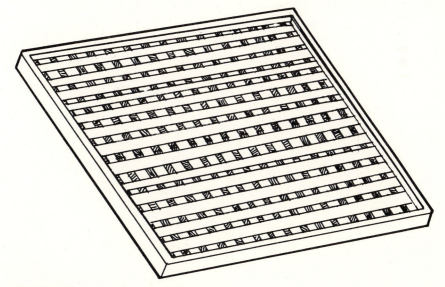

FIGURE 17.37
Masking Glass before Shipping

diagonally over the front of the painting at each corner and staple them to the back of the frame. An alternative to corner padding, but one that takes up more room in the crate, is to make an envelope for the painting out of the Bubble-pak. Cut a piece of corrugated cardboard large enough to fit the front of the painting and attach it to the frame sides with masking tape. Cut a length of Bubble-pak that will fold over and enclose both sides of the painting. Enclose the work in the Bubble-pak and tape it in place; to prevent condensation, do not make this enclosure airtight.

5. Place the picture face down inside the crate, and adjust its position so there is an equal amount of space all around the picture between it and the inside of the collar. Fill this space with rolls of Kimpak, Bubble-pak, or foam padding. Stuff all the spaces firmly until the work is snugly padded and cannot move around inside the crate.

6. Cut another piece of corrugated cardboard to fit on top of the picture and place it in the crate.

7. If there is a space left between the cardboard and the inside of the top cover of the crate, prepare two battens to hold the package tightly (Figure 17.38). The battens are screwed to the inside of the crate's collar.

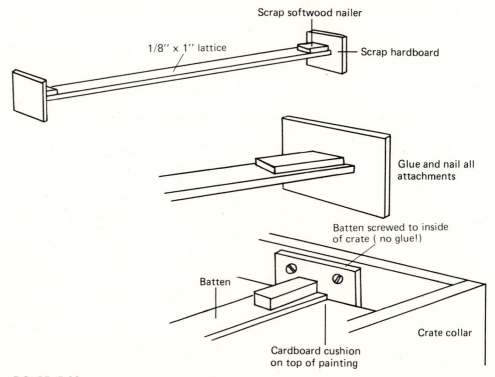

Scrap softwood nailer

1/8″ x 1″ lattice

Scrap hardboard

Glue and nail all attachments

Batten screwed to inside of crate (no glue!)

Batten

Crate collar

Cardboard cushion on top of painting

FIGURE 17.38
Attaching Batten to the Inside of a Crate

8. Attach the cover of the crate (Figure 17.39 shows crate construction and packing).

A crate for more than one picture can easily be built. Use ¾-inch (1.89-cm) plywood for the collar, and make the crate any depth necessary. When packing, follow all the steps outlined above up to step 6. Repeat steps 2 through 6 for each picture.

Instead of using battens to hold the work inside the crate, you can cut sheets of Bubble-pack to fill up the empty space.

A crate for many pictures of different sizes can also be built, although the construction is likely to be more complicated and the resulting box quite heavy. Each picture should have its own individual space within the crate. (See Figure 17.40 for a suggested scheme.)

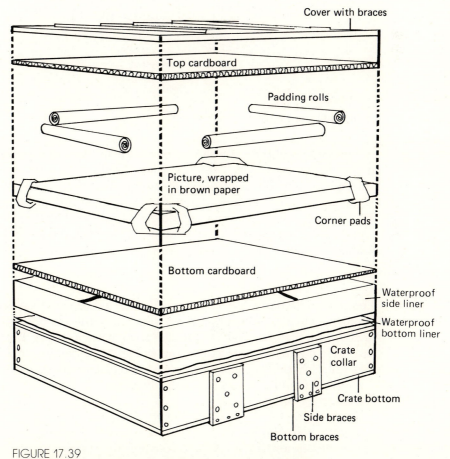

FIGURE 17.39
Exploded View of Crate Construction and Packing

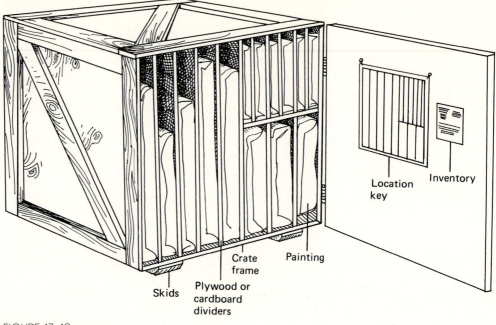

Location key · Inventory · Crate frame · Painting · Skids · Plywood or cardboard dividers

FIGURE 17.40
Multiple-Picture Crate

The outside of the crate should be clearly marked to identify its contents. Use arrows to indicate "Up," for the crate should always be standing on edge to relieve strain on the picture planes inside. Use the words "Work of Art" and "Fragile," and the symbols of a broken wine glass and an umbrella, to show that the contents are fragile and should be kept dry. If the work is to be shipped overseas, use the phrase "Use No Hooks" and the symbol of a hook with an X through it to indicate restrictions on crane use at the port.

SHIPPING

The size and weight of the crate will determine which carrier can handle the shipment. Smaller packages can be shipped by the United States Postal Service (USPS) or a private carrier, United Parcel Service (UPS). Both USPS and UPS have weight and size restrictions and will limit the amount of insurance coverage they will allow on the object. They may also place restrictions on the contents if it is a one-of-a-kind work of art. An advantage of these carriers is that they will deliver to the door.

Common carriers—ordinary freight trucking companies—will handle larger crates, but sometimes refuse to carry works of art. Insurance coverage is reasonable, however, and it is possible to convince the carrier that the crate is substantial and will prevent damage to the work. Common carriers will sometimes deliver to the door, but often require the recipient to pick up the shipment at a central distribution point.

Some common carriers specialize in shipping works of art, and provide the special handling occasionally needed by these objects. Workers for these companies have experience packing and handling art objects, and their trucks do not carry any other kinds of freight; some of these carriers will even ship uncrated work in specially padded vehicles. The rates for these shipments can be substantially higher than those charged by ordinary carriers, but the handling of the work is of the highest professional standards.

Whichever service you choose for shipping, be sure to be aware of the following variables:

1. Packing or crating requirements
2. Size and weight restrictions
3. Insurance limitations
4. Delivery arrangements

Always make sure that the recipient of the shipment understands what arrangements have been made for delivery of the work.

TRANSIT STORAGE

Sometimes the work being shipped must be stored for a day or two before delivery can be made. If this is a possibility, it is wise to find out what kind of storage facilities are being used. A warehouse with a controlled environment—at the very least the space should be heated—is preferable to a shed or open loading dock somewhere. Remember that works of art are fragile and can be damaged by rapid changes in atmospheric conditions.

CHAPTER 18

CONSERVATION AND RESTORATION

It is not our purpose here to instruct artists in *restoration,* the art and science of the repair of art works, or *conservation,* the art and science of the preservation of art works. Conservators, as they are known in this country, are professionals who have received highly specialized training and have considerable experience. Painters, if they are so inclined, can play a part in conservation by using quality materials and durable processes, but they should not really practice art conservation. In fact, probably more paintings have been irreparably damaged by amateurs—painters who thought they knew what they were doing—than successfully treated by professionally trained conservators. But it is useful, at least, for the artist to be aware of the kinds of harm paintings can suffer, and how these ills are treated. For those artists who might be interested in pursuing conservation as a profession, the end of this chapter lists the few professional training and internship programs in the United States.

All works of art are different and each, therefore, is treated as an individual case in a conservation studio. Some general procedures are followed in many cases, but to generalize where conservation practices are concerned can be dangerous; it can lead to assumptions about treatment methods. The following discussion of the damage that pictures may sustain, and the methods of treating it, is presented in the most general way, with the understanding that several types of defects or injuries may occur at once in a work, and that the conditions may alter the method of treatment. In other words, this is *not* a guide for the do-it-yourselfer.

INSPECTION OF THE WORK AND POSSIBLE CONSOLIDATION

All works of art that are to undergo restorative or preservative treatment must be thoroughly inspected. Color and black and white photographs of both sides of the work—the obverse, or front, and reverse, or back—are made before and after treatment.

376

A complete visual inspection under normal light is carried out, and the condition of the support and design layers is noted. If necessary, the work is also inspected under other kinds of light: infrared, ultraviolet, and by X ray, each of which can reveal information about the paint and support. In museums, a chemical analysis of the paint is often done to determine the authenticity of the work, or to place it in a historical context. All the information gathered from these inspections is recorded in writing in a separate file for each work; from the file, an individual plan for treatment can be developed. Only after consultation with the owner, including an explanation of suggested treatment, is the treatment attempted.

If the picture is in any sort of fragile condition, it must be consolidated before treatment can begin. Consolidation effectively stabilizes the design layer by immobilizing it under a reinforcing covering. The covering is usually small patches of very thin but strong mulberry paper applied as a patchwork over the fragile surface of the work, using a reversible glue. The mulberry paper can be further reinforced by a covering of thin muslin.

In all cases it is necessary to determine the solubility of the paint layer before consolidating it. Oil paint, for instance, cannot be consolidated with an adhesive that needs a strong aromatic solvent to remove it, since these solvents can affect the paint layer. A water-soluble glue may be used in this case, if there is no danger of loosening the ground from the support.

DAMAGE TO SUPPORTS

The type of damage that affects a work depends, in part, on the kind of support used. Paper, wood, and fabric are each susceptible to particular forms of disrepair.

PAPER SUPPORTS

Inherent faults in the paper can derive from its constituent materials, in which case not much can be done to restore the work. A cheap, acidic paper can be stabilized so that it will change little in the future, but it cannot be returned to its original state.

Mold Mold is characterized by brownish or gray-greenish spots or stains on the paper. Caused by too humid an environment, mold stains—also called foxing—can be treated by removing the work to a dry place and exposing it to circulating air and sunlight for a day to kill the organism. The object is sometimes placed in a closed container containing a fungicide, whose slow evaporation eventually kills the mold.

Stains Water stains or discolorations caused by atmospheric pollutants can sometimes be treated by bleaching the work with hydrogen peroxide vapors in a closed environment.

Acidic Papers These can be deacidified with a proprietary mixture called Wei T'o (available from Conservation Materials, Ltd.; see Appendix D). The solution, in three forms, is a dispersion of a buffering agent in volatile organic solvents. The solvents carry the buffer into the paper fibers, where it converts to magnesium carbonate, an alkaline reserve, by reacting with the water vapor and carbon dioxide in the air. The solution can be applied to the paper by brushing, spraying, dipping, or roll coating.

Insect Damage Silverfish, cockroaches, termites, and woodworms will all eat paper, and particularly enjoy animal glue sizes and vegetable gum binders. An insecticide is applied, and the work is removed to a safer environment.

Tears A patch can be made of a paper that is thinner than the paper on which the work was done. The patch has feathered edges, made by water-cutting and separating the fibers around the edges of the patch. The patch is attached with a weak reversible glue to the reverse of the object. Tests must be made to determine that the solvent for the glue does not affect the support paper or the design media.

Creases, Warps, Wrinkles These are caused by careless handling, folding, rolling, and so on. Depending on the nature of the media used in making the work, these physical defects can be reduced by exposing the object to a humidified atmosphere, by pressing under a moderate weight, or a combination of the two.

WOOD SUPPORTS

Warping This is caused by uneven tension between two faces of the work, or by uneven graining between the two faces. If the support is a grained structure such as a thick, solid wooden panel and the design layer is not in fragile condition, the panel can sometimes be straightened by exposure in a humidity chamber. When the work is removed from the chamber and dries out, the warp eventually reappears. The reappearance of the warp may be prevented or lessened by attaching a felt-lined aluminum channel brace around the perimeter of the support. Occasionally the conservator decides that attempting to remove the warp will cause more damage than leaving it alone. Cradling, the practice of attaching slotted braces to the rear of the panel running parallel to the grain, with smaller movable braces placed into the slots and running perpendicular to the grain, is rarely used today—it is one of those techniques that, though ingenious for its time, was discovered to have caused more damage than it prevented.

Cracks or Checks These splits in the wood can accompany warping, but can also be the result of the support's reaction to atmospheric changes. Sometimes the splits are filled with an epoxy or other inert consolidant, in order to stabilize the structure. These visual interruptions in the design layer can be lessened by in-painting.

Insect Holes Boring insects can honeycomb a support and leave it in a very weakened state. Treatment with an insecticide kills the insects. The channels and holes are then infused with a wax or epoxy consolidant to stabilize the structure.

Transferring Occasionally the support is so deteriorated that the paint films are actually supporting the panel—this occurs more often with pictures on textile supports, however. In this case, the design layer can be transferred to another support. First the paint layer is consolidated and immobilized by a covering of reversible adhesive (made with a solvent that will not affect the design layer) and thin rice paper. In some situations a muslin covering is used for added strength. The support is turned over and placed on a padded surface—if the paint has high impasto, the surface can be a reverse mold of the picture, to preserve the configuration of the surface projections. The panel is then carefully planed off the rear of the painting, down to the reverse of the ground; if the ground has deteriorated, even it is sometimes removed. While still immobilized, the paint layer is then attached to a new ground and support. Because of the delicacy and extreme risk of this operation, it is used only under the most unusual circumstances.

FABRIC SUPPORTS

The defects of fabric supports result from exposure to light and atmosphere. Embrittlement and general weakening are inevitable for the commonly used cotton duck and linen. Treatment of this kind of deterioration is usually accomplished by first stabilizing and consolidating the face of the picture, then attaching a new support to the back of the old. The operation is called *lining;* when an old lining is stripped from the back of a support and a new lining is applied, the procedure is called *relining.*

The new lining material has traditionally been new, smooth linen, of a weight similar to that of the old material. In the last two decades or so, the more stable synthetic fabrics, such as woven fiberglass or woven polyester sailcloth, have gained prominence; more recent developments make the use of light but very rigid honeycombed panels possible. These include cast polyester on aluminum honeycomb, or aluminum panel on aluminum honeycomb.

The procedure for lining begins with the usual close inspection of the picture, followed by stabilization and consolidation of the design layer if necessary. The picture is then removed from the auxiliary support, and the back is carefully cleaned; loose threads around tears are trimmed, but the original stretching edge of the picture is left intact. A strainer is prepared, and a new lining material (if it is a fabric) is stretched tightly on the frame. A wax and resin adhesive is prepared. This kind of adhesive is strong and penetrating but easily removed by gentle heating and/or the application of mild solvents.

The new support is placed face down on a release paper surface, which will not allow the adhesive to stick. The wax and resin adhesive is brushed into the rear of the new support and then spread out and forced into and through the fabric by gentle remelting with an iron. The temperature of the iron is set as low as possible, but warm enough to melt the adhesive.

The painting is likewise placed face down on a release paper surface, padded to prevent the flattening of thick paint, and the same wax and resin impregnation is carried out. The temperature of the iron is kept at its lowest setting to prevent the burning of the paint layers. When the back of the old picture has cooled, the new support with its coating of adhesive is aligned over it, and the two are stuck together using gentle heat and pressure. The strainer is then removed from the lining and the newly backed picture is restretched on its original chassis—although sometimes a new chassis is used.

A more recent method of lining uses a vacuum hot table, a table covered with seamless aluminum sheeting, heated from beneath by a series of electric elements. Suspended over the table is a frame holding a loosely stretched rubber blanket and a vacuum system connected to a vacuum pump. Newer lining tables are bigger, and do not use the suspended rubber blanket; instead, the vacuum system is incorporated into the perimeter of the table itself, and the rubber blanket has been replaced with a thick, transparent sheet of polyester film.

The picture is prepared in the usual way, but the new lining material is not stretched on a strainer. Rather, the adhesive is applied to both the picture back and lining, and the two are aligned and stuck together by hand. (There is a new material, a silicone-based, adhesive-coated woven fiber glass fabric that needs no such preparation. It is simply placed on the hot table, adhesive side up, and the painting is placed on it. The adhesive is activated by the heat of the table.) Release paper is placed on the hot table, and the lining and picture are placed face up on the paper. Strips of corrugated cardboard may be placed around the perimeter of the picture to act as channels to draw off excess adhesive. The table is then warmed just enough to melt the adhesive.

As the table is heating, the clear polyester film is placed over the surface of the table. If the object is large, the whole table is used; if not, small-diameter sausagelike tubes of sand-filled fabric can be placed around it, on top of the plastic film. A seal around the edge of the table is engaged, and the vacuum pump is turned on. Air is pumped from beneath the covering, to a pressure not higher than about 25 pounds per square inch (11.25 kg/2.5 cm^2), and the soft plastic film conforms to the surface irregularities of the picture. The heating elements are turned off and the picture is quickly cooled with fans while the vacuum continues to work. When all has cooled, the plastic film is removed, the cardboard is discarded, and the picture is taken off the table. It is then restretched on a chassis—a new one if necessary, the original if possible. Naturally, the process of lining varies from practitioner to practitioner and depends on the condition of the work.

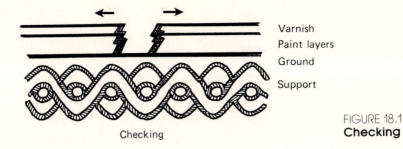

FIGURE 18.1
Checking

DEFECTS OF PAINT FILMS

Checking If the paint binder oxidizes completely or becomes brittle, either from stresses internal to the paint or from stresses external to the paint (atmospheric changes), cracks that follow the weave of a fabric support or the grain of a wooden support will appear (Figure 18.1).

Powdering The complete loss of the paint binder may leave pigment particles on the surface of the picture that can easily be knocked off. This particularly dangerous condition can be caused by excessive use of a thinner during painting.

Cleavage An area of the paint film may lift completely from the ground, or the paint and ground may lift completely from the support. This can be caused by any number of things: poor-quality mediums or paints, moisture in the ground, or mechanical damage (Figure 18.2).

Blind Cleavage This is a blisterlike condition similar to cleavage except that the paint may not be cracked on the surface. What cannot be seen may be dangerous for the life of the picture (Figure 18.3).

Cupping Small islands of paint crack through expansion of the support and then are pushed together when the support shrinks. When the flakes are pushed together, their edges can be raised above the plane of the picture, resulting in a cuplike profile (Figure 18.4).

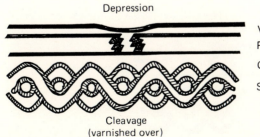

FIGURE 18.2
Cleavage (Varnished over)

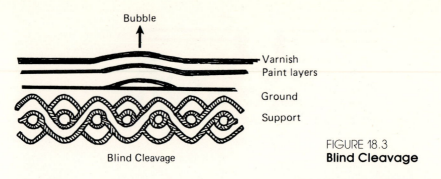

FIGURE 18.3

Blind Cleavage

Cracking   Also called *crackle* or *craquelure*. If the paint film or the ground loses its plasticity, many different types of cracking can occur. The damage can be caused by careless handling of the picture—rolling, for instance—or can come from the cyclical expansion and contraction of the support. Each condition can cause a separate and distinctive type of crack: traction cracks and alligatoring are examples.

Flaking   This can be caused by mechanical damage or atmospheric fluctuation, resulting in the dislodging of small chips of paint. This is a dangerous condition, since the whole picture may be in jeopardy.

Wrinkling   Also called reticulation. This can be caused by an excess of binder or vehicle in the paint film, or by an inferior binder, or, in oil paints by excessive use of a drier. Short of softening the film with very active solvent vapors, there is not much that can be done about this condition.

Bloom   This is more often a defect of the varnish layer, where moisture has become trapped between it and the paint film. The symptoms are a bluish- or grayish-white veil over the picture that obscures the image. It can be treated by drying the picture or, more commonly, by removing the varnish and revarnishing.

Fading   This can be caused by overexposure of the picture to ultraviolet light, but is also often the result of using inferior and impermanent pigments or other colorants. Other color changes can be caused by reaction of colorants to atmo-

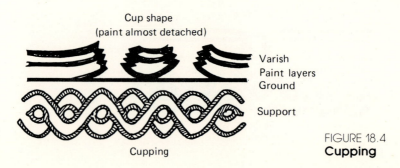

FIGURE 18.4

Cupping

spheric conditions, or other colorants or mixtures of colorants. Short of extensive retouching, which is usually advised against, there is nothing to be done about faded or changed colors.

CLEANING

Once the picture has been inspected, photographed, consolidated (if necessary), and lined (again, if necessary), it can be cleaned. This is a most delicate procedure, since the wrong use of the wrong material or method can easily destroy the picture.

Usually it is necessary first to remove any facing materials or excess lining adhesive. If no analysis of the paint film has been conducted, an inconspicuous corner of the work can be checked to see what effect various solvents have on it or the varnish layer, if any. Based on observation and experience, a selection of solvents to be used in the cleaning can be made. It is critical at this point that the conservator choose only those solvents which will remove surface dirt. A different set of solvents may be required for the varnish, if that is also dirty or yellowed and is to be removed. The conservator also selects solvents or mixtures of solvents that act as restrainers (also called "checks"); these solutions can instantly counter the action of the cleaning mixture and stop any damage to the picture.

Cleaning is a tedious process. No friction or vigorous mechanical methods are used. Solvents theoretically do all the work. Cotton or foam swabs are used to clean small sections of the picture at a time, and the swab is carefully examined to note the appearance of color, which could indicate that the paint film is being attacked. Swabs are discarded and replaced as soon as they become dirty. The restrainer is wiped over each section of the surface that has been cleaned to stop any further solvent action, and once the cleaning operation is completed the restrainer is used to buffer the entire surface of the work.

Naturally, different kinds of paints and paint and support systems require different approaches, and each work is treated as an individual case. There is no set system of cleaning that can be applied to all situations. This is why the diagnosis and treatment of the ills of art objects is work for the trained professional conservator.

REPAIR AND IN-PAINTING

Tears, holes, and lost areas of paint can be repaired by filling and leveling the voids with reversible putty mixtures such as stiff glue gesso. Depending on the media, it is sometimes necessary to isolate the paint film from repair operations with a thin coat of reversible varnish; sometimes it is not possible to isolate the picture in this way.

Once the voids in the picture plane have been filled, they can be treated to become less obtrusive. The process is popularly known as *retouching,* but is also called *in-painting.*

There is a great deal of disagreement about just what in-painting should accomplish. Some say it should be instantly recognizable as the work of another hand, but also very subtle, so as to do nothing to either add to or subtract from the artistic merits of the work. Others argue that in-painting can be entirely lost in the body of the work, indistinguishable from the original. The conservator's approach to this task can be determined by how extensive the damage is. It would be foolhardy and dishonest to try to replace—in the style of the artist—large areas of the missing image, but it might not be so bad to do this if the damage is confined to tiny, isolated spots.

A reversible paint is used for in-painting, so that it can be removed at a later time. The paint is rarely the same as that which was used to execute the original work, so that its removal will not affect the picture. Only those areas in which paint is lost are in-painted; original paint is not covered. Once the in-painting is completed, the entire picture is given a thin coating of a reversible spray varnish —if varnishing is compatible with the medium and/or the desires of the artist.

ARTIST AS CONSERVATOR

The foregoing should not be construed as instructions on how to repair paintings. It is reasonable for an artist to consider attempting conservation treatment on his or her own works, but not on anyone else's works.

Artists should advise their clients that if there is a physical problem with a painting, they should be given an opportunity to inspect it before the client goes to a conservator. The artist might be able to determine what went wrong and how to fix it—especially if there is a good label. At the least, an artist confronted with the prospect of a deteriorating painting that is only five or ten years old might stop and think a moment about quality materials and sound technique. That perhaps could be the most positive result of what could be an unsettling experience.

TRAINING PROGRAMS

It is unfortunate for the future of our cultural heritage that conservation training is not more actively supported in this country. In fact, there are only three professional conservation programs in the United States that provide scientifically based training. Several other small institutions offer additional training as internships to those who have completed the professional programs. There are also small schools which operate on the basis of apprenticeships; many fine conservators in this country were trained by apprenticing with well-known and respected conservators. In an apprenticeship program, however, it is possible to learn a great deal about how one person treats art objects, but very little about the science of materials. The following academically supported programs can provide sound training. Artists can make very good conservators, and interested aspirants are encouraged to write for more information. Be aware that the entrance requirements are stringent, and the competition for a limited number of spaces is very stiff.

Conservation Center of the Institute of Fine Arts
New York University
New York, NY 10021

Art Conservation Department
State University College at Buffalo
P.O. Box 71
Cooperstown, NY 13326
   (This program will move to the SUC Buffalo campus during the summer of 1987.)

Art Conservation Program
303 Old College
University of Delaware
Newark, DE 19711

The Center for Conservation and Technical Studies at the Fogg Art Museum, Harvard University no longer has a training program. It provides a limited number of internships for those who have completed at least two years of formal training in a conservation program.

Each of these programs has slightly different admissions policies, but generally they include one or two undergraduate courses in chemistry, a strong background in art history, and demonstrable manual dexterity (studio arts experience). Proficiency in a foreign language is also desirable.

The American Institute for Conservation of Historic and Artistic Works, Inc. (AIC), Kingle Mansion, 3545 Williamsburg Lane NW, Washington, DC 20008, is the professional society to which many conservators belong. Anyone can be a member of the AIC merely by paying the annual dues; only trained conservators who can demonstrate their competence before an examining board may be fellows of the AIC. This distinction is useful when seeking the services of a professional conservator, or when recommending one to a client. The AIC has also published a Code of Ethics and Standard of Practice that is a valuable reference for those considering entering the profession. In addition, the AIC has been lobbying to have conservators certified by a licensing board.

When seeking advice about conservation, or sending a client to a conservator, begin with the local museum. If the museum does not have a conservator on staff, write to the AIC.

APPENDIX A

PAINTING TOOLS AND EQUIPMENT

This section covers the auxiliary materials you will use when painting, but is also about some other tools, information, equipment, conditions, products, and situations you will encounter in general.

PALETTES

The word has a double meaning: it is the selection or range of hues employed in the painting, and the surface on which the artist mixes the colors.

The selection of pigments is important. There are vast lists of colors to choose from in every manufacturer's catalogue (and a quick glance at the pigment list in Table 7.1 should be enough to startle a beginner), so here is a limited list with which to start. A *limited palette* contains colors of relatively low chroma so that color harmonies are easily made. Students will find it instructive to use the following colors for a beginning painting:

Ivory black: a cool black that when mixed
    with white yields a cool, bluish gray.
Flake (lead) white: a warm, quick-drying
    white.
Yellow ochre: a dull yellow earth that
    when mixed with ivory black and
    flake white gives an olive green.
Light red oxide: a dull red earth color
    which when mixed with ivory black
    and flake white gives a dull purple.

These four colors have been used to produce subtle and interesting works by students in a beginning class. They allow the artist some degree of freedom from the difficulties of mixing high-chroma hues, while forcing him or her to make deliberate mixtures lest the result be muddied.

A slightly more advanced palette may contain, in addition to those pigments above, the following:

Cadmium red light: a bright, slightly
    yellow red, dense and opaque. Use the
    real cadmium pigment.

Alizarin crimson or natural madder lake:
   both alike in hue, a deep cool red.
Ultramarine blue: a relatively strong
   pure blue hue.
Cobalt blue: a cool blue indispensable for
   making clear purple mixtures with
   various reds. Do not use a substituted
   "cobalt blue hue."
Viridian: a weak, transparent, but useful
   green.
Chromium oxide opaque: the stronger,
   opaque version of viridian.
Cadmium yellow light (or lemon): a
   bright, strong, and opaque yellow.
   Use the real cadmium pigment.

These additions to the limited palette provide an extended range of chroma.

Before jumping to the next step, it is helpful to spend an afternoon mixing colors from the two palettes just given. Color charts reproduced in books are absolutely no substitute for finding out about color firsthand, and specific instructions about what to mix with what also do no good. Because one cadmium red may be quite different from another, to say, "Mix cadmium red with cobalt blue to get a deep purple" without specifying exact brands can be misleading. The best thing to do is to spend a few hours making all the mixtures possible from a range of colors, along with at least ten value steps for each of the mixtures. Try to avoid using black to make the dark values. Use the complementary hue instead, and remember that darkness is a relative term—one color is dark next to another, not by itself.

To extend the range of chroma even further, add these pigments:

Phthalocyanine blue
Phthalocyanine green
Arylide (Hansa) yellow

These very bright hues can disrupt the quiet, low-chroma palette first given. Use bright color judiciously, and do not confuse brightness with lightness.

The palette is also the surface on which one mixes the paints. There are several kinds: wooden, porcelain-coated steel, glass, or tear-off-and-throw-away paper, among others.

Wooden palettes, especially the arm-held kind (Figure A.1), are the traditional favorite. They are usually stained a dark reddish color, the better to see relative color mixtures. Arrange the colors in a organized fashion (Figure A.2) and leave the center clear for mixing. Instead of cleaning the paint off entirely at the end of a session, use a rag to rub some of the leftover paint into the wood. In time the palette will develop a natural gray patina that is excellent for making comparative color mixtures. An alternative to buying an expensive wooden palette is to make one from a well-sanded and shellacked piece of ⅜-inch (9 mm) thick plywood; shellac both sides to keep it from warping.

Porcelain-coated steel palettes are expensive but can be found as food-service trays in restaurant supply houses. The porcelain should be white. These palettes are easy to clean, but one must be careful not to chip the porcelain.

Glass palettes, at least ¼ inch (6 mm) thick tempered plate glass, are a favorite because they are easy to keep clean: Dried paint is quickly and efficiently stripped away with a

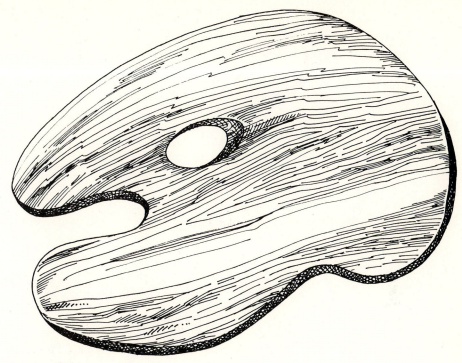

FIGURE A.1
Arm-held Wooden Palette

single-edged razor blade. This kind of palette should be securely fastened to a sturdy table top, not hand-held. Place a piece of white paper beneath the glass in order to see the colors; better yet, paint the table top with an acrylic emulsion artists' paint mixed to a neutral gray. Against a hueless neutral gray, the most subtle color mixtures are easily seen.

Tear-off paper palettes are convenient: At the end of the day the used paper is torn off, exposing a fresh surface on which to mix the next day's paints. These palettes are also a waste of money; with very little effort, one can make a far better and more durable surface on which to work.

BRUSHES

These long-handled implements are probably the most important tool an artist can purchase. It is therefore wise to buy the best brushes, since only the best will stand up to daily use and maintain their performance over the years. A cheap brush is not inexpensive—it is cheap.

Bristle Brushes

Fine bristle brushes come in many shapes and sizes, though this huge variety is a twentieth-century development. The bristle comes from hogs and boars raised in Switzerland, China, India, France, Russia, and the Balkan mountains of eastern Europe; the best bristle

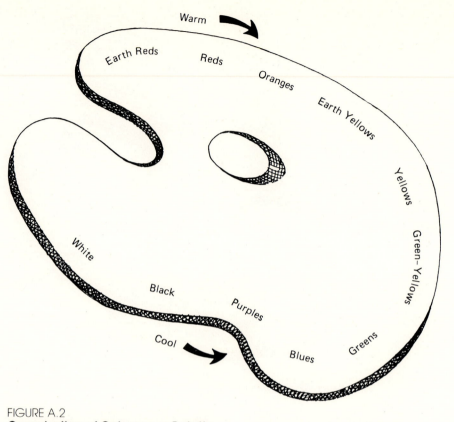

FIGURE A.2
Organization of Colors on a Palette

is from a 3-inch (8 cm) wide strip of hair running down the spine of the animal, from neck to tail, where it is long and springy. The length of the bristle may vary from 1 to 10 inches (2.5–25 cm) and can be black, brown, gray, or white. The kind used in the finest artists' bristle brushes are natural white, not bleached—bleaching can weaken the bristle. The significant feature of a good bristle is that its tip does not come to a point, like a hair, but rather has two or three points called flags (Figure A.3). The flags enable the bristle to hold more paint than a plain point. Bristle brushes that do not have flags may have been trimmed by the manufacturer: this is a sign of a cheap brush.

The bristles are bundled, cleaned, wrapped in a form, sterilized, sorted by length, and hand-tied into separate bundles for each brush. The various shapes of brushes (Figure A.4) are achieved by hand-tying the bundles, not by trimming the bristles. The bundles are then "cupped" into shape and set in a ferrule using a vinyl or epoxy resin adhesive. The size and shape of the ferrule, the best of which are made of seamless nickel-plated copper, will contribute to the shape and size of the brush. Unlike rubber-based, heat-cured compounds used to set the hairs or bristles of other brushes, the compounds used to set artists' white bristle brushes can be soluble in aromatic solvents. Care should be taken to avoid using these solvents with the best brushes: use only water, mineral spirits, gum turpentine, or alcohol.

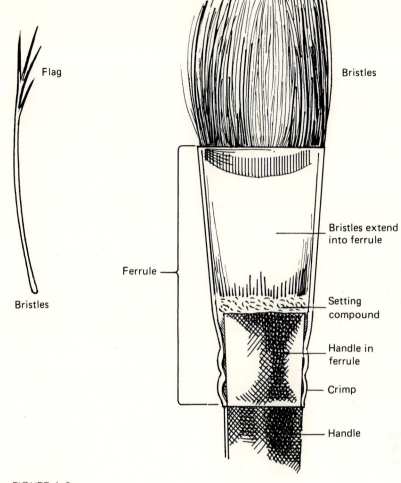

FIGURE A.3
Bristle Brush

Left: Bristle with flag.
Right: Brush head in handle, with terminology.

The set bristles, in the ferrule, are crimped to a hardwood handle. There are three crimps in the best brushes, two in the less expensive kind, and one (or none—just small brads) in the cheapest kind. The more crimps, the sturdier the attachment. The handles can be hardwood of any variety, but they must be straight-grained and free of defects. The handles are also usually lacquered, which can be a fault: Water used in cleanup can seep up through the bottom of the ferrule and down between the wood and the lacquer. Eventually the lacquer will crack because the wood swells in moisture, and the ferrule can loosen; the ferrule, with its precious cargo of fine bristles, can then fall off the handle.

Brushes are sized by number, with small numbers indicating small brushes and large numbers indicating large brushes. The sizing of brushes is not standardized: one com-

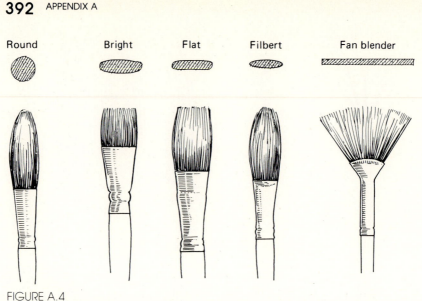

Round   Bright   Flat   Filbert   Fan blender

FIGURE A.4
Brush Shapes

Left to right: Round, bright, flat, filbert, fan blender.

pany's #6 can be quite a bit smaller or larger than another's. A good beginning selection of bristle brushes is a small round, a medium-sized round, a medium-sized flat, and a large flat.

Hair Brushes

Sable brushes can also be used in oil painting, mainly for glazing and applying fine details. The word *sable* is not a standard term, but refers to a class of which weasels, minks, ermines, martens, and kolinskies are members—these are all sables. Some brushes labeled *sable* are even made of camel, squirrel, dyed white ox hair, Russian fitch, goat hair, badger hair, or American skunk. The most reputable brushmakers are not so devious as to label all these as sables; some are labeled "sabeline," and some, believe it or not, are even labeled with their actual names.

The finest watercolor brushes are made of "100% Russian kolinsky sable," collected from the tip of the tail where the hairs are the longest. Russian kolinskies are favored because the animal, if wild, has survived a cold northern climate and therefore produces very long hairs. Domestic martens and other sables who have been raised in captivity produce shorter hairs because heavy coats are not needed for survival. This may be a fine distinction, but when one considers the price of true Russian kolinski hairs, several thousands of dollars per pound, and how it can affect both the prestige and reputation of the brushmaker and the price of the brushes, the distinction becomes clearer. Unfortunately, due to the difficulty of obtaining the hairs, no manufacturer is willing to guarantee in writing that its brushes are 100% Russian kolinski 100% of the time—they are usually mixes of Russian and other kolinski sables, but are always kolinskies, never other sable types.

Real sable hairs taper from the base, swelling into a belly, and then to a fine, microscopic point (Figure A.5). When they are set into a ferrule after the usual washing and bundling, their natural curve brings them together in a point. The top edge of the ferrule

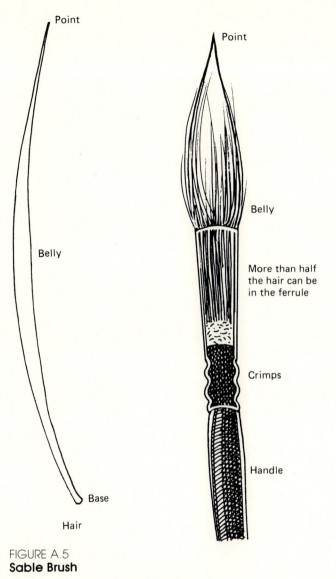

Point

Point

Belly

Belly

More than half
the hair can be
in the ferrule

Crimps

Handle

Base

Handle

Hair

FIGURE A.5
Sable Brush

Left: Hair with sharp point and belly.
Right: Brush head in handle, with terminology.

must be correctly placed to contact the bundle of hairs at about where the belly of each
hair occurs. This placement is crucial if the brush is to have and retain its characteristic
spring. When buying a sable brush, ask the dealer for a glass of water: flick the hairs against
the wrist to loosen the glue used to protect the brush when it is shipped from the maker,
swirl the brush about in the water until it is thoroughly soaked, and then sharply snap the
wrist to discharge the water. The brush should come to a perfect point, and the hairs

should spring into position without flopping over. Considering the expense of a sable brush, it is worth doing this test to demonstrate the quality of the product.

For glazing and detail work in oil or other heavy-bodied paints, do not buy the expensive sable watercolor brushes—they might not be ruined, but they may not perform as desired in watercolor after being washed in active solvents. Buy the long-handled flats, brights, or rounds, and do not pay too much for them. One or two will suffice for most purposes. For general information about other kinds of brushes, see Figure A.6.

Care of Brushes

Brushes should be cleaned after each day's painting. Use the correct solvent for the paint and remove as much of the color as possible. Wipe the brush on a cloth rag. Use a mild soap and lukewarm water; lather up the brush and swirl it in the palm of the hand. Rinse and repeat the lathering and rinse until no trace of color remains in the brush. Some of the particularly powerful organic pigments will stain the bristles or hairs. This is not serious—just be sure to get all traces of paint out of the brush, especially at the heel where the brush is inserted into the ferrule. Rinse, shape the brush, and put it away to dry. Brushes should not be stored upright in a pot: moisture will get down inside the ferrule and spread the hairs or bristles, or loosen the ferrule from the handle. Store the brushes flat, in a drawer or covered box, to keep dust from getting into them. Sable and other hair brushes can be stored in a box with mothballs, to keep moths from eating those expensive hairs.

Brushes that are stored carefully should retain their shape. If the bristles or hairs become splayed out or bent from careless storage, it may be possible to recover the original brush shape by the following method: (1) Wash the brush in hot, soapy water until the hairs or bristles soften. (2) Shape the brush—if the hairs or bristles are soft enough, they may retain this shape. (3) dip the brush into baby shampoo or cream rinse; allow it to soak for a minute. (4) Wrap the brush in a paper or waxed paper sleeve so it will hold its shape as it dries. (5) When the brush is dry, rinse out the soap or cream rinse.

A cheap brush will not last long, even if scrupulously cleaned daily. A good-quality

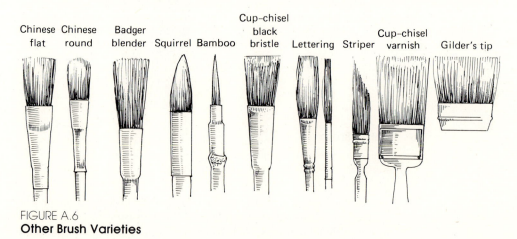

FIGURE A.6
Other Brush Varieties

Left to right: Chinese flat, Chinese round, badger blender, squirrel, bamboo, cup-chiseled black bristle, lettering brushes in goose-quill holders (2), striper, cup-chiseled varnish brush, gilder's tip in cardboard holder.

brush, if properly cared for, should last many years, even with daily use. Buy the best brushes possible, even when you are just beginning to learn painting.

KNIVES

Painting knives are for applying paint, particularly impasto effects, and for scraping paint off paintings in progress. Palette knives are for cleaning the palette. Spatulas and scrapers are for mixing pastes and scraping paint in large volumes. All these tools can be used interchangeably, of course.

Palette knives have handles and a flat blade that extends out from the ferrule and then bends down and out to keep one's knuckles from getting in the paint. One palette knife is all you need, though most painters have several—no one can resist buying new tools when browsing in an art supply shop (Figure A.7).

Painting knives come in myriad shapes and sizes (Figure A.8) and are distinguished from their cousins by the wire extension that projects from the handle. The wire makes the knives flexible and light. The blade should be tempered steel, so that it is both stiff and flexible. It should not be too sharp, lest it cut the fabric when scraping paint from a flexible support.

Be wary of buying too many knives. It is easy to become seduced by the thick, luscious slabs of impasto, and by the tricky effects some knives give. There is a place for knife painting, certainly, but the artist must always decide if the technical manipulations serve the concept of the work.

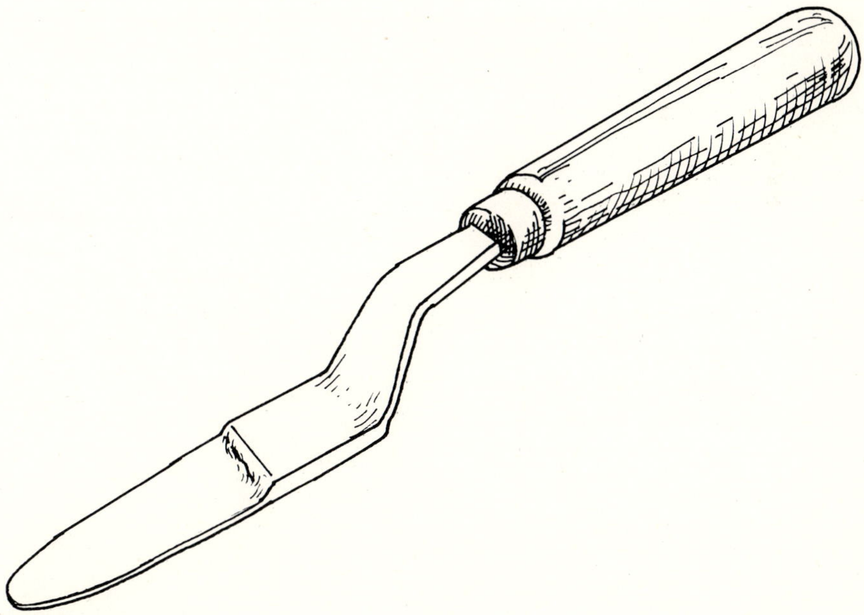

FIGURE A.7
Palette Knife

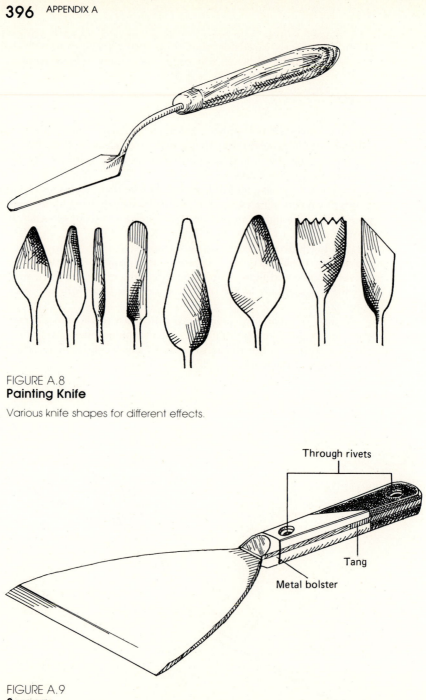

FIGURE A.8
Painting Knife

Various knife shapes for different effects.

FIGURE A.9
Scraper

Note the metal bolster where the handle is attached, the full-length tang, and through rivets in the handle. The same construction will appear in a quality spatula.

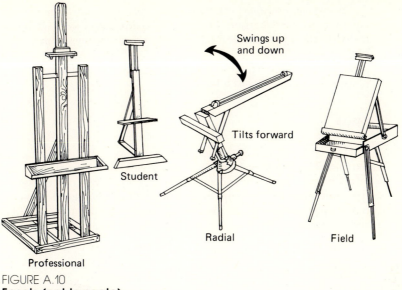

Swings up
and down

Tilts forward

Student

Radial

Field

Professional

FIGURE A.10
Easels (not to scale)

Left to right: Professional studio easel, student studio easel, radial easel, field easel (also called a French easel, folds up into a portable box).

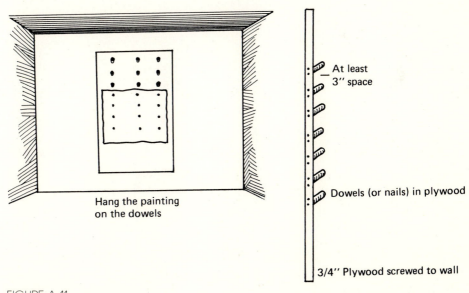

Hang the painting
on the dowels

At least
3″ space

Dowels (or nails) in plywood

3/4″ Plywood screwed to wall

FIGURE A.11
A Simple Studio Wall Easel

Spatulas and scrapers can be used in large-scale works or whenever a large volume of paint is to be moved around. Buy quality spatulas and scrapers in restaurant supply houses or hardware stores; the best have tempered carbon or stainless steel blades and a bolster where the blade emerges from the handle (Figure A.9). The tang should extend completely through the handle and be held in place by through riveting. One good spatula and one good scraper will last a lifetime.

EASELS

A large variety of easels, similar to the ones shown in the illustration (Figure A.10) can be purchased for studio or field use. A studio easel should be sturdily built of hardwood, steel, or aluminum, with heavy metal fasteners, and be versatile enough to handle a variety of sizes and weights of picture supports. Field easels, like the so-called French landscape easels, must also be sturdy and, for the price one must pay, should be made of hardwood and have stainless steel inserts and brass fittings; plastic and soft aluminum are not worth

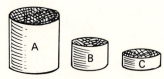
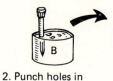

1. Get 3 cans. Can A is container Can B fits into can A. Can C fits over can A as a cover.

2. Punch holes in bottom of can B.

Jagged edges of holes point down. Will not damage bristles or hairs.

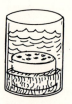

3. Put small can in large can.

4. Fill with solvent.

5. In use, heaver paint sludge falls to bottom.

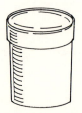

6. Cover when not in use.

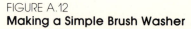

FIGURE A.12
Making a Simple Brush Washer

the $150 to $300 these easels can cost. You can avoid the whole issue of an easel if you have a studio. Some nails or dowels in a wall, as illustrated (Figure A.11), will hold a painting quite well.

LIGHTING

The section on color in Chapter 7 explains why cool north light is useful for lighting setups in the studio; it is a relatively steady light, albeit at a low level, that casts no strong, constantly changing shadows. But it is generally not a great kind of light to have falling on a painting in progress, because most galleries now light their shows with incandescent spotlights. You can make adjustments in studio lighting using a combination of fluorescent lights, incandescent spotlights, and colored theatrical gels, to suit most needs. One bit of advice—the lighting in a studio should be good, bright when needed, and adjustable.

MISCELLANEOUS ACCESSORIES

Palette cups, cans, bottles, rags, tables, and so on fall into this category. Palette cups attach to the palette and are used for holding small quantities of thinner or solvent, or mediums. Cans hold solvent for washing brushes. You can spend good money on a fancy brush washer, or make one for virtually nothing (Figure A.12). Glass bottles hold mediums, varnishes, and so on. They should be carefully labeled with the contents and dates of manufacture, and stored to avoid fire or health hazards. Colored wine bottles work well here—corks make good stoppers if they do not dry out. Paper towels are no substitute for fabric rags, and synthetic fibers are no substitute for absorbent cotton. Rough paper or synthetic can wear the bristles or hairs of a good brush. Buy clean used cotton diapers at a baby diaper service, or use worn-out cotton undershirts, sheets, or towels. Tables can be large or small, but they should be sturdily built; it helps when rearranging the studio (a frequent occurrence, it seems) if the table legs are fitted with casters.

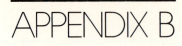

APPENDIX B

DRAWING MATERIALS

Drawing materials are often used together with painting processes, and have as long and involved a history as painting materials. Using contemporary terms it is practically impossible to separate drawing from painting, nor is it possible to give an entirely satisfactory explanation of just what "drawing" is. Simply, however, drawing can be said to be "a mark made on a surface." Since there has been so much recent interest in the use of alternative nontraditional media such as colored pencils and oil pastels, it is necessary briefly to survey the materials we use for drawing. The support most often used for drawing—paper—is also considered.

PAPERS

Light, portable, and flexible supports for drawing have always been a concern of artists. The first such support was probably made of beaten and flattened plant fibers—papyrus, or woven fibers—silk. The first mention of true paper as we know it is in the first century A.D. in China, during the first year of the Han dynasty. This paper is described as being made of "hemp waste, old rags, and fish nets."[*] These materials proved strong and durable, and in the ensuing centuries rag papers were the only ones artists found acceptable for their work.

Until the end of the eighteenth century, linen and cotton rags were the only materials used in papermaking. But by the beginning of the 1700s the demand for rags for fine artists' papers, coupled with the increasing use of paper for commercial printing applications, had quite exhausted the available supplies of raw materials. In the early 1800s a process was described whereby paper could be made from wood pulp. By 1803 Henry and Sealy Fourdrinier had refined an efficient and economical papermaking machine—originally invented by Nicholas-Louis Robert but called a Fourdrinier machine to this day—that increased the large-scale production of pulp papers. By then, fine rag papers had become as relatively expensive as they are now.

Papermaking

Whether the paper is made by hand from rag fibers or by machine from ground wood pulp, the process is essentially this: A slurry of rag or wood pulp and water is cast onto a screen and agitated, and the water is allowed to drain out. The agitation causes the fibers to felt together to form a sheet. The sheet is removed from the screen and dried. How the pulp is made, and from what materials, determines the paper's durability and strength.

HANDMADE PAPER. The process of forming the pulp is critical if you want to make a strong handmade paper. The plant fibers (cotton or linen) must not be ground up or

---

[*] Dard Hunter, *Papermaking: The History and Technique of an Ancient Craft* (New York, 1947), p. 52.

chopped too short, but rather individually separated by beating. The common household blender, often used in demonstrations of the craft, is a chopper, not a beater; it should not be used to make papers which are then expected to have wet strength, for it makes very short fibers. A machine called a Hollander beater is used to beat and separate fibers in most handmade operations (either that, or a hydropulper), and a great deal of pure, clean water is added to make the pulpy mass. The pulp, along with additives put into it during beating, is placed in a vat, and the mold is selected.

In the Far East, the paper mold may be a fine screen made of thin strips of bamboo tied together with thin brass wires and held in a frame. In the West, the mold is more often simply a fine brass wire screen, which can have a distinctive pattern and a watermark. Both pattern and watermark are used to identify the maker, or the mill. The perimeter of the mold is mounted with a detachable frame called a deckle, which is held in place during the paper-forming process by the papermaker's hands. The mold and the deckle together form a shallow trough that holds the pulp (Figure B.1). Molds can be any size that can be conveniently handled by one or two people, although in the past there were standard sizes which are sometimes still used:

Proprietary Name	Size
Antiquarian	31″ × 53″ (78 × 135 cm)
Double elephant	26½″ × 40″ (66 × 101 cm)
Elephant	23″ × 28″ (58 × 70 cm)
Imperial	22″ × 30″ (55.5 × 76 cm)
Super royal	19¼″ × 27″ (49 × 66 cm)
Royal	19″ × 24″ (48 × 61 cm)
Medium	17½″ × 22″ (44 × 60 cm)
Demy	15½″ × 20″ (39 × 51 cm)

The mold and deckle are dipped into the vat and filled with the pulp. With a back-and-forth and side-to-side motion, the papermaker distributes the pulp evenly across the surface of the mold and creates the felt, and then momentarily allows the water to drain from the screen. The deckle is removed from the mold and the now-formed paper is turned over onto a blotter—a procedure called *couching* (pronounced "kooching"). The pulp that bleeds out from under the deckle leaves a characteristic shredded-looking edge on four edges of the paper: what we call a "deckled edge."

Each sheet is added to the stack and separated from the others by a blotter; the pile of paper and blotters is called a *post*. The paper is allowed to dry in the post, according to the surface finish desired by the maker. Papers that will have a smooth surface are pressed under heated weights, and called *hot pressed. Cold-pressed* papers are finished under cold weights, which leaves a medium-rough surface (sometimes called *not*). For a paper with a rough surface finish, the sheets are not pressed (sometimes also called *not*).

MACHINE-MADE PAPER. A highly developed version of the original Fourdrinier process is used to make fine art papers by machine. The pulp and any additives are circulated in a deep, wide, narrow tank at one end of the machine, and thrown up onto a wide, long screen—really an endless belt—which moves the pulp toward the driers at high speed. The pulp is formed into a continuous sheet by the time it reaches the end of the screen, even though it is still about 95 percent water at that point. The driers are steam-heated stainless steel rollers that can be set to control the thickness of the paper. From the driers the sheet passes into a set of vertically arranged rollers called a *calender,* which gives

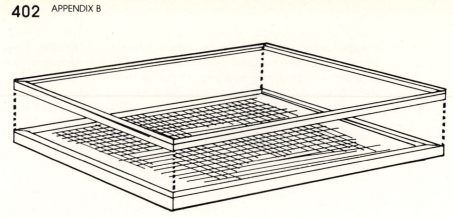

FIGURE B.1
Paper Mold and Deckle

The mold is like a screen.

the final desired surface finish to the paper. From the calender, the paper is gathered into a large roll.

All the surface characteristics of a handmade paper can be imitated by the machine process, except that machine-made paper has a grain direction that handmade paper—because of the random felting action of the mold-handler—lacks. The screen pattern of the mold, the deckled edge (only on two sides, where the pulp flows off the moving screen), and a watermark can all appear on the best of machine-made fine art papers. Perhaps the only difference between handmade and machine-made papers of equal material quality is a certain feel to the slightly irregular surface of the handmade paper—and, of course, the esthetic freight we are apt to attach to the concept of something that is handmade.

Permanence of Papers

The durability of a paper has to do not with how it is made, but with the materials used. With the beginning of the wood pulp industry and the invention of the Fourdrinier process, wood pulp papers became very popular and their use spread. Unfortunately, the cellulose in wood pulp is not pure. It contains ingredients such as lignin which react with oxygen in the air to cause the formation of acids. These ingredients can lead to the rapid deterioration of the paper. The very short life of newsprint, which is almost entirely low-alpha cellulose wood pulp, is a good example of how poorly this kind of paper lasts.

Linen and cotton fibers are still the most favored of the natural ingredients used in art papers; the longer, and therefore stronger, linen fibers are somewhat preferred over cotton. The so-called rice papers of the Far East, made predominantly of mulberry and other vegetable fibers, have very long fibers, which gives them great wet strength. The archival types are popular for use in printmaking and conservation. If the pulp made from the natural fibers is prepared by careful and repeated washing, it will contain no acids or other ingredients that might react with the atmosphere. Many papers are made with an alkaline buffer added to the pulp to counter any absorption of acidity which could occur in the course of normal exposure to our increasingly acidic environment.

Papers that contain 100 percent rag fibers are necessarily quite expensive, since there is a large demand for cotton and linen for other uses. Some papers are therefore only 75, 50, or 25 percent rag, the balance being cellulose or some other natural or synthetic material. These "rag content" papers may contain filler ingredients like chalk or kaolin to produce a surface similar to that of 100 percent rag papers. Furthermore, some art papers made today do not have any rag content; they are composed of synthetic materials like fiberglass or natural but impermanent materials that have been chemically stabilized. Besides fillers and buffers, the other ingredients that can be added to the pulp include pigments for color (dyes are not used in permanent papers unless they have passed lightfastness testing), and sizes to control the bleeding or spreading of liquid painting or drawing media. Alum should not be found in fine art papers.

With all the possible materials a papermaker can add to the product, the issue of permanence—and how to predict it—has become very confused. (A few of the older manufacturers, especially the European houses, rest comfortably on their centuries of excellent repute.) Watermarks in the paper sometimes indicate the rag content, but this is not always a reliable guide. A significant indicator of a paper's expected life, its pH, can be tested using the method outlined below.

PAPER pH. The potential of hydrogen, or pH, is measured with papers which indicate pH by means of a color change. pH can be acid, 0 on the scale, or basic (alkaline), 14 on the scale; 7 is neutral, neither acidic nor alkaline (Figure B.2).

MATERIALS

1. ColorpHast Indicator Strips (see Appendix D). ColorpHast strips do not bleed and they will not stain the paper being tested. They can be obtained in a variety of measuring ranges, but get the widest range—0 to 14.
2. Plastic film.
3. Distilled water.
4. The paper being tested.

METHOD (FIGURE B.3)

1. Lay a piece of plastic film under the paper.
2. Place a drop of distilled water on the paper.
3. Lay the sensitive end of the ColorpHast strip (a plastic strip with the indicating pad at one end) on the drop of water and move it around a bit to make sure it is completely wet.
4. Place another piece of plastic film on top of the pH strip.
5. Put a light weight on the film to make a firm contact between the pH strip and the paper.
6. After 5 minutes, remove the weight, plastic film, and pH strip. Read the pH of the paper by matching the color of the wet pH strip with the color chart on the ColorpHast Strip container. Papers with pH values between 8 and 10.5 are slightly alkaline; although they may absorb some acidity as they age, they are buffered

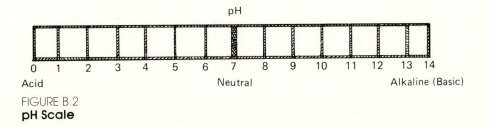

FIGURE B.2
pH Scale

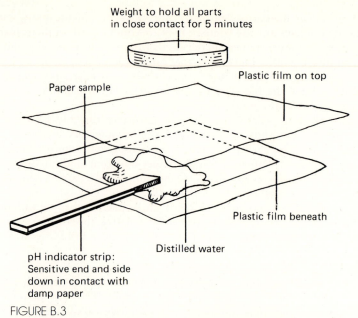

FIGURE B.3
Arrangement of Materials for Testing Paper pH

Used by permission of Dr. Richard D. Smith, President, Wei T'o® Associates, Inc., Matteson IL 60443 U.S.A.

against becoming too acid. Papers with pH values below 8 will become acidic as they age. Papers with a pH below 7 are already acidic and are deteriorating.

Weights of Papers

Weights of paper are determined by weighing 500 sheets (a ream) of the same kind of paper (that is, say, 500 sheets of 22- by 30-inch watercolor paper). If a ream of cold-pressed watercolor paper weighs 300 pounds, the paper is referred to as a "300-pound cold-pressed watercolor paper." The more substantial papers, with weights above 170 pounds, are generally better suited for wet drawing or painting media, while those below 170 pounds work well for dry drawing media. But there is no reason why any good paper cannot be used for any technique. Some manufacturers now refer to a paper's weight by grams per square meter: g/m^2.

Uses of Papers

For dry drawing techniques any kind of paper, with any kind of surface, can be appropriate. Usually, finely detailed drawing techniques require that the paper have a smooth surface, and harder surfaced papers will stand up to erasing. For wet media, the heavier papers will be able to stand repeated wetting without much distortion.

Surface preparation is unnecessary when most dry drawing techniques are used. The artist simply begins drawing on the paper, which can be in pad form or as single sheets pinned to a board. For a more resistant support, mount the paper on ¼-inch (6 mm) thick hardboard. A watercolor wash can be applied to the paper to give a colored surface on which to begin the work.

Papers used for wet techniques do not have to be stretched if they are sufficiently thick. Thin papers will often buckle and wrinkle in an unpleasant or uncontrolled way, and can be stretched on a board following the method outlined in the section on watercolor painting.

Rag papers can be used for collage techniques, and are far more durable and stable than the usual castoff scraps of labels and newsprint that one sees in this medium. Colored rag paper, or painted paper, also works well.

DRAWING MATERIALS

As with the surface on which drawings are made, the materials with which artists draw have a long and involved history. There is a huge variety of drawing materials available in supply shops, but comparatively few are reliably durable. Because ingredients and manufacturing methods for materials like colored pencils and colored markers are not standardized and are constantly changing, it is very wise—if you are concerned with the permanence of your work—to test them for lightfastness using one of the methods given in Chapter 7.

Dry Media

GRAPHITE PENCILS. Although the term "lead pencil" is the popular name for this instrument, a graphite pencil is made not of lead but of graphite, a crystallized form of carbon. (The term *lead* is used by manufacturers to differentiate between diameters of drawing materials. A lead is smaller than a crayon.) Graphite has been used for drawing or polishing since at least 2500 B.C., but the first wood-encased graphite pencil was developed in England in the mid-sixteenth century. By the end of the eighteenth century, Nicholas-Jacques Conté had developed the forerunner of the modern lead pencil by mixing ground clay and ground graphite into a dough with water, pressing the mixture into grooves, baking the dried sticks, and impregnating them with wax.

Today, graphite pencils are still made by mixing clays and natural graphite with a small amount of water and extruding the dough through a press to form the leads. The leads are cut into strands and fired in kilns at high temperatures. The fired leads are impregnated with wax and glued into cedar casings. The hardness of the lead is controlled by the proportion of graphite to clay in the dough: More clay and less graphite makes a harder pencil.

Drawing pencils are available in hardnesses ranging from 6H (the hardest) to 6B (the softest). Since the paper fibers shave the lead, and hard pencils contain clay to make them more resistant to the shaving, it is impossible to get a black mark with a 6H pencil. But a 6B pencil is not resistant to shaving, which makes it possible to make a very black mark with this soft lead. (Incidentally, the term *pencil* is actually the archaic word for *brush*.)

GRAPHITE STICKS. These are composed of the same materials as the graphite pencils, but do not have the wooden sleeves. The sticks are generally bulkier and capable of producing broad strokes of tone quickly. Graphite sticks can also be powdered by crushing, mixed with a little mineral spirits, and used as a rather greasy black inky drawing material; one can also draw with the dry powder. *Caution:* Do not breathe the dust.

Pentalic Corporation is now marketing a Czechoslovakian-made variety of graphite stick that is lacquered and can be sharpened like a large pencil. The lacquer coating keeps the hands clean.

VINE CHARCOAL. This kind of charcoal is made by slowly baking willow dowels (or other types of wood—formerly grapevines) until they are reduced to almost pure carbon. The sticks will produce lines and tones of infinite subtlety, as well as robust painterly effects. Vine charcoal sticks come in a variety of diameters and can also be obtained as rectangular sticks and blocks; the hardness of the sticks also varies. Vine charcoal can be powdered like graphite. *Caution:* Do not breathe the dust.

COMPRESSED CHARCOAL. This is compressed vine charcoal, available in pencil form as well as in sticks of different shapes, sizes, and hardnesses. The pencil form of compressed charcoal can be sharpened to a very fine point and is particularly suited to drawing meticulous detail. Compressed charcoal can produce very dense blacks.

CHALK. The word *chalk* is derived from the Latin *creta,* which in turn is the derivation of the French *craie,* or *crayon.* Perhaps this is why conté crayon is today sometimes called chalk. Conté crayon is a slightly greasy or oily kind of chalk, made with carbon black, various shades of earth reds or browns, or titanium white as the colorants. The crayons come in short sticks of various hardnesses that can be sharpened like charcoal sticks—by rubbing them against a sheet of fine sandpaper. Conté crayon marks are somewhat difficult to erase and can make a wide range of marks of varying delicacy.

Pastel Chalk. Although considered a paint, this chalk makes an excellent, fine, soft drawing material.

Blackboard Chalk. There are a great many ways of making this kind of chalk, from extruding natural calcium carbonate mixed with a small amount of gum, to molding calcium sulfate (plaster of Paris) into a stick form. Some blackboard chalks contain small amounts of clay (which can make them too hard to use on a fine paper) or petroleum jelly for making "dustless" chalks (which can make them less permanent). *French chalk* is not chalk, but talc; it is used to make tailor's chalks and should not be used for drawing, since the talc dust can be harmful if inhaled.

CRAYONS. If the Egyptians or Greeks are presumed to have developed the encaustic painting technique, then they may have also been responsible for making the first crayon, since the hardened encaustic mixture is very much like our modern crayons. In fact, a simple mixture of beeswax and pigment can make an effective, though somewhat soft and potentially brittle, drawing material.

Wax Crayons. Ordinary children's wax crayons are made of paraffin and stearic acid, melted and mixed with pigments or dyes (none of the ingredients can be harmful, by law), and molded. None of the children's crayons tested with the Blue-Wool Cards use permanent colorants.

Oil Crayons. A conté crayon can be considered an oil crayon, but normally the more colorful oil crayons, oil "paint sticks," and oil pastels fall into this category. Oil crayons and oil pastels are small, soft, pigmented, oil-impregnated sticks. Paint sticks are similar but much larger, and the name *paint sticks* is proprietary, used by Shiva to describe its product. Oil crayons can be built up to an appreciable thickness, scraped, thinned with mineral spirits, and brushed, and generally manipulated to a far greater degree than can wax crayons. The only drawback to these materials is that some of the colorants are extremely fugitive—some will fade, or disappear entirely, within a week of exposure to sunlight, according to results obtained from a Blue-Wool test. Furthermore, the formulas used to make them can change from batch to batch. It is advisable that these products be tested. Test each new box, since it can be different from the previous box from the same manufacturer. The "paint sticks" seem to be more reliable; they are labeled with generic pigment names for the colorants, and are offered in a much more restricted color range than the crayons and pastels.

Lithographic Crayon. A lithographic crayon is a carbon pigment impregnated with an oily and/or greasy vehicle. These come in pencil form as well as sticks, in both hard and soft textures, and are used for lithographic printing techniques—hence the name—although they can be used successfully for drawing.

METALLIC POINTS. Gold, silver, or aluminum wire can be inserted into a mechanical pencil holder and filed against a slightly rough surface to produce an image. *Silver point* is the traditional technique; gold and aluminum are less common. When the metal tarnishes (oxidizes), the image becomes darker. This is an extremely delicate medium, the range of values being particularly narrow and the possibilities for erasure and redrawing limited.

A base for metal point drawing can easily be made by coating a sheet of smooth drawing paper with a thin, evenly applied wash of zinc white (Chinese white) watercolor. The pigment particles are very fine and provide just the right sort of smooth but toothy and abrasive surface needed for this technique.

COLORED PENCILS. There are a tremendous number of different kinds of colored pencils in art supply stores. Many of them are made for temporary reproduction techniques, which can be a clue to their questionable permanence. Again, it is essential to test each new box of colored pencils for lightfastness, as composition and formulas change constantly.

Colored Pencils. Ordinarily these are made by impregnating the leads with a waxy binder, although some are bound with a thermosetting (heat-curing) resin. The leads are composed of pigments, toners, or metallic flakes—for "silver" and "gold"—and a little clay for hardness. The value range is rather narrow due to the hardness of some of the binders. Some brands offer better value ranges. Beware of proprietary color names, and test them for lightfastness.

Pastel Pencils. These pencils are somewhat like pastels, except that the pigmented sticks are encased in a wooden sleeve; they can be more easily sharpened and tend to crumble less. Usually pastel pencils (one brand is called a "colored charcoal pastel pencil," an unnecessarily confusing designation) offer a much greater range of values than regular colored pencils, mainly because they are softer. Beware of proprietary color names, and check for lightfastness.

Watercolor Pencils. Bound in either a water-gum binder or a water-soluble dispersion of oil, soluble soaps, and fatty acids, these pigmented leads are encased in a wooden sleeve. They can be used like a regular pencil, then brushed over with water to create washes. Beware of proprietary color names, and check for lightfastness.

MISCELLANEOUS. There are certainly many other dry drawing materials that can be used for making pictures, among them grease pencils, industrial crayons, and lumber marking pencils. Be sure to check the lightfastness of these products—and recheck new purchases—if you use them for permanent work; be aware that some industrial crayons use toxic lead chromate pigments.

Wet Media

Certainly any paint can be used as a drawing medium, but we normally think of the inks when referring to liquid drawing media.

INDIA INK. Actually, India ink was invented in China, but the source of the carbon pigment was India—thus the name. Traditional Chinese ink can be made simply by grinding with a mortar and pestle a small amount of normal-strength hot hide glue (see Chapter 2) with a proportion of carbon black, lampblack, or bone black pigment—lampblack is the finest textured. The proportions are approximately 1 part pigment to 2 or 3 parts vehicle, by volume. Grind the mixture until it is smooth, pour it into a shallow ceramic dish, and let it dry. To use, brush with water until the surface reliquifies. Or stir the mixture in the mortar until most of the water has evaporated and the ink is thick and stiff; mold it into a stick and wrap with waxed paper so it can dry slowly without cracking. To use, rub the stick in water on a slate ink slab.

Manufactured India inks are made of carbon black pigment ground in water with a little shellac—or other water-dispersed resin—to make them water-resistant. Most India inks can be considered reliably permanent in light. But do not confuse them with the other black inks made for technical pens; these inks are not water-resistant and worse, may not be lightfast. India inks can be applied in washes with a brush or with a very large variety of pens, including steel, crow-quill steel, lettering pens, bamboo pens, and reed and natural quill pens. Each type of pen gives a different characteristic line. It is worth experimenting with all of them to see the possibilities (Figure B.4).

COLORED INKS. There are two kinds of colored drawing inks that come in bottles. They can be used in drawing pens, air brushes, or with brushes and water; the dye-based inks can be used in technical pens.

Dye-based Inks. These colored inks form clear, transparent films suitable for glazing. Many of them use fugitive dyes, so it is necessary to test each new ink for lightfastness. One well-known brand advises that the colored inks in its line may not be permanent in light, but this warning appears only on the box of permanent black ink that accompanies the set: in a Blue-Wool Card test, all but the black ink made by this company faded to white.

Pigmented Inks. Pigmented inks resemble watercolor paints in that a water-based binder holds a very fine pigment dispersion, except that the binder is more water-resistant than the gum used in transparent watercolors. These inks may be more lightfast than most colored inks, but it is still wise to test each new purchase.

COLORED MARKERS. These are the familiar felt-tipped pens, in colored and black ink, which dry very quickly by the evaporation of the solvent that carries the colorant. Some are water-based, but the quickest drying ones use volatile solvents like xylene or toluene—these dry water-resistant. To get a fine enough dispersion that will flow through the fibrous pen tip, fugitive dyes are used for many of the products. Some companies do use permanent carbon for their black markers. So not only are some of the felt-tip markers hazardous because of their solvent content, but most are not for permanent artistic use. To be sure, test them for lightfastness.

There are a couple of new products which may meet the requirements of permanency: Golden Artist Colors' Fluid Acrylic Markers, which use acrylic emulsion paint in small plastic squeeze-bottles with mohair tips; and Hunt's Speedball Painters Opaque Paint Markers, which is the more familiar metal tube with a fiberous tip. Both claim that the colorants are lightfast and the vehicles are nontoxic; Golden's product has the generic colorant name on the label.

BALLPOINT PENS. Ballpoint pens use dyes for the colorant, so it is important to test them for lightfastness. One interesting advantage of a ballpoint pen is that an artist can draw for days without ever having to refill the pen point. This may be of no use, and less interest, if the drawing disappears in a year or two. Test for lightfastness.

Alvin has introduced their Graphic Pen, and assures the user that the ink used in this revolutionary ball-point pen is true pigmented India ink. The points are removable for cleaning in hot water, and the ink comes in cartridges for easy refilling. If this product passes lightfastness tests, which it should if real India ink is used, then here we have a technological break-through. Be wary of such labeling as "India ink," or "India ink

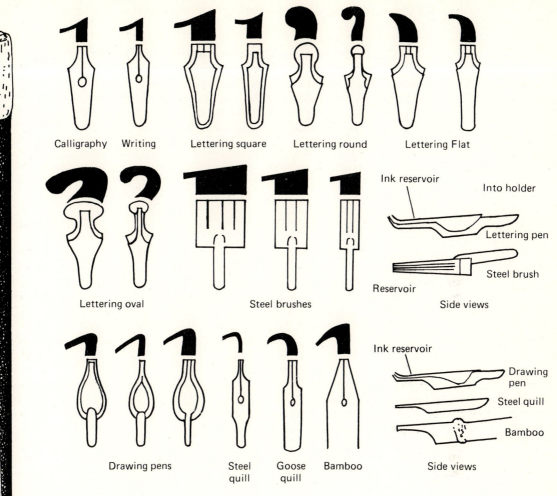

Pen holder

FIGURE B.4
Drawing and Lettering Pens

Left: Holder.
Middle top, left to right: Calligraphy, writing, lettering square (2), lettering round (2), lettering flat (2).
Middle center, left to right: Lettering oval (2), steel brushes (3), side view of lettering pen (*top*), side view of steel brush (*bottom*).
Middle bottom: Drawing pens (3), steel quill, goose quill, bamboo pen, side view of drawing pen (*top*), side view of steel quill (*middle*), side view of bamboo (*bottom*).

density,'' however; the quotation marks are a clear signal that the real pigment is not being used.

Note: With all the recommendations to ''test for lightfastness,'' you might get the impression that these materials should not be used for artwork. Not so. They should be used with caution, if you are concerned about permanence. A work that is sold for money carries with it an implied warranty about its fitness. A professional artist with integrity will certainly be concerned that the client—collector, dealer, agent, museum, gallery—be able to look at and enjoy the work for a long, long time.

APPENDIX C

GLOSSARY

Many of the words defined here are used in a nonstandard way by artists. An attempt has been made to reduce technical language to the minimum, but in some cases its use is unavoidable. The abbreviation P/CD means Paint/Coatings Dictionary.

Acrylic Emulsion   A water dispersion of polymers or co-polymers of acrylic acid, methacrylic acid, or acrylonitrile. Paints made with the acrylic emulsion as a binder have a variety of other ingredients added to control the performance of the paint. Acrylic emulsions dry by evaporation of the water *and* film coalescence; the dried layer is consequently filled with voids and is quite porous.

Acrylic Solution   A solution of acrylic resin in a volatile solvent. Paints made with an acrylic solution binder resemble oil paints more than those made with an acrylic emulsion binder. Acrylic solutions dry by evaporation of the solvent and form continuous, solid films.

Acute Hazard   A hazard producing a symptom of injury immediately, or after a short period of exposure.

Additive Color   Color that results from the mixture of two or more colored lights, the visual blending of separate spots of transmitted colored light (as in color television), or by the visual blending of flickering hues (tree leaves seen from a distance).

Agglomeration   A condition of paint in which individual pigment particles cluster into undispersed lumps. The spaces between the particles are filled with air.

Aliphatic Hydrocarbons   Generally, higher boiling point petroleum-distilled solvents than aromatic hydrocarbons, composed primarily of paraffinic and naphthenic hydrocarbons (P/CD).

Alkyd   Synthetic resin formed by the condensation of polyhydric alcohols with polybasic acids (P/CD).

Allergenic   Substance that is capable of causing an allergic reaction. It is a term used in ASTM D 4236, the voluntary health labeling standard of the American Society for Testing and Materials for artists and the artists' materials industry.

Anhydrous   Free from water.

Archival   Refers to a material that meets certain criteria for permanence such as lignin-free, pH neutral, alkaline-buffered, stable in light, and so on. The term is not precisely defined, since a constantly changing environment may negate standards for durability and permanence.

Aromatic Hydrocarbons   A class of organic compounds that have an unsaturated ring of carbon atoms (P/CD), considered generally more volatile and active solvents than aliphatic hydrocarbons.

Binder   The nonvolatile adhesive liquid portion of a paint that attaches pigment particles and the paint film as a whole to the support.

Bleeding The action of the binder, vehicle, or solvent used in a paint system that causes diffusion of color into an area where it is not wanted.

Bloom A condition of paint and varnish films characterized by the insidious appearance of a bluish or whitish veil over the image, usually beneath the transparent film. It is thought to be caused by humidity and temperature changes. Bloom can be avoided by varnishing on dry days.

Canvas Any closely woven cloth. Paintings may be referred to as "canvases."

Cartoon A planning device in mural painting, often a full-scale line drawing of the design, without color.

Casein A natural protein obtained from cow's milk.

Chassis Another name for the auxiliary support on which a textile is stretched. Also called a stretcher or a strainer.

Chroma The relative intensity or purity of a hue when compared to grayness or lack of hue.

Chronic Hazard A hazard producing a symptom of injury only after prolonged exposure.

Collage A technique of picture making in which the artist uses materials other than the traditional paint, such as cut paper, wood, sand, and so on. The items are glued to the painting support and incorporated into the design or composition.

Colloid Solution A gel-like solution, as compared to the more common liquid or syrupy types.

Colour Index An internationally recognized reference text used for the identification of colorants according to type (dye, pigment), hue, chemical composition, or process of manufacture, published by the British Society of Dyers and Colourists and the American Association of Textile Chemists and Colorists.

Combustible Referring to any liquid with a flashpoint between 100 and 150°F (38 and 65°C).

Co-polymer A polymer in which the molecule is of more than one type of structural unit.

Cradle Originally, a system of attached and immovable battens interleaved with sliding battens, the whole screwed and glued to the rear of a solid wooden panel to keep it from warping or splitting. Today, the word may refer, incorrectly, to any auxiliary support for the back of a panel.

Direct Painting A style or technique of painting in which the final image is achieved with as little manipulation of the painting surface as possible.

Dispersion Applied to paint, a smooth, homogeneous mixture of heterogeneous ingredients; the process of dispersal, in which pigment particles are evenly distributed throughout the vehicle.

Drier A material that accelerates or initiates the drying of an oil paint or oil by promoting oxidation. "Top driers," which cause the surface of a film to dry before the interior, can be most harmful to paint films. "Through driers" can cause the whole film to dry at once, and so are safer.

Drying Oil An oil that, when spread into a thin layer and exposed to air, absorbs oxygen from the air and converts into a tough, leathery film.

Emulsion A liquid system in which small droplets of one liquid are immiscible in, but thoroughly and evenly dispersed throughout, a second liquid (P/CD).

Encaustic Literally, "to burn in." A painting technique in which the binder is melted wax; the wax carries the pigment to the support, where it cools and hardens. The paint is melted into the support with a heat lamp to increase its adhesion.

Explosive Referring to any liquid with a flash point below 10° F (−12° C).

Extremely Flammable Referring to any liquid with a flash point below 20° F (−7° C).

Flammable Referring to any liquid with a flash point between 20 and 100° F (−7 and 38° C).

Flash point The lowest temperature at which a liquid gives off vapors that can be ignited by an open flame or spark.

Flocculation A condition of paint in which individual pigment particles cluster into lumps. The spaces between the particles are filled with vehicle, unlike in agglomeration, where the spaces are filled with air. The lumps may project above the surface of a spread-out film of the paint.

Fresco A painting technique in which the pigments are dispersed in plain water and applied to a damp plaster wall. The wall becomes the binder, as well as the support for the paint. Also called affresco.

Frit A powdered, colored material that when fired at high temperature fuses into a continuous film, as hard and brittle as glass, that is often a different color from the original powder.

Gesso A white ground material for preparing rigid supports for painting, made of a mixture of chalk, a little white pigment, and glue. Also called glue gesso or Italian gesso.

Glaze A very thin, transparent colored paint applied over a previously painted surface to alter the appearance and color of the surface.

Gouache A technique of painting with opaque watercolor.

Grissalle A monochromatic painting, usually gray.

Ground The coating material, usually white, applied to a support to prepare it for painting.

Gum A plant substance, like sap, that is soluble in water.

Hue The perceived color of an object, identified by a common name such as red, orange, yellow, green, blue, purple.

Hygroscopic Absorbing or attracting moisture from the air.

Impasto A style of paint application characterized by thick, juicy slabs of color.

Imprimatura A thin, transparent veil of paint—or a paint-tinted size—applied to a ground to lessen the ground's absorbency or to tint the ground to a middle tone.

Indirect Painting A style or technique of painting in which the final image is built over an underpainting by means of transparent or semi-opaque applications of paint that do not completely obscure the underpainting.

Key Toothy grounds that allow succeeding applications of paint or a drawing material to grip them mechanically; a basis for attachment other than adhesiveness.

"Lacquer Thinner" A widely misused term referring to any kind of mixture of various aliphatic and/or aromatic solvents used to dilute or dissolve lacquers.

Lake A dye that has been chemically or electrically attached to a particle and hence does not bleed or migrate.

Latex A dispersion in water of a solid polymeric material.

Levigating A method of water-washing pulverized pigments or sand to clear the particles of dissolved salts or organic matter.

Lightfast Referring to a substance that has passed a test in which it is exposed to a known amount of light over a measured period of time. Lightfast materials resist fading.

Lignin A natural and acidic adhesive material found in wood that acts as a binder for the wood fibers.

Marouflage A technique for attaching, with glue, mural-size paintings on paper or fabric to a wall.

Masstone The top tone or body color of a paint seen only by reflected light.

Mat A stiff paperboard with a window cut out of the center, attached to a backboard. A mat forms a protective sandwich for a work of art by separating it from direct contact with the glass that covers it and the frame that surrounds it. Archival matboard is sometimes called museum board.

Matte Flat; nonglossy; having a dull surface appearance. Also spelled *matt.*

Migration The action of a pigment or dye moving through a dried film above or below it.

Monomer A low molecular weight material that can react with similar or dissimilar materials to form a polymer.

Museum Board High-quality, multiply paperboard that is made of cotton rags or buffered cellulose to ensure its chemical stability and neutrality.

Mosaic The technique of making a picture out of small units of variously colored materials (bits of glass, stone, ceramic tiles) set in a mortar.

Palette The surface on which a painter's colors are mixed; also, the range of colors a painter uses.

Pentimento A condition of old paintings, particularly oil paintings in which lead-containing pigments have been used. The upper layers of the opaque paint become transparent, revealing earlier layers.

Pigments Particles with inherent color that can be mixed with a transparent adhesive binder to form paint.

Plasticizer The ingredient added to the vehicle that allows the paint either to flow or to be easily redissolved.

Polymer A series of monomers strung together in a repeating chain-like form. A polymer is usually thought of as two monomers, but could be more.

Precipitate An inert particle to which dyes can be laked.

Preservative A material that prevents or inhibits the growth of microorganisms in organic mixtures.

Primer *See* ground.

Radial Sawing A method of sawing boards in which the saw cuts are perpendicular to the growth rings of the log.

Refractive Index The numerical ratio of the speed of light in a vacuum to its speed in a substance.

Refraction The bending of light rays from one course in one medium to a different course as it passes through another medium of a different refractive index.

Relative Humidity The amount of water vapor in the air, shown as a percentage of the maximum amount the air could hold at a given temperature.

Resins A general term for a wide variety of more or less transparent, fusible materials. In a broad sense, the term is used to designate any polymer that is a basic material for paints and plastics. Resins dissolve in organic solvents, but not usually in water (P/CD).

Saponification The process in which a paint binder, under moist and alkaline conditions, becomes transparent or discolored.

Scumble The technique of applying a thin, semi-opaque or translucent coating of paint over a previously painted surface to alter the color or appearance of the surface without entirely obscuring it.

Sgraffito A technique in which the surface layer of a design is incised or cut away to reveal a ground of contrasting color.

Silicate A material, such as sand, that is composed of a metal, oxygen, and silicon.

Sinking-in A condition in which either the oil paint is thinned too much with mineral spirits or with gum turps or the ground is too absorbent or too unevenly absorbent.

Size A material applied to a support as a penetrating sealer, to alter or lessen its absorbency and isolate it from subsequent coatings.

Specular Reflection Mirror-like reflection, such as the apparently white reflections from a colored glass bottle.

Strainer A type of wooden chassis for textile supports that has rigid, immovable corners.

Stretcher A type of wooden chassis for textile supports that has expandable corners.

Stucco A surface finish composed of Portland cement, lime, sand, and water.

Subtractive Color Color resulting from the absorption of light.

Support The basic substrate of the painting; the carrier of the image: paper, cotton duck, linen, panel, wall, and so forth.

Tangential Sawing A method of sawing boards in which the saw cuts run at a tangent to the direction of the growth rings of the log.

Tempera   A technique of painting in which water and egg yolk or a whole egg and oil mixture form the binder for the paint.

Thermoplastic   Capable of being repeatedly softened by heat and hardened by cooling (P/CD).

Thermosetting   Having the property of setting into a relatively infusible state when heated (P/CD).

Thixotropic   Referring to a material that is thick and viscous while at rest but will flow if brushed, stirred, or shaken, resuming its viscous state when the agitation stops.

Toner   An unlaked dye that can bleed or migrate through dried paint films.

Tooth   A random, small-grained but even texture. Tooth provides for the attachment of succeeding layers of paint or drawing material.

Transmittance   Of light, that fraction of the light that is not reflected or absorbed, but passes through a substance (P/CD).

Undertone   The color of a paint seen when it is viewed in transmitted light or when the paint has been spread into a transparent glaze film; it may be very different from the masstone.

Value   The relative lightness or darkness of a hue. Black is low value; white is high value.

Varnish   Generally, a more or less transparent film-forming liquid that dries into a solid film after application.

Vehicle   The entire liquid contents of a paint, including the binder and any additives (solvents, driers).

Vinyl Resin   Any resin formed by the polymerization of compounds containing the vinyl group, derived from ethylene.

Volatile   Evaporating rapidly or easily.

Watercolor   A technique of painting using a binder made from a water-soluble gum. Watercolor paints may be transparent or opaque.

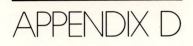

APPENDIX D

SOURCES OF SUPPLY

Mention of a product or a company is not an endorsement of the product or the company. Each individual must decide whether the product or service is appropriate for the intended use. This is by no means a comprehensive list, but a starting point. This appendix is organized in the following way:

1. *For each chapter, a material that has been mentioned is listed, along with the source.*
2. *In a separate, alphabetically arranged list on pages 421–426, the address and other information about the source is given.*

CHAPTER 1   Supports

Solid Wood Panels
Local specialty hardwood mills
Some local lumberyards

Die Boards
Eggers Plywood Company
Some local specialty hardwood mills

Plywood
Local lumberyards

Museum Board
Andrews/Nelson/Whitehead
Art materials supply shops
Process Materials
Strathmore Paper
Westfall Framing

Chipboards
Local lumberyards

Hardboards
Local lumberyards
Masonite Corporation

Cored Boards
Fine Arts Stretchers and Services
Process Materials

Cotton Duck
Art materials supply shops
Fredrix Artists Canvas
Selwin Textile Company
Utrecht Manufacturing
Winsor & Newton

Linen
Art materials supply shops
Fredrix Artists Canvas
Selwin Textile Company
Utrecht Manufacturing
Winsor & Newton

Polyester and Polyester/Cotton Blends
Fredrix Artists Canvas

Polypropylene
Fredrix Artists Canvas

Ready-made Stretcher Bars
Art materials supply shops

Heavy-duty Ready-made Stretcher Bars
Some art materials supply shops
Utrecht Manufacturing

Custom Stretcher Bars
Fine Arts Stretchers and Services
I.C.A. Spring Stretchers
James J. Lebron
Starofix (Luca Bonetti)

Stretcher Cleats and Crossbar Cleats
Grumbacher

CHAPTER 2 Sizes and Grounds

Hide Glue
Art materials supply shops
Fezandie and Sperrle (Tricon Colors)
Grumbacher
Utrecht Manufacturing

Be Square #175 Microcrystalline Wax
TALAS

Methyl Cellulose
Conservation materials
Dow Chemical (Methocel K4MS)
TALAS

Acryloid Acrylic Solutions
Rohm and Haas

Rhoplex Acrylic Emulsions
Rohm and Haas

PVA Emulsions
Borden Chemical (Elmer's Glue)
Hardware stores (Elmer's Glue)

Lead White Paste
Triad Paint and Chemical

Barrier Creams and Handcleaners
Handi-Clean Products (Doktor Handi-
  Clean)
Lab Safety Supply (Cover-Derm)
Mentholatum Company (Barracaide)

Barium Sulfate
See Pigments

Alkyd/Oil Primers
Winsor & Newton

Acrylic Emulsion Primers (Gesso)
Grumbacher
Hunt Manufacturing
Liquitex
Martin/F. Weber
Utrecht Manufacturing

Titanium White, Zinc Oxide,
Precipitated Chalk
See Pigments

CHAPTER 3 Binders

Linseed Oils
Grumbacher
Liquitex
Utrecht Manufacturing
Welch, Holme and Clark
Winsor & Newton

Safflower, Poppyseed, Soybean,
and Walnut Oils
Welch, Holme and Clark

Beeswax, Carnauba Wax
Fezandie and Sperrle (Tricon Colors)

Gum Acacia (Gum Arabic)
Fezandie and Sperrle (Tricon Colors)
Winsor & Newton

Casein
Fezandie and Sperrle (Tricon Colors)
Fisher Scientific

Vinyl Resins
Borden Chemical

Acrylic Resins
Rohm and Haas

Alkyd Resins
Reichhold Chemicals

Silicates
Du Pont
Union Carbide

CHAPTER 4 Solvents and Thinners

Protective Devices: Masks, Gloves,
Goggles, Barrier Creams
Lab Safety Supply

CHAPTER 5   Varnishes

Damar Resin
Art materials supply shops
Fezandie and Sperrle (Tricon Colors)
Utrecht Manufacturing

Mastic Resin
Fezandie and Sperrle (Tricon Colors)

White Shellac Solution
Hardware stores

Acrylic Resins in Solution and Emulsion
Rohm and Haas

Ketone Resin Varnishes
Winsor & Newton

Silicone Varnish
Conserv-Art

CHAPTER 6   Balsams, Driers, Retarders, Preservatives

Venice Turpentine, Driers, and Retarders
Art materials supply shops
Grumbacher
Liquitex
Winsor & Newton

Preservatives
Conservation Materials

CHAPTER 7   Pigments

Blue-Wool Textile Fading Cards
TALAS

Retail Pigment Suppliers
Bocour
Fezandie and Sperrle (Tricon Colors)
Grumbacher
Perma-Color
Winsor & Newton

Wholesale and Raw Materials Suppliers of Pigments
American Cyanamid
American Hoechst
Blythe Colours
Ciba-Geigy
Du Pont
Ferro
Harmon Colors
Harshaw
Hercules
I.C.I. Americas
Kohnstamm
Mearl
Mineral Pigments
Pfizer
Reckitts Colours
Reichard-Coulston
Sandoz
Shepherd Chemical
Sun Chemical
Whittaker, Clark and Daniels

Colored Gels
Edmund Scientific

Humidity Indicator Cards (product #5B015H01)
Multiform Dessicants

Munsell Book of Color
Munsell Color

Natural Color System
Scandinavian Colour Institute

Uniform Color Scales
Optical Society of America

CHAPTER 8   Painting Techniques and Makir

Glass Mullers
Fezandie and Sperrle (Tricon Colors)

Blank tubes
Bocour
Pearl Paint
Teledyne-Wirz

Brushes
Langnickel
Grumbacher
Isaby
Liquitex
Raphaël
Simmons
Strathmore
Utrecht Manufacturing
Winsor & Newton

Chapter 9   Oil Paints

Oil Paints
Blockx
Bocour
Grumbacher
Holbein
Hunt
Lefranc et Bourgeois
Liquitex
Maimeri
Martin/F. Weber
Old Holland
Rowney
Schmincke
Sennelier
Shiva
Talens
Utrecht Manufacturing
Winsor & Newton

Chapter 10   Synthetics

Acrylic Solution Paints
Bocour
Maimeri Restoration Paints (blend of
    synthetic and natural resins)

Acrylic Emulsion Paints
Bocour
Chromacryl
Golden
Grumbacher
Holbein
Hunt

Lascaux
Liquitex
Martin/F. Weber
Rowney
Shiva
Utrecht Manufacturing
Winsor & Newton

Alkyd Paints
PDQ
Talens
Winsor & Newton

CHAPTER 11   Water-Thinned Paints

Transparent and Opaque Watercolors
Bocour
Grumbacher
Holbein
Hunt
Lefranc et Bourgeois
Liquitex
Rowney
Utrecht Manufacturing
Winsor & Newton

Glycerine
Local pharmacies

Casein Paints
Shiva

CHAPTER 12   The Temperas

Egg-Oil Emulsion Paints
Rowney
Sennelier

CHAPTER 13   Encaustic

Encaustic Supplies
Fezandie and Sperrle (Tricon Colors)
    (wax, pigments)

CHAPTER 14   Wax Soaps

Wax Soap
Siphon Art (Dorland's Wax Medium)

Wax and Oil Crayons
Grumbacher
Holbein
Niji
Sakura (Cray-pas)
Shiva (Markal Paint Sticks)

CHAPTER 15   Pastels

Pastels
Grumbacher
Rowney
Sennelier
Talens

CHAPTER 16   Mural Techniques

Enamel Frits
Dick Blick

CHAPTER 17   Picture Protection

Spray Packs
Art materials supply shops
Conservation Materials
Precision Valve

Mat Cutting Tools
Art materials supply shops
Light Impressions (Dexter, C & H)
Westfall (Alto Ez)

Marking Gauges
Hardware stores

Hinging and Hanging Tape
Conservation Materials
Light Impressions
TALAS
Westfall Framing

3M #415 Double-Faced Polyester Tape
Conservation Materials
TALAS

Museum Board
Andrews/Nelson/Whitehead
Art materials supply shops
Light Impressions
Process Materials
Strathmore Paper
Westfall Framing

Plastic Framing Spacers
Frame Tek (Framespace)

All-Flex
Flex-Fast

Styrene Glazing
Westfall Framing

Ultraviolet-Filtering Plexiglass
Rohm and Haas

Denglas
Denton Vacuum

Acid-Free Corrugated Cardboard
Process Materials

Fome-Cor
Monsanto

Humidity Indicator Strips
Multiform Dessicants

Mylar Film
Du Pont

Print Storage Boxes
Light Impressions
Hollinger
TALAS

Bubble-Pak
Sealed Air Corporation

Kimpak
Kimberly and Clark

Glas-Kraft Waterproof Paper
Glas-Kraft

APPENDIX B   Drawing Materials

Papers
Art Supply Warehouse
New York Central Supply
Pearl Paint
Shiva
Strathmore
Utrecht Manufacturing

ColorpHast pH Indicator Strips
Conservation Materials

Wei T'o® Deacidification Solutions
Conservation Materials
TALAS

NAMES AND ADDRESSES

Alvin
Box 88
Windsor, CT 06095

American Cyanamid Company
Pigments Division
Bound Brook, NJ 08805

American Hoechst Corporation
Industrial Chemicals Division
PO Box 2500
North Somerville, NJ 08876
  and
129 Quidnick Street
Coventry, RI 02816 (Organic Pigments)

American Society for Testing and
  Materials
1916 Race Street
Philadelphia, PA 19103

Andrews/Nelson/Whitehead
31–10 48th Avenue
Long Island City, NY 11101

Art Supply Warehouse
360 Main Avenue (Route 7)
Norwalk, CT 06851

Artransport, Inc.
2706 South Nelson Street
Arlington, VA 22206

Blockx (Belgian)
U.S. distributor:
  Pentalic Corporation
  132 West 22 Street
  New York, NY 10011
  *Brochures and 4-color printed color chart;
    minimal technical information.*

Blythe Colours, Ltd.
Cresswell
Stoke-on-Trent ST11 9RD
England

Bocour Artist Colors, Inc.
1 Bridge Street
Garnerville, NY 10923
Brochures; minimal technical information.

Borden Chemical Division, Borden, Inc.
Thermoplastics Division
511 Lancaster Street
Leominster, MA 01453

Chromacryl (Australian)
U.S. distributor:
  Chroma Acrylics
  40 Tanner Street
  Haddonfield, NJ 08033
  *Brochures and color charts; minimal
    technical information.*

Ciba-Geigy Corporation
444 Saw Mill River Road
Ardsley, NY 10502

Cities Service Company
Columbian Chemicals Division
3200 West Market Street
Akron, OH 44313

Conserv-Art
John G. Shelley Company, Inc.
Art-Sciences Division
16 Mica Lane
Wellesley Hills, MA 02181
Excellent technical information.

Conservation Materials, Ltd.
240 Freeport Boulevard P.O. Box 2884
Sparks, NV 89431
Catalogue available.

Daniel Smith, Inc.
Fine Artists' Materials
4130 First Avenue South
Seattle, WA 98134
Catalogue available.

Denton Vacuum, Inc.
8 Springdale Road
Cherry Hill, NJ 08003

Dick Blick
Box 1267, Route 150 East
Galesburg, IL 61401

Dow Chemical Company
Dow Chemical U.S.A.
2020 Dow Center
Midland, MI 48640

Edmund Scientific
101 E. Gloucester Pike
Barrington, NJ 80007
Catalogue available.

E.I. Du Pont de Nemours and Company,
   Inc.
Tatnall Street Building
Wilmington, DE 19898

Eggers Plywood Company
Two Rivers, WI 54241
   and
Eggers Hardwood Products Corporation
Neenah, WI 54956

Ferro Corporation
Color Division
4150 East 56 Street
Box 6550
Cleveland, OH 44101

Fezandie and Sperrle
Leeben Color
Division, Tricon Colors, Inc.
16 Leliarts Lane
Elmwood Park, NJ 07407
Catalogue available.

Fine Arts Stretchers and Services, Inc.
1064 62 Street
Box 380
Brooklyn, NY 11219

Fisher Scientific Company
711 Forbes Avenue
Pittsburgh, PA 15219

Sam Flax, Inc.
111 Eighth Avenue
New York, NY 10011

Flex-Fast, Inc.
Box 4176
Greenwich, CT 06830

Frame Tek
2134-C Old Middlefield Way
Mountain View, CA 94043

Fredrix Artists Canvas, Inc.
Tara Materials, Inc.
Box 646
Lawrenceville, GA 30246
Catalogue and samples available.

Glas-Kraft
Railroad Street
Slatersuill, RI 02876

Glidden
Durkee Division, SCM Corporation
Pigments and Colors Group
3901 Glidden Road
Baltimore, MD 21226

Golden Artist Colors, Inc.
Box 91, Bell Road
New Berlin, NY 13411
Excellent technical information; handmade
color charts.

M. Grumbacher, Inc.
460 West 34 Street
New York, NY 10001
Good technical information; extensive
catalogue.

Handi-Clean Products, Inc.
301 Swing Road
Greensboro, NC 27402

Harmon Colors
Specialty Chemicals Division
Allied Chemical Corporation
PO Box 14
Hawthorne, NJ 07507

Harshaw Chemical Company
1945 East 97 Street
Cleveland, OH 44106

Hercules, Inc.
910 Market Street
Wilmington, DE 19899

Holbein (Japanese)
U.S. distributor:
    Hopper-Koch, Inc.
    13 Lexington Green
    Ridgewood Estates
    South Burlington, VT 05401
Minimal technical information; catalogue
available.

Hollinger Corporation
3810 South Four Mile Run Drive
PO Box 6185
Arlington, VA 22206

Hunt Manufacturing Company
1405 Locust Street
Philadelphia, PA 19102
Good technical information; catalogue
available.

I.C.A. Spring Stretchers
344 South Professor Street
Oberlin, OH 44074

ICI Americas, Inc.
Specialty Chemicals Division
Wilmington, DE 19897

Isaby
LaBrosse et Dupont
12, Rue Léon-Jost
75017 Paris, France
Also available from:
    La Brosse et Dupont
    623 South State Street
    Appleton, WI 54911

Inter-Society Color Council, Inc.
c/o Office of the Secretary
Therese R. Commerford
U.S. Army Natick Laboratories
ATTN: DRDNA-ITCP
Natick, MA 01760

Kimberly and Clark
2001 Marathon Avenue
Neenah, WI 54956

H. Kohnstamm and Company, Inc.
161 Avenue of the Americas
New York, NY 10013

Lab Safety Supply Company
3430 Palmer Drive
PO Box 1368
Janesville, WI 53547-1368

A. Langnickel, Inc.
253 West 26 Street
New York, NY 10001

Lascaux (Swiss)
Alois K. Diethelm AG
CH-8306 Brüttisellen, Switzerland
Very good technical information; color charts.
U.S. distributor:
    Fine Arts Stretchers and Services

James J. Lebron
31-56 58 Street
Woodside, NY 11377

Lefranc et Bourgeois (French)
U.S. distributor:
    Strathmore Paper Company
Very good technical information; color charts.

Light Impressions
439 Monroe Avenue
PO Box 940
Rochester, NY 14603

Liquitex (formerly Permanent Pigments)
Binney and Smith Artist Materials
1100 Church Lane
PO Box 431
Easton, PA 18042
*Excellent technical information; catalogue
    available.*

Maimeri (Italian)
U.S. distributor:
    Charvoz-Carsen Corporation
    5 Daniel Road East
    Fairfield, NJ 07006
*Good technical information; catalogue
    available.*

Martin/F. Weber Company (formerly
    Weber)
2727 Southampton Road
Philadelphia, PA 19154-1293
Fair technical information; general catalogue.

Masonite Corporation
29 North Wacker Drive
Chicago, IL 60606

Mearl Corporation
41 East 42 Street
New York, NY 10017

Mentholatum Company, Inc.
Buffalo, NY 14213

Mineral Pigments Corporation
7011 Muirkirk Road
Beltsville, MD 20705

Monsanto Company
800 North Lindbergh Boulevard
St. Louis, MO 63166

Multiform Dessicants, Inc.
1418 Niagara Street
Buffalo, NY 14213

Munsell Color
Macbeth, Division of Kollmorgen
    Corporation
2441 North Calvert Street
Baltimore, MD 21218

New York Central Supply Company
62 Third Avenue
New York, NY 10003
Extensive catalogue; special papers catalogue.

Niji
Yasutomo and Company
500 Howard Street
San Francisco, CA 94105.

Old Holland (Dutch)
Oudt Hollandse Olieverwen Makerij N.V.
2584 CH Kanaalweg 107
Scheveningen, Holland
*Fair technical information; handmade color
    charts.*
Available at:
    David Davis Fine Arts
    539 La Guardia Place
    New York, NY 10012

Optical Society of America
1816 Jefferson Place NW
Washington, DC 20036

PDQ Artist Oil Paint Company
6059 Larchmont Court
San Jose, CA 95123

Pearl Paint Company, Inc.
308 Canal Street
New York, NY 10013
Extensive catalogue.

Perma Colors
Division H. Mark McNeal Company, Inc.
1626 East Boulevard
Charlotte, NC 28203
Catalogue available.

Pfizer Minerals
Pigments and Metals Division
235 East 42 Street
New York, NY 10017

Precision Valve Company
PO Box 309
Yonkers, NY 10702

Process Materials Corporation
301 Veterans Boulevard
Rutherford, NJ 07070
Excellent technical information.

Raphaël (French)
U.S. distributor:
  Dismart, Inc.
  22 West 21 Street
  New York, NY 10010

Reckitt's Colours, Ltd.
Morley Street
Hull HU8 8DN
Yorkshire, England

Reichard-Coulston, Inc.
15 East 26 Street
New York, NY 10010

Reichhold Chemicals, Inc.
525 North Broadway
White Plains, NY 10603

Rohm and Haas
Independence Mall West
Philadelphia, PA 19105

George Rowney and Company, Ltd.
  (English)
PO Box 10
Bracknell RG12 4ST
Berkshire, England
*Good technical information; extensive
  catalogue.*

Sakura (Japanese)
U.S. distributor:
  Sandford's
  Bellwood, IL 60104

Sandoz Colors and Chemicals
Atlanta, GA 30336

Scandinavian Colour Institute
Riddargatan 17
Postadress Box 14038
S-104 40 Stockholm, Sweden

H. Schmincke and Company (German)
GMBH and Co. KG
Otto-Hahn-Strasse 2
4006 Erkrath-Unterfeldhaus
Dusseldorf, West Germany
Good technical information and catalogue.
  Available at:
  Sam Flax, New York

Sealed Air Corporation
2030 Lower Homestead Avenue
Holyoke, MA 01040

Selwin Textile Company, Inc.
15 West 38 Street
New York, NY 10018

Sennelier (French)
34, Rue Lebrun
75013 Paris, France
Available at:
  David Davis Fine Arts, Pearl Paint
  Company

Shepherd Chemical Company
4900 Beech Street
Cincinnati, OH 45212

Shiva, Inc.
4320 West 190 Street
Torrance, CA 90509

Robert Simmons, Inc.
45 West 18 Street
New York, NY 10011

Siphon Art (Dorland's Wax Medium)
Ignacio, CA 94947
　Available at:
　New York Central Supply

Starofix
Luca Bonetti
154 West 18 Street
New York, NY 10011

Strathmore Paper Company
Westfield, MA 01085

Sun Chemical Corporation
Pigments Division
411 Sun Avenue
Cincinnati, OH 45232

TALAS
Division, Technical Library Service, Inc.
213 West 35 Street
New York, NY 10001-1996

Talens (Dutch)
U.S. distributor:
　Morilla Company
　211 Bowers Street
　Holyoke, MA 01040
Catalogue.

Teledyne-Wirz
Fourth and Townsend Streets
PO Box 640
Chester, PA 19016

Triad Paint and Chemical Corporation
810 Evergreen Avenue
Brooklyn, NY 11207

Union Carbide Corporation
Chemicals and Plastics
270 Park Avenue
New York, NY 10017

Utrecht Manufacturing Corporation
33 35 Street
Brooklyn, NY 11232
Good technical information; catalogue.

Welch, Holme and Clark
1000 South Fourth Street
Harrison, NJ 07029

Westfall Framing
PO Box 6607
Tallahassee, FL 32314

Whittaker, Clark and Daniels, Inc.
1000 Coolidge Street
South Plainfield, NJ 07080

Winsor & Newton, Inc. (English)
U.S. office:
　555 Winsor Drive
　Secaucus, NJ 07094
*Excellent technical information; extensive
　catalogue.*

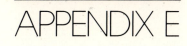

APPENDIX E

METRIC MEASUREMENT CONVERSIONS

To Convert From	To	Multiply By
LENGTH		
inches (in.)	centimeters (cm)	2.54
feet (ft)	centimeters (cm)	30
yards (yd)	meters (m)	0.9
millimeters (mm)	inches (in.)	0.04
centimeters (cm)	inches (in.)	0.4
meters (m)	feet (ft)	3.3
meters (m)	yards (yd)	1.1
AREA		
square inches (in.^{2})	square centimeters (cm^2)	6.5
square feet (ft^2)	square meters (m^2)	0.09
square yards (yd^2)	square meters (m^2)	0.8
square centimeters (cm^2)	square inches (in.^{2})	0.16
square meters (m^2)	square yards (yd^2)	1.2
WEIGHT		
ounces (oz)	grams (g)	28
pounds (lb)	kilograms (kg)	0.45
grams (g)	ounces (oz)	0.035
kilograms (kg)	pounds (lb)	2.2
VOLUME		
teaspoons (tsp)	milliliters (ml)	5
tablespoons (tbsp)	milliliters (ml)	15
fluid ounces (fl oz)	milliliters (ml)	30
cups (c)	liters (l)	0.24
pints (pt)	liters (l)	0.47
quarts (qt)	liters (l)	0.95
U.S. gallons (gal)	liters (l)	3.8
milliliters (ml)	fluid ounces (fl oz)	0.03
liters (l)	pints (pt)	2.1
liters (l)	quarts (qt)	1.06
liters (l)	U.S. gallons (gal)	0.26

TEMPERATURE

$C° = (F° - 32) \times .555$

$F° = (C° \times 1.8) + 32$

BIBLIOGRAPHY

American Society for Testing and Materials. 1986 Annual Book of ASTM Standards, Section 6, Vol. 06.01, *Paint—Tests for Formulated Products and Applied Coatings.* Philadelphia: American Society for Testing and Materials, 1986.

Billmeyer, Fred W., Jr., and Max Saltzman. *Principles of Color Technology,* 2d ed. New York: Wiley, 1981.

Cennini, Cennino. *The Craftsman's Handbook 'Il Libro dell' Arte,* trans. Daniel V. Thompson, Jr. New Haven, CT: Yale University Press, 1933; New York: Dover.

Chaet, Bernard. *An Artist's Notebook.* New York: Holt, Rinehart and Winston, 1979.

Chieffo Clifford T. *The Contemporary Oil Painter's Handbook.* Englewood Cliffs, NJ: Prentice-Hall, 1976.

Cohn, Marjorie B. *Wash and Gouache.* Cambridge, MA: Fogg Art Museum, Harvard University, 1977.

Constable, W. G. *The Painter's Workshop.* London: Oxford University Press, 1954; New York: Dover, 1979.

Crown, D. A. *The Forensic Examination of Paints and Pigments.* Springfield, IL: Charles C. Thomas, 1968.

Doerner, Max. *The Materials of the Artist and Their Use in Painting,* rev. ed., trans. Eugen Neuhaus. New York: Harcourt, Brace & World, 1949; © 1962 by Eugen Neuhaus.

Gettens, Rutherford J., and George L. Stout. *Painting Materials: A Short Encyclopaedia.* New York: D. Van Nostrand, 1942; Dover, 1966.

Hiler, Hilaire. *The Painter's Pocket Book of Methods and Materials,* 3rd ed. rev. London: Faber and Faber, 1970.

Hunter, Dard. *Papermaking, The History and Technique of an Ancient Craft.* New York: Knopf, 1947.

Hurvich, Leo M. *Color Vision.* Sunderland, MA: Sinauer Associates, 1981.

Jensen, Lawrence N. *Synthetic Painting Media.* Englewood Cliffs, NJ: Prentice-Hall, 1964.

Kay, Reed. *The Painter's Guide to Studio Methods and Materials.* Englewood Cliffs, NJ: Prentice-Hall, 1983.

Keck, Caroline K. *A Handbook on the Care of Paintings.* New York: Watson-Guptill, 1965.

Koretsky, Elaine. *Color for the Hand Papermaker.* Boston: Carriage House Press, 1983.

Kühn, Dr. Hermann. "Artists' Colors," *CIBA Review* 1963/1, pp. 3–36. Switzerland: CIBA, Ltd., 1963.

Laurie, A. P. *The Painter's Methods and Materials.* New York: Dover, 1967.

Le Blon, J. C. *Coloritto,* with an introduction by Faber Birren. New York: Van Nostrand Reinhold, 1980.

Levison, Henry W. *Artists' Pigments: Lightfastness Tests and Ratings.* Hallandale, FL: COLORLAB, 1976.

Long, Paulette (ed.). *Paper—Art and Technology.* San Francisco: World Print Council, 1979.

Massey, Robert. *Formulas for Painters.* New York: Watson-Guptill, 1967.

Mayer, Ralph. *A Dictionary of Art Terms and Techniques.* New York: Thomas Y. Crowell, 1975.

Mayer, Ralph. *The Artist's Handbook of Materials and Techniques,* rev. New York: Viking, 1982.

Mayer, Ralph. *The Painter's Craft.* New York: Penguin Books, 1976.

McCann, Michael. *Artist Beware.* New York: Watson-Guptill, 1979.

McCann, Michael, and Gail Barazani (eds.). *Health Hazards in the Arts and Crafts.* Washington, DC: Society for Occupational and Environmental Health, 1980.

Newman, Thelma R. *Plastics as an Art Form,* rev. ed. Radnor, PA: Chilton; Ontario, Canada: Thomas Nelson & Sons, Ltd., 1969.

Overheim, Daniel R., and David L. Wagner. *Light and Color.* New York: Wiley, 1982.

Paint/Coatings Dictionary. Philadelphia PA: Federation of Societies for Coatings Technology, 1978.

Patton, Temple C. (ed.). *The Pigment Handbook.* New York: Wiley-Interscience, 1973.

Permanent Pigments. *Enduring Colors for the Artist.* Cincinnati, OH: Binney and Smith, Inc., 1975.

Rainwater, Clarence. *Light and Color.* New York: Golden Books (Western Publishing Company), 1971.

Ruhemann, Helmut. *The Cleaning of Paintings: Problems and Potentialities.* New York: Praeger, 1968.

Smith, Merrily A., comp. *Matting and Hinging of Works of Art on Paper.* Washington, DC: Preservation Office, Library of Congress, 1981.

Society of Dyers and Colourists and the American Association of Textile Chemists and Colorists. *The Colour Index,* 3rd ed. Bradford, England, and Research Triangle Park NC, 1975.

Sward, G. G. (ed.). *Paint Testing Manual,* 13th ed. Philadelphia: American Society for Testing and Materials, 1972.

The Tate Gallery. *Paint and Painting.* London: Winsor & Newton/The Tate Gallery, 1982.

Thomas, Anne Wall. *Colors from the Earth.* New York: Van Nostrand Reinhold, 1980.

Verity, Enid. *Color Observed.* New York: Van Nostrand Reinhold, 1980.

Wehlte, Kurt. *The Materials and Techniques of Painting.* trans. Ursus Dix. New York: Van Nostrand Reinhold, 1982.

Williamson, Samuel J., and Herman Z. Cummins. *Light and Color in Nature and Art.* New York: Wiley, 1983.

Woody, Russell. *Painting with Synthetic Media.* New York: Reinhold Publishing, 1965.

INDEX

Absorption, 124–126
Acetate fabrics, 17
Acetone, 89, 95, 103
Acid-free papers, 18, 402
Acidic papers, 377–378
Acid-refined linseed oil, 60
Acrylic emulsion, 411
Acrylic emulsion gessoes, 221
Acrylic emulsion grounds, 42–44,
    52–56, 268
  as irreversible sizes, 35–36
  and stretching of textiles, 22
Acrylic emulsion paints
  binders for, 144, 232, 235, 237
  commercial, 237
  on dry fresco wall, 302
  homemade, 232–234
  in markers, 408
  for murals, 282, 302, 307
  painting techniques for, 234–237
  pastel combined with, 279
  pigments for, 121
  protecting works done in, 322,
    327
  retarding drying of, 113
Acrylic fabrics, 17, 56
Acrylic polymer emulsion gesso, 18
Acrylic polymer emulsion paints,
    9–10, 69, 107
Acrylic resins, 68–69, 79, 106–107
Acrylic sheets, 346
Acrylic solution paints
  binders for, 144, 227–228, 268
  cleaning paintings done with, 326
  commercial brands of, 229
  homemade, 228

for murals, 282
painting techniques for, 228–229
pastels combined with, 279
varnish required for works done
  in, 322
Acrylic solutions, 68–69
  defined, 411
  size from, 35, 53–56
  varnish from, 100, 110
Acryloid A-21, 229
Acryloid B-67MT, 35, 100,
  106–107, 268, 280
Acryloid B-72 or B-67, 106
Acryloid F-10, 106
Acryloids, 69
Acute hazard, 411. *See also* Health
  hazards
Additive color, 125–126, 411
Adhesive
  binder as, 57
  for collage, 68, 107, 236
  polyvinyl acetate emulsions for,
    305
  wax-resin, 27–28
Agglomeration, 121, 208, 217, 266,
  411
Air brushes, 408
Albumen, 66, 256
Alcohols, 390
  denatured, 12–13, 88, 94, 105
  as fire hazard, 13, 32, 229
  for surface preparation, 12–13
Aliphatic hydrocarbons, 86–87, 411
Alizarin crimson, 120, 141, 143, 148
Alkali-refined oil, 60, 214–215, 260
Alkyd, defined, 411

Alkyd grounds, 41
Alkyd paints
  binders for, 330
  commercial, 231–232
  for murals, 282
  painting techniques for, 231
  pastel combined with, 279
  retarding drying of, 113
  varnish required for works done
    in, 322
Alkyd resins, 69, 80, 108, 230
Alla prima style (direct painting),
  221, 235, 246, 412
Allergenic substance, defined, 411
Alligatoring, 382
Alum, 403
Aluminum hydrate, 133, 214
Aluminum panels, 379
  size and ground for, 54
  as substrate for acrylic polymer
    emulsion paints, 9–10
  surface preparation for, 12–13
Aluminum points, 407
Aluminum stearate, 133, 214
Alvin Graphic Pen, 408
American Association of Textile
  Chemists and Colorists, 412
American Institute for Conservation
  of Historic and Artistic Works,
  Inc. (AIC), 385
American Society for Testing and
  Materials (ASTM), 145, 148,
  411
Ammonia, 50, 251–252
Ammonium carbonate, 67,
  251–252, 271